THE PATTERN *of* AUSTRALIAN CULTURE

THE PATTERN OF
AUSTRALIAN
CULTURE

EDITED BY

A. L. McLEOD

LOCK HAVEN STATE COLLEGE
PENNSYLVANIA

❖

CORNELL UNIVERSITY PRESS

ITHACA, NEW YORK

CORNELL UNIVERSITY PRESS

First published 1963

Library of Congress Catalog Card Number: 63-14902

PRINTED IN THE UNITED STATES OF AMERICA

BY VAIL-BALLOU PRESS, INC.

PREFACE

❧

IN his recent study of ideas and institutions in early nineteenth-century Australia, *Australia's Colonial Culture* (1957), Dr. George Nadel pointed out a number of serious lacunae in Australian scholarship; one of them is an "intellectual history"—a comprehensive study of the growth of the arts and sciences and an assessment of their place in the development of an Australian national identity. The great difficulty of such an undertaking is no doubt the explanation for its not having been attempted. If attempted by a sciolist, the result would be valueless; if undertaken by an individual conscious of the complexity of the task, the project would certainly not be completed for many years.

C. Hartley Grattan, in a Foreword to Dr. Nadel's book, expressed the hope that "a history of the Australian mind"—a study that would describe and evaluate the contributions of Australians to the arts, sciences, and "cultural institutions" of society—would soon be written. Its continued absence, Grattan suggested, was a severe handicap to an informed understanding of the country and its people. It is the purpose of this book to provide just such an intellectual history of Australia as has been found missing. It is intended for the informed general reader rather than for scholars and academicians.

The Pattern of Australian Culture is the third in a series published by Cornell University Press. The earlier books, both edited by Professor Julian Park of the University of Buffalo (now the State University of New York at Buffalo), are *The Culture of France in Our Time* (1954) and *The Culture of Contemporary Canada* (1957). In its scope the present volume differs somewhat from its predecessors, as it was thought that an account of only the contemporary achievements of Australia in the arts and sciences would be inadequate and perhaps misleading. In order to understand the present it is necessary to understand the past, runs the old adage. This is especially true of the present state of Australian culture, since it is so inextricably associated with the colonial past. Besides, since there is no account of Australia's cultural infancy, it seemed both mandatory and convenient to present a picture of the country's cultural achievement over the course of its entire—though brief—history. The three books are, however, similar in content. The book on French culture contains chapters on law and religion, which are not included in *The Culture of Contemporary Canada*. On the other hand, the book on Canada has chapters on literary scholarship and on French-Canadian culture. In *The Pattern of Australian Culture* such work in the area of literary scholarship as is worthy of discussion or mention has been considered in the chapter on literature; religion, because it cannot be regarded as a cultural force in Australia (and because there have been no significant contributions to theological literature), has been omitted. A chapter on the culture of the indigenous peoples of the Australian continent has been considered essential. In addition, chapters on the Australian contributions to the English language, on historiography, and on recreation—often thought a substitute, in Australia, for the more conventional cultural pursuits—have been included in an effort to present as complete a picture of the total social and intellectual milieu of Australia as is feasible within the limits of a book of this type. In other respects the contents of the three books in the series are the same.

The bibliographies appended to the chapters are intended as guides

PREFACE

for further reading for those who would like to pursue their interests; they do not necessarily represent the authors' sources.

It is a pleasure to acknowledge the receipt of a grant-in-aid from the State University of New York Research Foundation, which has met the expenses incurred in the preparation of the manuscript for the press.

A. L. McL.

Lock Haven, Pennsylvania

ACKNOWLEDGMENTS

❖

GRATEFUL acknowledgment for permission to reproduce copyright material is made to the trustees of the Mitchell Library, Sydney (for photographs of Christopher J. Brennan, Henry Handel Richardson, and Henry Lawson); the trustees of the National Art Gallery of New South Wales, Sydney, and the trustees of the Queensland Art Gallery, Brisbane (for reproductions of paintings); P. R. Stephensen (for excerpts from *The Foundations of Culture in Australia*); Miss D. E. Collins (for excerpts from "A Ballade of an Anti-Puritan," by G. K. Chesterton); and the following publishers, who have kindly allowed quotations from the works listed:

Angus and Robertson, Ltd.: *Poetical Works of Henry Lawson; A Vision of Ceremony*, by James McAuley; *Poems*, by Hugh McCrae; *The Collected Verse of A. B. Paterson; One Hundred Poems*, by Kenneth Slessor; *The Birdsville Track*, by Douglas Stewart; *Phoenix Wings*, by Harold Stewart; *Woman to Man* and *The Two Fires*, by Judith Wright.

Bulletin Publishing Co., Ltd.: *Maoriland, and Other Verses*, by A. H. Adams.

ix

ACKNOWLEDGMENTS

Columbia University Press: *The Australian Way of Life*, edited by George Caiger.

Edwards and Shaw, Ltd.: *Poems*, by A. D. Hope.

Lothian Publishing Company: *Collected Poems*, by John Shaw Neilson; *Poems*, by Bernard O'Dowd; *Poems*, by Frank Wilmot.

Melbourne University Press: *Moonlight Acre*, by R. D. FitzGerald; *The Escape of the Notorious Sir William Heans*, by William Hay.

Oxford University Press: *Cobbers*, by Thomas Wood.

It has proved impossible in some cases to trace the present copyright holders of brief passages quoted, and we apologize to any who have been inadvertently omitted.

CONTENTS

❧

THE PATTERN *of* AUSTRALIAN CULTURE

INTRODUCTION

A. L. MCLEOD

THE growth of an identifiable and characteristic culture in a new land is unpredictable; it follows no particular and established sequence or timetable and is governed by no known, immutable laws.

In one country art may flourish while literature languishes; in another, theatre and music may burgeon while science and philosophy remain in the fetal stage; in yet another religion may permeate—even motivate and direct—all creative expression that comprises culture. The only essentials for the development of an indigenous culture would appear to be the passage of time, adequate leisure, and that social permissiveness which allows relatively uninhibited development of an individual's yearning to be creatively expressive. Cultural maturation is most swift where, in addition, there is widespread and official encouragement; where the public is literate, is interested in painting and sculpture and architecture, is interested in entertaining new ideas, is inclined to discuss, is neither censorious nor self-satisfied—where, in sum, there is a congenial atmosphere.

1

PATTERN OF AUSTRALIAN CULTURE

In matter of time, Australia has had almost too little opportunity to develop a national culture of any great originality or distinction —just six generations. Yet what has been achieved in this short span is deserving of the attention of the remainder of at least the English-speaking world; it has had high commendation from disinterested critics whose authority gains respect for their opinions.

The equable climate of Australia, a short work week, and generous provision for public holidays and vacations allow considerable opportunity for those who help to create the national culture to pursue their interests and for the remainder of the society to become acquainted with what has been created. Leisure and the climate are certainly the important factors which account for the widespread popular interest in painting, especially landscapes and seascapes, and for the predominance of plein-air painters. Although there may not be the large markets and munificent rewards for creative efforts that are to be found overseas—and hence relatively few professional men of letters, composers, independent thinkers, and nonacademic pure scientists—there are, by way of compensation, also few *salons*, poseurs, dilettantes, and asocial, misunderstood "geniuses." Australian culture is, therefore, largely the product of the leisure activities of its creators; patronage is exceptional.

Generally speaking, Australians are culturally permissive. Literary censorship, such as it is, is fitful and irregular, insubstantial and not any worse than that in most countries—though the situation in the state of Queensland is at the moment somewhat unenlightened and puritanical. Disapproval is customarily shown rather by public opinion than by legislative repression, and it should be acknowledged that at times public opinion is not at or even near the forefront of contemporary cultural endeavor. But this "cultural lag" is a universal phenomenon. Sociological evidence suggests that it has always been so.

One of the most difficult forces for the creative thinker or artist to contend with in Australia is the oppressive lack of interest of the government, except (and this has been recent) in the field of science and, to a lesser degree, in education and music. Politicians seem always to be willing to give priority, in matters of fiscal consideration, to railroad carriages and balanced budgets rather than to opera houses, libraries, and universities. There are small literary fellowships

INTRODUCTION

maintained by the Commonwealth government, minimal subsidies for books for public libraries, token grants in support of symphony orchestras, and grudging endowment of art galleries by the state governments; but all of these are scandalously niggardly. Museums, art galleries, educational institutions, libraries, and research organizations all function on shoestring budgets. All give the impression that they are regarded by the government as necessary—though hard to justify—appendages of modern society. Government buildings are austere: there are no murals and original paintings, such as are to be seen in almost all United States public buildings, no sculpture except an occasional statue of a former viceregal or historical figure. When an opera house was finally approved for Sydney (after heated advocacy of low-rent public housing instead), it was financed principally from state-operated lotteries rather than from large-scale appropriations from the treasury. There is no Australian equivalent of the British Council, the Canada Council, the French Academy, and the numerous semiofficial cultural bodies in the United States.

If the government is not notably forward in supporting the cultural forces of Australia, neither are business, industry, and individuals. There are no great privately endowed philanthropic foundations comparable to the Carnegie Corporation, the Ford Foundation, and the Rockefeller Foundation in the United States or the Shell and Leverhulme Trusts in Britain. Though there are many persons of immense inherited and earned wealth, few have given very generously to support the institutions of public culture.[1] The privately endowed universities of India, Europe, and the United States are not understood in Australia; and the concept of graduates (and even nongraduates) supporting their universities

[1] The universities of Sydney, Melbourne, and Adelaide have a number of partly endowed professorships, but the other universities have very few. A recent appeal for public endowment of a chair of Australian literature in the University of Sydney resulted in the receipt of £20,000 of the required £80,000. One of the younger universities has named its library in honor of the donor of a gift of just £5,000. There are, of course, some notable benefactions: the Waite Institute of the University of Adelaide, the Hackett Bequest of the University of Western Australia, the Felton Bequest of the National Gallery of Victoria, and the Walter and Eliza Hall Institute in Melbourne. In recent years Professor Harry Messel has obtained generous support for the Nuclear Research Foundation of the University of Sydney, and during 1962 that university received a bequest of over £1,500,000 in support of a school of fine arts.

3

financially is almost alien to the established Australian custom. In few places in the world can a small donation to a cultural organization earn so remarkable a reputation for munificence as in Australia.

The leaders of business give sparingly in support of scientific and humanistic research foundations and are virtually unknown to have endowed orchestras, galleries, museums, scientific expeditions, university professorships, or creative arts fellowships. The Melbourne newspaper, the *Age*, has endowed a chair of fine art at the University of Melbourne, and one or two of the large corporations have provided student scholarships, but these are so exceptional as to cause comment. Few business and professional leaders purchase books of intellectual content or the work of Australian artists for their business premises and homes. As one recent British visitor has observed: "I have been into many rich and beautiful houses in Sydney where there were, quite literally, no bookcases and no books." If private libraries are rare, public ones are not especially good. Australian libraries are, by overseas standards, of quite miserable proportions. Accordingly, research is difficult. The largest public libraries, those in Sydney and Melbourne, and the Fisher Library of the University of Sydney house somewhat more than a half-million books. The other public and university libraries are Lilliputian. It is often observed that Australians are among the world's most enthusiastic book buyers; this is the result, in part, of the absence of numerous and satisfactory public libraries. The only book collector of consequence, David Scott Mitchell, bequeathed his collection of Australiana to the New South Wales Public Library in 1907; it is the basis of what is now the best library in the world devoted to Australiana and the Pacific.

In the absence of generous and tangible support by the government, business, and wealthy individuals, it is surprising, indeed, that Australia can already boast of a considerable cultural achievement. Of course, there are those few who aver that there is, in fact, no distinctive Australian culture. One Australian, Clement Semmler, writing in the March, 1960, *Australian Quarterly*, stated the case for this segment of opinion. But it is certainly a minority viewpoint, and it could not be said to represent the thinking of many Australians or of overseas *cognoscenti*.[2]

[2] Aspects of Australian culture are being studied and taught in several over-

4

INTRODUCTION

A recent British sojourner in Australia, J. D. Pringle, has published his observations on Australian life and manners in *Australian Accent* (1958), a work more to be noted for its inconsistencies of observation and its distinguished acerbity than for its penetrating criticisms. In it Pringle at times endorses Semmler's comment. He writes:

> Everything seems to discourage intellectual effort in a nation where intellectual effort has never been highly regarded. If, then, culture is to be judged by the general standard of education and the arts among the population, once again it must be said that Australia has little or none. Indeed, there is a terrifying crudity in the manners and pursuits of the masses, whose intellectual interests seem entirely limited to the study of racing form.

Pringle must be aware of the weakness of his argument. It has never been considered a sound measure of a nation's culture to consider the "general standard of education and arts" and the interests of the lowest social stratum. If this were a valid measure, we should be forced to come to insupportable conclusions about the Philistinism of England, Europe, the Orient, India, and North America, for in all these places the great mass of the population is woefully uneducated and inappreciative of the arts. Furthermore, the fact that the English working class is hopelessly addicted to darts and pubs, television and soccer pools is no true sign of deep-down general cultural degeneracy or of intellectual *rigor mortis*. Fortunately, Pringle corrects himself elsewhere when he expresses in the most unreserved lyricism his delight in Australian art and theatre personnel and in the prospects for cultural achievement in the immediate future.

Much nearer the point are those who see in Australia a situation similar to that which obtains elsewhere in the Western nations at present: a largely uneducated, uncultured mass and a "two cultures" bifurcation at the top. One part of this cultural elite, perhaps the smaller, is well informed—in Matthew Arnold's phrase—of "the best that has been thought and said" in the world and is comprised, generally speaking, of graduates of the arts, law and medical faculties of the universities and the art schools; the other, perhaps the

---

seas universities—Leeds, Duke, Pennsylvania State, and Uppsala, for example. Professor Liljegren at Uppsala has even inaugurated an Australian Studies monograph series.

larger and more influential part, is composed of the graduates of the technical and semi-professional faculties and institutes who, since they are among the *doyens* of society, politics, and business, are unconcerned about their Philistinism. This latter group, the "cultural yahoos" as Pringle calls them (in happy imitation of the felicitous phrasing of Australian poet-satirist A. D. Hope), are not all merely passive; some are often, it seems, vocally and vociferously anticultural. It is commonly thought that Australian politicians, who often take pride in being self-confessed "low-brows," regard any sign of cultural attainment or awareness as politically disadvantageous. Their Philistinism, as Professor R. G. Howarth pointed out in his widely discussed lecture "The State of Culture" in 1950, is vigorously cultivated.

Tocqueville, who observed that the democratic nations "will cultivate the arts which make life easy in preference to the arts whose object is to adorn it," would seem to be contradicted by the state of Australian culture. In this militantly democratic country the arts most concerned with making life easy—science, architecture, and industrial arts—are the least developed and influential; those which can only be regarded (in Tocqueville's terminology) as adornments—historiography, literature, philosophy, painting, and vocal music—are the most highly developed and commendable.

In his *Notes towards a Definition of Culture*, T. S. Eliot issued a caveat that we should not identify religion with culture. There is little need for his warning in Australia. Although religion has, at various times and in many countries, been the primary and pervasive influence in philosophy, science, and the creative arts, it has been singularly absent as a cultural force in Australia. The reasons for this may, of course, be found in the circumstances under which the country was settled; convicts in penal settlements in obscure corners of the world have never been renowned for their devotion to matters of the spirit, especially when the penal system has been supported by the church itself. Again, the clergy in Australia are by and large unintellectual, poorly educated, and either unable or unwilling to write and preach on matters of concern with conviction or originality. The church has remained remarkably well separated from the state, and also from the mainstream of ideas and culture in general. Most Protestant clergy are trained for just two years in small

6

denominational seminaries, where they encounter little or no intellectual stimulation, and then care for lower-middle-class congregations. Catholic priests take a six-year seminary course, but are little better educated and fail to exert any real intellectual force on their working-class parishioners. Few clergymen—Protestant or Catholic —hold even a first degree from a university. It is not to be wondered, then, that the intelligentsia are largely independent of the church in Australia. Australian literature has no obvious marks of religious inspiration; there are no novels that come to grips with matters of religious or philosophical speculation; there have been no masses from Australian composers, no *Pietàs*, stained-glass windows, or important religious sculpture from Australian artists. Worse still, there has been no notable Australian theologian. The only churchman to attain scholarly eminence, Archbishop Eris O'Brien, has gained his reputation not as a theologian but as a historiographer. If and when Australia produces a Karl Barth, a Paul Tillich, and a Reinhold Niebuhr, and trains an erudite clergy, the influence of religion on the general culture may be more noticeable.

Writing in *The Australian Way of Life* (1953), the Reverend K. T. Henderson observed:

As to the intellectual prestige of Christianity, it may be said that in Australia, as throughout the world, the authority of the Christian tradition has been shaken by successive eruptions of hostile philosophic dogma, withering established beliefs with the fiery breath of scientific prestige. . . .

To people dwelling within a culture in which the specific influence of religion is becoming indistinguishable, the notion of a culture vitalized by religion will seem fantastic. . . . A culture without religion would have seemed just as incredible and impossible to our forefathers, primitive or civilized, as a culture fused with religion seems to the "average, sensual man" in Australia today.

Henderson claims to have been able to see, a decade ago, "at the subarticulate levels, more religious influence within cultural activities than appears on the surface"; there has, in the interim, been no overt sign of a religious renaissance. But some observers claim to have been able to discern a growing hedonism, a vital "Cult of the Present Moment" and of the enjoyment of the outdoors. "It would be hard to point to anything which is specifically Australian, except, perhaps, the universal enjoyment of the pleasures of an outdoor life," writes Pringle. It is this aspect of Australian culture that Edgar Waters has limned so satisfactorily. Culture not only determines the types of recreation developed by a nation, it also reflects the trend of its national life, so that the recreational forms become a part of the whole social and cultural pattern. "A people's play is a fair test of a people's character," wrote S. A. Barnett in *Towards Social Reform.* "Their recreation more than their business or their conquests settles the nation's place in history."

Australian culture is largely the result of two brief periods of intellectual, creative activity. The first, which occurred from about 1880 until Federation, saw the establishment of a truly national identity. The second, which commenced about 1948, has seen a truly remarkable and rapid cultural maturation. In the first period were laid the foundations of all those arts and intellectual enterprises that have since flourished. At its worst the period was marked by intellectual plagiarism; often it was sensibly adaptive; at its best it was truly imaginative, creative, original. Most significantly, this first period gave indication that Australian culture would not be just a pale imitation of then contemporary British culture. (It could not be expected, of course, that it would be uninfluenced by its very source.) British in inspiration and genesis it could not help being; but indistinguishable from British it no longer remained. By the time of Federation an Australian ethos had appeared; it was to be found in language, literature, art, and all the other facets of cultural achievement.

But no sooner had this first flush of cultural independence appeared than it was brought to a lamentable and sudden end by a series of malign circumstances: depression, world war, depression, world war. It is no wonder that P. R. Stephensen could write in 1935, in *The Foundations of Culture in Australia,* that "no one who can think at all is satisfied with Australia's intellectual status and the achievements of culture in Australia today." The contrast between the legendary 1890's and the dolorous 1930's was indeed a sobering one; the two periods represent almost precisely the zenith and nadir of intellectual and artistic achievement to that time. Stephenson continued in his vitriolic tone:

Australian culture has become so stultified, smug and puerile; . . . the exultant outburst of Australian creativeness of the 'nineties (in politics as well as in literature) had a damper put on it so that the Australian

8

national fire, for thirty years or more, has merely smouldered when it might have blazed. . . . In Australia we have had no fearless social critics and thinkers even remotely comparable with Shaw, Wells, Chesterton, Mencken, Nathan and Lewis: the smugness here has been quite undisturbed and has settled down into lethargic self-contentment. The purveyors of bromides, from press, pulpit and university, have administered their sedatives without meeting any perceptible resistance from their patients. . . . In no other country in the civilized world is the literary genius so badly treated, so humiliated and crushed and despised and ignored as in Australia.

Stephensen was one of those whom Kipling so poignantly termed the "angry young men." In other circumstances, he might have become Australia's Mencken or Chesterton, but he did not. His criticism was not on the same level as theirs; it was motivated by unacceptable and unorthodox views, and it lacked the wit and wisdom that made Mencken's or Chesterton's criticisms palatable, if not lastingly influential or effective. Stephensen acknowledged his bias in his frank and alerting Preface, where he confessed that his book was composed "with a consciousness that all cultural achievement in Australia is threatened by militarism and bureaucratic fascism." This opinion did not, and would not today, find any considerable endorsement; but it is an interesting example of the jeremiads of the time and especially of those by humanists whose very existence seemed threatened by the social and economic naïveté of the era. It is questionable whether Australia had, in fact, any writers of international stature—let alone genius—in the period in which Stephensen wrote, and certainly they labored under no more onerous conditions than did their counterparts elsewhere. The Australian feeling for A. B. ("Banjo") Paterson, C. J. Dennis, and Henry Lawson, which at times reached what now appears to have been an unreasonable, quasi-reverence, is some indication that Stephensen's values were not essentially sound. If he had wanted encouragement for the unworthy, for the inartistic, he would have been guilty of supporting a practice that he regarded as pernicious and one against which he not infrequently inveighed. He openly opposed the solidarity of the second-rate, the hegemony of the halfhearted, for, he wrote,

A nation culturally passive—culturally self-classified as second-rate—culturally dependent on another nation—in brief, culturally abject—is

9

one which will exalt mediocrity and drive genius into silence or exile: precisely what Australia has done for almost forty years past.

In recent times, the painter, Albert Tucker, has expressed similar sentiments. His famous parting pasquil, "I am a refugee from Australian culture," is often repeated, but as an indication of delight in his epigrammatic, sardonic wit rather than by way of serious criticism. And it should perhaps be noted that Tucker has recently returned to Australia.

Stephensen's rancor is undisguised; he lacks the sardonic wit of Tucker. He is petulant—petty at times—and too denigrating, too caustic, when he continues:

Australia, the country that produces geniuses—for export—and kills them slowly but surely if they stay here. . . . Bland and smug, the second-rate minds have made Australia safe—for themselves. The nasty, unpalatable and very deplorable truth which we must now swallow is that Australia, for one reason or another, has become a cultural backwater, stagnant and culturally green-slimed.

Looking back on the 1880's and 1890's, however, the contrast was disheartening.

On the subject of the export of talent, Stephenson's viewpoint has always been supported by both commentators and facts. Writing in *Some Australians Take Stock* (1939), J. V. Connolly reported that, of the Australian Rhodes scholars to 1927, "more than a third of the total have not been persuaded to place their training at the disposal of the country from which they were selected"—and there is little reason to believe that the situation has changed materially since.

While this observation is limited to a somewhat special category of talented persons, it confirms the generally accepted impression that Australia is constantly losing men and women of artistic or intellectual capacity and achievement. The number of Australians who hold university appointments overseas is remarkably large when considered in relation to the small population of their homeland; the number of Australian writers, actors, and artists to be found in England, Italy, and the United States is surprisingly large and seems to be growing. Most of the artists have migrated to the world's great cultural centers for the obvious and compelling—irresistible— reasons of greater opportunity and more frequent, closer contact with the celebrated leaders in their respective areas of interest. The academic expatriates are often the result of the overproduction of specialists in Australian universities or of the absence of the opportunity to practice specialized professions and to cultivate the non-utilitarian branches of learning that are consequent upon the country's state of development.

Australia is now experiencing its second cultural florescence. For the past fifteen years there has been an astonishing productivity in all the branches of culture, and much of it has been of sufficient quality to attract international attention and win world-wide acclaim. The earlier period, in retrospect, seems to have been too artfully engineered, too artificially sustained. The present one seems to be more genuine, more likely to be sustained and to sustain. It augurs well.

Jack Lindsay, long an expatriate in London, has recently commented that "Australian culture is now gaining the breadth and depth . . . where writers can work out their inner conflicts with full fruitfulness inside it." The atmosphere is now conducive, it seems, to cultural creation and expression in a manner hitherto unknown in Australia. Even Pringle felt obliged to allow that "one of the most striking things about contemporary Australia is the comparative vigour of the arts and sciences." The following pages record Australia's cultural achievement up to the present time.

THE SOCIAL FABRIC

RUSSEL WARD

AUSTRALIA was probably the last continent to be occupied by human beings, and it certainly was the last to be discovered by Europeans. It seems quite likely that the ancestors of the aboriginal inhabitants arrived via Southeast Asia at the beginning of the New Stone Age, perhaps about ten thousand years ago. Numbering probably about 300,000 at the time of European contact, they were a nearly black-skinned people, identified by some anthropologists as a fourth and separate race of mankind, the Australoid. Cut off by the surrounding oceans from all but the slightest contact with other human groups, their culture remained extremely primitive—in the sense made familiar by the late modern Australian archaeologist, V. Gordon Childe. Even today the handful of survivors who have not been detribalized by contact with the white invaders still live entirely by wandering in search of natural foods, as all mankind did ten thousand years ago.

Available evidence suggests that the aborigines were among the most unwarlike folk known to history. Sporadic contact with

Indonesian fisherman may have helped to make the northern coastal tribes more bellicose than others, but none seem to have learned to carry on warfare in the sense that this term is understood by all civilized, and nearly all other, peoples. Individuals were often killed, sometimes by men of a different tribe or group, for breaking taboos believed in by all the tribes in a large area; but this practice seems akin, and possibly ancestral, to what more developed societies mean by punitive judicial action. By custom also, two tribes would meet at a traditional place where, after exchanging insults and challenges, the men would hurl spears at each other and dodge the missiles with great skill. These "tribal wars," as early European observers called them, sometimes continued for hours without more than a few superficial wounds being sustained by either party. Usually if someone was severely wounded or killed, the "war" was at once abandoned for a year or more until the next formal meeting. But this practice seems more akin to the Olympic games or an international football match than to warfare. There is no evidence that any of the 370-odd aboriginal tribes ever thought of exterminating or enslaving another or of permanently annexing part of another's tribal territory. It may be that true warfare arises only when the discovery of stockbreeding and agricultural practices, or contact with other folk who have made these discoveries, provides portable wealth worth fighting over. At any rate, the pacific disposition of the aboriginal race has probably had some effect on modern white Australians. When their hunting grounds were taken from them by the early settlers, naturally the aborigines sometimes replied to violence and misusage with violence; but their resistance was so sporadic and ineffective that men seldom had to go armed on the Australian frontier. Perhaps, too, the fact that practically all Australians are descended from one national group (the British) has made for peaceful behavior. At any rate, compared with the situation in the United States, for instance, there has been extremely little physical violence in Australian life and culture. Although two world wars have shown that Australians fight against outsiders no less courageously than do other peoples, they have always been extraordinarily slow to shed each other's blood.

There is strong, but not conclusive, evidence to suggest that a Chinese fleet may have touched the northern coastline, near the present site of Darwin, in the early fifteenth century. It is possible that Portuguese sailors sighted the shore during the next hundred years; but the first certain European landing was made by a Dutchman, Willem Jansz, on the northwestern coast of Cape North Peninsula in 1606. During the seventeenth century Abel Tasman and other Dutch navigators roughly charted the western coastline between Cape York and the head of the Great Australian Bight and the southern coast of Tasmania, but the relatively well-watered southeastern part of the continent remained unknown until its discovery by the son of a Yorkshire laborer, Captain James Cook, who landed near the present site of Sydney in 1770. Here, eighteen years later, the first permanent European settlement was made.

European or "White" Australia has always been, basically, a provincial British society. That this should be so was determined by the continuous stream of immigrants, books, ideas, fashions, and institutions from "the Old Country"—or "Home," as a very few Australians still call Great Britain. Even after the six separate colonies became completely self-governing under the British Crown, the major ones in 1856 and the others at intervals until 1890, the colonists began only slowly to think of themselves as a separate and unified nation. Until the last quarter of the nineteenth century the six colonies were, physically no less than politically, separate settlements, and communication between them was most readily effected by sea. Yet a recognizably distinct and distinctive Australian culture developed from 1788 onward, and the differences between it and its British prototype became increasingly evident during the nineteenth century to visitors, if not always to Australians themselves. These characteristic differences sprang from two main sources: first, from the strange nature of the new environment and the struggle of the immigrants to adapt themselves to it and, second, from the fact that the emigrants came in disproportionately large numbers from certain parts of Britain and certain classes of British society. We shall look first at the geographic environment.

The southern continent is roughly the same size and shape as continental United States, but, because it is situated a thousand miles or so nearer to the equator, Australia is very much drier. Her only considerable river basin, that of the Murray-Darling in the southeast, is comparable in extent and fertility to the basin of the Rio

14

Grande rather than to that of the Mississippi-Missouri. From the point of view of fertility and rainfall, Australia compares with northern Africa, including the Sahara but excluding much of the tropical West African coast. The Great Dividing Range, which parallels the long eastern coastline, forms the backbone of the continent. At its loftiest point in the south, this range rises to only about 7,000 feet. Nevertheless, it is high enough to trap most of the moisture brought by the prevailing winds from the Pacific. Thus, the great majority of Australians live, and will probably always live, on the narrow and broken, but comparatively well-watered, coastal plain extending from Adelaide around the southern and eastern shores to North Queensland. On the western side of the range the rainfall diminishes rapidly. In most places it is barely sufficient to support any kind of agriculture beyond a line drawn about two hundred miles inland. Westward beyond this lies a belt of country another two or three hundred miles wide which, when improved with artesian bores and dams to conserve surface water, makes fair pastoral land. Westward again beyond this belt most of the land is too parched to support any kind of permanent human occupation until a few sheep and cattle stations appear again near the western coast thousands of miles away. The extreme southwestern corner of the continent also enjoys sufficient rainfall to support a small agricultural population. Altogether, about a third of the Australian land surface receives water enough to support agriculture, but much of this is mountainous and infertile. About a third will support a sparse pastoral population. About a third is desert, useless for the foreseeable future except for the occasional outcrop of mineral ores rich enough to pay for their transport to the coast.

In any consideration of the springs of Australian culture, the sheer size and emptiness of the country are worth stressing. So is its isolation and remoteness from the rest of the inhabited globe, particularly its remoteness from Great Britain and other countries of European-type civilization like Canada and the United States. In the early days news and supplies often took nine months or more to reach Australia. Until the overland telegraph line from Adelaide to Darwin was finished in 1872, news and letters took at least a month in transit. This remoteness helped in forcing Australians to generate a positive national self-image. The vastness of the ancient, nearly empty land also, perhaps, helped to turn their imagination inward. Australia, after all, is the only place in the world where the boundaries of a nation-state are the same as those of a continent. In 1911 C. E. W. Bean, later the historian of Australia's part in the First World War, wrote:

The Australian, one hundred to two hundred years hence, will still live with the consciousness that, if he only goes far enough back over the hills and across the plains, he comes in the end to the mysterious half-desert country where men have to live the lives of strong men. And the life of that mysterious country will affect Australian imagination much as the life of the sea has affected that of the English. It will always be there to help the Australian to form his ideals; and one knows of no land where they have a more definite ideal than in Australia, or where the whole people, men, women, and even youngsters, are more consciously employed in working it out.[1]

It is improbable that, when Bean wrote this, he was familiar with the "frontier thesis" of the American historian, F. J. Turner; yet Turner held the same view of the sources of what was distinctively *sui generis* in American culture. As he wrote in an early article: "What the Mediterranean Sea was to the Greeks, breaking the bond of custom, offering new experiences, calling out new institutions and activities, that the ever-retreating Great West has been to the Eastern United States." An explicit comparison between the role of the Australian and American frontiers was made by Francis Adams in 1892, a year before Turner delivered in Chicago his celebrated paper, "The Significance of the Frontier." Poet, novelist, journalist, and critic, Adams was a gifted and widely read young Englishman who spent the years from 1884 to 1889 in Australia. Although he never visited the United States, he anticipated Turner's vision of the "noble frontiersman" as the promoter and exemplar of nationalism—of all that was specifically American or Australian, and most removed from Old World influences—in the life of the two new countries. Adams' comparison is worth quoting at some length:

The gulf between colony and colony is small and traversable compared to that great fixture that lies between the people of the Slope and of the Interior. Where the marine rainfall flags out and is lost, a new climate, and in a certain sense, a new race begin to unfold themselves. The "fancy" stations on this side of the Great Dividing Range produce some-

[1] *The Dreadnought of the Darling* (London: Rivers, 1911), pp. 317-318.

headed by R. G. Menzies, whose campaign had been based largely on the promise of strong anti-Communist action.[3] Accordingly, in October, 1950, the Menzies government passed an act which gave it power to dissolve the Australian Communist party and to declare seditious, under certain conditions, citizens or organizations deemed to be aiding or abetting communism. The Communist party, with the support of some major trade-unions, challenged the legislation in the High Court which, by a majority of six judges to one, ruled that the act was constitutionally invalid. The Commonwealth government then decided to seek popular assent to a constitutional alteration by which the "Anti-Communist Act" would have been validated. Held in September, 1951, the referendum resulted in a win for "No." A small majority of citizens voted against giving the government increased powers to deal with communism, in spite of the fact that the "Yes" case had been supported by the great majority of newspapers, radio commentators, and so forth. Needless to say, the vast bulk of the Australian electorate was almost as strongly opposed to communism as were contemporary Americans; but it is hard to imagine a similar national referendum in the United States in 1951 having had a similar result. Probably the Australian bias toward collectivist attitudes goes less than halfway toward explaining the poll figures. It was perhaps more important that, because the Australian frontier experience is so much more recent, the trend toward conformity has gone much less far in Australia than in America. In the terminology of David Riesman's book, *The Lonely Crowd*, it would seem that the "inner-directed" type of character is still more common in Australia than the "outer-directed."

Of course, these differences are merely ones of shading and emphasis. There are many rugged individualists in Australia, as there are many sturdy levelers and some socialists in the United States; but if we would understand Australian culture, it is important to remember the *relatively* strong emphasis placed on collectivist attitudes and ideas. In 1928 Carter Goodrich, an American visitor to Australia, first pointed to the source of this difference in an article in the

[3] The early workers' parties in Australian politics are referred to as "Labour" parties; the first government representing workers' interests called itself the "Labour" government; the present political party is officially the Australian Labor Party, though the accepted Australian spelling in all other uses is "labour."

19

November issue of *Economic Record:* "Certainly the United States owes its individualism largely to its small man's frontier; I think it is not fanciful to suggest that Australia owes much of its collectivism to the fact that its frontier was hospitable to the large man instead." Because of the material conditions of the life he knew, the Australian bushman tended to be less interested in freedom to make his individual way to the top than he was in freedom to "stick together with his mates" for their collective good and the discomfiture of "those wealthy squatters." Thus, the Australian labor movement has been, and still is, relatively much stronger than its American counterpart, and collectivist and even socialist attitudes are much more widely tolerated in Australia than in the United States. Further, because these attitudes have long been associated with nationalist aspirations, they have loomed much larger in Australian writing, art, law, and other forms of cultural expression than they have in America. With these qualifications about the nature of the Australian frontier experience in mind, let us return to its effects on the nation's outlook.

We suggested above that the isolation and the sheer size and emptiness of the island continent helped to foster in men's minds a positive national image. Australians are like Americans in having, for the most part, few doubts about what they are like and about what characteristic attitudes, values, and manners are—or ought to be—specifically Australian. It seems that the people of similar new countries, much smaller in size or less remote from powerful neighbors, have more difficulty in coming to feel at home in a new land. New Zealanders and Canadians, for instance, tend to define their respective self-images with some difficulty and in negative rather than positive terms. When asked to sketch roughly his national stereotype, the New Zealander usually answers, not with a positive statement that most of his countrymen *are* people of such and such a sort, but with two negatives. "Well, we're not as rough and crude as you Australians, of course. No convicts. We're much more like the English. But we're not really as genteel and formal as the English either. We are something in between." Similarly, though Canada's area and emptiness are quite comparable with Australia's, her remoteness is not, and Canadians often seem to feel spiritually overshadowed by the great republic bordering them to the south and by the motherland a few days' voyage away across the Atlantic—not to mention the complications arising from the existence of her great body of French-Canadian citizens. Confronted with the same question, Canadians tend to reply: "You must not for a moment confuse us with the Americans. We are not nearly so materialistic, brash, and so on. We are more like the British. But we are not really as stuffy and old-fashioned as the British either. We are something in between."

To say that the imagination of Australians has tended to be colored, if not dominated, by the vastness of "the great outback" is by no means to suggest that most Australians are hard-bitten and taciturn bushmen more at home in a saddle than a drawing room. In fact, today the great majority of Australians live in the large coastal cities, and Australia has always had a relatively higher proportion of urban dwellers than any other comparable country. Today nearly half of her ten million citizens live in Sydney and Melbourne. Recently there has been some reaction away from outback themes and inspiration in all forms of art, in none more than in poetry. This reaction has made Australian culture a good deal more sophisticated; yet it is not difficult to show that the old motif is still potent, though in a more mature and unself-conscious form. A. D. Hope is one of the three or four living Australian poets whose work posterity may place in the first rank—by world standards and without any special pleading for regional values. His verses are certainly more sophisticated and cosmopolitan than those of most of his Australian contemporaries. Yet one of his best-known poems, "Australia," clearly bodies forth the deep-seated national attitude expressed overtly in the passage from C. E. W. Bean quoted on p. 16:

> Yet there are some like me turn gladly home
> From the lush jungle of modern thought, to find
> The Arabian desert of the human mind,
> Hoping, if still from the deserts the prophets come,
>
> Such savage and scarlet as no green hills dare
> Springs in that waste, some spirit which escapes
> The learned doubt, the chatter of cultured apes
> Which is called civilisation over there.

A similar preoccupation lies behind the work of Patrick White, the greatest Australian novelist. He is disgusted by many aspects

21

of the leveling, collectivist outlook which inspired Bean and other earlier writers, but he is equally concerned with this outlook and fascinated by the unique environment which did so much to evoke it. His characters are preternaturally lonely, in a spiritual sense, like the people in the paintings of Bob Dickerson and so many other modern Australian artists, just as the pioneers of the inland were so often physically lonely. But for White the equalitarian mateship which the pioneers developed in reaction to the loneliness is at best insufficient, at worst a superficial sham which actually emphasizes the isolation of sensitive souls. In *Voss*, White's hero explores the human condition and his own soul by leading an expedition into the endless wastes of the interior. The paintings of Russell Drysdale illustrate the same preoccupation with the consciousness—perhaps subconsciousness would be more accurate now than when Bean wrote—of that "mysterious half-desert country" at the back of the Australian mind.

So much for the uniqueness of the Australian environment and the immigrants' reaction to it. What specific cultural values and assumptions did the immigrants bring with them? That is, from what regions and classes of the British Isles did most of them come?

European or "White" Australia was founded mainly because the victory of the American colonists in their War of Independence deprived Great Britain of a suitably remote dumping place for her convicted criminals. The first fleet, under the command of the able Captain Arthur Phillip, R.N., reached Sydney Cove on January 26, 1788. It carried about 1,100 souls, of whom about nine-tenths were convicts and most of the remainder marine corps soldiers. Transportation of convicts to the eastern mainland continued until 1840, to Van Diemen's Land (later Tasmania) until 1852, and to Western Australia from 1850 to 1868. Altogether, about 160,000 convicts were transported from Britain. Relatively few of them were women, and only about a thousand were political prisoners sentenced for radical or unconventional views. The great majority were simply habitual criminals, who worked for the government or for private employers to whom their services were "assigned." Most of them were thieves from the great English cities, especially London, but there were also many poachers, rick-burners, and other agrarian offenders from the countryside and from Ireland. Many of the Irish convicts, though sentenced usually for ordinary crimes against property, tended to see themselves as patriotic rebels since so much of the property in their country was owned by its English rulers. Future generations of Australians have tended to see them—and to a lesser extent their English and Scottish fellow convicts—in the same charitable light.

Rum and tar were the prevalent odors in early Australia. The first four governors were naval commanders armed with almost absolute powers, and the first staple industries were whaling and sealing. For perhaps the first forty years the colonists looked in imagination outward to the Pacific and homeward across more miles of ocean to Britain. In 1813, after many abortive attempts, the Great Dividing Range was crossed, and by 1830 the great rush of pastoralists to the western plains beyond the mountains was well under way. Thenceforward, sheep and cattle raising provided Australia's staple exports, and men dreamed dreams of the inland rather than of the ocean.

From the beginning, a few of the soldiers and officials sent to administer "the prisoners' country," as the convicts themselves and some contemporaries called it, stayed in Australia. There was little love lost between them and their charges. From about 1830 onward, the fortunes to be made in the pastoral industry, with the help of cheap convict labor, attracted an increasing number of respectable and relatively well-off immigrants, and after transportation to the eastern mainland ceased in 1840, many shiploads of assisted pauper immigrants were brought out to alleviate the almost continuous labor shortage. Nevertheless, until the mid-century probably most Australians were convicts, or ex-convicts, or the offspring of one or more convict progenitors. And the majority of assisted migrants, coming from very much the same social strata in Britain as the convicts, very rapidly assimilated themselves to the mass of the eastern Australian population.

Thus, early Australian society was, in some important respects, perhaps even more class-conscious than British society of the period. In 1822 one observer, James Dixon, wrote that the immigrant to New South Wales would "land in a country possessing two distinct sorts of mankind. He will find that he can hardly avoid attaching himself to one party. . . . Perhaps in all societies, it is in some

23

measure the same, but here it is more strongly felt." [4] The "two distinct sorts of mankind" were the "exclusionists" or "pure Merinos" —the colonial upper class, whose members jealously guarded themselves from any social contact with convicts or the associates or descendants of convicts—and the "emancipists," and they in practice included also their offspring and those who associated with them on familiar terms. This division in early Australian society was accentuated by the existence of only a very small middle class. Almost all consumer goods, except meat and some other basic foods, were imported in bulk and often bought wholesale by pastoralists and other employers for sale to their workers. Colonial manufacturers and retail traders made up a very small portion of the community. The New South Wales census of 1841 listed 4,477 pastoralists, importers, bankers, and professional men and 50,158 mechanics, laborers, servants, and other manual workers. Between these two groups there were only 1,774 "shopkeepers and other retail dealers."

The wealthy and articulate minority for a long time continued to think of themselves as Britons in temporary exile. Generally literate, they usually kept up connections with "Home." Often they sent their sons there to be educated, and sometimes they retired there after making their fortunes in Australia. For many of them in the first half of the last century, even to think of themselves as Australians savored of disloyalty. Transplantation to the new country, however, affected the great bulk of the population very differently. Most of them, especially those of Irish descent, had less reason to love the old country than had the exclusionists and much less chance of visiting or returning to it, even had they wished to do so. As one assisted immigrant girl from London said in 1846: "Oh, what a difference there is between this country and home for poor folks. I know I would not go back again. I know what England is. Old England is a fine place for the rich, but the Lord help the poor." [5]

Thus the great majority of the population, derived from a British working-class background, came to look upon Australia as their

[4] *Narrative of a Voyage to New South Wales* (London: Longman, Hurst, 1822), p. 92.

[5] Quoted in Margaret Kiddle's *Caroline Chisholm* (Melbourne: Melbourne University Press, 1950), p. 243.

home much earlier than did the small group of middle-class colonial employers and transient officials. From this situation sprang the still marked tendency for nationalist and even chauvinist sentiment in Australia to be associated with the social, cultural, and political left rather than the right. This tendency was early strengthened by the large number and pervasive influence among Australian working people of Catholic Irishmen. Before 1851 nearly one-third of the population of New South Wales came from Irish stock and, owing to the appalling poverty of contemporary Ireland, the vast majority of them were unskilled or slightly skilled working people. Most of these Irish-Australians, like their counterparts in the United States in the last century, naturally hated England. Naturally, too, they were among the first to feel strong attachment to the new land of plenty which usually provided more jobs at good wages than men to fill them. If nationalist Australian patriotic sentiment was felt, by Englishmen and Australian conservatives, to weaken imperial loyalties, this was all the more reason for Irish-Australians to nurture local patriotic feeling. Even today there are probably still a few conservatives who feel in their hearts that Australian patriotism consists overwhelmingly, if not solely, in loyalty to Great Britain.

This early dichotomy in the first-settled and most populous convict colonies of New South Wales and Van Diemen's Land had interesting long-term results on Australian society. Until the last decade or two of the nineteenth century, culture (in the narrower and more formal sense of that word) tended naturally to be almost a monopoly of the more cultivated and well-to-do minority. Yet, for this very reason, literature, painting, and art were little more than a rather anemic and artificial provincial reflection of their English exemplars. Before about 1890 formal culture expressed little that was specifically or distinctively Australian. Even when men addressed themselves to local themes they tended to see them through the borrowed spectacles of English cultural conventions. Meanwhile, the less cultivated mass of colonists, thoroughly acclimatized in Australia, evolved a distinctive pronunciation of English speech, salted with a large number of expressions taken from thieves' slang and from their reactions to the new environment; but they produced little beyond a few surviving folk songs and tales to give permanent expression to the developing Australian ethos. There are signs that this ethos might have achieved more formal cultural expression some thirty years earlier than it did if gold had not been discovered in 1851. Just at this time, when the old exclusionist-emancipist dichotomy had practically broken down and when native-born Australians seemed about to become a majority of the population, gold attracted a vast rush of new immigrants.

Between 1851 and 1861 the population almost trebled, rising from 405,350 to 1,145,580. Most of the newcomers had at least enough money to pay the high fares demanded for a ticket to El Dorado, and in those days possession of money was very much more closely correlated than it is now with possession of education and culture. Most of the new immigrants were middle-class or lower-middle-class people, among whom were many skilled tradesmen, artisans, clerks, and a sprinkling of professional men. Most of them, too, were more or less deeply imbued with liberal and radical ideas derived from the British Chartist movement or from the ferment of aspirations which had led to the European revolutions in 1848. To the incipient Australian democratic-nationalist ethos, deeply tinged as it was with collectivist, egalitarian, working-class attitudes, the newcomers added a more respectable, bourgeois, individualist component. Light secondary industries mainly concerned with food processing, clothing, housing, and agricultural implement making sprang up. Secondary schools, universities, libraries, and art galleries appeared in the cities, which began to be something more than crude, coastal, administrative, and trading posts, siphoning manufactured goods into, and wool out of, the interior of the continent. Australian society became more complex and, at least relatively, more sophisticated. Responsible government and a wider measure of parliamentary democracy than existed almost anywhere else at the time were established in the major colonies in 1856. These advanced political institutions worked more smoothly than they might have without the large urban middle class, which was so greatly strengthened, if not quite created, by the new immigrants. For instance, by 1860 most colonies had achieved virtually universal male suffrage and vote by secret ballot. The latter measure came to be known later in America and Britain as the Australian ballot. Such reforms usually took place twenty years or more earlier than in Great Britain, as did the extension of the franchise to adult women in 1902. Yet the inception of these reforms was associated with far less bitterness and tension than was the case in most European countries.

Thus, the effect of the gold-rush immigration was to accelerate the growth of liberal, democratic institutions, but at the same time to delay the emergence of a distinctively Australian national sentiment and culture. Society became more urbanized and more cultivated, but also, at least temporarily, more "English." The most important social effect of the gold rush was to augment greatly the numbers and influence of middle-class people and "English" attitudes, for in Australia whatever is formal, respectable, cultivated, or conservative has always tended to be associated with English values, and whatever is free and easy, rough, untutored, or working class in origin has tended to be associated with "Australianism." It would, however, be quite wrong to imagine that, in this period from about 1860 to 1890, two consciously opposed social groups faced each other as the exclusionists and emancipists had done in the 1830's and early 1840's. From the mid-century onward, new chum immigrants and Old Australians mixed freely. They rapidly came to share a common outlook as "Jimmy Grants" and the native-born influenced each others' manners and outlook. The period was one of fairly steady economic prosperity and expansion, during which it is hard to see even the beginnings of organized political parties based on class or regional interests. Practically all colonial politicians claimed to be liberals, though, to paraphrase Orwell, some were in practice more liberal than others. Members of parliament for the most part voted on each specific issue as it arose, as conscience, private interest, or extraparliamentary pressure groups dictated. The result was that governments, grouped temporarily around influential leaders, rose and fell with almost Gallic frequency. Yet, between 1860 and 1880, two issues which had lasting effects on the nature of Australian society were fought out to the same conclusions in all the colonial parliaments. These were the struggles over the control of the land and over the nature of the educational system. We shall examine each in turn.

By the middle decade of the nineteenth century most of the best land had been taken up for pastoral purposes under long-term lease, and the great flockmasters—they were called "squatters" at the time—had become easily the most influential group in Australia,

27

both socially and politically. Most of the politicians elected under the new democratic franchise belonged, in the ironic words of a contemporary, to "the wealthy lower orders—lawyers, journalists, officials, publicans, and traders of the metropolis." Many of these men, motivated no doubt partly by self-interest, wished to clip the squatters' wings. They did so by promoting the struggle to "unlock the lands." Much, though not most, of the land held on lease by the squatters was quite well-watered enough to support, if subdivided, a very much denser population of small farmers. As easily won surface gold became scarce, many ex-miners and others sought an alternative and more secure means of making a living. Their voices and votes swelled the agitation. In 1861 John Robertson's government in New South Wales passed two land acts which allowed any bona fide agriculturist to select before survey up to 320 acres of state land on payment of a small deposit, whether it was leased to a squatter or not. By living and working on the land, the selector could acquire its freehold over a period of time—or so the framers of the acts hoped. Similar laws were passed in Victoria and in the other colonies, but the prosperous yeomanry which had been the subject of so much political oratory was not established so quickly or easily. In South Australia, and to a lesser extent in Tasmania, peculiar geographic and historical conditions had created a relatively stable and prosperous wheat-farming industry even before the selection acts of the 1860's. In Victoria the legislation did succeed in placing some good lands in the hands of genuine small-scale farmers, but even more of the best country fell into the freehold possession of the great pastoral proprietors and companies. In New South Wales and Queensland this unlooked-for result was even more apparent. High transport costs and lack of skill and capital combined to frustrate the petty agriculturalists until railways began in the 1890's effectively to serve the potential wheat-growing areas. In fact, it was not until 1899 that New South Wales grew enough wheat to feed its own citizens.

In the long run, the aims of those who had sought to lessen the power of the squatters were achieved. By the time of the First World War most of the big pastoral estates had been subdivided again and again, and the process has continued since. A large class of self-employed farmer-proprietors did come into existence, however slowly and painfully. The squatters retained, as they still do, much of their social prestige, but their political power and influence were reduced to something more nearly commensurate with their numbers in the community. At the same time, small-scale proprietors —both rural and urban—professional men, and others strengthened middle-class influence so much that by the first decade of this century when the Labor party became a power in the land, it proved to be possibly even less "revolutionary" and more "patriotic" in action than its British counterpart.

Before 1860 the education of Australian children had been left largely to the churches and to a few enterprising persons who set up as private schoolmasters or tutors. Colonial governments had offered subsidies to the schools of all religious denominations, but some clerics, particularly in South Australia where nonconformity was very strong, rejected any kind of government aid lest it should bring with it government interference. The result was that nearly half of the country's children grew up barely literate. Reformers proposed that the governments themselves should set up their own school systems, but there was argument over the place of religious teaching in the proposed national schools. Catholics, who comprised about a quarter of the community, held more firmly than any other denomination that religious instruction must be an integral part of education, but they tended to see as a Protestant plot proposals that the national schools should teach, in an unsectarian way, the dogmas common to all Christians. While church leaders disputed, acrimoniously but inconclusively, radical and liberal opinion grew more convinced that the only practicable solution was for the state to set up its own system of entirely secular schools, leaving the churches to provide their own denominational schools for those of their adherents who wanted them and could afford, or felt bound in conscience, to pay the necessary fees. By 1880 all the eastern colonies had established systems of state-controlled, secular education. School attendance was compulsory in the sense that parents who did not send a child to any other school, religious or private, had to send him to the state school. Supported by government revenues, these state schools charged no fees at all after the first few years of their existence.

Those who had fought for the secular system thought that nearly all children would soon be attending the government schools, as in the United States, but this is not quite what happened in Australia. Catholic church leaders denounced the government schools as "seed-plots of future immorality, infidelity and lawlessness," and, by prodigious efforts, set up a comprehensive system of religious schools of their own. Most of these schools charged very low fees, and the vast majority of Australian Catholic children attended them, as they still do, while the vast majority of Protestant children attend the state schools. Even before the government schools were established, however, all the larger churches had founded a few more or less fashionable secondary schools of their own in the capital cities. These church schools are sometimes called "great public schools," being modeled closely on the so-called great public schools of England, and their number has increased—though not relatively as rapidly as that of the government secondary schools—up to the present day. These schools, which charge high fees, have tended to act as a brake on the very strong leveling tendencies in Australian life. They are relatively more influential than the military-style preparatory academies and other private schools in America, but less so than the "great public schools" in Britain.

With the last decade of the nineteenth century the post-gold-rush era of expansion came to a sudden and painful end. The country was rocked by three catastrophes, still often known as the great strike, the great depression, and the great drought. Only Western Australia, which enjoyed a gold boom during the nineties, escaped. Yet, despite—or perhaps partly because of—these trials, the decade also saw immense growth in national cultural awareness and activity. It is not a very great exaggeration to say that Australian culture—as opposed to a provincial reflection of English culture—was born in the nineties.

Much of the preceding prosperity, particularly in Victoria, most populous of the colonies at the period, had been built on money borrowed too recklessly from British investors by governments and private entrepreneurs. Overseas wool prices began to fall rather sharply after 1886. Many employers sought to protect their incomes by lowering wages, while employees reacted accordingly. The already strong trade-union movement spread rapidly to embrace many previously unorganized men working in unskilled or semiskilled occupations in industries such as grazing, mining, and transport. The

30

great strike was really a series of strikes and lockouts which extended with intervals from 1890 to 1894. In most of the disputes the fundamental bone of contention was what the employers called "freedom of contract"—the right they claimed to employ anyone they chose at mutually agreed-upon terms. The trade-union leaders demanded the closed shop—their right to bargain collectively with employers for high wages and to exclude nonunionists from industry. Particularly in the pastoral industry and in Queensland, feeling was very bitter, and there were a few hotheads on both sides who talked of the possibility of civil war. There was some violence, but little or no actual loss of life. All the colonial governments sided, though not always openly, with the employers, and the unions were crushingly defeated. Not so crushingly, however, but that they had regained their former strength by the time of Federation in 1901.

Meanwhile, defeat turned the minds of trade-union and radical leaders in other directions. Two shiploads of idealists, led by William Lane and Mary Gilmore, went to Paraguay to found an unsuccessful socialist community which they called New Australia. Mary Gilmore, long a prominent Australian poet, was one of those who returned after a few years. The frustration of industrial action stimulated the majority of trade-unionists to think more about politics. Many of them joined the embryonic labor parties which became extremely powerful during the next decade. Distrust of the mighty prompted the labor movement to exact from aspiring members of parliament a pledge that they would always cast their votes in accordance with labor policy, as determined in advance by a meeting of Labor party members. The existing free-trade and protectionist parties bitterly denounced this "regimentation of members' consciences by outside bodies"; but in self-defense they had to tighten up the organization and discipline of their own parties. By 1909 the Labor party was so strong in the federal parliament that the other two parties fused to oppose it.

The great depression may also have stimulated the rapid growth of the Labor party. Between 1891 and 1894 most of the banks in Australia failed outright, suspended payments for a period, or were reconstructed in some way. Unemployment rose to previously unheard-of levels. Some of the people whose livelihood had disappeared joined the 80,000 or so who went to Western Australia during the decade, drawn by the rich gold discoveries in that previously backward colony. Others no doubt voted for the new political party which often denounced the shortcomings of capitalism and always professed to stand for the interests of the working man.

Reeling from the effects of the strike and the depression, the country was further tried by the most prolonged drought in its recorded history. For seven years most districts had poor and patchy rainfall, and many in the north and the interior had practically none. When the drought finally ended in 1902, it is said that outback children were terrified by the unknown sound of rain rattling down on the galvanized iron roofs of the homesteads.

These trying experiences made some thoughtful Australians ask new questions about themselves and their country, their relationship with it and its relationship with the rest of the world. A more important cause of the nationalist cultural awakening was probably the fact that native-born Australians for the first time heavily outnumbered immigrants. The percentage of the total Australian population born in the United Kingdom declined during the period as follows: 1861, 53.18 per cent; 1871, 40.44 per cent; 1881, 30.66 per cent; 1891, 25.86 per cent; 1901, 18.00 per cent. It is safe to say that nearly all of those not born in the United Kingdom were native-born Australians—that, for example, in 1890 roughly three-quarters of the people knew no other country, climate, or customs than those to which they had been born. It was natural for them to feel dissatisfied with their colonial status and to begin dreaming of a single Australian nation.

These aspirations were forwarded by such organizations as the Australian Natives' Association which was founded in Victoria in 1871 and became very influential in the 1890's. At the same time the separate settlements had expanded inland from their isolated beginnings until the four capitals of the most populous mainland colonies, New South Wales, Victoria, Queensland, and South Australia, were linked by rail in 1888. External events, moreover, gave some cause for concern. In 1883 rumors of German plans to occupy New Guinea provoked Queensland to raise the Union Jack at Port Moresby. Although Sir Thomas McIlwraith's government proposed to pay for the administration of the new colony, the British government disapproved this action. In 1884, when Germany did annex northeastern New Guinea, Queenslanders and many other Australians felt they had been let down by Colonial Office bungling; but Britain was able to reply that the Australian colonies must find a means of speaking with one voice if they wished to be heard in Whitehall.

The patriotic awakening found its most obvious expression in literature, art, and politics. For the first time there arose a generation of Australian writers who owed little to English models. Most of them contributed to the *Bulletin*, a radical, nationalist Sydney weekly journal, founded in 1880, which circulated in all the colonies and especially in the back country which was felt to be the symbolic home of truly Australian values. The *Bulletin* came to be known as "the Bushman's Bible" and wielded an immense influence on Australian attitudes up till about the time of the First World War. On August 31, 1903, even the remote and august London *Times* recognized the *Bulletin*'s importance: "It is hard to overestimate the extent to which this journal modifies the opinions (one might almost say the character) of its readers. . . . Its candour verges on the cynical, but the Australian has no objection to humour in his politics or grimness in his jests."

The greatest of the new writers were Henry Lawson, A. B. ("Banjo") Paterson, and Joseph Furphy. All wrote mainly, though not exclusively, of outback life, and their verse owed as much to the anonymous, orally transmitted yarns and ballads of the common Australian folk, who had long acclimatized themselves in the new land, as it did to overseas literary influences. At its best, their work was vigorous, racy, and absolutely true to the emerging national ethos. At its worst, it was slipshod, brash, and sentimental, protesting far too much its independence and Australianism. Furphy, for instance, prefaced his great novel, *Such Is Life*, with the statement that it was in "temper democratic, bias offensively Australian." To many men of the time the two adjectives seemed synonymous, and most apparently felt in their bones that the true or "typical" democratic Australian was the bushman. A stanza from one of Lawson's poems in the *Bulletin* of August 27, 1892, sums up the outlook of these men in its most exaggerated form:

Ye landlords of the cities that are builded by the sea—
You toady 'Representative,' you careless absentee—

I come, a scout from Borderland, to warn you of a change,
To tell you of the spirit that is roused beyond the Range;
I come from where on western plains the lonely homesteads stand,
To tell you of the coming of the Natives of the Land!
   Of the Land we're living in
   The Natives of the Land,
For Australian men are gathering—they are joining hand in hand.
Don't you hear the battle coo-ey [6] of the Natives of the Land?

The new writing of the nineties, like the new painting by such men as Tom Roberts and Sir Arthur Streeton, was tremendously popular. It held up to Australians for the first time a mirror in which all could observe the pleasing spectacle of themselves limned large. Although the population was then only about 3,500,000, the *Literary Year Book* probably did not exaggerate when it wrote of Paterson's *The Man from Snowy River:* "The immediate success of this book of bush ballads was without parallel in Colonial Literary annals, nor could any living English or American poet boast so wide a public, always excepting Mr. Rudyard Kipling." The cultural upsurge of the nineties played a considerable, if imponderable, part in bringing about formal national unity in 1901 when the six colonies federated to form the Commonwealth of Australia. So, of course, did the ambitions of political horse traders, of certain business groups, and of producers seeking a wider market than was afforded by each separate colony. Yet the first federal parliaments up to the time of the First World War did give legislative form to much that was basic in the emerging national ethos. These laws were passed mainly by liberal (protectionist) or labor parties mutually supporting each other, but the generally more conservative free-trade group, the official opposition for most of the period, usually agreed with the principles, if not the details, of the legislation. The nationalist awakening, based on a contemporary recognition of what the past had produced, was at least equally concerned with utopian visions of a future in which the new nation, unsullied by the inherited follies and vices of the Old World, would be something like a model commonwealth for the common man—the white, Australian common

⁶ Coo-ey or coo-ee: An aboriginal word taken into English by the early settlers. It is shouted in a long-drawn-out way and on a high note with a rising inflection and is used as a greeting or hail when people are seeking others at a distance in the bush.

man, of course. Many, even including many politicians, seem to have felt more or less coherently the aspirations voiced by another contemporary writer, A. H. Adams, in his poem, "The Australian":

> Once more this Autumn-earth is ripe
> Parturient of another type.
>
> While with the past old nations merge
> His foot is on the Future's verge.
>
> They watch him as they huddle, pent,
> Striding a spacious continent,
>
> Above the level desert's marge
> Looming in his aloofness large.
>
> .   .   .   .   .
>
> He sees beyond your hazy fears;
> He roads the desert of the years.
>
> .   .   .   .   .
>
> So, towards undreamt-of destinies
> He slouches down the centuries.

The last line hints at the rather tepid respect with which Australians traditionally are supposed to regard hard work or even any form of unnecessary activity, such as standing up straight if there is a handy post to lean on.

Implicit in Adams' verses, too, are the delusions of racial grandeur felt by so many people of European descent, and by none more than Australians, before the Second World War had shown the depths of the moral abyss to which racism leads. Adams' lines remind us not only of the radical democratic aspirations of the *Bulletin*, but also of its slogan, "Australia for the Australians—The cheap Chinaman, the cheap nigger, and the cheap European pauper to be absolutely excluded." But to the men of the time an isolationist racism seemed to be not a contradiction of the liberal, collectivist democracy which the emergent Commonwealth meant to many, but rather the prime condition of its being. Early Commonwealth laws have sometimes been considered in two groups—one which aimed at strengthening nationalist sentiment and security and one which sought to raise living standards and strengthen social security—but in practice the most important legislation was usually concerned with both ends.

35

Thus, the first national parliament confirmed and strengthened the existing practice of all the colonies by passing the Immigration Restriction Act in 1901. By providing devices for the exclusion of colored migrants, this act implemented what has long been known as the "White Australia Policy." Its aim then was nationalistic—to preserve what was known as "racial purity"; but much of the argument used to support the policy, both inside and outside parliament, was economic. Australia's high standard of living must be protected from the depressing effects which would surely follow the introduction of cheap Asian, African, or Polynesian labor.

The most characteristic and important legislation of this period was that implementing the policy of New Protection, initiated by the native-born Liberal prime minister, Alfred Deakin. In its primary, narrower sense, this legislation sought to protect struggling Australian industries from powerful foreign or British competitors; but however great its need, a given firm was to receive government help only if it could show that its employees would receive in high minimum wages and good working conditions an equitable share of the resultant prosperity. In a far broader sense, New Protection soon came to mean a wide range of laws which implemented or extended the democratic-nationalist aspirations held to be fundamental in the Australian way of life. This, for reasons suggested above, was more collectivist and egalitarian, less individualistic and competitive, than its American counterpart. In 1904, for instance, the Commonwealth government set up a court for "the prevention and settlement of industrial disputes extending beyond the limits of any one state." H. B. Higgins, its first president, was a courageous and wise reformer. In 1907 he handed down his epoch-making "Harvester judgment."

H. V. McKay Ltd., a large firm of agricultural implement makers, sought an exemption from excise duty under the New Protection laws. To gain this indirect subsidy, the firm had to show the court that the working conditions of its employees were fair and reasonable. Higgins heard a great deal of evidence and refused the exemption on the grounds that the wages paid by the firm were not high enough to meet "the normal needs of the average employee regarded as a human being living in a civilised community." From this judgment sprang the concept of the basic wage. All manner of minor alterations and additions to the legislation have been made since 1907, but the basic wage has remained a fundamental pillar of the Australian way of life. No adult male, working the full hours of the legal working week (40 since 1947), may be paid less than the minimum wage, no matter how unskilled his work or how unskillfully he performs it. Trade-union vigilance has helped to ensure that the law is carried out. Indeed, Albert Métin, a discerning French visitor of 1901, named his book on Australian life *Le Socialisme sans doctrines*. Australia was not a socialist country, of course, but by the time of the First World War she had advanced farther than perhaps any other land along the road to the welfare state. To this extent, the utopian dreaming of the nineties was justified by future events. There was a slowing of the rate at which state paternalism advanced after 1914, and today Australia lags in many such fields behind certain Scandinavian countries and even Great Britain. But the direction of the movement and the basic assumptions do not appear to have changed significantly.

The First World War brought experimental social legislation to a temporary halt. It also split the traditionally isolationist Labor party, most of whose members were opposed to conscripting men for military service outside Australia. So, as it turned out when they twice voted on the issue in the referendums of 1916 and 1917, were most of the electors. But the same electors returned anti-Labor or Nationalist governments to the federal parliament throughout the interwar period, except for one short-lived and conspicuously unsuccessful term of Labor party rule in 1929–1932. In the 1920's there was some optimistic expansion, but the world-wide depression of the thirties quickly halted it. The large queues of unemployed understandably resented any competition for the few jobs available, and immigration, even of Britons, fell away to almost nothing. Australia's self-centered tendency to isolationism, disturbed briefly by the "War to End Wars," was reinforced by the bitter depression years. On the whole, the interwar period was one when the country marked time. Many citizens felt disillusioned after the heady visions of the 1890's and 1900's, yet contemporary experience suggested to them little more than a continuing, sour acceptance of the traditional attitudes whence the visions had sprung.

It is too early to write with any certainty about the effects of the

Second World War on the Australian ethos, but not too soon to notice current trends springing from important material changes that accompanied and followed the conflict. First, the war accelerated, if it did not cause, something like an Australian industrial revolution. Previously, secondary industries had been growing slowly under the Commonwealth government's protective tariff, but the depression of the 1930's showed all too clearly that the country still rode substantially on the back of the primary producer. During and after the Second World War, however, Australia became the major manufacturing nation of the Southwest Pacific area. In the twenty years between 1938 and 1958 the number of factories and factory employees doubled, while the real value of secondary industrial production increased nearly three times, and power units used nearly quadrupled. Consumer goods like motorcars, refrigerators, and washing machines, formerly luxuries imported from abroad, were made in such quantities as to supply the home market and leave a substantial surplus for export.

Second, as no other previous event had done, the war ended much of Australia's physical and spiritual isolation. The fall of Singapore and Japanese air raids on Australian ports, not to mention the grueling New Guinea campaign, forced even the most provincial isolationists to realize that henceforth Asian neighbors would have to be reckoned with in one way or another. Moreover, for the first time since the gold rush of the 1850's, nearly all Australians came to know personally at least some foreigners. Hundreds of thousands of American soldiers and quite a number of Dutch, Indonesian, Chinese, and other war refugees passed through the country. Many of them lived there for years and were welcomed in Australian homes. In addition, the gas ovens of Belsen and Maidenek caused many Australians, like other people, to revise the racist assumptions they had held for so long. After the war all political parties agreed in supporting the unprecedented immigration program which was made economically possible by the continued industrial boom. Well over a million selected British and European migrants have been settled in the continent since 1946. They are known, both officially and in ordinary daily usage, as New Australians, not as "Pommies," "Dagoes," "Reffoes" (short for "refugees"), and so forth, as was the case before the second war. Gallup polls show that, though no political party will yet query the sacred cow of the White Australia Policy, a small majority of citizens is coming to favor a controlled quota system for Asian and other non-European migrants. The extent to which these changes in the traditional Australian outlook on racist matters will prove permanent remains to be seen. Students and other young people accept newcomers, even Asian and African visitors, in a way that astonishes most of their parents and horrifies many surviving grandparents; yet tolerance of newcomers might be severely tested if a depression were to make jobs really scarce again.

Meanwhile, the migrants have brought with them many new industrial skills and a higher valuation of education and culture (in the narrower sense) than was common in prewar Australia. University student enrollments, for instance, have quadrupled since 1939. Society has become considerably more urbanized, more complex, and more sophisticated. Probably, too, business has become more competitive. It more often happens now than it did before the war that a building will be finished within a few months of the contract date, or that a wrist watch, left for repairs, will be ready on the promised day; but to North American visitors at least, such examples of drive and efficiency still seem shockingly rare. For though many New Australians have sought security in a most un-Australian way—by working inordinately hard for more than forty hours a week—many more have quickly absorbed, in trade-unions and elsewhere, much of the traditional Australian outlook which is by no means confined to trade-unionists. Many graziers, for instance, still endorse by their own practice the sentiments of one intelligent and well-descended squatter who has no time for pasture improvement, though he tried it for some years. His wool check doubled, but his expenditure on seed, artificial manures, extra labor, and so on almost doubled too. He paid income tax at a higher rate. In the end, he realized that he was producing twice the amount of wool for perhaps an extra £1,000 or more a year—but at the same time working almost twice as hard as before the experiment. The last consideration was decisive in its abandonment.

The current influx of new men, money, and ideas is, after all, relatively by no means as great as was that of the gold-rush decade a century ago. Then it seemed to most contemporaries that the whole of Australian life had been transformed; so much so that some historians wrote of the second or "real" foundation of Australia in 1851. In the longer-term historical view, however, the influence of already existing local traditions on the gold seekers has seemed as great as or greater than, the changes wrought on the local outlook by the newcomers. Time may prove the same to have been true of today's immigrants. It is certain that most of their teen-age children speak English with a broad Australian accent, as though born to the manner; and I have often been intrigued in the classroom to find these young Reimersmas or Komorofskies riding on with "The Man from Snowy River" even more wholeheartedly than their Old Australian classmates.

In this chapter we have tried to sketch the origins and nature of the social matrix out of which a specifically Australian outlook has grown. In other words, by characterizing Australian culture in the broadest anthropological sense, we have sought to explain the distinctive tone of Australian culture in the narrower sense. In doing so, we have necessarily stressed those aspects of life which are specifically or characteristically Australian. Inevitably we have underemphasized, or even ignored, those more numerous aspects of the Australian scene which are more or less common to all English-speaking, British-derived societies. For this imbalance we shall not be forgiven by many respectable Australians who, now as in past days, like or need to stress their generalized British identity; but we may hope to have made Australia and the Australian way of life easier for an outsider to understand. Further, by stressing the more distinctive elements in the Australian tradition we help to explain also those elements opposed to them. One could hardly understand, for example, many of the characters in the novels of Martin Boyd and of Henry Handel Richardson without knowing what it is that these sensitive, cosmopolitan souls were reacting *against*. In some forms of art the reaction has been almost as strident as was the original cultural expression of an Australian ethos in the 1890's, when some patriots seriously proposed that citizens should express approbation on public occasions by giving three coo-ees instead of three cheers. Since the Second World War the tension between the old and the new, the imported and the homemade, the "British" and the "Australian" has come considerably nearer to a mature resolution such as that reached by American culture in the last half-century or so. At the same time, there are signs that this fruitful tension may be replaced by another one—that between old Anglo-Australian traditions and new American influences.

BIBLIOGRAPHY

Allen, H. C. *Bush and Backwoods.* 1959.
Clark, M. *Sources of Australian History.* 1961.
Crawford, R. M. *Australia.* 1952.
Fitzpatrick, Brian. *The Australian People.* 1946.
Grattan, C. Hartley. *Introducing Australia.* 1949.
Greenwood, G., ed. *Australia: A Social and Political History.* 1955.
Harris, Alexander. *Settlers and Convicts.* Ed. C. M. H. Clark. 1953.
Hancock, W. K. *Australia.* 1945.
Kiddle, Margaret. *Men of Yesterday.* 1961.
Palmer, Vance. *The Legend of the Nineties.* 1954.
Shaw, A. G. L. *The Story of Australia.* 1955.
Ward, Russel. *The Australian Legend.* 1958.
White, Patrick. *Riders in the Chariot.* 1961.

LITERATURE

CECIL HADGRAFT

THE earliest Australian literature was already old. This was a necessary consequence of history. Poetry began in Australia as an imitation, rather belated, of typically eighteenth-century forms and themes. It remained imitative for nearly a century.

A sprinkling of verses appeared in the official newspaper, the *Sydney Gazette*, soon after its establishment in 1803. The first thin trickle of verse came from Michael Massey Robinson (1747–1826), a convicted blackmailer, pardoned after arrival, who from 1810 to 1821 wrote odes celebrating public occasions. The convict was followed by a judge, Barron Field (1786–1846), friend of Charles Lamb, who produced the colony's first volume of verse in 1819. Field's verse was as poor as his law, and today only the professed student recalls more than the following two lines of it:

> Kangaroo, Kangaroo!
> Thou spirit of Australia.

Field found Australia sometimes comic, but always distasteful. Others found it repellent. There was no reason why they should love it—they had not wanted to go there. The native-born was likely to have a different opinion. Such was William Charles Wentworth (1792–1872), the first and still among the greatest of Australian statesmen. After his matriculation at Cambridge, he wrote *Australasia*, which took second place to Winthrop Mackworth Praed's entry in competition for the Chancellor's Medal in 1823. Wentworth writes in couplets, in diction worn faceless by a century of use, but with an affection for his distant homeland which, with the help of the anthologists, has kept him remembered as a poet. He looks forward to colonial and national glories: should Britannia, bow'd by luxury, yield its pride of place,

> May this—thy last-born infant—then arise,
> To glad thy heart, and greet thy parent eyes,
> And Australasia float, with flag unfurl'd,
> A new Britannia in another world!

But all this was, in a way, occasional verse, written by a man with something more important to do. The next two were men who wanted rather badly to be honored by their country for their poetic devotion to it. Both were derivative, both tended to see the Australian scene through the spectacles of their reading in English poetry; but both had something in them of the poet dedicated to a calling.

Charles Harpur (1813–1868), whose life was a punctuated catalogue of misfortunes, had read his Milton, his neoclassics, his Wordsworth—but to more than some purpose. His blank verse, too reminiscent of his great master, falls away into sandy wastes; his descriptions are redolent of Augustan phrasing. His best work is found in his narratives, where he can capture, for instance, the excitement and tension of an escape from hostile aborigines. His historical place is as the first Australian poet with some bulk of work; and in one poem he greenly suggests what at the end of the century was to appear as the bush ballad. This short verse-tale of Harpur's, "Ned Connor," with its flavor of "The Rime of the Ancient Mariner," has a bush setting, some movement, and a gathering speed, but its formality is rather far from the colloquial roughness of the bush ballad.

Harpur's admirer, Henry Kendall (1839–1882), weaker in character and as unfortunate, but luckier in his friends, reveals a greater variety. Like Harpur he is full of echoes, and his poetry recalls Tennyson, Arnold, Byron, and Swinburne in varying degrees. This

43

tendency to repeat others—and himself—is one of his two obvious failings; the other is his addiction to the "poetical" word, his belief that *splendid, sublime, stately,* and other such vaguely connotative words will produce the adequate response. Kendall is best read in a selection; for instance, Tom Inglis Moore's *Selected Poems of Henry Kendall,* which contains an Introduction that, though perhaps too kindly, is likely to remain the standard estimate. The variety in his verse stretches from lyric to satire (this last a little unexpected in its trenchancy), with elegy, narrative, description, and humor along the way. Despite his faults of vagueness and bathos, Kendall remains among the sweetest of our singers, pensive and nostalgic, finding often in the voice and hue of creek and mountain the echoes and reflections of his own inner melancholy:

> I think I hear the echo still
>   Of long forgotten tones,
> When evening winds are on the hill,
>   And sunset fires the cones.

The last poet of any concern in this period offers considerable contrast to Harpur and Kendall. They were both born in Australia, knew and loved its coastal areas, and tried with what powers they had to render its softness or its ruggedness, its music or its silence. Adam Lindsay Gordon (1833–1870) arrived in Australia at the age of twenty and remained English to his death. A myopic roughrider, he wrote little description. Careless in verse as in life, he told of risks taken, dangers overcome, the excitement of the chase. His chief importance is that a few of his narratives set the fashion which the *Bulletin* later fostered into the bush ballads. He has been the subject of one of the queerest incidents in our literature. A few misguided enthusiasts, hero-worshiping Gordon, finally stormed Westminster Abbey, so that in Poets' Corner there now stands a bust of Gordon inscribed "Poet of Australia," an odd memorial to one who was never of Australia and—so some may think—was barely a poet.

The poetry of this period, then, leans heavily on that of England. Consequently, when it describes the new and sometimes bizarre land, it lacks ways to capture the essential quality. It will, for instance, use words like *dell,* where the associations now seem to us grotesquely inappropriate. In a way, wherever they were born, the poets of this period are like English poets put down in Australia.

The early novelists were more successful in their picturing. They encountered a land enormously larger than Britain, endowed with strange fauna and flora, often drought-stricken in the interior, reluctant and hostile, where sheep were to spread over its holdings, where gold was later to be found lacing its veins, and where the bushranger and the aborigine were normal subjects of talk and fiction. These differences were the staple of fiction, and to some extent they have remained so.

The first novel was *Quintus Servinton* (1830–1831), the product of Henry Savery (1791–1842), a businessman of Bristol transported to Tasmania for uttering fraudulent bills. A long, detailed work, it is in the main an autobiography. Its value lies in its priority, the picture it gives of certain aspects of the convict and social systems of the period, and its general readability. Formal and old-fashioned in the telling, it can nevertheless still wake interest.

From this first novel to the 1880's, a period of half a century, about three hundred works of fiction dealing with Australia were published. Of this bulk only a student of the period is concerned with more than half a dozen. Even the members of a recognizable genre, the guidebook novels, covering the years 1840–1860, are not remembered individually. They served, under the guise of fiction, as introductions to the country for newcomers. They deal with life on the land—costs of stocking a run, seasons, dangers (snakes, bush fires, aborigines, and the like), the people, and the customs. Over this information a relish of adventure is spread with a fairly lavish hand.

Of the still-remembered novels, the first is *Ralph Rashleigh* (1844–1845), surviving only in manuscript until its publication in part in 1929 and in full in 1952. Its author, thanks to the investigations of Colin Roderick, has been identified as one James Tucker (1808–1866), a weakly vicious criminal transported for blackmail, who put into the first half of this story much that he experienced himself. It may be read as a partial exculpation: Do the guilty deserve all this? It records an aspect of convictism different from Savery's—that of the shackles and the cat, of degradation and injustice. The second part of the book is drawn from tales of aborigines that Tucker had heard and from his imagination.

Three other novels remain, all on the stock themes of the age—

45

pastoral life, convictism, and bushranging. *The Recollections of Geoffry Hamlyn* (1859) by Henry Kingsley (1830–1876), brother of the more famous Charles, is a novel of exile, of a group of Englishmen who come to Australia to make their fortune, succeed, and gratefully return to England. It is not that they dislike the new land —indeed, there are almost lyrical passages of description—they simply feel it is hardly the place in which English gentlemen would wish to stay. This attitude was not uncommon.

Very different from the sunny artlessness of *Geoffry Hamlyn* is *For the Term of His Natural Life* (1870–1871 as a serial; a few years later in a shortened version; 1929 in full). Its unlikely author was Marcus Clarke (1846–1881), who arrived in Australia as a rather unstable youth in 1863 and wrote this astonishing production when he was only twenty-four. It is the most powerful Australian novel of the last century and still keeps its place among the first half-dozen. The atmosphere is one of unrelieved brutality, an impression that Clarke derived from his reading in the Tasmanian penal records. Its chief figure, Rufus Dawes, unjustly condemned and as unjustly tormented, perishes tragically at the moment of seeming deliverance. Like Tucker, Clarke blacks the chimney: such things did happen, but the novel suggests a system more horrible than historical warrant affords.

The fourth novel, *Robbery under Arms* (1882–1883 as a serial; 1888 in 3 volumes), takes rustling and bushranging for its themes. Its author, Thomas Alexander Browne (1826–1915), wrote this and his other novels under the pen name of Rolf Boldrewood. Perhaps read today more by adolescents than by adults, the novel has a lively excitement and colloquial gusto and supposedly was written by one of the participants when in prison. For the social historian, it is of interest as containing a group of recognizably Australian characters.

These novels capture the feel and movement of their times and in some ways serve almost as historical documents. Aspects of Australia live in their pages. The poets, with a keener eye for natural surroundings, are not so successful. Their comparative failure is due to language; their diction draws a thin veil between reader and reality.

The drama of the period is relatively unimportant. Theatrical activity began as early as 1789, but the writing of plays did not come till later. Nineteenth-century Australian drama was imitative of the contemporary English drama, and many of the plays written were set in England. But from 1825 on there was an occasional play set in Australia, and generally in these there was some attempt to comment on the new country. Verse was sometimes used, the language was removed from reality, action was sensational, and characterization was "stock." Comedy, when it occurred, was provided by English cockney types, but the setting and story were sometimes local.

Most of this applies to the first dramatist, David Burn, an English naval officer who in 1842 published a volume of plays (none of which is concerned with Australia), but who left also the manuscript of *The Bushrangers,* which deals with convict days in Tasmania. Charles Harpur, the poet, also wrote a literary melodrama mainly in verse (1853) with the same title. It is too wordy to be a good melodrama and is not good enough poetry to be a dramatic poem. More interesting is a play by Walter Cooper, a lawyer, who, in *Colonial Experience* (1869), made a genuine attempt to investigate the colonial temperament by contrasting its rough, independent humor with the attitudes of various affected types of migrants. Something of the Australian independence appears also in the work of P. A. Dutruc. From his play, *Fame and Fortune in Twentyfour Hours* (1878), comes the following dialogue:

Boaster. The aristocracy! In Sydney! With one or two exceptions, where are they to be found?

Augusta. Well, sir! Besides our shepherd-kings and princely merchants, have we not many knights whose titles are the more honourable because they owe them not merely to birth or chance, but to their own merit?

The imitation grows less and the original material more as the century advances. By the eighties actor-managers were emerging who looked for Australian material to put on and who themselves sometimes wrote it.

The poets of the period from 1880 to 1914 may be loosely gathered into three groups: the "public" poets, commemorating or reprehending and often looking hopefully to the future; a smaller group that it is a little misleading but very tempting to call "aesthetes"; and the largest group, the bush balladists, themselves of more than one type.

The most notable of the "public" poets was James Brunton Ste-

47

phens (1835–1902), a cultured Scot, metrically deft, who wrote some of the best comic verse and a narrative, "Convict Once," that has been both overpraised and undervalued. He also wrote a few poems exhorting his new fellow countrymen, which cover a quarter of a century and begin with hope and aspiration:

> So flows beneath our good and ill
> A viewless stream of Common Will,
> A gathering force, a present might,
> That from its silent depths of gloom
> At Wisdom's voice shall leap to light,
> And hide our barren feuds in bloom,
> Till, all our sundering lines with love o'ergrown,
> Our bounds shall be the girdling seas alone.

Stephens later urges the separate states to forget their jealousies and to federate as a dominion. In a third poem he offers a hymn of triumph as though the dominion had already come into being. He lived to see his hopes realized, dedicating his "Fulfilment" to Queen Victoria. But the note of warning, something of a favorite tune with public poets of the time, is sounded also; the future of the Federation lies in his readers' hands:

> But not so ends the task to build
> Into the fabric of the world
> The substance of our hope fulfilled.

George Essex Evans (1863–1909) was the most vocally hortative of the group. Like Stephens he shows variety—humor, narrative, public verse. Inferior to the elder man in skill, he equals his force with a coarser vigor and writes of figures and incidents of the time. Although he is in the main not deluded by visions of the future, he still echoes the slightly overblown sentiments of nationalism and patriotism:

> This is the last of all the lands
> Where Freedom's fray-torn banner stands,
> Not wrested yet from freemen's hands.

Perhaps his very lack of sensibility makes him the more representative of such contemporary attitudes.

Not one of these "public" poets was born in Australia. But they appear to have had some sense of obligation before reaching the new land, and on arrival they found causes and movements to engage their dutiful enthusiasm. The resultant verse may inspire, but it is unlikely to be inspired. It is Australian in a political or national manner, and it has native idealism; but it hardly represents in an everyday fashion what comes home to men's business and bosoms.

Of the small group who seem to stand aside from the Australian scene, the best known is Victor Daley (1858–1905), an Irishman who reached Australia at the age of twenty. The conventional idea of Daley as a Bohemian—a facile writer of an idealized past, of nostalgia and lost love, all in a diction of the type prevalent in England in the nineties—is now sixty years old and seems certain to prevail. The attempt made, in a volume collected years after his death—*Creeve Roe* (1947)—to show him as essentially a democratic singer lashing abuses, has proved futile. It is ironic that in one poem, "Corregio Jones," he reprehends Australian painters for their neglect of native subjects and their fondness for the past—in short, for doing with paint what he was doing with words. Today Daley reads like a diluted Dowson.

The other member of the group—if indeed it can be called a group as it had no overt aim—is Roderic Quinn (1867–1949), more robust but more unequal than Daley. His "Currency Lass" still is remembered as catching, with some rhythmic dexterity, a sort of macabre, ballad-like quality. Both Daley and Quinn show a greater formal competence in verse than any earlier poet except Brunton Stephens. In the period they blossom like thin-rooted exotics.

Their robust opposites are the bush balladists. These are not to be confused with the writers of the old bush songs. Most bush songs, and probably the best, were composed before 1860, the end of the gold-rush days. The authors are, in general, unknown. (Douglas Stewart and Nancy Keesing's collection, *Old Bush Songs and Rhymes of Colonial Times* (1957), which contains over two hundred and covers a period almost up to yesterday, lists about three-quarters as anonymous.) The words, as often as not, are modified versions of songs already known, and the tunes had existed previously. The themes, sometimes treated humorously, sometimes nostalgically, sometimes seriously, range from convictism to bushranging to the hard life in the outback. Sociologically, they provide treasure for the student; from the literary point of view they are rather poor stuff. But they capture something of the early outlook and to that extent are folk poetry. But they are not, despite assertions to the contrary, "the stones upon which all the later edifice rests." Indeed, had they never existed at all, it is difficult to see that our literature from the eighties on would have been at all different.

The bush ballads are another matter. They are mostly narratives by known authors; they were read and often enough recited. Their forerunners were occasional: Harpur wrote an approximation to a bush ballad, Kendall a couple, and Gordon three in language a little formalized and romanticized, but John Farrell was perhaps the earliest who may justly be called a balladist. The spate began about the middle 1880's. Most of the seeds lay in Gordon's efforts, but it is doubtful if we should have had the harvest but for a weekly periodical, the *Bulletin*.

The foundation of this paper was the most important single happening in Australian literary history in the last century. The *Bulletin* was founded in 1880 by J. F. Archibald and J. Haynes. After a period of indecisive aims, Archibald—in some ways hardly a literary man, but in most ways a highly gifted editor—laid down the principles it was to follow for over a generation. It was to break with the past and the memories of convictism and officialdom and to assert the principle of nationalism; in doing all this it accepted and paid for contributions from its very numerous readers. It was democratic, brash, vitally alive, and enormously influential. It is not too much to say that the bush ballad and the Australian short story were its children.

To its staff Archibald, in 1894, added A. G. Stephens (1865–1933), the most potent critic, if not the best, that this country has had. The few volumes of criticism Stephens has left are no indication of his importance; for most of his work was in his reviews on "The Red Page" of the *Bulletin*, in the letters he wrote to writers, and the influence he exerted on them. He knew practically all the literary men of the period, and however perverse he may occasionally have been, he encouraged and fostered talent when it came his way; Shaw Neilson, for instance, owed him much, and Joseph Furphy's work would almost certainly not have appeared when it did—perhaps only by lucky accident ever—but for his insistence.

Henry Lawson (1867-1922)

Christopher J. Brennan (1870-1932)

Henry Handel Richardson (1870-1946)

LITERATURE

In the pages of the *Bulletin* the bush ballad found a home. The prime example of a balladist is A. B. ("Banjo") Paterson (1864–1941). By far the most popular poet ever to have written in Australia, he produced what may be considered the typical bush ballad—a rousing, swinging narrative of events and men of the outback. Though he began writing in the nineties, he looks back to the eighties or earlier and rather heroicizes his figures. These range through most of the types: the station owner, shearer, horseman, swagman, trooper, and so forth. The picture of the country is idealized to correspond with man and incident, and when drought and flood intrude, they magnify this virile and adventurous saga. Paterson's best poem is "The Man from Snowy River," and it remains the bush ballad par excellence. His "Waltzing Matilda" has become the unofficial Australian national anthem.

A contrast appears in the poems of Henry Lawson (1867–1922), the greatest writer of the Australian short story, but not a typical balladist. If Paterson paints rather too rosy a picture, Lawson redresses the balance with his descriptions—he wrote few narratives —of outback disaster and depression. The poems of the two men reflect both their lives and their temperaments—Paterson in fairly easy circumstances and apt to see the outback he knew so well as brighter than it was; Lawson always struggling and embittered, viewing (at least in verse) the outback, which he knew less well than Paterson, in darker shades.

The rather bookish, romantic balladist appears in W. H. Ogilvie (1869–1963), who writes like Scott transferred to Australia, in diction that often appears alien to the rough reality he describes. Edward Dyson (1865–1931) deals with the life and fellowship of the prospector. E. J. Brady (1869–1952), a balladist by concession, is one of the few Australian poets of the sea. Barcroft Boake (1866–1892) survives by virtue of one poem, "Where the Dead Men Lie," a grim and somber threnody.

These varied writers of the ballad were a few among scores. In their fashion, the balladists were (though it may seem odd to say so) conventional. Rough diction, rough galloping meter, rough but kindly men, sardonic humor, and wry acceptance—these were parts of a stock in trade. Readers devoured it all with perhaps a half-conscious awareness that things and men of the outback were really not quite like that. Implicitly it was assumed that in the outback was to be found the true spirit of Australia.

The bush ballad bloomed in Paterson. As years passed, the tradition became a little worn at the edges. After the First World War a newly written bush ballad seemed artificial, an imitation of past fashion. No ballad, early or late, could aspire to be considered great literature, but the type served, and still does, as the expression of a former Australian ethos or even an ideal.

The novel, the predominant form in the colonial period, changed and declined as the century drew to its close. Though Boldrewood still wrote, he wrote less vigorously; and the novel often turned from the open air and physical adventure to the city and the doings of women. Three women retailed such events. Ada Cambridge (1844–1926), the wife of a parson, came to Australia in her twenties and moved from parish to parish for the rest of her long life. Although class-conscious and with a veneration for gentle birth, she gave pictures of the "new" woman of the period, doubting and a trifle unconventional. "Tasma" (Jessie Couvreur) (1848–1897) was brought to Australia as a child, but left in her early thirties. As a novelist, she is noted for her repeated use of a plot involving badly matched couples—an echo, perhaps, of her own unhappy marriage. Rosa Praed (1851–1935), born in Australia, with a family background of pastoral affluence and political experience, portrayed both these aspects in a lengthy series of novels that were often spun out beyond material warrant. The fads of the age, occultism and mysticism, appear in her work.

Not one of these women survives as more than a minor novelist, but together they throw light on contemporary attitudes. Their novels are among our earliest urban fiction; they also picture the life of the squatter; they are, for their time, often daring and questioning; and, perhaps most important for the social historian, they show the changing relationship of Australian and Briton. The snobbish Australian subservience to English pretensions is still portrayed, but the novelists often enough provide worthy, manly Australian heroes. Even wealthy Australian parvenus are shown as not wholly despicable.

The strength of the period lay, however, not in the novel, but in the short story. Here, as with the bush ballad, the influence of the *Bulletin* was paramount. It demanded or encouraged a terseness, a realism, an Australian note; and writers responded to the demand. Except for a story by Tasma that anticipates Lawson, the nineties mark the beginning of the Australian short story. Its writers wrote best of what they knew best, and so they tended to mark out individual areas for themselves.

William Astley (1855-1911), who wrote as Price Warung, produced five volumes of tales, most of which deal with the convict system at its worst. With democratic and humanitarian sympathy, Warung hated the brutalities he retailed, and the *Bulletin* encouraged this denigration of older days.

Equally brutal, but greater as a craftsman, is Barbara Baynton (1862-1929), who lives by three or four short stories out of the eight she wrote. They are the cruelest Australian tales ever written, though the cruelty resides not so much in physical grossness as in spiritual and emotional callousness and degeneration. As Warung makes a reader feel that he hates "the system," so Baynton makes a reader feel that she hates the outback—and perhaps even the people in it.

The town factory was depicted in the slangily humorous and sometimes grotesquely pathetic stories of Edward Dyson, the ballad-ist. The setting and the characters were of a kind that Dyson thought neglected, and he set himself to remedy the lack.

In the stories of Arthur Hoey Davis (1868–1935), who used the pen name of Steele Rudd, the small farmer or "cocky" appears, with his humor and resignation and resentment in the face of drought and disaster, his small triumphs, and his often unsung stoicism. Rudd knew the life, for he had worked on a farm in southern Queensland as a lad. The sketches he produced, gathered later into too many volumes, are a hayseed family saga.

By far the greatest of the group, indeed still the greatest Australian writer of short stories, was Henry Lawson, born in a tent on a New South Wales gold field. With limited education and opportunities, Lawson led a wandering and rather unruddered life, and he degenerated in after years into an improvident retainer dependent on the generosity of friend and publisher. Much misfortune was his own fault, but a great deal he had some justification in resenting.

This bitterness he vented in his verse; in his stories he was too good a craftsman to let it color his presentation unduly.

Lawson writes mostly of certain areas of outback New South Wales, and his main characters are the men on the track, "humping their bluey" (carrying their few belongings rolled in a blanket), trudging across the waterless, at other times waterlogged, plains from one station to another, looking sometimes for work, sometimes only for the meal traditionally handed out by the station owner. Men went in pairs, for the distances made it dangerous to travel alone. The theme that pervades much of Lawson's fiction, set in such areas and among such characters, is that of "mateship." It does not necessarily mean friendship, for mates did not have to be friends. The custom had a history that perhaps began in convict days when hostility to brutal authority served as a bond. Lawson's version—the first articulate version—is in some of his stories a little sentimentalized and in a couple of his later writings can be downright embarrassing. He did not create the conception, he crystallized it.

As a master of pathos and humor, he is at his best a sort of natural genius. This is not to say that his tales are artless. They may appear so, but they are the results of a practiced as well as innate talent. He can, for instance, delay an ending, sustaining a sequence of two or three possibilities over a space of ten lines or so until the apparently inevitable conjunction of word and situation arrives. When he is not in control of his medium he can be maudlin in his pathos and gimmicky in his humor. But his eye and ear are often so sensitive and the results so faithfully recorded in the laconic "yarn" that part of the reality he knew is imperishably caught. Although some of it may seem a little old-fashioned today, his work is the most sensitive revelation of the emotional attitudes which prevailed then and some of which still persist: dissatisfaction with things as they are, distrust or even hatred of law-enforcing agencies, a mixture of contempt and affection for the outback life, cynicism mingled with naïve idealism, an acceptance of the second best that even becomes an impatience with the search for perfection, and a jealousy of those more privileged.

Verdicts on Lawson's literary position still vary. Some critics rank him with Chekhov and Katherine Mansfield; others say he is the best of the Australian writers of the short story, but more important in his day than now. Those critics most favorable to Lawson today tend to be elderly and were young or mature men when he was alive. Younger readers are generally less sympathetic. This is perhaps significant—tastes have changed, memories and legends of a past period have faded, and this would seem to indicate that Lawson suffers, unfairly in a way, from belonging to his age. Just as his stories concern a class of people that has gone, so they concern an age that is past. Of course, all fiction is in the same case; but the greatest survives because it transcends the time it was written of and the characters it depicted. If it has not this quality of the universal, then it begins to "date," and something of this is beginning to happen with Lawson. He is simply so faithful in his pictures, so Australian—and of a certain period—that his reputation is likely to decline.

Both the bush ballad and the short story were essentially Australian, and the best of them were written by the native-born. They answered the needs of their nationalistic era, which in the *Bulletin* found a voice that was at times not merely Australian, but even anti-English. A major work of the same tenor appeared in 1903—*Such Is Life* by Tom Collins, pen name of Joseph Furphy (1843–1912). Furphy submitted his bulky manuscript to A. G. Stephens, who advised the excision of sizable portions that later appeared in volumes as *Rigby's Romance* (1946) and *The Buln-Buln and the Brolga* (1948).

The setting of *Such Is Life* is the Riverina (southwestern New South Wales and northwestern Victoria), the period the eighties, the chief characters bullock drivers, the minor ones practically all types likely to be found there at the time. The work is partly a vividly descriptive guidebook, partly a series of character sketches, partly a sequence of interwoven stories that at first sight can confuse and perplex an unsuspecting reader. Furphy's ingenuity in such interweaving, in his concealing and revealing of clues, and in the over-all linkage, has aroused admiration in many modern critics: what was once leveled against the book as a fault has now become a subject for praise. But even Furphy's warmest admirers would not adduce this as his chief claim. Although certainly not "the greatest Australian book," as an American critic once hailed it, it has become an Australian classic of its own kind, read for its pictures of an age, for its portrayal of Australian democratic sentiments, for

55

its humor of the most diverse kinds, and for its pathos—this last especially evident in the masterly handling of a traditional theme, the child lost in the bush. It is, on the other hand, a highly idiosyncratic book because of its intricate pattern, its oddities of style and outlook, and its essential topicality. Even readers of some sensitivity have been repelled by it, and it will continue to be a subject of argument for a long time to come.

The nationalistic note appears also in the plays. This period was fertile in melodramas, which often were written by workers in the theatre, notable being the actor-manager Alfred Dampier, who collaborated with various others, most successfully with Kenneth Mackay in *To the West* (1896). E. W. O'Sullivan's *Coo-ee, or Wild Days in the Bush*, was written in 1906. O'Sullivan earlier had written *The Eureka Stockade*, handling the theme of the miners' revolt in the gold-rush days—a theme which has since figured in a number of left-wing plays. These plays are alike in their melodramatic qualities: the action is sensational, the characters exaggerated, the motivation unconvincing, and the long arm of coincidence shamelessly overexercised. But these writers were growing conscious of Australia as a field for drama. The action is set in Australia, though it is the extraordinary event and the theatrical setting, seen through English eyes, that are portrayed. And there is an attempt to distinguish Australian vocabulary and idiom and to depict the local or colonial character; the true Australian was seen as a simple, manly fellow, who might swear a little, but was reliable and honest, and he was contrasted with an affected or untrustworthy migrant character.

In contrast to the writers of melodramas there were, as far back as the eighties, a few who tried to handle realistic settings and social problems in the kind of play that recalls Robertson and Pinero. *Polling-Day, or Wooed and Won* (1883) by Benjamin Hoare is a comedy of political corruption, and Sutherland's *Poetical License* (1884) must have seemed very advanced in its day for its outspoken treatment of the parent and child relationship. William Cuneo's bushranging story, *Westman's Jackeroo* (1900), studies the adventurer type without romanticizing him, and Agnes Gwynne's *A Social Experiment* (1908) satirizes an attempt to run a sheep station on socialist lines. Montague Grover's short plays, *The Minus Quan-*

tity and others, published from 1910 on, are full of conventional theatrical gimmicks, but the writer is genuinely studying life in its complications.

The notable feature of the plays is their variety of kinds; their one common element, distinguishing them from the plays of any other country or time, is the introduction, almost without exception, of a character whose business it is to assert Australian individuality—crudely, with bumptious, aggressive overstatement, but with something of what is now a recognized trait. In sense of theatre, the plays indicate that the country could have stood on its own dramatic feet if the managers, actors, and public had not depended on the imprimatur of overseas popularity.

The poets of the Federation period mark a new era quite distinctly. They were, with all their faults, much more mature in outlook and technique than their predecessors and dwindling contemporaries; and, with the exception of Bernard O'Dowd and to a lesser degree Mary Gilmore, they had little of the nationalistic note of the "public" poets or the Australian note of the balladists.

Seven of these poets call for discussion. One of them lived till recently, Mary Gilmore (1865–1962), who was created a Dame of the Order of the British Empire in 1936. Her gifts retained their freshness, and her last volume, *Fourteen Men* (1954), bears witness to the flowering tenderness and pity which in most of her work is instinctive. She is the poet of love, if that word is given a wide meaning—love of woman for child, of wife for husband, of observer for bird and flower, of a human being for the past to which we are all in debt. The objects of her regard are neglected things—the hunted and forgotten aboriginal tribes, the lonely shepherd, even the convict bowed under his task or straining against bonds and blows. She is, then, rather like a national conscience.

Her most delicate and successful effects are with sounds. She can capture the susurration of wings (swans, for instance, appear frequently in her verse), the clang and hoot of flocks of birds, even the void of silence. It is tempting to label her verse as a woman's verse: it has the reactions thought characteristic, it is pitiful and loving, it is patient and suffering, and it trusts in resurgence. These qualities reflect her sympathies and beliefs; for long, especially since

57

the turn of the century, she played a part in the growing labor movement. She still lives as a memory of an age more radiant than our own in its hope for human betterment.

One of these poets has obvious affiliations with former Australian writers: the note of adjuration, heard earlier in Brunton Stephens and Essex Evans, reaches orchestral volume in the poems of Bernard O'Dowd (1866–1953). Born into the Roman Catholic faith, he came under the scientific and socialistic influences of the eighties and nineties; and his intellectual doubts caused him to abandon, with hesitation and reluctance and yet with finality, many beliefs of his youth. Soundly educated, he read closely and widely; he was an admirer of Walt Whitman and corresponded with him; he sharpened his considerable intelligence on the problems of legal drafting; and he used poetry rather as an instrument for exhortation than as the record of experience.

His influence and reputation, once considerable, have decreased, perhaps unduly; his aspiration has a forcefulness that puts him rather by himself. Probably, indeed, this clangor and sense of hortative mission are the very things that have, apart from some modern critical hostility, worked most against him. His reserves of verbal felicity or imaginative insight were never considerable, and so he remains more as a voice heard in one's childhood than as a living force. Even his learning, like his aims, is obtrusive, sowing his verse with recondite allusions and images that stand like grotesque granitic boulders in the field he plowed.

Writing after the federation of the states, he looks forward with mingled hope and doubt to the future of the Commonwealth:

> Last sea-thing dredged by sailor Time from Space,
> Are you . . .
> A new demesne for Mammon to infest?
> Or lurks millennial Eden 'neath your face?

These lines from "Australia," his best-known sonnet, suggest his particular quality: an intellectual and national enthusiasm that can occasionally glow into incandescence.

The greatest poet of the seven, indeed by consent of most critics the greatest poet the continent has produced, is Christopher Brennan (1870-1932). He was primarily a scholar—an honors graduate of the University of Sydney, a postgraduate student in Germany (where his chief interest lay in the French symbolists), and eventually an associate professor of German and comparative literature at his old university. His learning was regarded by his contemporaries and by many later as extraordinary in its scope. As a figure he riveted attention and was the subject of legendary tales—great in bulk, aquiline of nose, black-maned, largely smoking and drinking, volubly talking. A modern critic may wonder if something of this effect has colored the verdict on his poetry, which at the hands of some admirers has been elevated into comparison with that of the greatest in this century.

His verse was collected in 1960. Formerly it was accessible only in anthologies and in the volumes, hard to find except in the larger libraries, that he published at irregular intervals. For some critics this anthologizing has worked in Brennan's favor: he is so uneven, it has been asserted, that his stature is enhanced because we read only his best. Others believe that Brennan must be read as a whole since his poetry forms a massive structure that, however defective in parts, has few equals in its architectonic effect.

Something may be said in favor of both views. But whatever the conclusion, it is undoubtedly true that there are obvious contrasts in Brennan. He is certainly massive in effect; at the same time he is the victim of a phraseology that seems old-fashioned and often pretentious or even strident. He is far more profound and powerful, and at the same time more subtle, than his Australian contemporaries, while (perhaps in consequence) he almost always lacks that appearance of spontaneity which delights and transports in such poets as McCrae and Neilson.

Brennan's life after his return to Australia in 1894 became progressively less contented, and he ended his days, after dismissal from the university, in sporadic dissipation. The philosophy adumbrated in his most important volume, *Poems* (1913), bears some relation to his life until that point. It has been analyzed with sympathetic insight by G. A. Wilkes as a search for a lost Eden. In his expression of this, Brennan traces the vain valuation of love, the despair of the soul's night, the skeptical appraisal of the philosophic (and therefore human) analysis of reality, and the resignation in accepting the universal process of becoming.

These spiritual and emotional experiences are couched in terms not

59

easy of access. Brennan's knowledge of psychology (he is astonishingly modern in outlook), his reading in myth, legend, and literature, and his capacity for symbolic suggestion gave him a verbal armory that he used with great lavishness. The result has been a great deal of puzzled and even resentful explanation, and even Wilkes's authoritative explication has not met with complete acceptance. Some of Brennan's poems, then, are still open to dispute. The surface effect may be strikingly empathetic (as in "Lightning"), or subtly evocative and delicately nostalgic (as in "Sweet Silence After Bells"), or filled with a kinesthetic and tactile imagery (as in "Fire in the Heavens"), and a first reading may give a first agreement. But the significance that is almost certainly symbolized, the place that it occupies, and the part it plays in Brennan's deployment of ideas are not so readily apprehended.

As a technician he is full of sins and redemptions. He is capable of prosaic lines, but more often of mouthed declamations and outmoded, hollow stridencies; phrases such as "antient amplitude" and "mailed miscreant unchaste," for instance, are no uncommon apparitions. But he can also give us—what is not always the lucky or fashioned fate of scholarly poets—the phrase or word where etymological overtones enrich enormously the texture of implication. In

> Those metal quiring hymns
> shaped ether so succinct

the last word gains from our—and Brennan's—awareness of its derivation.

As an Australian poet, he hardly reflects the country he lived in. There are a few passages where knowledge from outside the poems allows us to identify a spot, but the local relevance has little importance in evaluation; it would not affect our reading in the least if his poetry had been written in Timbuktu. Brennan is, then, a poet in the European tradition. He is far distant from Australian preoccupations with the outback or with nationalistic aspirations. He is not clear; he has no narrative, except that of ratiocinative processes; he describes no significant physical actions. He is, in short, the poet of impassioned speculation.

This puts him much aside from his Australian period and surroundings. We have to wait until R. D. FitzGerald before we encounter a poet who bears any relation to him in tendency, however different in outlook. In the years, then, from the first settlement to the sesquicentenary, he is on his own. Over a century had elapsed before Australian poetry reached an adult development. Brennan's *Poems* is the first Australian volume of verse that any critic would venture to appraise as a significant part of the corpus of poetry written in English.

Given the background and upbringing of the next of these seven, few would have dared to predict poetry as the result. John Shaw Neilson (1872–1942) had a hard youth, a meager education, and in thirty years had gone through some two hundred jobs, all of them manual labor. His eyesight grew continually weaker; at last he could hardly see to write and often dictated his verse to an unlettered and wondering companion. Out of that unpromising soil blossomed some of the most delicate poems in Australian literature. All poetry appears in a measure miraculous, but Neilson's by contrast with his scanty opportunities seems even more astonishing. It is, for instance, apparently quite simple; and this we might expect. But the surface simplicity is no mere artlessness: it appears to be a spontaneous *cri de coeur*, but it is very often, as we know from records and manuscript readings, the result of careful revision. A. G. Stephens of the *Bulletin* encouraged Neilson and even suggested alternative versions of lines—which Neilson did not always accept. Again, as the surface technique conceals an art that is really not simple or naïve, so the surface meaning, ostensibly pellucid, has undertones and suggestions that are very rich in their implications. Even his descriptive passages, where he catches the essential quality that makes a thing—bird or beast or fruit—unique, are careful pieces of complex art:

> Across the stream, slowly and with much shrinking
> Softly a full-eyed wallaby descends.

The danger that attends such verse as Neilson's is a collapse into bathos. It cannot be denied that Neilson is occasionally a victim. Then the simplicity can dissolve into mawkishness and the childlike becomes the childish. The charm that sufficed before—sinew and strength absent—now cloys like diluted honey. At his most successful, however, as in "Love's Coming," Neilson is an unpredictably magical poet:

> Without hail or tempest,
> Blue sword or flame,
> Love came so lightly
> I knew not that he came.

The poem for which he is known everywhere in Australia is "The Orange Tree," a capturing of elusive mood—the child's developing from attention to listening to identification, the man's coarser sensibility providing a contrast. Slighter than Wordsworth's "Immortality" ode, it is thematically reminiscent of it and suggests by imagery what Wordsworth describes by comparison or philosophic disquisition:

> Listen! the young girl said. There calls
> No voice, no music beats on me;
> But it is almost sound: it falls
> This evening on the Orange Tree.

In a comment on the poem Neilson later wrote, "There was . . . something which I tried to drag in, some enchantment or other." In most of his poems he attempted the same task, and with varying success. In this poem, to which no excerpt does justice, he superlatively succeeded.

In contrast with the others, Hugh McCrae (1876–1958) has an air of not belonging to this world of today. Son of a poet, he was a magnificent figure of a man, and to his extreme age preserved his vikinglike look. Rebellious against constraint, whether of domestic or commercial ties, he avoided the company of other than personal friends.

His poetry, often classified as belonging to the school of Vitalism, corresponds. He turns to the stories and legends of the past, to history or myth. Through his pages centaurs and satyrs strut, nymphs and dryads gambol, hunters gallop in the chase. His favorite bird is the eagle. This suggests an air of vivid unreality, and it is true that McCrae seemed to regard the world of facts and figures as something outside his concern; but this is merely a statement of his themes, not an evaluation.

Through his verse there runs an intense love of life and its overt activity. When he looks below the vibrant surface he uses nature as a reflection of his moods, and these are mostly optimistic. The archer in the path, in one such poem, aims his arrow; the poet momentarily

hesitates and then springs to the attack; the arrow whistles harm-
lessly overhead, and the threatening visitant vanishes. Fear, in other
words, is our own creation, and action will dissipate it. Even when
death and tragedy enter his pages, the extraordinary and the bizarre
offset any effect of despair.

He is mostly a very positive poet. An air of joyousness fills his
work. Much of this results from his mastery of empathetic and
kinesthetic imagery. Few of his lines are so well known as the conclusion of his "Ambuscade," where the stallions, warned of the approach of centaurs, gallop to the rescue of the mares:

> A roar of hooves, a lightning view of eyes
>   Redder than fire, of long straight whistling manes,
> Stiff crests, and tails drawn out against the skies,
>   Of angry nostrils, webbed with leaping veins,
> The stallions come!

Easily wise after the event, we may yet think of McCrae as
fitting into his period. Too competent and too paganly robust to
have appeared earlier than the nineties, he would be an oddity after
the Second World War. In the Australian twenties, with their reaction against nationalism in art and with their Dionysian cult, he
occupied a prominent position. He is among the most individual of
our poets, the lusty exponent of a *joie de vivre*, never preaching,
expressing no social program or national ethos, little concerned with
any morality, but responding to the urgency of physical demand.

Personal and social tensions strain in Frank Wilmot (1881–1942),
who adopted the name Furnley Maurice in 1905 to get his verse into
the *Bulletin* past the presumedly biased eye of A. G. Stephens. He
was diffident and often noncommittal, but in booklets and periodicals
he published over four hundred poems. He held fairly firm liberal
or socialist views, but his verses on social questions generally stop
short at comment rather than push on to advocacy of action. He
knew the experimental work of Pound and Eliot, but his own techniques remained traditional until the early 1930's.

He wrote too much for what he had to say, probably because of
a reluctance to revise, so that themes seem to recur. The early poems
depend largely on the stock response to obvious attacks on a reader's
sympathies and reliance on "poetical" adjectives like *eternal*. He
had, in short, the courage of a man—but not that of an original poet.

In 1916, in the middle of a war that called out the extremest feelings, he published "To God: From the Weary [later changed to Warring] Nations," where, for once, his courage finds adequate expression:

> God, let us forget
> That we accused of barbarous intent
> The foe that lies in death magnificent.
> How can we hate forever, having proved
> All men are bright and brave and somewhere loved?

But his ambivalence, perplexing and distressing to his friends, produced another poem, in which war is lauded as an inevitable instrument of justice.

Maurice's reputation depends today on his *Melbourne Odes* (1934), a collection of urban poems where tension in theme appears, reflecting in part the unresolved conflicts of the poet. The city is built on trade and on huckstering, but into the sky rise the towers the traders have built; into the agricultural show, dusty and tawdry and yet evocative, pour the products of the areas outside the city; and as the folk go homeward,

> Drenched with the colour of unexperienced days,

they are brought back to industrial realities. It is in these poems, with their more direct vision and their more realistic diction, that Maurice both consciously and unconsciously exhibits the results of his study of modern poets such as Eliot. Maurice led no movement, answered no problems, showed no way. He suddenly found his way, and he had his prayer answered—that God would let him do his best things last.

Derivative yet independent, dubiously nationalistic yet different from patriots like O'Dowd, there remains the enigmatic poet William Baylebridge (1883–1942) who was born Blocksidge, under which name he wrote some of his early poems. Baylebridge is in one way like Maurice: he developed from an apprentice to a much more competent craftsman. But whereas Maurice turned to models late in his career and then rather suddenly became a poet, Baylebridge worked on models from the start. The imitations he produced gave little promise of future success. That is the weakness of literary prophecy; for Baylebridge was indefatigable, and some measure of achievement was his reward. Even his sonnets, so obviously Shake-spearian, can often be effective in their phrasing.

Throughout his life Baylebridge presented a puzzling façade to the world of readers. He had means to indulge his tastes, he published his volumes in private and often limited editions, and these often contained revised versions of earlier work. His bibliography—some volumes, for instance, announced but apparently never printed—and his text still remain problems.

The puzzle is seen also in his later work and the social and national philosophy it seems to have been intended to embody. He has been labeled a Nietzschean, a perfervid nationalist, a would-be Nazi or Fascist. Analyses of the last volume, *This Vital Flesh* (1939), a sumptuous limited edition, are in consequence often contradictory. Sometimes the verses are terse, gnomic utterances, sometimes ultra-Miltonically magniloquent, sometimes caustic and vitriolic. Much of his prose is as mannered as his verse. He stands aside from the pre-vailingly democratic tendencies of many of the writers of the nine-ties and the earlier portion of this century; and this, together with his other traits, distinguishes him as one of our most idiosyncratic poets.

Only O'Dowd among the poets of this period is vociferously Australian. His counterpart among the novelists is Miles Franklin. The other novelists may use the Australian setting, but the note of defensive or insistent nationalism is absent from their work. Although fewer than the poets, they include the first novelist with any claims to be regarded as great. This is Henry Handel Richardson (1870–1946).

Until the later works of Patrick White appeared, it was a com-monplace of Australian criticism that she stood preeminent among our novelists. Developing late, she drew copiously, even consumingly, upon her own background and experiences until these were seem-ingly exhausted. As if to demonstrate her own contention that "to a writer, experience was the only thing that really mattered," her last novel, *The Young Cosima* (1934), drawn from musical history, proved a comparatively mediocre book.

The daughter of Dr. Walter Lindesay Richardson, she was chris-tened Ethel Florence and attended the Presbyterian Ladies' College in Melbourne. From her school days there she drew *The Getting of*

Wisdom (1910). When seventeen she was taken to Leipzig to study music. Her knowledge of music, the city in its varying moods, odd characters encountered, and the story of two young lovers provided the basic material for *Maurice Guest* (1908), which for some critics, at least, remains her superlative work as an artist. But for the emotional intensity of unrequited passion she again turned to her adolescent years, when (in her own words) "I fell desperately, hopelessly in love, with a man fifteen years my senior." The picture of obsession in this novel is unequaled in Australian writing.

Her greatest, if not her most perfect, work was some years in incubation and writing—*Australia Felix* (1917), *The Way Home* (1925), *Ultima Thule* (1929). The trilogy is now known as *The Fortunes of Richard Mahony*. It is partly a historical picture of Victoria in the last century from the fifties on, partly an elaborated and penetrating study of the decline of Mahony himself. For some readers the portrayal of the changes in Mary, his wife, is of equal interest, tracing the ripening of a gentle and tremulous girl to a radiant woman and the hardening—if not coarsening—under misfortune to an almost remorseless wife and nurse.

But Mahony must appear to most readers the center of engrossed attention. Prickly and sensitive, responsive and yet withdrawing, tender but proud, he changes by degrees into an irritable and dissatisfied man, content with no milieu that he finds himself in. His changes of fortune are depicted in the first two volumes. In the third, his descent begins, has its momentary and delusive recoveries, and then hastens pitilessly downward. He becomes deranged, is confined to an asylum, is released to his wife's care, and dies almost speechless. It is a harrowing story, and for sheer eviscerating pathos it has no rival, near or remote, in Australian fiction. It was the story of Richardson's father.

More than one verdict on this powerful novel is possible. If it could be considered as a purely imaginative work, it would be the creation of a strange and fascinating personality. But there, so it seems, this verdict should be questioned, for other things must be taken into account. In the first place, Mahony is a picture of Richardson's father gathered from diaries, reminiscences of those who knew him, and her own childhood memories of him (he died when she was nine). He dies from arteriosclerosis, an organic malady that has a very poor prognosis. The third volume of the trilogy exhibits this illness with almost clinical faithfulness. Well over half a hundred symptoms are recorded, so that the reader feels almost as if witnessing a medical examination, hearing the verdict, and following with helpless pity an inexorable course to insanity, paralysis, and death. The picture that results is hardly a creation, but rather a reproduction. And from the point of view of emotional effect the result is pathos, not tragedy.

This diagnosis of Mahony's illness has been made by a physician, and it seems to rule out any assertion that the novel portrays the working out of character into action. It is not Mahony's character, but his illness, that determines how he shall act.

Richardson's production depended, it may then seem, upon her own personal experiences, and she was quite openly affirmative on that score. For the most part she had enough to draw upon, and when it could be turned into great art, she was capable of the feat. She has given us a vivid and humorous depiction of adolescence; an almost perfect work of art in *Maurice Guest*, where love of a particular kind is shown as obsessive and fatal; a long and profoundly moving picture of a man brought to his death by physical weaknesses over which he has no control, a picture that has so many intimately human affiliations of family life and wifely devotion that it is by consent of most critics acclaimed as her greatest if not most perfect novel. That is *The Fortunes of Richard Mahony*. And when memories of experience were exhausted, she drew upon books to write the story of a musical genius that by comparison with her other works appears almost mechanical.

She used all of herself, and when her remembered experience was depleted she had little creative imagination to draw on. For that reason she can hardly be ranked among the great masters of fiction. But no other Australian novelist has moved us so deeply or has pierced home so poignantly to some of the basic relationships that we live by.

The town novel was delayed in full development. In the eighties and nineties Rosa Praed provided pictures of Brisbane, and Tasma of Melbourne; but a vivid portrayal of parts of Sydney, for instance, waited until the new century. When it did appear, it had many flaws and a redeeming virtue. It gave a partial picture of one of the seedier areas and the more lawless elements; it was written in a style that often verged on the melodramatic; it seldom penetrated far beneath the human skin; and it offered no character creations of normal everyday people. This novel was *Jonah* (1911), written by a man who visited the area in search of color—Louis Stone (1871–1935).

Stone excels when he has eccentric characters, startling incidents, and odd areas to depict. His book is full of faults, and they often do not seem to matter. Through it there pulses a sort of galvanic life, and in it move some characters that Dickens might not have been ashamed to create. One is Jonah, the larrikin; but the superlative example is Mrs. Yabsley, a female Falstaff, huge, sweating, voluble, full of horse sense expressed in the colorful language of her class— a group belonging to areas where the "pushes" (gangs) prowl: "There's no mistake, secrets are dead funny. Spend yer last penny to 'elp yer friend out of a 'ole, an' it niver gits about; but pawn yer last shirt, an' nex' day all the bloomin' street wants to know if yer don't feel the cold." This book is Stone's claim to be remembered. He can capture the grotesque with a style that is often grotesque. And, like Dickens, he can drop into the story the minor character with a startling life and a sort of spasmodic and fantastic vitality. When the theme does not permit this, Stone fails; his other novel, containing middle-class folk in middle-class areas, seems almost comatose by contrast. But *Jonah*, now a minor Australian classic, still remains exuberant.

Three stock themes of Australian fiction of last century—con- victism, bushranging, and the pastoral life—still served novelists at the start of this century, and in fact continue to do so. The brutali- ties of the penal system were exploited to the full. That there was another side to that medal, however dirty, was hardly noted; there were educated convicts as well as the scum of English slums, and life for these in the colonial settlements could be almost normal except for some galling restraints. This aspect of convictism appears in the major work of William Gosse Hay (1875–1945), which complements the accounts by writers like Tucker and Clarke.

Hay had leisure to write, he studied the Tasmanian records, and over a period of thirty-six years he produced six novels, all except one concerned with some aspect of convict life. These novels exhibit a sort of family relationship quite apart from the theme. Their heroes bear a resemblance to one another, grotesque and vital minor characters are found in each novel, tension gathers like the strain in a stretched wire until it tinglingly snaps, escapes by varying methods are frequent, disguises are almost *de rigueur*, and the style is a highly idiosyncratic medium that is Hay's and nobody else's.

All this may read like a recipe for melodrama. In a way it is. Hay is a fantastic, a romantic, a cloak-and-dagger man, and some of his writing is kin to the cruder Victorian (and Australian) stage effect. But though he is all this, he is something more as well. What this is may be seen in his best novel, *The Escape of the Notorious Sir William Heans* (1919). The hero, transported to Tasmania for abduction, finds the restrictions imposed on him unendurable, and he determines on escape. Twice he fails; the third attempt is successful. There is, then, a surface thrill of expectation of action. No reader is disappointed there. Woven into the story is the account of a personal animosity between Heans and his archadversary, a police officer. As well as being individually incompatible, each is in love with the same married woman. These characters are adequately adult.

The reader in search of some rarer or more exotic flavor will find it in the revelations of emotional states. Hay does not tell us these, he shows us. We are invisible attendants upon the characters and their meetings. We cannot take part, we cannot provoke reply or reaction. This rather unusual manner of presentation is enriched— or tainted, some would say—by the style. This probably owes something to Meredith; it is indirect, allusive, repetitive:

Now that he had got these, this man, said Heans, is not really interested in a position of eminence. It crosses him to aim fine and kindly, without change, praise, or cessation; and if he must put a sheath on that venomed instrument, his tongue (always phonetically right), the good folk, to whose level he had won, must permit him, for sheer boredom, to wear it in his cheek.

In Hay's hands the repetition of word and phrase can infuriate some critics to indignant protestation. Yet, like Carlyle's staccato lightnings, his style can abruptly and brilliantly illuminate:

There was an uproar in the hall at that moment, and the drawingroom door opened with a clatter and a swish. A man with bushy little whiskers, a depressed moustache, and a jocular little voice, whirled into the room. He bundled heartily to the window and lugged the blind half-down, saying "Too much light for this climate."

Perhaps it does not make for comfortable reading—if comfortable reading is what one wants.

Yet even admirers of Hay's fiction—and they are numerous—are not going to claim that this way of writing is suitable for anyone but Hay. It is something of an oddity in our literature, and some tastes reject it unhesitatingly. These critics, however, often fall into the error of assuming that Hay does not know how to write, that he writes as he does because he is an offbeat tyro. There is not the least reason to accept this. Hay knew what he was doing, he ran the risk of repeating *grey* and *yellow* as applied to faces; other passages in his work reveal him as a careful and painstaking craftsman. So with Hay it is a case of paying for our enjoyment with outlays of patience.

He is certainly the most unusual of our historical novelists, and, if certain allowances are made, among the few successful ones. He is interested in the people of the period, not merely in the period; his command over—or exploitation of—tension is extreme; and, gnarledly mature himself, he writes for readers who are also grown-up.

The Australianism of the ballads appears in few of the novels of this period. The most eccentric example is *My Brilliant Career*, written by Miles Franklin (1879–1954) when she was still in her teens. Published in 1901, it has been labeled the first Australian novel, the stress lying on *Australian*. But the national quality is colored very strongly by the personality of the author, for she has a marked individuality, more than a few prejudices, and a style that with its oddities is entirely her own. Lawson valued the book and wrote a preface; A. G. Stephens summed it up in his characteristic way: " 'Miles Franklin' is one of these incomprehensible ugly ducklings who has luckily escaped from the creek, and is delightedly taking her swan-swim in the river of literature." She was, he pointed out, searching for a fuller life than a farm afforded.

A sequel, *My Career Goes Bung*, though written shortly afterwards, was not published until 1946. The nodosities are more prominent in this, and she hits out rather more wildly at her *bêtes noires*.

Her feminist views are no whit softened, and all in all the flavor of eccentricity has become so marked that the charm has mostly gone.

In spite of all that one can say against these two novels, they still have a place by reason of their freshness. And they are forceful and individual. Many readers believe that *My Brilliant Career* is more likely to preserve Miles Franklin than her serious and ambitious novels, in which her democratic Australianism remains. *All That Swagger* (1936), a historical saga covering a century from the early 1830's, has the typical faults of its type—too much historical detail, especially in the beginning, and too much explanation and discussion of factors, influences, and what not to clarify the pattern of events for the presumably dull reader. The saving grace is the figure of the old pioneer, who bursts through these pages as Miles Franklin does through the pages of her first novel.

The twenty or so years between the early and later novels of Miles Franklin saw the appearance of some novels by "Brent of Bin Bin." This timing is one of several reasons for believing that these two figures are the same, or that Miles Franklin at least revised Brent's work or collaborated in the writing. Between 1928 and 1956 six novels by Brent appeared. The first two, *Up the Country* (1928) and *Ten Creeks Run* (1930), are by common consent the most satisfying.

The whole series is a sequence chronicling certain related outback families, and it stretches in time from the 1840's to the 1920's. If one reads the volumes in order, a sense of contraction on the one hand and of diffusion on the other tends to be felt. The earlier volumes deal in spacious fashion with outback life, where the families are affluent with their great holdings, men are masculine and meet mishap and fortune with equal mastery, women have large families, and a general sense of plenitude and freedom prevails. Perhaps it is a trifle glamorized, but it has a spaciousness that is very appealing. But the later novels move into cities, into houses, into rooms. The characters seem smaller, not so much confined as more meager in emotional and spiritual outlook. Some are almost querulous, and their arguments and complaints are a far cry from the early assurance of men easily able to deal with the world outside.

The diffusion in these volumes is the effect partly of spread of

71

time, partly of the dilution of values. The early volumes often are packed with the most varied incidents, so that hardly any time seems wasted, and what happens, though improbably crowded, is significant in the development of country or character. But as the time comes closer to the present, fewer things fill more pages, and these things are often enough trivialities. The early volumes are occasionally like Kingsley's *Geoffry Hamlyn* (at least its Australian sections) written in a more modern and less poeticized style. As such they are ebullient pictures of the old pastoral life. But there are too many volumes in the Brent series.

Just as the *Bulletin* in the nineties helped poets and short-story writers to be independent of English tradition, so the little theatres did something to sponsor independent playwriting. From 1908 on, amateur groups appeared in the capital cities, putting on the best plays of the modern European theatre, which the commercial theatres were not showing, and trying out newly written Australian plays. Thus a more critical theatre audience was created, the local writer was enabled to keep abreast of current trends in the European dramatic renaissance, and he had a chance to see his own work and that of his countrymen performed.[1]

A few short-lived groups devoted themselves principally or exclusively to Australian work. The first, founded by William Moore in 1909 and running annual "Australian Drama Nights" in Melbourne until 1912, discovered several playwrights of talent, most importantly Louis Esson; and Esson, with Vance Palmer, founded the Pioneer Players in Melbourne in 1921. They lasted only till 1924.

Such playwrights, impressed by the work of Yeats and Synge in the Abbey Theatre in Dublin, sought to achieve similar results in their own work. They set their plays in typical Australian environments—the bush, the city slum, and social and political circles. They tried to catch the speech of the people they knew who lived in these areas. Thus, Esson's one-acts, *The Drovers, Dead Timber,* and *Andeganora,* and his three-act, *Mother and Son,* are set in the bush, and the characters speak in the colloquial idiom appropriate to their

---

[1] Eunice Hanger, lecturer in English in the University of Queensland, has annotated the sections on the drama. Lecturer, dramatist, producer, and critic, Miss Hanger has collected numerous unpublished playscripts by Australians and is writing a book on trends in modern Australian drama.

LITERATURE

education within that environment. Similarly, his slum plays, his one-acts, *The Woman-Tamer* and *The Sacred Place*, and a full-length, *The Bride of Gospel Place*, are generally true to their locale. One feels less sure about his historical play, *The Southern Cross*, one of many attempts to tell in dramatic form the story of the Eureka Stockade. But Esson's plays never received professional production, and they remain unpolished and lack the controlled craftsmanship that might have come with revision in the theatre.

The same is true to a greater extent of the plays of Vance Palmer, who is better known as a novelist. He wrote some one-acts, the best of which are *The Black Horse* (1924) and *Ancestors*, and a number of full-length plays—comedies, including *Christine* and *The Happy Family*, and a historical play, *Hail Tomorrow* (1947). The comedies are set in the bush, and one feels that Palmer has been careful to make his detail authentic; but the speech is always too busy with telling the story, emphasizing aspects of character, and providing atmosphere to give us that shock of recognition that delights because it is unexpectedly true.

Other playwrights who emerged through the little theatres and the writers' theatres were Katharine Prichard and Sydney Tomholt, and generally we may say that their work is of the same kind, with some overemphasis on the hardships of bush life and of the under-dog in all walks of life. They write most effective speech when their characters are poorly educated.

Plenty of high-flown speech was used in some of the verse plays of the period 1900–1930. So far as the verse goes, these are not negligible. The best are those of Jack Lindsay, written in the twenties, published in London, and not affected by the aims of Esson and his realistic group. Apart from such examples, the direction of the period was toward realism, expressed in plays largely dependent on the little theatres for production.

Both quantity and quality of writing have been considerable in recent years. The number of competent poets has never been so great. The editors of *The Penguin Book of Australian Verse* (1958) chose poems from fifty-nine poets of this century, of whom about a dozen are no longer living. The list was not long enough to suit reviewers; some twenty additional names of living poets were re-

73

proachfully or indignantly placarded as inexcusable omissions. In simple arithmetic, this suggests that there are nearly seventy good poets at present writing in this continent of ten million people.

There are, of course, more than seventy—if "good" means having claims to inclusion in a Penguin twentieth-century anthology. But both editors and critics were right. There is a hard core of names, on four of whom all critics would agree—Judith Wright, R. D. FitzGerald, A. D. Hope, and Kenneth Slessor. But after that any choice is going to be invidious.

Here, for instance, are two defensible groups to fill out the round dozen: (1) Douglas Stewart, Nancy Keesing, Vincent Buckley, John Manifold, Francis Webb, John Thompson, David Campbell, David Rowbotham; (2) James McAuley, John Blight, Harold Stewart, Roland Robinson, Geoffrey Dutton, Rosemary Dobson, Ray Mathew, Randolph Stow. A third group, easy to compile, would contain names that many critics would prefer to some of those chosen. Such being the difficulties of anthologists, the writer of a sketch of our literature must simply be content to add to the agreed four a few representatives that his taste imposes, and then resign himself to the inevitable accusation of critical insensitivity.

To classify the poets of the period satisfactorily seems impossible. Groupings may be made, but they serve merely as devices of convenience; there have been "schools," if the term is loosely used, and some poets today hold similar views on the purpose and techniques of their art; but there is surprising diversity of individual performance.

So far as experimentation is concerned, Australian poets since the thirties have been of three kinds—those who have espoused allusiveness and even opaqueness and some devices of "modernistic" poets; those who have rejected and indeed attacked such experiments; and those who have remained traditional or orthodoxly individual.

Of those rejecting the more extreme experiments, the most influential is A. D. Hope (b. 1907), professor of English at Canberra and certainly the most technically accomplished poet now living in Australia. His work presents him as a double Janus figure. One face of one figure is set determinedly toward clarity: among other things a reader recalls an annihilating attack on the opacities of Max Harris, a caustic review of a novel by Patrick White, and a parody on Hop-

74

kins, which takes that poet to task for his idiosyncratic handling of
English. The other face is not so readable and has caused some of his
verse to be charged with obscurity. The surface effect is for the most
part clear enough; but it often symbolizes a more significant yet
elusive reality.

One face of the second figure is set, if not with determination
perhaps with a sort of compulsion, toward sexual imagery. This aspect has awakened much fascination in youthful readers. Some of
these poems, for instance "Imperial Adam," are elaborated, sumptuous, and even luscious:

> The pawpaw drooped its golden breasts above
> Less generous than the honey of the flesh;
> The innocent sunlight showed the place of love;
> The dew on its dark hairs winked crisp and fresh.

Some poems—one hesitates to call them love poems, for suggestions
of fulfillment are so sparse—deal with physical relations. Here many
readers feel a note of frustration or incompleteness. Such poems
seem deprived of any woman. There are, indeed, two persons present, but both are the poet; he is the participant and at the same time
the watcher—an autovoyeur who never applauds. The other face
is that of the moralist. Hope is the finest satirist the literature has yet
seen. Fastidious, impatient, suffering no fool or rogue gladly, he finds
the contemporary scene an inevitable target for his barbs. His "Australia" affords a representative quotation:

> And her five cities, like five teeming sores,
> Each drains her: a vast parasite robber-state
> Where second-hand Europeans pullulate
> Timidly on the edge of alien shores.

His prolific verbal dexterity of phrase and rhyme appears as patent
in these satires as in his more serious poems, and sometimes it is so
rich that it even seems to take away from the satiric effect. The poet
enjoys hating—it is almost an emotional indulgence—and the reader
participates in the orgy.

Hope's great competence makes him a master of the prodigious
squib, a superlatively adroit affirmer of the negative. If one may
ungraciously complain after the satisfaction he affords, it would be
to lament that he has not given us more of such verse as "Medita-

tion on a Bone." This is a poem stripped bare as the bone he writes on, instinct with a bitter and unusual poignancy that is glimpsed on the sudden lifting of the mask that some suspect this poet always wears.

Influenced by Hope—at any rate a holder of some of the same critical tenets—James McAuley (b. 1917) has written mainly two forms of poetry, the satiric and the religious. Some of his satire has been influenced by his religion (he is a Roman Catholic convert) and is molded in the spirit that Dryden gave many of his attacks. The force of McAuley's satire is considerable, and the beliefs whose validity he assumes drive his pen in deep. Oddly enough in a writer who, like Hope, is impatient of much modern experimentation in poetry, his own poems yield examples of the enigmatic and the esoteric. Here, unlike Hope, he presents difficulty not by general, but by particular implication: it is a matter of the unusual and allusive word and phrase.

His bright, hard, and yet sensitive and penetrating diction suffers a change in his second book, *A Vision of Ceremony* (1956). This contains most of his religious verse, and the theme has influenced his style. Sincerity of belief demands, so McAuley maintains, a treatment that should concern itself with naked truths rather than with personal doubts:

> Scorn then to darken and contract
> The landscape of the heart
> By individual, arbitrary
> And self-expressive art.

A reader, thinking of Donne and Hopkins, may wonder.

But the style has gone further. Augustan verse, admirably used by McAuley for satire, can even in his modern hands result in some odd mistimings when turned to other purposes. These lines from "Palm" are an extreme example:

> But mostly, stilled to trance, O palm,
> Your paradisal plumage rears
> Its fountain, and amidst the calm
> A milky flowering spathe appears;
>
> Which an ascending youth incises
> Deftly with a bamboo knife,

Whence a fermenting fluid rises
Like joy within the common life.

Great religious verse has possessed on the one hand an Edenlike simplicity (which McAuley has not), on the other a tortured and complex force (which McAuley has renounced). The application of a critical credo has limited the religious verse of this poet, an effect the very opposite of that desired.

McAuley's kinship to the eighteenth century and his distrust of certain "modern" trends took a startling form in 1943. He collaborated with his friend Harold Stewart in composing some bogus verse, ostensibly esoteric and experimental, with the ambiguous title *The Darkening Ecliptic*. This was sent to Max Harris, a member of the avant-garde. Harris and many others swallowed the bait; the verse was printed, and the presumed author, "Ern Malley," was acclaimed as "a poet of tremendous power." When the trick was revealed, the victims were gleefully pilloried by the newspapers. Three not necessarily exclusive reactions to the jape were, and still are, current: that it was all a brilliant hoax, the bubble of solemnity was pricked, and nobody was much the worse; that some of the bogus verse was really respectable poetry, the authors not being able to control the mental associations that made their own writings good poetry; that it was all rather a pity, since the laughter resulting tended to cover not only the objects of the trick, but also any experimental poets. Whatever view one holds, the affair remains the most successful literary hoax in our history.

The second of the two "Ern Malley" hoaxers, Harold Stewart (b. 1916), is also a craftsman of considerable polish and virtuosity. His first volume, *Phoenix Wings* (1948), passed with little notice, but it displays his unusual control over aural imagery. In his second volume, *Orpheus* (1956), Stewart tells the myth of the descent and return. Two changes have occurred. The theme is no longer a love story or a nature myth, but a psychological comment on the subconscious springs of poetical activity. It is interesting to recall this when reviewing Stewart's part in the "Ern Malley" affair. The second change is a wit transformation. Stewart uses a five-lined stanza of tetrameters, with a varied rhyme arrangement; and the language is a modernized Augustan:

77

PATTERN OF AUSTRALIAN CULTURE

> With cloven hoof and pointed ear
> Capricious urges leap and leer.

Dexterously neat, brilliantly sophisticated, with a flavor of Prior or Gay, Stewart is an unusual figure in Australian literature.

The nationalistic tendencies in poetry, together with the idiom of expression, have oddly fluctuated. Last century English poetry and the memories of English poetry and the English scene came between poets and the Australia they saw. The bush ballads went to the opposite extreme: language and theme were pressed into the service of a convention, vigorous, national, and yet in its extremes a little bogus. The other poets addressed themselves to exhortation. The early years of the new century produced only one poet of note who resembled these—O'Dowd. The rest were poets first, Australian poets second, if at all.

But the ballads were still being written and have continued to make belated appearances until this period; the last ones of Ogilvie, for instance, were published in 1937. A deliberated doctrinaire reaction against nationalism in verse showed itself in the twenties. The vehicle was *Vision*, a short-lived quarterly. The moving spirits were Norman Lindsay and his son Jack, and poets like Kenneth Slessor and Hugh McCrae contributed vitality to the Vitalism that has been used by some critics as a label for the group. The setting tended to move back to a poetically pagan era, and here the decorative genius of Norman Lindsay provided illustration. In *Vision* appeared (though more playfully than in other pictures) his satyrs and his bronzed men, arrogantly male, strenuously clasping the characteristic Lindsay women, slit-eyed, long-chinned, mildly afflicted with goiter and elephantiasis. The general air of riotous life should have stimulated everybody. But *Vision* was too extreme, or too precious, or even too good for its period, and only four issues came out.

One poet who outgrew this niche of the twenties is Kenneth Slessor (b. 1901). The poems he contributed to the vociferous *Vision* were often like McCrae's—vital, but to us now occasionally old-fashioned:

> Good roaring pistol-boys, brave lads of gold,
> Good roistering easy maids, blown cock-a-hoop
> On floods of tavern-steam, I greet you! Drunk
> With wild Canary, drowned in wines of old.

78

LITERATURE

His limited output is contained in *One Hundred Poems* (1944; 1957 with omissions and additions). In spite of the small number, the poems range variedly. There are, for instance, the early dealings with historical or legendary scenes. In a very few, a sardonic eye dwells on Australian settings—here, "Country Towns":

> At the School of Arts, a broadsheet lies
> Sprayed with the sarcasm of flies.

But this note is rare with Slessor—the visible world is for him a constant stimulant, food for the senses to enjoy. Even soiled clothing is an experience in a sort of sensuousness, in "William Street":

> Ghosts' trousers, like the dangle of hung men,
> In pawnshop-windows, bumping knee by knee.

And it awakens the unexpected response:

> You find this ugly, I find it lovely.

His most notable poems, such as "Five Visions of Captain Cook," have dealt with the sea—those who early voyaged on it:

> So, too, Cook made choice,
> Over the brink, into the devil's mouth,
> With four months' food, and sailors wild with dreams
> Of English beer, the smoking barns of home;

those who, like the old salt in "Captain Dobbin," left it:

> But the sea is really closer to him than this,
> Closer to him than a dead, lovely woman,
> For he keeps bits of it . . .
> What you might call a lock of the sea's hair;

those who died in it:

> I felt the wet push its black thumb-balls in,
> The night you died, I felt your eardrums crack,
> And the short agony, the longer dream;

and the poet himself, who saw a bubble on its surface as the fragile mirror of a world momentarily free of time and time's destructive power:

> Leaning against the golden undertow,
> Backward, I saw the birds begin to climb
> With bodies hailstone-clear, and shadows flow,
> Fixed in a sweet meniscus, out of Time.

79

These frequent extracts from Slessor are not an expediency to escape the task of comment. They serve to stress his quotability. In his small body of work the level of craftsmanship is very high, and almost any page affords examples of his capacity at or near its best. He is a poet drunk on things. So it is surprising and disappointing to find that he has decided to stop at certain points. He stopped writing some years ago, at the verge of the "modernistic" techniques, and only one or two brief poems have appeared since. There are, it is true, some passages in his work, as in "Five Bells," where the meaning does not readily yield itself to inspection, but on the whole he is brilliantly and illuminatingly and sensuously lucid.

Slessor's professed concern is with sheer verbal virtuosity. He is an admirer of Tennyson, and his own lines contain words upon which the lines seem to pivot. What Chesterton said of Tennyson— that in a Tennysonian line such a word is like the keystone of an arch, which would fall into ruin without it—is not quite so true of Slessor, who tends to spread his risks. Nevertheless, lines of much this tenor can be found:

> The lighted beach, the sharp and china sand,

and

> Crow-countries graped with dung,

and

> Between the sob and clubbing of the gunfire.

One may call his credo ostensible, for it holds a suggestion of limitation, of deprecation. Admirably adapted to quotation as they are, his verses are not a scattering of "gems," but (especially the later ones) a coherent body of artistry shot through with a reserved pity and a sardonic regret for our mortality—and his own.

In all these poets the note of reflection necessarily is heard, but philosophical poetry as such has made only occasional appearances. An early major example was the work of Brennan. The only modern to be compared with him in that sphere is R. D. FitzGerald (b. 1902), whose poetical career has stood normal expectation on its head: instead of beginning with narrative and moving sedately with age to poetry of reflection, he began, after some short poems, with philosophical verse and later turned to narrative. But there is no real dislocation; the narratives provide particular examples of the philosophical themes.

The best and most famous of his philosophical poems is his "Essay on Memory," one section of his *Moonlight Acre* (1938). A long poem in couplets, which in FitzGerald's hands are sometimes hardly noted as couplets, it is an eloquent and strangely vivid dissertation upon causality. The memory that he writes of is symbolized by the rain:

> Rain in my ears: impatiently there raps
> at a sealed door the fury of chill drops.

The room is the self. To it the past is often only a blur of sound. In the succession of verbally created independent moments, held in the mind because the mind can conceive or verbalize them, there is the sequence of the past. But the sequence is not one of individual unrelated instants: they are linked in a chain that is unbreakable, though we may not recognize this. Memory for FitzGerald, then, is not our transient recollection, but a sort of infinite memory, the relation of all to the past that has created each present; it is in effect necessity, ineluctable cause and effect. We ourselves perceive only the surface of the process and cannot predict—indeed, we often enough misinterpret the past. Any trust we have in our future must be manifested in our choice of action:

> then, launched above that steep,
> venture shall cant bold wings and with their sweep
> splinter such clogging silence as they met
> in older abyss where time slept stirless yet.

This considerable and complex poem has taken its place in our poetry. It is surprising in at least one technical device: FitzGerald is dealing with an essentially abstract theme, and he has chosen the most material of imagery to express it—imagery that concerns touch, muscular tensions, forces that are to be felt. This is found unexpectedly and brilliantly adequate, for as even the short extracts given suggest, the sense of plastic influence is inherent in them as in the conception the poet is molding, or by which he is molded.

FitzGerald's turning from this conceptual poetry to poetry of action is susceptible of two possible explanations: that he had exhausted his philosophical stores and was obliged to resort to narra-

81

tive; or that, having stated his thesis, he proceeded to illustration. Those who value his poetry will choose the second explanation. In *Heemskerck Shoals* (1949), the rumination of Tasman, the Dutch explorer, the approach is tentative. In *Between Two Tides* (1952), it is more direct. A story of the South Seas, of island conflict, it is a study in particular choices. Told in a series of enveloped narratives—stories within stories within stories—it is prefaced and concluded by reflection. The action is vivid, but it is often shown to be nugatory or sterile. FitzGerald's latest poem, *The Wind at Your Door* (1959), looks back to an incident in colonial history, the flogging of a convict. All concerned were partly guilty, partly innocent. And to all of them we in the present are bound and indebted:

> That wind blows to your door down all these years.
> Have you not known it when some breath you drew
> Tasted of blood?

This body of work by FitzGerald can, then, be regarded as a more coherent sequence than may at first appear: an author's credo, followed by the exemplifications and qualifications with which he has chosen to illuminate it. In subtlety, if not profundity of thought, his poetry can bear comparison with Brennan's.

One poet who may serve as the all-rounder, spreading his talent over a wide field of writing, is Douglas Stewart (b. 1913), editor, reviewer, critic, anthologist, short-story writer, poet, dramatist. In verse he has moved from lyric to description. His prentice pieces, as so often with young poets, have a touch of the portentous; although poetry is a serious business, he demonstrates this too obviously. In his second phase he is seriously playful, as though he felt he could relax after learning. And like a disclaimer, many of the poems are put into the mouths of his subjects—bunyip, cricket, lizard, an old fossicker, magpie, and the rest. Descriptive poems are found in *The Birdsville Track* (1955), the best sequence of desert pictures we have. Here the dead bullocks:

> Cleaned by the wind, by hot sun dried,
> With folded legs and heads turned back
> Just as they lived, just as they died,
> Hollow and gaunt and bony-eyed
> They stare along the Birdsville Track.

Judith Wright (b. 1915)

Patrick White (b. 1912)

In his last poem, "Rutherford," he reveals an unexpected gift for reflection.

In lyric, Australian poetry has naturally enough been most prolific. Of the poets listed at the beginning of this section, all but one or two are essentially writers of this kind, all varying widely in theme and form, and ranging in age from about thirty to fifty. At the moment only a few (Thomas Shapcott and David Malouf, for example) are in their twenties still.

Among the living lyrists the finest, indeed the finest of all Australian lyrists, is Judith Wright (b. 1915). Her first volume, *The Moving Image* (1946), was hailed with surprised delight as poetry of almost unbounded promise, full of fresh imagery and delicate response of a kind not offered before. Here were aspects of Australia reinterpreted, seen as if for the first time by an eye unjaded, unjaundiced, pristinely tender. Not every reader has believed the promise wholly fulfilled; but her later volumes are still the work of a poet of distinction.

Her poetry began as the inner reaction to externals and has moved in the direction of an inner reaction to internals. The freshness of the first volume never wholly vanishes, but the stress has come to dwell rather more in reflection. This change has been due partly perhaps to an increasing deafness, partly to the impact of war on a nature to whom life and love have so intense a significance that the mounting threat of nuclear destruction acts like a blight on the human spirit. This particularly applies to a poet for whom at first, as for Gautier, the visible world existed. The later change, to an identification or empathetic absorption of the self with all that is, may be adaptation as well as natural development.

A great deal of her verse concerns the need for fulfillment, and it finds an answer in different ways. Her poems of pregnancy and motherhood are answers of a woman. Her "Woman to Man," which gives the title to her second volume (1949), is the most perfect work of this kind in all our poetry—the blossoming of the expectant woman:

> The eyeless labourer in the night,
> the selfless, shapeless seed I hold,
> builds for its resurrection day—

> silent and swift and deep from sight
> foresees the unimagined light—

and in the last stanza an efflorescent and startling change to the
particular transfigures poem, poet, and reader alike:

> This is the maker and the made;
> this is the question and reply;
> the blind head butting at the dark,
> the blaze of light along the blade.
> Oh hold me, for I am afraid.

In "Twins" she suddenly sees beneath appearance the significance
of identity, an answer to the individual loneliness:

> How sweet is the double gesture, the mirror-answer . . .
> and moving in its web of time and harm
> the unloved heart asks, "Where is my reply,
> my kin, my answer? I am driven and alone."

One frustration of fulfillment—the sense of separation, or separation itself—is our own doing; and only we ourselves can give us
our self-knowledge. This is another answer. These are not proffered
as solutions to the ills of our society, but implied as individual poetic
reactions. As she has continued to write, the poet has tended to look
toward the quietness—or even the quietude—and acceptance that
age, with life's experience behind it, can confer on us.

This may suggest that Judith Wright's poetry is troubled and torn
by the conflicts that life and the threat of extinction awaken. It is
true that the threat hangs over some later poems, and a reader may
feel wonder that a sensitive personality should not have been drained
dry by it. But, on the whole, her verse is full of hope. Pictures of
drought, of dearth, of physical and spiritual malaise appear, but they
are counterbalanced by rebirth. Even change which brings decay,
though resented humanly, is accepted poetically as a necessity. This
is part of her paradox. In her verse appears the tension of contradic-
tions and opposites: love of the union which yet demands disparates
for its very existence; the perfection of calm, but the necessity of
human activity even if only in the art that mirrors it; loss of the self
in that nothing which completes the self.

She has contrived often enough her perfections. It is, then, a measure of her truth that nevertheless she almost despairs of art. That art

is one of the few permanent realities—the conceptual and its expression—this she does not deny: art is "thought's crystal residue." But she dwells in her later verse more and more on the difficulty of snaring reality in the meshes of language:

> Word and word are chosen and met.
> Flower, come in.
> But before the trap is set,
> the prey is gone.

Judith Wright's readers will not be deterred by such disclaimers. She has grown in her own fashion and developed her own language, and the Australian flavor has tinged unobtrusively her reaction to the Australian scene.

It is possible that we have been rather impatient of our poets in their slow development to this compromise or balance. When Burns writes

> Bye attour, my gutcher has
> A heich house an' a laich ane,
> A' forbye my bonie sel,
> The toss o' Ecclefechan!

we may not be much enlightened, but we do not overly object. When A. B. Paterson writes

> The tarboy, the cook and the slushy, the sweeper that swept the
>   board,
> The picker-up, and the penner, with the rest of the shearing horde,

some tend to feel that he is dragging in the Australian background and idiom.

One aspect of this problem—the assimilation of the Australian background and its conveyance in an adequate form—though rather a side issue, has awakened dispute. This is the work of the Jindyworobaks (or, more briefly, Jindies). Their founder, Rex Ingamells, in his manifesto, *Conditional Culture* (1938), made two points. The first was the danger for the Australian poet in using words with inappropriate associations; if *castle* were part of a comparison, then an aura of age, battlements, chivalry, and so forth immediately became felt and could discolor the Australian atmosphere. The second was that we should be in greater cultural debt to aboriginal lore. These original inhabitants of Australia are, in the view of the Jindies, the only people with direct and living connection with the soil. The essential spirit of the Australian landscape can therefore be found in their art. Even through their language will seep this spirit. And so we find in some Jindyworobak poetry lines like these:

> Far in moorawathimeering,
> safe from wallan darenderong.

This is admittedly an extreme example, but it offers a warning: it is as dangerous to borrow from the aborigines as it was from the Romantics. Australian poets have to fend for themselves. In the last thirty years they have managed very well.

The body of Australian fiction of the last thirty years cannot be anatomized in detail. One tendency, however, at least among some novelists, is discernible—to deal with bulk, whether of groups of people or extent of space or period of time. This is evident in the historical novel.

This genre, long a favorite of Australian authors and thought by some critics to be a measure of literary or national immaturity, offers a choice of themes: pastoral life, exploration, convictism, mining. This century has not seen much decrease of the type.

The theme chosen by Brian Penton (1904–1951) was a mingling of pastoral and convict. To this he added his own ingredient of bloody violence in incident and style. He intended to write a trilogy. Of the two volumes that he completed, the first, *Landtakers* (1934), traces the gathering power of Derek Cabell and his reluctant toughening. A newcomer from England, Cabell hates both the people and the land. But at last he comes to accept both, having grown into a man like the men he once feared and detested and having become inured by habit to the landscape and even, oddly enough, made more sensitive to its desolate beauty. This change in attitude, though not an invariable one, has been common enough in both our history and our fiction.

If the first volume is Cabell's rise, the second, *Inheritors* (1936), is his fall. At the start of this novel the bitter and resilient patriarch rules his family (except his daughter) as he controls his animals. It is natural and ironic that the beloved child should leave him, that the son he rather despises should at the end, as Cabell tires and fails, rule him. The unscrupulous and vicious but courageous old man is presented as the public-spirited pioneer.

86

In both novels, especially the first, the violence is extreme: that apparently was a necessity for Penton the man and the writer. In both novels, especially the second, the irony is pervasive: that apparently was a necessity for Penton the newspaper editor. Both novels have been underrated.

A rather different kind of historical novel appeared with Eleanor Dark (b. 1901). More thoughtful and penetrating than Penton, she devoted much time to her sources, so that her novels might serve as reliable secondary source material.

She began, however, with the psychological novel. Her startling early work, *Prelude to Christopher* (1933), is a series of interwoven flashbacks—reviews of former years by the figures in the story. Artificial as the device may seem when used in this inclusive fashion, it manages to convey a vivid sense of reality. This interest in psychological relations was to lead to three more novels, all concerned with emotional stress and change. As she wrote, Eleanor Dark tended to intrude upon the stage. She held with firmness certain views on one's duty in the human predicament; and she used some characters as if she were demonstrating to her readers what life could teach, what should be learned, and what the penalties were for inattention. This didactic quality is not uncommon in our serious fiction of this century.

Moving, then, from psychology, she turned to history. Her three novels of this type cover the first twenty-five years of the early Australian settlement. *The Timeless Land* (1940), the title of which suggests the theme and the link that holds the story together, conveys with insight the struggles of the first governor, the relations of aborigines to the white newcomers, and the slow growth of adjustment to and acceptance of the new land. The second, *Storm of Time* (1948), concerns the internal conflicts of the colony, the struggles between the governors and the military personnel. Although the novels are long, they deal with a small area and population, so that as historical novels they are detailed to a degree. The third stage in her recountal, *No Barrier* (1953), has a sense of outward movement both in feeling and in theme—the crossing of the Blue Mountains, which released the settlers from confinement to the narrow coastal strip.

These novels are literally historical; indeed, for much of the story

87

the author could, if required, have pointed to documents. For some critics this is a virtue; for others it is an indication that Australian fiction has not grown up. But Eleanor Dark mostly escapes the bias that actuates those novelists trying to prove a case that supports their political beliefs. She is, in addition, a far better writer, a wielder of prose that can at times become almost transparent. And she has a penetration into the motives and passions of men and women that saves her from giving us pasteboard figures. Of the historical writers of this period she is the most considerable.

Only one other novel compares with Dark's work in historical fidelity. This is Barnard Eldershaw's *A House Is Built* (1929), the work of Marjorie Barnard (b. 1897) and Flora Eldershaw (1897–1956). This carefully planned novel traces the history of a family in Sydney from the forties to the eighties. In spite of a few passages that give history in the fashion of a textbook, it does convey a sense of human growth. In addition, it is an elaborate exposition of the ironical workings of fate in human affairs—in marriage, in business, in reputation, in death. Only the overuse of convenient coincidence —the very pervasiveness of the irony itself, as though a thesis were being demonstrated—takes away from this effectiveness.

The strongly egalitarian feelings that have flavored much Australian writing from the eighties on still make themselves felt, though the writers who deal in them, who almost derive from them lessons to be conveyed, have mostly finished their work and are being replaced by those interested in personal problems and tensions. But their solid and serious work has its recognized and valued place.

Too conscientious a craftsman to let political or even democratic sympathies render his novels tendentious, Vance Palmer (1885–1959) by choice of theme—at least in his last novels—reveals some of the principles valued. He spreads his talent over a wider field than most of our writers—poetry, drama, short story, novel, essay, criticism. In all these he emerged as the eminently competent professional.

He never wrote a great novel or a bad one. He knew his people, his country, his language, and himself. It is not absurd to say that perhaps he knew them too well, or was too conscious of knowing them so well. At all events, he stuck very closely to what he knew, so that life appears transcribed in his pages, but not transformed.

He held his hand when depicting characters, so that secrets remained unrevealed. He stopped short at a crisis—or perhaps life's ordinariness stopped him—so that often there was no explosion, but merely a subsiding. The best of his earlier novels is *The Passage* (1930), set in a small township on the Queensland coast.

His last three novels, *Golconda* (1948), *Seedtime* (1957), and *The Big Fellow* (1959), deal with themes that Australian fiction has most surprisingly lacked—industry and politics, especially labor in politics. They give accurate pictures of a mining town, of social and political life in Brisbane, and of the rise to political power of Macy Donovan. These are the most effective novels of their kind in our writing. It merely stresses the scarcity of such novels to say that Palmer's are not very vital—and this in fiction covering a field where the bitterest feelings are engaged and the most devious maneuvers are part of the normal round.

Another novelist holding much the same views as Palmer is Katharine Prichard (b. 1884), nearly all of whose eleven novels are more obviously slanted than his. She has taken her fiction with seriousness: it is her message to her readers. To encompass reality, she has moved widely over Australia, lived in the places and among the people she depicts, and even traveled with a circus to ensure an accuracy in detail that few others would care to achieve at such cost.

The people she describes are mostly those who work with their hands—farmers, miners, timber getters, workers on a station. Her most popular and most successful novel is *Coonardoo* (1929), the pathetic story of an aboriginal woman in the Northwest. In these earlier works her sympathy with the underprivileged is manifest. Some readers may find it obtrusive, but the pastoral charm of setting atones for much.

Like Palmer, she devoted her last three novels to a sort of exposition; but whereas Palmer subdued his message to the canons of artistry he always preserved, Katharine Prichard gave rein to her political commitments. This trilogy—*The Roaring Nineties* (1946), *Golden Miles* (1948), and *Winged Seeds* (1950)—in some passages resolves itself into a history of gold mining in Western Australia. Characters are not created (as in *Coonardoo*); they are, as it were, named—and so, sometimes as mouthpieces, sometimes examples, they express the sympathies and opinions of the author.

89

The earlier novels of Katharine Prichard must wake gratitude in any responsive reader: she is a novelist so honest in outlook, so direct in intuition, and at times even so artless in the expression of her faith and hope. She worries over the state of society. But in her last three novels a reader uneasily senses that she may love causes so much that the fiction becomes a means to an end.

In one novel intrusive and insistent life pushes aside the causes the novelist has every intention of advocating. In *Capricornia* (1938) Xavier Herbert (b. 1911) covers the Northern Territory, an area little known to most Australians, and incredibly he has not exaggerated the grotesquely unprincipled yet fantastically funny events and persons that proliferated there. But it is a book that occasionally cracks apart. On the one side is Herbert the defender of the underdog—half-caste or aborigine—on the other, Herbert the vital observer, squeezing laughter from caricatures and names (Pondrosass and the rest), reveling in accident, turning even sudden death into macabre and explosive humor. It is a novel written in tearing high spirits, with the advocate every now and then slowing down the pen that the artist is wielding.

The vitality dried up in *Seven Emus* (1959), but revived in *Soldiers' Women* (1961). One may ask, as some have done, how many hands have worked on Herbert's fiction; the manners, for instance, of *Capricornia* and *Soldiers' Women* are very different, but the surge and exuberance can have come only from Herbert himself. The contrast is violent between some astonishingly vivid characters and the style, which in this last novel runs a gamut from threadbare cliché to blowsy ornament, sometimes only a maudlin tear distant from the modern equivalent of Peg's Paper. Parts are like Amanda Ros, full of chest-thumping fustian. But some sections grip like fishhooks. The book is diffuse, occasionally embarrassing, too long —and one reads it to the very end.

The depression of the thirties, it might be thought, would be an obvious choice for writers flaying the injustices of capitalist democracy. But not much fiction is set in that period. One writer who does use it is Kylie Tennant (b. 1912). Her three novels of this sort —*Tiburon* (1938), *Foveaux* (1939), and *The Battlers* (1941)—paint respectively the drabness of a western township with its unemployed, life in the suburbs, and the itinerant workless.

90

As with Katharine Prichard, the very overtness of intention tends to defeat its own purpose. The novels are never tracts, but something of the pamphlet finds its way into them. A contrast, where humor replaces the insistence of sympathy, is *Ride On Stranger* (1943). Brilliantly and even startlingly satiric, and with laughter flavoring any message into acceptance, it is a skit on the oddities of Sydney. It is one of the ironies of these novels by serious reformers that humor may more vividly silhouette abuses and injustices than a direct and serious portrayal.

Not many of the novelists can lay claim to distinction or sophistication of style. Of those who can, most except Patrick White are of less stature than those who cannot. This general deficiency is more pronounced in the novelists of this period than in earlier novelists. Clarke was melodramatic, Hay was odd; but they had at least a personal quality. Many substantial novels of the last thirty years have been amorphous in expression, and to read them is at times rather laborious.

One stylist is Christina Stead (b. 1902), whose first novels had a coruscation that gave promise of a major talent. She wrote a few novels with Australian settings, the best being *Seven Poor Men of Sydney* (1934), and then turned to pictures of the American scene. The impression then left was that her voluble inventiveness of phrase was to be devoted to supplying a popular market. There has been no indication of a return to the art of her early work.

Another is Martin Boyd (b. 1893), half English in outlook, half Australian in theme, whose novels devour the material that his own family relationships plentifully provided. His style, polished in ease, sparkling in wit, malicious in tenor, is that of some contemporary English novelists—for example, Anthony Powell. A repetitiveness of theme suggests a lack of invention, but any one of his novels by itself is an urbane pleasure.

One criticism made, especially outside Australia, is that of traditionalism. It has been leveled mainly at the poetry, but some applies to the fiction as well. It applies not at all to the next and last novelist to be considered, the most experimental to have written in Australia. This is Patrick White (b. 1912), born and partly educated in England. He wrote his first three novels in England, his last three after his return to Australia in 1948. In *Happy Valley* (1939) he uses the

91

stream-of-consciousness device and an extension of it that has been termed the "communal" stream-of-consciousness. As he has continued to write, he has incorporated his techniques more smoothly: they are felt to be necessary, not adjunctive.

The story is a study in choices. The characters react according to their natures and find their satisfactions in renunciation, acceptance, or cold grasping at opportunity. Even suffering, a recurrent theme in White's fiction, can be an emotional or spiritual satisfaction.

In *The Living and the Dead* (1941), with an English setting, the flashback technique is employed and the opening scene concerns the ending of the story. It is a picture of a small family in the thirties, with the approach of 1939 and its possibilities of redemption darkly adumbrated.

The third novel, *The Aunt's Story* (1948), remains for many readers the favorite among White's studies of the human situation. In three parts, the story tells of the lonely and withdrawn home life of Theodora Goodman (the Christian name is significant—gift of God), her stay in a sort of temporary world of illusion, symbolically eccentric, in a Mediterranean *pension*, and her ultimate withdrawal into the world she has chosen to inhabit. It is an extraordinary picture of the movement to schizophrenia, clinically accurate, with the early symptoms delicately noted. It is the one novel of White's where little suffering or renunciation is felt; for Theodora goes willingly into her new world as one prepared, a postulant to derangement.

After the Second World War, White deliberated whether to remain in England or to return to Australia. He took the second choice for various reasons. He found in his own country "the Great Australian Emptiness," and he has remained in the hope "that one may be helping to people a barely-inhabited country with a race possessed of understanding."

One may paraphrase this—all too crudely—as the hope of writing novels that will do something to raise Australian literary taste. The first novel he wrote after his return, *The Tree of Man* (1955), perhaps made the aim too overt. A. D. Hope, the most pungent critic in the country, made a scathing attack upon it. The review may be deplored, but one can understand Hope's reaction. The novel, covering the life of a fairly simple couple in their pioneering home, retails their numerous Wordsworthian experiences, and in addition very often offers comments that underline the implications of these experiences. Many readers found this stress—almost this explication—objectionable. White, they felt, did not trust his readers. Some luminous passages, where he forbore to explicate, made the comments the more marked by contrast. It was this portentous quality of stress and style that exacerbated Hope. No other of White's novels has evoked such extremes both of praise and blame.

Voss (1957) added a new dimension to White's work. A highly and sometimes ambiguously symbolical work, it is partly a study of a personality, partly the tracing of the soul's redemption. Voss himself, rather a Nietzschean figure at the start, has puzzling Christlike traits in the later parts of the book.

Not all were converted. Enthusiasm for the book was greatest in the United States, rather less in England, both excessively great and absurdly small in Australia. But even in the United States dissentient voices were heard: one critic dismissed it as "a tricky failure," a verdict based unsoundly on its style. He quoted the well-known opening: " 'There is a man here, miss, asking for your uncle,' said Rose. And stood there breathing." The device of punctuation in the second sentence was, the critic held, unwarranted. One can only reply that the implications and stress will be different if the punctuation and syntax are different. White is seeking certain effects, and he uses certain means to get them. If other methods do not work as well, then it is futile for a critic to object to the means: he must turn his attention to the effects.

His latest novel, *Riders in the Chariot* (1961), is set in the semi-urbanism that White particularly detests, inhabited by the semiliterate whose grosser forms of the Australian idiom he catches with a loving fidelity indistinguishable from hatred. In this milieu live, emotionally apart, the four characters that are his concern. White elaborately distinguishes them from one another by background, intelligence, race, religion, capacity, and even color. Their bond is their faithfulness to the truth that is in them; and each seeks, or awaits, the fullness of a vision momentarily and partially glimpsed. Their linkages, accidental at first, grow closer until they are finally seen as the Biblical group of the Deposition.

93

The symbolic significance, as in *Voss*, may sometimes seem strained or artificial. And the device of differences that stress by contrast the community of search and the validity of illumination (This is so, this is true, for it happens to those so diverse) has the flavor of a thesis demonstrated by complicated patterning. One may feel afterwards that it is a gifted essay in analogical coincidence. But as one reads, it is easy to be persuaded. That is the tribute one pays to a sensitiveness of style in atmospherics and a tact in exoticism that White has never exhibited so fully before.

It is a measure of White's impact on his countrymen that even those who object to him feel constrained to write voluminously about him. No other Australian author has in his lifetime been the subject of so much critical discussion. It is rash to summarize in little space a writer who is so variable a phoenix; but one may venture to say that, in spite of the different methods he has employed and the different themes he has developed, search is implicit in all his writing. It is not for the explanation of suffering—though this has been written on frequently—but rather a search for fulfillment. Practically all his main characters achieve their own versions of it, and all pay for the achievement in their individual fashions—abnegation, service, endurance, insanity, submission, humiliation, death. His novels are a work in progress, the Ways of Fulfillment, an elaborate exploration in the form of fiction.

In this century, with the exception of Judith Wright and possibly Mary Gilmore, the best Australian poets have been men; it is almost as true that with the exception of Patrick White and possibly William Gosse Hay the best Australian novelists have been women.

Australian literature has been more notable this century in poetry than in fiction. Only brazen hardihood would suggest that here lie the elements of a syllogism.

In the other form of fiction, the short story, no modern has equaled Lawson. The nearest is the late Vance Palmer, who links the *Bulletin* period and this. The modern Australian short story is, of course, of more than one kind, but the tendency of the best has been to glimpse some facet of personality under stress. Dal Stivens is a notable example, and Marjorie Barnard's *The Persimmon-Tree* (1943) is the classic of this type. Here the difference from Lawson is observable; Lawson was concerned chiefly with the picturing of

94

a class in a certain period, but since his readers accepted and extended the portrayal, his work expressed much of the national ethos. No modern, perhaps because of modern complexity, has done—perhaps can do—as much as this. Again, the well-made, rounded short story, which the lesser writers of the earlier period produced, is not so characteristic of the moderns who, as it were, prefer to accept rather than to make. This is no comment on their skill; indeed, Lawson and Baynton aside, the moderns as a group are superior. Cecil Mann and John Morrison, for instance, essentially masters of narrative structure, still pierce beneath the skin.

The emotional atmosphere of certain classes is captured in the stories of Gavin Casey, whose "Short Shift Saturday" remains a superlative norm of resigned depression. Not far behind is the work of Peter Cowan. More lively, written from intimate knowledge, are the Jewish stories of Judah Waten. The "area" writers—if the term is generously interpreted—include Frank Dalby Davison, whose technique may owe a little to the influence of Vance Palmer, but whose humane sympathy remains his own. The "authentic fragments" of Katharine Prichard are mostly from Western Australia. Brian James, with vivid memories refreshed by visits, portrays the life of the small township. The stories of Ray Mathew give glimpses of writer and artist, cafe and boardinghouse, in Sydney. A difficult theme for any writer—the emotional reactions of children—is delicately handled by Alan Marshall and Margaret Trist. Rather on his own by reason of his conscious and iridescent style, Hal Porter picks his way among offbeat situations. This thin listing, personal and necessarily biased, will satisfy no reader; it may, however, serve to indicate some of the variety.

In drama the thirties saw the beginning of a series of play competitions, organized by little theatres, by eisteddfods, and by the Playwrights' Advisory Board, as well as by the Australian Broadcasting Commission in its search for radio plays. The competitions led to better craftsmanship within the limits of the well-made play, to experiment with verse form, and to more successful reproductions of the living speech idiom.

Many playwrights emerged in the period. Alexander Turner set plays on the Murchison gold field in Western Australia, and contrived to evoke vividly the atmosphere of fatalism of the district;

George Dann set plays in the coastal and country districts of Queensland, using an aborigines' settlement in his best play, *Fountains Beyond* (1944); Dymphna Cusack ranged widely, from a girls' school to an amenities center for soldiers in Melbourne; Betty Roland set a tragedy, *The Touch of Silk* (1942), on a lonely farm, while Lynn Foster studied a family saga of station life in *There Is No Armour* (1945); Henrietta Drake-Brockman's *Men without Wives* (1938), is set in the sparsely populated Northern Territory, and her *Hot Gold* (1946), on the West Australian gold fields. There were, it can be seen, more bush plays than city plays.

In the dialogue, there is a steady trend toward more authentic realism, the speech growing out of the setting; that is, characters speak as they do because they belong to a certain place and way of life. Although the most convincing speech comes mostly from the less-educated characters, playwrights do achieve good flowing dialogue that sounds true, for a mixed group; *Royal Mail* (1939) by Alexander Turner, for instance, opens with a flawless piece of dialogue. But though most of the playwrights could manage this for moments, they never seemed able to sustain the easy flow for the whole play. The first time this was done was in Ray Lawler's *The Summer of the Seventeenth Doll* (1955), where good craftsmanship and an original plot, characters that had not appeared before, and above all dialogue that was true to character and that conveyed a humor, fresh and recognizably local, resulted in a play which had immediate commercial success in its own country. Since then, this play has been imitated: *The Shifting Heart* by Beynon, *Fire on the Wind* by Coburn, and *The One Day of the Year* by Seymour, are plays that with less general acclaim than Lawler's have used the superficial elements of his technique.

The most interesting experimental work has been the verse plays of Douglas Stewart. During the forties he produced two radio plays, *The Fire on the Snow*, dealing with Scott's expedition to the South Pole, and *The Golden Lover* (both 1944), based on Maori legend, and two stage plays, *Ned Kelly* (1943), which uses Australia's best-known bushranger, and *Shipwreck* (1947), the story of Pelsart's wreck off the West Australian coast in the seventeenth century. Stewart has been the most successful writer of history plays. He sacrifices strict accuracy for dramatic concentration, keeps the number of scene changes, climaxes, and characters within the range of practical theatre, and uses the speech of his own time, lively and colloquial though in verse. He achieves intensity by skillful manipulation of verse and speech rhythms and lifts into figure with a poet's ease when he wants vividness. The two radio plays, the first tragic and the second comic, have been successful everywhere and cover a considerable range of dramatic effects possible only in verse drama.

Catherine Duncan is the only other notable verse playwright, and is known chiefly by one play, *Sons of the Morning* (1946), set in Crete during the evacuation of the Australian troops.

These plays, all published or commercially produced, use the speech and method of the well-made realistic play. But a number of our playwrights within the last ten years are experimenting with techniques closer to the trends of recent European rather than English drama and are making more imaginative use of speech. So far they have had only limited amateur production and have not been published.

Ric Throssell stands out as author of a considerable body of drama. His best is *The Day Before Tomorrow*, which handles the theme of a country dealing with the aftereffects of an atomic war. This is a playwright on top of his craft, using technique in a professional manner. The same is true of John Naish. In *The Paul Davis Affair* he has a setting in a totalitarian state of the future: the first and third acts are realistically set in a suicide center, while the second act breaks away from realism, using symbolic *décor* and props.

There have been a number of efforts to avoid the three-act structure. *Image in the Clay*, by David Ireland, is arranged in five scenes, each of which reaches a climax before the end. The scene drifts away, giving the effect that the whole action is true, not an artificial stage effect. Ireland's second play, *The Virgin of Treadmill Street*, is in twelve scenes. The most sophisticated, toughest writing we have yet had from a playwright, it well illustrates the advance in technique over the last few years: exposition imperceptibly shading into development, atmosphere being evoked without our feeling conscious of tricks.

Ray Mathew's *A Spring Song* is in six scenes, each scene finishing gently, so that one imagines the characters living on after the curtain comes down. In this bush play, as in his more strictly realistic *We Find the Bunyip,* he does not resort to uneducated Australian and to slang, but catches individuality by repetition and pattern. His Sydney play, *The Life of the Party,* produced in London in 1961, handles sophisticated characters with a similar technique, but in a play on the Kelly theme he has tried a semifantasy style, letting the actors come out of character to address the audience.

A Man Is a Mountain, by Kevin McNamara, is another city play, and experiments in speech and in atmospheric effects. The characters answer the unspoken rather than the spoken words of others.

Another playwright who uses effective patterns of speech is J. P. McKinney, in his bush play, *The Well.* Here the playwright does not give us a resolution of conflict, but leaves us with the feeling of the continuity of life, of people getting up next morning as usual, after the drama is over.

Standing quite apart from all these, and with a European rather than an English or Australian flavor, is *The Ham Funeral* by Patrick White, written fourteen years ago but produced only in November, 1961. It is distinguished by its freedom from the conventional pattern and by its penetration below the surfaces of speech and behavior to explore a young poet's quest for the complete life.

Thus the plays of this period display a branching out in many directions. There is more courage in the selecting of settings and in the writing of dramatic speech; there is more originality in the variety of forms attempted; there is an enormous advance in sheer craftsmanship. By way of these things, there is greater depth, more penetration into the nature of human beings.

Criticism of the literature has probably never been so active and organs to publish it never so numerous and so literate: *The Bulletin, Southerly, Meanjin, Quadrant, Westerly, Overland, Australian Letters, Nation, The Melbourne Critical Review, The Australian Quarterly, Australian Book Review*—to name the best known. Two huge histories—one by Morris Miller (1940), revised, condensed, and alphabetically arranged by F. T. Macartney (1956); the other by H. M. Green (1961)—and a shorter account by the present writer (1960) cover the literature from the beginnings to the fifties. The critics themselves are so many that limited space would invidiously condense comment into a selective catalogue. The major figures are given in the bibliography. To any list should be added the name of the only essayist nationally known, that of Walter Murdoch.

As in the United States, the universities in this period have played a major role in criticism; most of the critics are university graduates, and many are on the faculties of universities. Again, the American custom of having a poet on the campus recently commenced in Australia with the appointment of poet and critic James McAuley as reader in English in the University of Tasmania.[2] Academic interest has become official—there are lectureships in Australian literature, and the first chair in the subject has been established at the University of Sydney. The universities administer the money and invite the lecturers in the Commonwealth Literary Fund lecture scheme, which has now operated for twenty years.

This fund also provides for more general lectures, where adult education authorities are in charge, makes grants to writers undertaking certain works, and partially supports the publication of some literary volumes.

The whiff of paternalism is not offensive: writers helped are not expected to provide any *quid pro quo* apart from the work they produce. Not every official choice, of course, has been happy; but a literary gamble is no bad thing—the bet is not a large one.

The various production in all fields of writing continues. On one day in August, 1961, for instance, an Australian publisher issued six books of verse, one by each of six poets. It may have had the slight flavor of a stunt—production had been held up by managerial eruptions—but the event was significant enough.

In quality alone, the best of Australian writers this century have had their equivalents in other Commonwealth countries—the Canadians, Pratt and Klein; the South African, Campbell; the New Zealander, Katherine Mansfield. But in quality and volume combined, it seems indisputable that the Australian yields to no other of the Commonwealth literatures.

---

[2] There have been several poets (such as John le Gay Brereton, Archibald Strong, Christopher Brennan, R. G. Howarth, and A. D. Hope) on the regular lecturing staffs of Australian universities, but McAuley had no obligation to perform the usual university teaching duties. He was later appointed to the chair of English.

BIBLIOGRAPHY

General

Ewers, John K. *Creative Writing in Australia.* 1962.
Franklin, M. *Laughter, Not for a Cage.* 1956.
Green, H. M. *Australian Literature, 1900–1950.* 1951.
——. *A History of Australian Literature, 1789–1950.* 2 vols. 1961.
Hadgraft, Cecil. *Australian Literature.* 1960.
Matthews, J. P. *Tradition in Exile.* 1962.
Miller, E. Morris. *Australian Literature: From Its Beginnings to 1935.* 2 vols. 1940.
——. *Australian Literature: A Bibliography to 1938. Extended to 1950.* Edited, with a historical outline and descriptive commentaries, by Frederick T. Macartney. 1956.
Palmer, N. *Modern Australian Literature, 1900–1923.* 1924.
Rees, L. C. *Towards an Australian Drama.* 1953.
Roderick, C. *An Introduction to Australian Fiction.* 1950.

Critical Essays

Buckley, V. *Essays in Poetry: Mainly Australian.* 1957.
Eldershaw, Barnard. *Essays in Australian Fiction.* 1938.
Elliott, B. R. *Singing to the Cattle, and Other Australian Essays.* 1947.
Green, H. M. *Fourteen Minutes.* Revised and brought up to date by Dorothy Green. 1950.
Johnston, Grahame, ed. *Australian Literary Criticism.* 1962.
Macartney, F. T. *Australian Literary Essays.* 1957.
Phillips, A. A. *The Australian Tradition.* 1958.
Stephens, A. G. *The Red Pagan.* 1904.
Stewart, D. *The Flesh and the Spirit.* 1948.

Studies of Individual Authors

Chisholm, A. R. *Christopher Brennan: The Man and His Poetry.* 1946.
Dutton, G., ed. *Australian Writers and Their Work.* Irregular. 1961– .
Elliott, B. R. *Marcus Clarke.* 1958.
Franklin, M., and Baker, K. *Joseph Furphy.* 1944.
Gibson, L. J. *Henry Handel Richardson and Some of Her Sources.* 1955.
Green, H. M. *Christopher Brennan.* 1939.
Hughes, R. C. J. *Brennan: An Essay in Values.* 1934.

100

LITERATURE

Kennedy, V., and Palmer, N. *Bernard O'Dowd*. 1954.

Macartney, F. T. *Furnley Maurice*. 1955.

Moore, T. Inglis. *Six Australian Poets*. 1942.

Palmer, N. *Henry Handel Richardson*. 1950.

Palmer, V. *A. G. Stephens: His Life and Work*. 1941.

——. *Frank Wilmot (Furnley Maurice)*. 1942.

——. *Louis Esson and the Australian Theatre*. 1948.

Roderick, C. *In Mortal Bondage: The Strange Life of Rosa Praed*. 1948.

Stephens, A. G. *Chris. Brennan: A Monograph*. 1933.

Wilkes, G. A. *New Perspectives on Brennan's Poetry*. 1953.

Anthologies

Australian Poetry. Annual. 1941– .

Coast to Coast: Australian Stories. Biannual. 1941– .

Green, H. M., ed. *Modern Australian Poetry*. 1952.

Jindyworobak Anthology. Annual. 1938–1952.

Mackaness, G., ed. *An Anthology of Australian Verse*. Second edition. 1952.

Stewart, D., and Keesing, N. *Australian Bush Ballads*. 1955.

——. *Old Bush Songs and Rhymes of Colonial Times*. 1957.

Thompson, J., Slessor, K. and Howarth, R. G., eds. *The Penguin Book of Australian Verse*. 1958.

Verse in Australia. Annual. 1958– .

Periodicals

Australian Letters. Quarterly. 1957– .

The Australian Quarterly, 1929– .

The Bulletin. Weekly. 1880– .

Meanjin. Quarterly. 1940– .

Overland. Quarterly. 1954– .

Quadrant. Quarterly. 1956– .

Southerly. Quarterly. 1939– .

Westerly. Three times a year. 1956– .

LANGUAGE

SIDNEY J. BAKER

THE Australian has a good deal of difficulty in disguising his origins when he goes abroad. Even if he labors strenuously to acquire the social pattern of another environment, he does not find it easy to submerge the qualities that have gone into making him what he is. True, in another setting, the passage of time will wear away the rough edges of his manner and habits and speech (and do not let us deceive ourselves by forgetting that some people feel that these things are well worth being worn away); but complete transformation is almost impossible.

Today, precisely a century and three-quarters after the first white people settled in this country, the Australian has gone a long way toward abandoning efforts to disguise himself when he is overseas. But it was not always so. Probably only in the past generation has a mood of avowal operated generally. Throughout the nineteenth century and early in the present century many Australians who journeyed abroad felt the sense of apologetic worthlessness which Ray Lawler has woven into his play, *The Piccadilly Bushman*. There were good reasons for this—Australia's convict beginnings, its vastness, its concentration on practical activities, its many cultural deficiencies.

But there was another side to the picture. Those Australians who could afford to journey abroad to Places Where Things Happened left behind them many people who either could not raise traveling money or felt little desire to quit Australia. It is worth looking closer at these stay-put Australians. They were here, and they were glad of it. Not for more than fleeting instants did they feel what Australian author A. A. Phillips calls "the Cultural Cringe." That "cringe" was basically a high-brow attitude, and whether the forelock-pullers overcame it or not made little difference to those who had more practical things to think about.

And how practical were those things? At the outset, they were the rawest, crudest essentials of life. Here was a handful of people at the far end of the earth, rejects from a parsimonious England, who were faced with an alien and harsh environment and burdened with all the distresses that an out-of-sight-out-of-mind policy could inflict. The first, most practical issue they faced was merely staying alive. One of the most easily perceivable manifestations of this was the nature of the slang used by our reluctant "Pilgrim Fathers." It was almost exclusively concrete. Indeed, not until more than a century later did any significant group of abstract terms or phrases appear, and we do not have to ponder long over these expressions (for example, *Buckley's chance, to crack hardy, wowserism, rafferty rules, to whip the cat*) to realize that many of them are fundamentally earth-bound. That fact not only assures us that the inventors of these terms had little interest in nonpractical affairs, but that their "low-browism" had become confirmed by generations of relentlessly practical activity.

Between 1788 and 1868 nearly 160,000 convicts were shipped to Australia from Britain. Most of them had been schooled in the argot of English jails, and much of that argot remained with them long after they arrived in Australia.

We are fortunate in possessing a fairly detailed record of the slang imported to this country and the way Australian influences imposed early changes upon it. This is a "Vocabulary of the Flash Language," compiled in 1812 at Newcastle, N.S.W., by a convict

103

named James Hardy Vaux during what he describes as his "solitary hours of cessation from hard labour." This "Vocabulary" was included in Vaux's *Memoirs* (1819). Admittedly, not much in it can be described as authentically Australian, but there are many pointers to the way our language was to go. Here are some of the English importations: *grab*, meaning to seize; *grub*, food; *to kid*, to deceive; *lark*, fun or sport of any kind; *nuts on*, infatuated with; *prime*, good; *pull*, an advantage; *to queer*, to spoil; *throw off at*, jeer at. And here are a few of the terms recorded by Vaux which Australia has since modified: *awake*, "to see through or comprehend," which occurs in the modern form, "I'm *a wake-up* to you!"; *chum*, "a fellow prisoner in a jail, hulk, etc.," which later appeared in *new chum*, a recent immigrant (1839), *new chumism* (1854), and *new chumhood* (1883); *gray*, a composite halfpenny or other coin having two heads or two tails, which is used in *two-up* (gambling) slang today for a two-tailed penny; *push*, "a concourse of people, a crowd," which later became the larrikin equivalent of "gang"; and *leary*, for "fly," cunning, or alert, which Australia later converted to *lairy* with a different meaning.

But there were more important developments than these. As the lexicographer, Noah Webster, wrote in his Preface to the *American Dictionary of the English Language* (1828):

Language is the expression of ideas; and if the people of one country cannot preserve an identity of ideas (with the people of another) they cannot retain an identity of language. Now, an identity of ideas depends materially upon the sameness of things or objects with which the people of the two countries are conversant. But in no two portions of the earth, remote from each other, can such identity be found. Even physical objects must be different.

The unique nature of the Australian environment, its flora and fauna, its aborigines, the problems and tasks it forced on its inhabitants, produced a vast mass of linguistic innovations. After the Blue Mountains were breached in 1813, what had begun as a trickle of new offerings around Sydney became an avalanche. Thus, the Australian speaker who had begun by taking into his everyday vocabulary such words as the aboriginal *boomerang, kangaroo, koala, kookaburra, gin* (an aboriginal woman), and *gibber* (the g is hard), and who had found that his own experiences led to the creation of *stockyard* (1796), *stockman* (1803), *bush* (1801), and *bushranger* (1805), was faced with countless new interests. And as those interests broadened, so did the list of words he either invented or adapted from abroad to describe them: *outback, station, run, gully, scrub, creek, squatter, pastoralist, paddock, boundary rider, overlander, jackeroo, bushwhacker*, and hundreds more. His borrowings from the aborigines included not only *billabong, humpy, coo-ee, corroboree, dillybag, bunyip*, and *waddy*, but scores of essential words like *dingo, wallaby*, and *wombat* (animals), *budgerigar, galah*, and *currawong* (birds), *barramundi, mulloway*, and *wobbegong* (fish), and *coolibah, jarrah*, and *mulga* (trees).

Most of this was more or less in the linguistic order of things, but not all. Take the word *squatter*, for example. Today the Australian *squatter*, a large landholder in the outback, mainly occupied in raising sheep or cattle, is the acme of financial respectability. It was not always so. The original *squatter* was a freed convict, or ticket-of-leave man, who built a bark hut on unoccupied land and (as Charles Darwin reported in *Voyage of the Beagle*) "buys or steals a few animals, sells spirits without a licence, receives stolen goods —and so at last becomes rich and turns farmer; he is the horror of all his honest neighbours." A pamphlet issued by the South Australia Company about 1839 referred to "the mere squatter . . . content to lead a savage life in the wilds remote from the decencies of society, with no company but his felon dependents." Even as late as 1851, J. F. L. Foster, author of *The New Colony of Victoria*, calls the word "a barbarous appellation."

The early history of this term is a rather necessary reminder, not only that many such expressions had extremely earthy beginnings, but that a large number of people who put these words into currency were unrepentant proletarians. Here we encounter two issues of major importance. The first is that, until the discovery of gold in 1851 which led to a change in social focus, much of Australia's work force pursued a seminomadic existence in the outback—a valuable point made by Dr. Russel Ward in *The Australian Legend* (1958). The second is that, at least until the 1870's, many Australians were educationally deprived. It is somewhat difficult to establish clearly the extent of this educational privation, but the school commission of 1854–1855 reported: "We are under the impression that the average time spent at school by each child cannot far exceed two years." Since only half of Australia's children at the time had any schooling at all, the apparent fact that the more fortunate youngsters had two years of systematic instruction obviously had a major influence on the development of proletarian methods of speech. We cannot be surprised to learn that between 1844 and 1854 nearly half the marriage certificates registered were signed with crosses. As late as 1866, Henry Parkes declared that "it is very probable that there are 100,000 children [in New South Wales] under fourteen years of age destitute of all instruction whatever." The combined effects of large-scale lack of education and itinerant work hunting in the outback encouraged the development of slang and its widespread propagation.

Those who recoil from the part Australia has played in befouling the "pure well of English" should resist the temptation to be astonished at what has happened. Here are two of many comments:

1) On the wide use of slang—from *What I Heard, Saw and Did at the Australian Goldfields* (1853) by C. R. Read: "Such dreadful and horribly disgusting language may be heard expressed by children on the diggings that I do not imagine could be surpassed by the most hardened adults on Norfolk Island, and this does not rest with boys alone, but by little girls from eight to ten years of age."

2) On Australian pronunciation—from the *Report of the School Commission* (1855): "Little care is apparently taken [in N.S.W. schools] to correct vicious pronunciation. . . . This inattention has a tendency to foster an Australian dialect which bids fair to surpass the American in disagreeableness."

Since it is only in the past generation that the population of Australia's capital cities has exceeded that of the remainder of the continent, the prolonged influence of the outback is not to be underestimated. If now, for the first time in Australian history, the rich idiom of *wool-barbers, ringers, swagmen, poddy-dodgers, rouseabouts,* and *bush-dwellers* shows signs of becoming submerged by urban growth, we cannot be altogether surprised.

If, today, some observers are tempted to see bush traditions as static, it was certainly not always so. The influence of gold was immediately perceivable in the changing nature of popular speech, and there was ample reason for C. R. Read to urge, in 1853, that Englishmen going to the Australian diggings should search their souls and ask themselves "if they can stand a little colonial slang."

In view of its ultimate destiny, no term is more significant at this period than *digger*, describing a man who dug for gold. More than sixty years later, it was transferred to the Australian soldier in the First World War, was capitalized, and, together with its abbreviation, *Dig*, became something of a national accolade. It was revived in the Second World War and retains its military application today.

Among the many derivatives spawned by the original *digger* were *diggerman* (1854), *diggeress* (1855), *diggerdom* (1855), and *diggerism* (1857). Scarcely less important than *digger* was *fossicker* (1853), derived from an English dialectal word *fossick*, which found an easy place in the gold-seeker's vocabulary. Over the years, this has also undergone big changes. Today we not only *fossick* for something when we search for it, we *fossick it up*, or we *fossick around*, and *fossicking*, searching (originally, searching for surface gold), is a useful present participle.

There were, however, many terms that have disappeared from general use, like *reefer, cradler, dryblower, sandscratcher*, and *nuggeter; leader*, an alluvial gold claim or vein of gold; *deep leader*, a man who works a deep alluvial claim; *Gympie work*, singlehanded hammer and drill work (a Queensland use, after a town in that state); *wash*, soil from which gold is extracted by washing; *monkey shaft*, a small trial shaft in a mine; *burnt stuff*, a stratum of ironhard rock or compacted clay and rock encountered during digging; *hungry quartz*, an unpromising quartz reef; *shicer* and *duffer*, an unproductive mine. Many gold-seeking terms were taken from the United States—*prospector, to prospect*, and *prospecting*, although the noun *prospect* (for "an examination or test of mineral richness in a locality, or of material from which ore, etc., is to be extracted") appears to be Australian.

Among the scores of words which became current in Australia following the discovery of gold, few were fated to earn a larger place in our gathering national consciousness than *miner's right*, a license to dig for gold. It originated in the newly established state of Victoria in 1852 when an act of parliament was passed imposing payment of a license fee on all diggers. Under the direction of C. J. LaTrobe, who was appointed governor of Victoria in 1851, strict

107

measures were taken to ensure that every digger had a *miner's right*, and *license-hunting* or *digger-hunting* described the methods of checking enforced. LaTrobe's administration bred riots at Beechworth and Castlemaine and led eventually to the stand by miners at Eureka Stockade in 1854.

LaTrobe's second Christian name was Joseph, and from this were developed the terms *joe*, a police trooper, and the cries *Joe!*, *Joe-Joe!*, and *Joey!*, warnings used by diggers at the approach of troopers. There were other variations, among which T. McCombie lists in his *Australian Sketches* (1861): "To *joey* or *joe* a person on the diggings, or anywhere else in Australia, is grossly to insult and ridicule him." Two years later B. A. Heywood reported that *joe* was becoming "the chaff for new chums" and was being hurled at new arrivals on the gold fields. By the 1860's it had found its way across the Tasman Sea to New Zealand and, as late as 1871, C. L. Money reports in *Knocking About New Zealand:* "The word *joe* expresses the derision usually bestowed on new chums on the diggings." From a historical viewpoint, *joe* and its derivatives were among the first indigenous terms to commemorate the name of a person. Later, of course, there were to be many more, varying from *game as Ned Kelly*, foolhardily courageous, and *Buckley's chance*, little or no chance at all, to *Granny Smith*, the name of a species of apple.

Gold brought many people to Australia. It also provided wealth for many of the people who had previously moved from place to place in the outback seeking work. The itinerants had produced a great deal of slang of their own—*damper* (1826); *bush biscuit* (1845), a thin damper; *bush life* (1839); *bullock dray* (1847); *eye blight* (1826); *have a shingle short* (1847), to be silly; *splitter* (1841), a timber cutter; *steamer* (1820), a dish of stewed kangaroo flavored with pork; and many more—but few of these people had been able to acquire enough wealth to settle and develop their own land. Soon the outlook changed. More money, more people, and increasing demands for primary products made it possible for many of the wanderers to find niches for themselves.

Up to the middle of last century a great deal of the land taken up was in the hands of the *squattocracy* (a term which dates from 1846), but then smaller landholders began to move in. The *cockatoo*, a small farmer, who, according to legend, was "just picking up the grains of a livelihood like cockatoos do maize," became a recognizable rural figure. This word *cockatoo* came into use about 1850 and remained current until the end of the century when *cocky*, which had appeared in 1884, took over. Thus, we hear of *cockatoo settler* (1869), *cockatoo farmer* and *cockatoo squatter* (1873), and *cockatoo selector* (1893). *Cocky* remains in use today and has acquired even wider applications than it had formerly—for example, *cane cocky*, a grower of sugar cane, *chicken cocky*, a poultry farmer—but *cockatoo* is now used almost exclusively to denote someone who *keeps nit* or *nitkeeps* (keeps guard) while some illegal activity is afoot, such as playing *two-up* or *heading 'em*.

From the early 1860's many large properties were broken up by official edict to allow the *cockies* to move in. One result was bitter antagonism between the *squatter* and the *free selector;* and to preserve the land he had occupied, the *squatter* introduced methods variously known as *land dummying, dummyism, peacocking, spotting*, and *gridironing*. The *gridironer* earned his name by purchasing good farming land in strips—after the fashion of a gridiron—so that intervening land was rendered worthless and might be bought at the *gridironer's* pleasure. The *peacocker* was somewhat similar: he held on to the best portions of a district and left the worthless sections (especially those without water frontages) to people with smaller means. This practice was known as *eyepicking*, and we find frequent references in old Australian books and journals to *picking the eyes out of the country*. (The phrase, which refers to the ocelli on the tail of a peacock, has survived, and today we can *pick the eyes out of* anything by selecting the best of what is available.) *Spotting* is a synonym for *peacocking*. Another ruse adopted by the squatter was the employment of a *dummy* or *medium*. Under the law, a buyer of government land at auction was required to attend in person and to swear that he was selecting land (the original *backblocks* or blocks of land in the outback) for his own use and benefit. The *dummy* took up land ostensibly for his own purposes, then handed it back to the squatter for a fee. These ruses allowed many large landowners to retain control of much of their original holdings.

One result was that land hunger drove some adventurers far out into the *back-of-beyond*, where they occupied even larger areas of land. So there were now three major influences in outback life: the old squatters, the cockies, and the new squatters *way out, back of Bourke, west of sunset,* and so on. Since most of them could supply at least seasonal work, Australia's proletarian itinerants went out once more, as they had done before the discovery of gold, but now in greatly increased numbers, into the Mallee, the Channel Country, west and north Queensland, the Center, and the Northern Territory.

The symbol of these laborers is the *swag*. The original English use of the word *swag* was to denote stolen property, but by 1812 (the record was made in Australia by Vaux) it also described "a bundle, parcel or package." As a bundle made of a rolled blanket within which were personal effects, the *swag* became a possession of special importance to the itinerant. We hardly need any other assurance of how the nature of Australian life changed after the heady 1850's when we learn that the expressions *to swag it* and *swagging* were first used in 1861. It should not be forgotten, however, that those early *swagmen* or *swaggies* were work-seekers and not tramps or hobos. Since less than a quarter of Australia's population lived in her capital cities at that time, the paths of the unemployed inevitably led inland.

The linguistic fertility of the years between 1860 and 1900 must represent one of the most impressive manifestations of social awakening that has ever occurred. Here are a few examples:

From sheepmen: *jumbuck,* a sheep; *woolshed,* a large building on a station where sheep are shorn; *penner-up, tarboy, fleece-picker, broomie,* shearing-shed workers; *boss-over-the-board,* a woolshed manager or overseer; *ringer* and *gun-shearer,* an expert shearer; *to dump,* to press wool in a bale; *to double-dump,* to press two bales of wool together for transport; *a dump,* two bales of wool so pressed together; *a blow,* a stroke with hand shears when shearing a sheep; *daggers, tongs, jingling johnnies,* hand shears; *smoke-oh,* a period of rest, a spell from work, in fixed woolshed breaks; *eaglehawk,* to pluck wool from a dead sheep; *cocky's clip,* the equivalent of shaving a sheep; *to box,* to mix mobs of sheep; *to cut out,* to complete shearing at a shed; *nowler,* a sheep difficult to shear because of burr and dirt in the wool; *monkey-dodger,* a sheep station hand (from the use of *monkey* to denote a sheep); *hermit,* a sheep which becomes attached to a spot and will not budge; *snob,* the last sheep in a day's work in a woolshed (a play on the word "last" as used by a cobbler, a boot repairer, or *snob*); *bell-sheep*, as for *snob*; *spade press*, a make-shift wool press; *mob*, a flock of sheep; *fly-strike*, infestation of sheep by blowflies; *kelpie* and *barb*, types of sheep dogs; *Polwarth*, an Australian breed of sheep first developed in the 1880's.

From cattlemen: *cleanskin*, an unbranded head of stock; *scrubbers*, *pikers*, *myalls*, cattle that have run wild in the scrub and deteriorated in condition; *windsplitters*, *razorbacks*, *hatracks*, lean and scraggy cattle; *bangtail muster*, a periodic counting of herds; *stag*, a half-grown bull, an imperfectly castrated bullock; *poddy*, a hand-fed calf (also used for a hand-fed lamb or foal), whence *poddy-calf* and *to poddy*, to rear by hand feeding; *poddy-dodger*, a person who steals unbranded calves; *duffer*, a cattle thief, whence *duffing*, cattle thievery; *staggering bob*, a young calf; *ropeable*, an excitable head of stock (whence the general use, meaning violently angry or savagely ill-tempered as applied to a person); *ringer*, a stockman (this is distinct from the use of *ringer* in shearing); *blue heeler* or *bluey*, a type of cattle dog; *Illawarra shorthorn*, a breed of cattle developed in Australia; and a number of synonyms for the *bullocky* (driver of a bullock wagon) and his kind, such as *bull puncher*, *ox persuader*, *buffalo navigator*, *cow conductor*, and *bullocker*.

From horsemen: *brumby*, a wild horse; *crocodile* and *alligator*, any horse; *to prop*, to come to a sudden halt, especially when traveling at high speed; *to plant* (of a horse), to remain perfectly still (there was an older use of *plant* as a verb meaning to hide stolen horses or cattle; whence *planter* and *planting*); *buckjump*, to ride a bucking horse, or said of a horse that bucks; *pigjump*, used somewhat similarly; *to buck* and *bucker*, said of a horse that bucks; *buck a hurricane*, said of a horse that bucks wildly; *get shanghaied*, to be thrown from a horse; *rough ride*, to ride a partly broken horse; *hang up a horse*, to tie a horse to a fence or rail; *turn on a cabbage leaf*, said of a horse than can turn smartly.

General: *stock route*, a route or track along which stock, especially cattle and sheep, are driven; *stockrider*, a horseman who tends cattle or sheep on the move; *stockwhip*, a whip used by a cattleman or someone driving a bullock team or horses; *stock and station agent*, a man handling the sale of stock and properties in the outback; *boundary rider*, an employee of a station who patrols boundaries to prevent the straying of stock and, if necessary, to repair fences;

111

overlander, a man driving stock over long distances; *jackeroo*, a station hand who is being trained for managerial status; *bowyang*, a strap or string tied below the knees of a worker's pants to keep the cuffs off the ground; *tucker*, food, whence *to tucker*, to eat, *tuckertime*, time for eating, *tuckerbox* or *tuckerbag*, a box or bag in which food is carried; *babbler* (a truncation of the rhyming slang *babbling brook*), cook; *baitlayer* or *poisoner*, a cook; *johnny cake*, a small damper baked in the embers of a fire; *jump-up*, a mixture of flour and water boiled into a paste with sugar; *billy*, a tin can in which water is boiled for tea or in which cooking is done, also *billy-can* and *billypot* (from the aboriginal *billa*, water, which occurs in *billabong*, a large pond); *quart pot*, a large billy; *post-and-rails*, strong and often poor-quality tea made in a billy; *jack the painter*, strong bush tea.

From swagmen: *bluey*, as for *swag*, named from the blue-colored blanket most commonly carried; *drum, roll, parcel, curse, shiralee, Matilda*, assorted terms for a swag; *to hump a swag* (or *bluey*, etc.), to carry a swag; *to waltz Matilda*, used similarly (the popular song "Waltzing Matilda" disguises the fact that the original form of this expression was *to walk Matilda*); *to push the knot*, to carry a swag; *toe rags* or *Prince Alberts*, originally rags which an outback itinerant wound about his toes or feet (the still current *toe-ragger* is a term of contempt); *sundowner*, a swagman who managed to dodge working for his food by arriving at a station at sundown; *drummer*, a swagman; *waler*, a tramp who lived on the New South Wales side of the Murrumbidgee River at a time when north of the river was known as *Sydneyside* (residents of Sydney are still called *Sydneysiders*) and the south as *the other side* or *totherside* or *Yarraside* (the Yarra River runs through Melbourne); *on the wallaby*, tramping in the outback, similarly with *on the sunshine track; the long paddock*, the open road; *Wagga blanket*, a covering made by cutting open a chaff or flour sack and hemming it roughly.

Many of these terms (and hundreds more like them) were interchangeable between one group and another and, as a result, it is often difficult to determine their precise origins.

In addition to outback slang, another influence began to appear as urban pressures put such new expressions into currency as *larrikin*, a street tough or hoodlum (derivations included *larrikinism* and *larrikiness*); *bludger*, originally a harlot's bully, later anyone who imposes on others, a loafer or idler, a general term of contempt (whence *bludging*, the practice of imposing on others, *to bludge*, to loaf or impose on another, and *a bludge*, a period of loafing or of operating some minor racket); *cobber*, a friend, companion, workmate; *dinkum*, true, vouched for, honest (whence *fair dinkum*, *square dinkum*, *dinkydie*, *dinkum article*, *dinkum oil*, *dinkum Aussie*, etc.); *to barrack*, to shout or jeer at, to interrupt noisily, especially in a sporting event (whence *barracking*, the practice, *barracker*, one who barracks, *barrack for*, to support or encourage); *cronk*, ill, of poor quality; *johnhop*, a policeman; *to poke borak*, to tease, make fun of; similarly with *to poke mullock*; *graft*, work, especially hard work, whence *grafter*, a hard worker; *guyver*, affectation, "side," spurious talk; *hoot*, money, ready cash.

The word *larrikin* merits closer attention. It came into use in Melbourne a little before 1870 and in the early days of the *pushes* found wide currency in Australia. The 1911 edition of the *Encyclopaedia Britannica* reports: "As may be seen from the novels of Rolf Boldrewood and other writers, [Australia] possesses an ample store of slang peculiar to itself; but of this *larrikin* is the only word that has found its way into general use in the mother country." Actually, *larrikin* is not an original Australianism. It had been current in Cornwall more than a generation earlier (it is recorded in F. W. P. Jago's *Ancient Language and Dialect of Cornwall*, [1882]) and had probably also been used in Ireland. What had occurred was that Australia had found a place for the term and that it had been lifted out of English dialect, acquiring enough currency to mislead English observers into thinking that it was an antipodean original. Much the same thing happened with many other terms that became firmly rooted in Australia, among them *dinkum*, *to barrack*, *cobber*, *fossick*, *smoodge*, *skerrick*, and possibly *wowser*. Definitions not already given: *smoodge*, to make love to, to kiss, to flatter, to curry favor, whence *smoodger* and *smoodge up to* (someone); *skerrick*, a small amount of anything, a small sum of money, especially used negatively as *not a skerrick*, *without a skerrick*, *he hasn't a skerrick*, he's penniless; *wowser*, a killjoy, a blue-ribbon, a puritan.

The combined effect of indigenous invention and adaptation from abroad in the last quarter of the nineteenth century put a vast array

113

of new words and phrases into use in this country. A direct result was the publication of various collections of Australian slang, the most notable of which were *The Detectives' Handbook*, published in 1882 or earlier, Karl Lentzner's *Wörterbuch der englischen Volkssprache australiens*, published in Leipzig in 1891, Cornelius Crowe's *Australian Slang Dictionary* (1895), Professor E. E. Morris' *Austral English Dictionary* (1898), and Joshua Lake's Australian supplement to the 1898 edition of *Webster's International Dictionary*. Although all these collections have shortcomings, some of them of an extremely misleading nature, their appearance stresses the point that, less than a century and a quarter from the beginnings of settlement in Australia, the country's idiom had grown to formidable dimensions. The process was destined to continue, with increasing emphasis, into the twentieth century. The first of the post-Federation lexicographers were S. E. O'Brien and A. G. Stephens. Between 1900 and 1910 they compiled a valuable collection, but this was never published and remains in typescript form in the Mitchell Library, Sydney, entitled "Material for a Dictionary of Australian Slang." An Australian supplement to the 1912 edition of Macmillan's *A Modern Dictionary of the English Language*, W. H. Downing's *Digger Dialects* (1919), successive commentaries in the *Encyclopaedia Britannica*, Eric Partridge's *Slang Today and Yesterday* (1930), and my own *Dictionary of Australian Slang* (1941), *The Australian Language* (1945), *Australia Speaks* (1953), and *The Drum* (1959), and other publications show the richness and continuing expansion of Australia's slang.

Much of what was originally slang, of course, has now become fully orthodox—*stock route, squatter, station, run, jackeroo, humpy, wowser*. Other terms have become obsolete or obsolescent: who today, except in historical studies, hears of *emancipists, currency lads, cornstalks, pipes, Botany Bay swells, cabbageites*, and *colonial experiencers?* Even such a word as *bonzer*, first rate, which leapt into prominence early this century and bred a wide variety of alternatives such as *boshter, bosker, bonster, bontoger, bontosher, bonsterina, bonzerino, bonziorie*, and *bonzo*, has largely faded from use. *Sheila* (girl friend) has replaced *cliner* and *donah; ridge* has pushed out *ryebuck; bodgie* (hoodlum) has almost eliminated *larrikin*.

As Australian life expanded, new words and phrases developed,

114

edging out old expressions, eroding away old meanings, and replacing them with new applications. The convict days, the gold era, the spacious years of nomad life in the outback have gone, and with them many hundreds of slang terms which Australian speakers once used freely. And as urban populations, secondary industry, and internal networks of transport and communication have grown, so Australian life has taken new directions. But this is not all. Among the most substantial influences brought to bear on Australian life have been major wars.

Australian soldiers who went to the Boer War—they were variously called *Bushmen, Cockyolly Birds, Contingenters,* and *Tommy Cornstalks* at the time—have left no clearly recognizable marks on the language. But the effects of Australia's participation in the two World Wars have been considerable. Enduring today, although they first earned attention in the First World War, are such terms as *Aussie,* an Australian or Australia; *possie,* a position; *bludge,* to loaf or dodge duty (the earlier use of *bludger* for a harlot's bully has already been noted); *furphy,* a rumor or lie; *to hum,* to cadge, and *hummer,* a cadger; *maggoty,* angry; *pom,* an Englishman (an abbreviation of the earlier *pommy*); *to ring it,* to be a coward or *ringtail; shrewdy,* a cunning person; *to souvenir,* to purloin; *upter,* no good (from *up to putty, up to mud,* etc.); and *ziff,* a beard. Downing gives a valuable collection of soldiers' jargon in his *Digger Dialects,* which had the distinction of being the first dictionary of war slang published after the First World War. Another authoritative list was given in the 1920 edition of *Aussie,* the soldiers' magazine issued during and just after the war.

In the Second World War Australian servicemen put hundreds of terms into general use, although actually some of these expressions had begun to appear before the war—for example, *had it,* hopeless, exhausted, finished (which was used in the Northern Territory long before it went abroad); *animal,* a contemptuous description of a person; *drongo,* a fool; and *come the raw prawn,* to attempt to deceive or hoodwink someone. Here is an assortment of other war words: *wouldn't it!,* an exclamation of disgust or disapproval (also *wouldn't it root you!, wouldn't it rip you!, wouldn't it rotate you!*); *troppo,* silly, insane, with special reference to the type of insanity or eccentricity promoted by service in tropical climates; *pull your*

head in, shut up! mind your own business! (also *pull your skull in!*);
gigglesuit, fatigue dress; *panic hat*, steel helmet; *to promote*, to borrow or scrounge (something); *on the nose* (or *bugle* or *trumpet*),
objectionable, unpleasant, worthless; *to dice*, to reject, throw away;
galah, a fool, especially a silly chatterer; *give the game away*, to
abandon interest in any activity or pursuit; *to go* (or *shoot*) *through*,
to go AWOL, to disappear; *to bash*, a general utility verb which
occurs in varied forms such as *earbash*, to talk wearisomely, *spine-
bash*, to loaf, especially supinely, *have a bash at* or *give* (something)
a bash, to make an attempt at, *bash it up you!* a phrase equivalent to
"You know where to put it!" or, more moderately, "Go to the
devil"; *punisher*, a wearisome talker, *an earbasher; to laugh*, to complain, especially used in the meiotic instruction *Stop your laughing!*
Stop making a fuss! Stop *whingeing!; wog*, an Arab; *lurk artist*, an
expert in manipulating some dodge or minor racket; *nohoper*, a
person without merit or unworthy of confidence; *yike*, a row or
argument, a fight, a brawl, more or less equivalent to some of the
uses of *blue*.

Although many war terms were forgotten almost as soon as the
war ended, most of the examples above survive today and have
moved into general use. They form part of the large body of Australian slang which has acquired its durability from its proletarian
origins. This is one of the most important features of slang, of course,
but as mentioned earlier, it has had special force in Australia where
the main crucible of slang invention and use has always been the
proletariat. If we look back over our social history we become aware
that exceedingly few expressions have been imposed from above.
True, of course, it is possible to point to the modern development
of such expressions as *The Movement*, that is, the Roman Catholic
political organization in Australia, *a grouper* (a member or supporter
of right-wing Labor party industrial groups), and *unity ticket*, but
these have been sustained largely by working-class usage.

Apart from a few favored inheritors of wealth, Australia has always been a working-class nation, and its slang has thrived and expanded particularly at times when men were thrown together in
large numbers. As a result, our slang is essentially masculine, like
our ironic humor.

Australian humor is worth examination, not only because it is intimately linked with the development of the Australian character, but because little research has been done on it. One reason for this lack of research is that the Australian sense of humor is difficult to illustrate. At its pungent best it leans heavily on the use of terms which find little favor among censors. Thomas Wood puts the matter fairly clearly in *Cobbers* (1934):

The native-born [joke] is gold, pure gold. It is worth hearing. It comes pat, faintly mocking, hiding a sting in its tail. It is exactly what you might expect from that thin-lipped Australian mouth. . . . But the best stories will never be published. Too broad? Not necessarily. Too vigorous. Too full of words you must not print. The words that won the War. The Big Five. Australian stories need them all and use them lavishly. The effect is stunning.

This element of unprintability is important, but it is not the sole reason Australian humor is mainly reserved for oral performances. It is also heavy with irony. This means that the circumstances for its production are never static. It emerges mainly in special situations in the form of wry comment, and to explain the nature of any of these situations would usually require long-winded detail which would kill the essential crispness of the example. If concessions are made to the blanks, these illustrations may clarify the issue a little:

Here is a description of a man with dirty teeth: "With one white tooth he'd have a —— snooker set!" You have to know the game of snooker (pool) to realize that it has only one white ball; all the rest are colored.

A worker complains about the cramped quarters in which he is expected to work: "I wouldn't lease this hole to a —— witchetty grub!" Witchetty grubs are the larvae of several species of longicorn beetle and are often found in holes in dead wood.

Outline of a romantic triangle: "A is shook on B, B is shook on C, and C is shook on his —— self!" It is only necessary here to note that *shook on* means "infatuated with."

These samples allow us to make several deductions. In the first place, the use of some of Wood's "Big Five" assures us that this humor is basically masculine. Second, we note the deft use of Australian slang or terms which are widely known in Australia. Third, the terseness. Fourth, the conjunction of seemingly remote images—

117

teeth and snooker, a workplace and a witchetty grub, love for others and self-adulation. Fifth, the sharp climax.

It can also be observed that the Australian is a humorist rather than a wit, an ironist rather than a cynic.

In an examination of *The Development of an Australian Social Type* (1932), P. R. Cole said that Australian humor "has a special quality of its own, that of inversion. . . . The Australian humorist regularly says the opposite of what he means." Is this so? Occasionally, yes; but only occasionally. Thus, the Australian speaker tends to say that a man *performs* when he is indulging in a frenzy of anger or vituperation; we call a wild confusion or a potentially difficult task a *picnic;* we say *Stop laughing!* when we admonish someone who is complaining; we say a thing is *not good enough* or *not too wonderful* when we mean that it is extremely bad; we call a violent argument a *session* or a *bit of a blue.*

Perhaps it would be truer to say that these are examples of understatement rather than meiosis. The issue becomes a little clearer when we examine a not uncommon, and always genial, comment by one man to his mate: "You're not a bad old bastard—for a bastard!" Here, the word "bastard," which has promoted countless disputes throughout the world in its time, is rendered innocuous by the speaker's tone. Indeed, there is hardly a vulgarism the Australian cannot use in two ways, and his tone of voice (which cannot be adequately denoted in print) is an infallible index to whether he is using the term genially or provocatively. The same comment goes for most of his understatements. It also weighs significantly in such an exchange as this between a wife and husband. The wife (new dress, new hairdo, and so on) says invitingly, "Well, say something nice." The husband looks away as though deep in thought and after a minute replies, "Righto! Braised prawns!"

The illustrations given above are all brief, but there is a more loquacious form of Australian humor. This is mainly used to pull the legs of overseas people who have no close knowledge of Australia, and it involves rhapsodic improbabilities about saber-toothed koalas roaming the streets of Sydney at night and terrifying the peasants (the koala or native bear is both harmless and gentle), man-eating bull-roarers which infest the mountain billabongs (a bull-roarer is an aboriginal instrument and billabongs, lagoons, are not found in mountains), goanna farms (a goanna is a type of Australian lizard), and prickly-pear plantations (the prickly pear is a noxious cactus).

Since heavy emphasis is placed on the use of local imagery, and so much depends on the tone of the speaker's voice, much of Australia's humor is not exportable. Within the boundaries of the country, however, it has extremely wide currency and is likely to be encountered almost anywhere.

For reasons which, again, are consonant with Australia's development, there has always been a close link between what can loosely be described as our upper and lower classes. In consequence, much of our slang is well known to both strata and has always tended to be national property rather than localized or dialectical. So, too, with our accent.

Let us move, now, a little out of the field of slang words into the lively arena of metaphor. As mentioned earlier, many of Australia's metaphors have an earth-bound quality that is likely to puzzle rather than impress overseas observers. But if the allusions in some of them are baffling and imaginative, and color seems to be spread a little thinly, they are nonetheless highly utilitarian—a point which is adequately shown by the fact that Australians recognize them immediately when they are used in the correct contexts.

Some similes: *happy as Larry*, extremely happy; *bald* (or *balmy* or *miserable*) *as a bandicoot*, extremely bald (balmy, miserable); *full as a goog*, extremely drunk (*goog* means egg); *silly as a bag of worms* (or *as a two-bob watch*, a watch costing two shillings, or about twenty-five cents), extremely silly; *rough as bags*, extremely rough or crude; *tough as fencing wire*, extremely durable; *all over someone like a rash*, said of a skillful contestant or fighter; *like a stunned mullet*, stupid, silly.

Negative comparisons: *no good to Gundy*, worthless, no good at all; *not worth a bumper*, worthless (here *bumper* denotes a cigarette butt); *rafferty rules*, no set rules of conduct in any specified activity; *a roll Jack Rice couldn't jump over*, a large roll of bank notes; *you don't have to be dead to be stiff*, said of someone who is extremely unlucky (here *stiff* means out of luck).

Assorted descriptions: *all laired up*, meticulously dressed or overdressed (also *all tizzied up*); *within coo-ee*, near at hand, within

119

calling distance; *the daddy of them all*, the best, most outstanding in a group; *dead ring of*, highly similar to; *over the edge*, unreasonable (also *over the fence*); *extra grouse*, extremely welcome or attractive; *up a gumtree*, in a quandary; *close to the knuckle*, vulgar, indecent, or approximating thereto; *in the cactus*, in trouble; *blinded with science* (figuratively or actually) said of a triumph of brains over brawn; *home on the pig's back*, easily completed; *fair crack of the whip*, said of fair dealing; *this side of the black stump*, a measure of comparison, as in the best (worst, biggest) that you are likely to encounter in Australia; *better than a kick in the crutch* (crotch), something a little better than the worst; *up against one's duckhouse*, said of a setback to one's plans.

Exclamations: *break it down!* be reasonable!; *dickin (on)!* be reasonable! cut it out!; *don't wake it up!* let sleeping dogs lie!; *don't do anything you couldn't eat!* don't bite off more than you can chew!; *fair enough!* a general expression of approval or acquiescence; *fair go!* be reasonable; *hooray!* and *hooroo!* goodbye!; *it's a gig!* it's extremely good; *more hair on your chest!* good on you!; *pigs!* a derisory or contemptuous term; *pull your head in!* shut up!; *how's your rotten form!* how lucky you are!; *send her down, Hughie!* an exclamation of approval when long-awaited rain falls (here *Hughie* denotes God); *shove it!* a contemptuous ejaculation of dismissal (also *stick it!*); *stone the crows!* an ejaculation mainly indicating exasperation or surprise (also *starve the bardies! stiffen the lizards!*); *there's no doubt about you!* a rather nonsensical phrase of admiration or good will; *upya!* an ejaculation of rejection or indifference (also *up you for the rent!*); *whacko!* good! hurrah!; *what's this, bush week?* a derisory phrase usually indicating that the speaker is not deceived by another; *when you're on a good thing, stick to it!* don't abandon a lucky break; *wouldn't it!* an exclamation of disgust or disapproval; *you beaut!* a phrase mainly used to denote approval, but often ironical.

Verb phrases: *to put the acid on*, to bring pressure to bear on, to ask (an employer) for a raise in wages, to seek a favor; *to put the hard word on* (of a male), to ask a woman for sexual submission; *to argue the toss*, to dispute an order or decision; *to get off one's bike*, to become violently angry; *to give it a burl*, to make an attempt at some task or undertaking; *to crack hardy*, to put on a courageous face against misfortune; *to go crook*, to complain, to protest; *to bung* (or *stack*) *on an act*, to protest violently and at wearisome length; *to curl the mo* (moustache), to exult over; *to dingo on*, to betray, to let down; *to do one's block*, to become extremely angry; *to drink with the flies*, to drink alone; *to drop one's bundle*, to panic, to give up trying; *to give someone the drum*, to tip off someone, to explain the facts; *to be financial*, to have adequate money; *to get on someone's works* (or goat), to irritate or anger a person; *to get the spear*, to be dismissed from a job; *to go lemony* (or *hostile*) *at*, to show anger toward, to protest at; *to go to the pack*, to go to pieces, to lose morale; *to pull on*, to undertake; *to take a screw at*, to inspect; *to do a get*, to leave; *to roar up*, to reprove; *to cut the rough stuff*, to act with restraint; *to put in the boot* (figuratively or actually), to kick someone when he's down; *to make a box of*, to confuse, to mar; *to work* (something) *back*, to return something to its rightful place or ownership.

For reasons which are not altogether dissociated from the Australian's indifference to authority (as represented here by orthodox English) and his natural vitality, his slang has developed so extensively since the turn of the century that a survey such as this cannot give more than general hints as to its nature. Consider this assortment of terms, for instance: *berley*, nonsense or humbug (originally, ground bait used by fishermen); *barney*, a row or argument; *boong*, an aboriginal, any person with black skin; *chat*, to advise; *chip*, to reprove; *kidstakes*, pretense, nonsense; *to let on*, to admit, betray; *lowheel*, a prostitute; *Old Dart*, England; *old identity*, an old, especially a noted, inhabitant of a locality; *pie-eater*, a worthless or contemptible person; *plonk* or *bombo*, cheap wine; *shickered*, drunk; *to skite*, to boast, to show off; *snakey*, bad tempered; *squib*, a coward; *weekender*, a weekend or holiday cabin or cottage; *whinge*, to complain. Whereas most of these are national possessions, recognized and used almost everywhere throughout the land, the past few generations in Australia have witnessed the growth of a great deal of group jargon. This fragmentation is an important sign of the extent to which social development has occurred and is occurring, for it reaches into almost every corner of Australian life.

For example, on the Queensland cane fields you meet such essential words as *hairy mary*, *trash*, *borer*, *to arrow*, and *to crow's nest*.

Among jail inmates you hear of *brat*, a seventh-class prisoner, that is, one under twenty-six years of age; *head*, a privileged jailbird; *hominy gazette*, a source of jail rumor; *kangaroo*, a warder (by rhyme on *screw*). On our many surfing beaches you hear such words as *dumper, howler, back shoot, down the mine, shark tower, surfer, surf-reel, surf-ski, patrol*, and *march past*. From waterside workers come *blood donor*, a worker who supplements a gang as required; *bull*, a company man who, under the *bull system*, in which *wharfies* (longshoremen) had to front the stevedore "would *sling* (pay a bribe) to the foreman"; *delo*, a delegate for a branch of the Waterside Workers' Federation; *disso*, a disability case, who is fit only for wharf, not ship work; *floater*, as for *blood donor; a name not dry on the book yet*, said of a new wharfie; *panno*, a foreman in charge of a gang of workers (short for *pannikin boss*); *vet*, a man over sixty-five who works irregularly. From horse riders: *bat*, a whip carried by a rider (also *mop* or *stick*); *gin*, a saddle; *jug handle* or *Wagga grip*, a leather strap or binding through the pommel of a saddle; *ratbag*, an overexcitable horse; *warrigal*, an outlaw horse or wildly behaved station hack (also *yarraman*). From pearlers: *barrack*, an irregular, pearly formation on a pearl shell known to the precious-gem trade as "baroque"; *lay*, a bonus of so-much-per-ton-of-shell-raised paid to pearl divers; *settings*, small pearls; *stone*, a pearl of quality.

Consider now a different development in which various areas make separate contributions on a single theme. Winds, for example: *cock-eye bob*, a cyclone on far north coasts; *willy-willy*, a fierce, but usually brief squall in the inland; *southerly buster*, a southerly gale (especially in New South Wales and Victoria); *black northeaster*, a violent northeasterly gale on the east coast; *Fremantle doctor*, a sea wind which lowers temperatures around the Perth-Fremantle area after a hot day. And trains: *Spirit of Progress*, Victoria; *The Fish*, New South Wales; *Sunshine Express*, Queensland; *The Trans*, the transcontinental train between Perth and Adelaide; *The Ghan*, the train from Adelaide to Alice Springs; *Leaping Lena*, the train from Darwin to Birdum.

A few terms are mainly limited in use to certain areas: *emu-bobbing*, the picking up of fallen timber (from this outback use the term became current among servicemen in the Second World War to describe the task of picking up scraps of paper and cigarette ends in a camp); *kewing* (*queueing* or *cuing*), the shoeing of cattle for crossing stony far northern country; *Kimberley mutton*, roast goat as eaten in the Kimberley area of Western Australia; *stud*, a lubra, or aboriginal woman, who becomes the mistress of a white man in Central or Northern Australia. Expressions like these are rarely heard outside special areas, but some Australian terms are even more limited in use. Here are a few illustrations:

Anting is the practice followed by many birds of rubbing ants or other acidulous substances, ranging from vinegar to aromatic leaves, beneath their wings and tails; whence *to ant* and *anting*. (The term was first used by Australian ornithologist Alec H. Chisholm in 1935.)

A *blow* is a large area on or near which aborigines lived. The quotations which follow describe the nature of *blows*. From an article, "The Surface Archaeology of Wooloomanata," by A. Massola, in the *Victorian Naturalist* of May, 1961:

In this territory [near Geelong] there was an abundance of game and edible roots . . . and the natives were able to camp almost anywhere on it. Like all coastal natives, however, they preferred to camp on sandy spots. These sandy patches, on which no vegetation seems to grow, are generally referred to as *blows*. This one has an area of four or five acres.

From *Roll the Summers Back* (1961) by J. A. Porter:

Water was the greatest problem. In some places a supply was obtained at the foot of one or other of the great granite *blows*. These are like a great, upturned saucer, perhaps hundreds of yards across. They form a catchment like a huge concrete roof from which even a light shower will give a considerable run-off.

Lerp is a chemical substance derived from *lerpamyllum*, or *lerpamillum*, secreted by lerp insects. It is one of the few aboriginal words to have won a place in scientific terminology; in its original use, *lerp* meant sweet and was applied by aborigines to the scalelike sugary or waxy secretions of most species of insects of the family Psyllidae.

Sironized is a term used since 1959 to identify washable woolen fabrics that do not need ironing made by the Commonwealth Scientific and Industrial Research Organization by a new process.

Wonk is a "bush bass" or bass viol made from a tea chest, a sapling, and a piece of stout fishing line, as used in a mock band (*wonk* is also used by aborigines to denote a white man, much as *boong* is used by whites to denote a native).

Since the Second World War an important new influence has entered this field of limited jargon. More than a million migrants (the description *New Australians* dates back to 1926) have arrived in Australia in less than twenty years. This intake, representing about 10 per cent of the country's population, is quite likely to have a linguistic effect, but it is too early, as yet, to say what terms will survive. Indeed, we will probably have to wait a generation to see the impact in perspective. One point is worth making, however: Australians have a well-developed ability to absorb external influences without great changes being imposed on them. To date, the changes wrought by New Australians have largely concerned food and drink, through restaurants, wine and espresso bars, and delicatessens. Few people who have lived through our culinary twilight will mourn such modifications.

In recent years another influence has been brought to bear on Australian English by the introduction of television. Since many of Australia's television programs originate in the United States or are imitations of American programs in which the will to succeed is all too often offered as a substitute for talent, the potential American influence is considerable. However, this is by no means new. We had much of it in Hollywood films long before television, and those films did not make any sizable inroads on either Australian idiom or character.

Placed as we are between the linguistic pressures of Britain and America, we have absorbed much from both without hindering our native flair for wordmaking. Here are just a few of the American originals that have had spells of popularity in Australia: *blurb, B.O., baloney, call girl, carry a torch, crew cut, falsies, gimmick, heebie-jeebies, hillbilly, hot rod, the mostest, oh yeah, okeydoke, oomph, pash, play it cool, phony, pussyfoot, sez you, screwy, sheba, shoot the works, so's your old man, square, superduper, take a powder, tin lizzie, vamp, whoopee, yak,* and *yen.*

Just as Americans have taken some of our indigenous expressions and done unmentionable things to them (a few examples will be given later), so Australia has wrenched some Americanisms out of

124

shape. Even our aborigines have helped. In outback townships aboriginal jazzmakers sing a song that includes the lines:

> He borrowed a sub and headed straight for the pub,
> That boy he ain't no mug,
> And very soon
> He had all us coon
> In the mallee, cutting a rug.

There are several expressions here which deserve attention, but I would like to concentrate on the last three words. In America, *cut a rug* means to dance, specifically to jitterbug. Australia's town-dwelling aborigines have adapted it to mean "to let off steam, to cut a dash, to get rip-roaring drunk." Any dancing involved is purely incidental.

In a slightly different way, we have taken the American *payola*, meaning graft, blackmail, or extortion money, and produced an interesting local variation in *lurkola*, meaning much the same thing. This is an extension of the Australian *lurk*, a dodge, racket, or scheme. The American *dingus*, a thingumejig, has been given a specific use in Australian journalism as *dinkus* (sometimes *dink*) for a small line block mainly used to fill out space in a feature article. The American *dead ringer*, a duplicate, a person who closely resembles another, appears in Australia as *dead ring of*. Although somewhat similar in appearance and sound, the American *leary*, wary, suspicious, is altogether different in application from the Australian *lairy*, flashily dressed, vulgar in manners.

An American friend of mine who spent some years in Australia reports that similar variations are to be found in other usages. In the examples that follow many, although not all, of the Australian equivalents (given in parentheses) originated in Britain. Thus, Americans use *bingo* (the game known in Australia as *housie* or *housie-housie*), *clothespin* (*clothes peg*), *good for you!* (*good on you!*), *go to pieces* (*go to the pack*), *pari-mutuel* (*totalizator* or *tote*), *safe-cracker* (*safebreaker*), *slot machine* (*poker machine*), *stag party* (*buck party*), and *sugar bowl* (*sugar basin*).

Mention of the word *tote* (an Australian machine patented by George Julius in 1917) reminds us of the quite impressive array of new words derived from Australian innovations and inventions: *stump-jump plough* (1877), *Australian crawl, Australian ballot*

(1856), *Owen gun* (1941), *hula hoop* (1957), *Australorp* chickens, *kelpie* dog, the football code called *Australian Rules, cuddleseat,* a form of baby carrier invented during the early 1940's, and *wobble-board,* a form of "musical instrument" made from Masonite, measuring two feet by three feet, which, when wobbled, "gives off a gloop-gloop sound like water going down the drain," as *Time* reported on September 26, 1960.

Particularly because of wide contacts between Australians and United States servicemen in the Second World War, many Australianisms have found their way to America. For example, among Australian originals in the *Dictionary of American Slang* (1960), by Harold Wentworth and Stuart Berg Flexner, are *also ran, billy, bodgie, bonzer, Chink, cobber, digger, dinkum, drum, googly, jack-eroo, larrikin, possie, push, sundowner, tote, whip the cat,* and *wowser.*

The American rights to some of these can be disputed on the simple issue of dates. For instance, *also ran,* a failure, was current in Australia before 1916, but has been in American use only in recent years; *bonzer,* good, excellent, was used in Australia in 1904, nearly forty years before Americans borrowed it; *Chink,* a Chinese, was used in Australia in 1879, more than twenty years before it reached America; *cobber,* a friend, was used in Australia in 1895 or earlier, but is of only recent and rare use in America; *cow,* an objectionable person, thing, or event, dates back to 1915 and was almost certainly picked up by Australian servicemen in France from the French slang use of *vache* (cow) for a policeman, a nasty fellow.

Similar points can be made about sundry incorporations in Sir William Craigie's *Dictionary of American English* (1934–1944). Here are a few of the words claimed by Craigie as American, but which have been found to have earlier textual records in Australia: *Australian,* adj., pertaining to Australia, Australian date, 1814 (U.S. date, 1856); *boomer,* something notable or impressive, 1860 (1887); *bullpuncher,* a cattleman, 1872 (1874); *brush,* bushland, 1799 (1881); *buck,* of a horse that bucks, 1838 (1864); *buckjumper,* a bucking horse, 1838 (1878); *bush,* forested land, 1803 (1827); *bushranger,* 1805 (1830).

Wentworth and Flexner's definitions for some of the Australian words they include appear unusual to Australian eyes: *billy,* "a

126

bucket or large can used for heating wash water or for cooking";
bodgie, "a male jitterbug"; *googly*, "a bomb"; *jackeroo*, "a cowboy";
push, "a gang of tramps or thugs"; *sundowner*, "a strict disciplinar-
ian, a martinet"; *wowser*, "a formal person, a stuffed shirt." Australians will not need to be told that there is little similarity between
their uses of these terms and the meanings allotted to them in the
United States. But since they have imposed similar mutilations on
many Americanisms, they have no right to be critical of what happens to their slang when it is transplanted to another environment.

For a long time past, Americans have been liberal users of terms
with internal rhymes: *drape-shape, itsy-bitsy, killer-diller, reet-
pleat, walkie-talkie*. Such duplications (with the possible exception
of *stump-jump plough*) have been current in Australia for not much
longer than twenty-five years and have probably been shaped largely
by American influences. However, quite a few of the Australian
offerings seem to be current mainly in Australia, although American
terms have been incorporated in some of them. Samples: *cop-shop*,
a police station; *cobber-dobber*, a person who betrays (*dobs in*)
a friend; *yeller-feller*, a half-caste aboriginal; *fuzzy-wuzzy*, a New
Guinea native (this term became current in the 1940's); *grouse
mouse*, an attractive girl (*mouse* is American in this sense, but
grouse, meaning excellent, is Australian); *ridge widge*, used similarly (*widge* is short for *widgie*); *square lair*, an awkward and clumsy
although flashy young man; and such expressions of approval as
great, mate! and *big, dig!*

Whereas we can suspect that American influences have either
directly or indirectly done a good deal to shape these terms, the
same cannot be said of the widespread use of hypocorisms (reduced
words with *-ie* or *-y* endings) in Australia. The development of
hypocorisms seems to be common in Britain as well as in America,
but some of the Australian examples are extremely old: *billy, cocky,
humpy, pommy*, and *lairy*. Worthy of particular note is our strong
preference for combining *zz* sounds with the *-ie* and *-y* suffixes, as
in *Aussie*, Australia or Australian; *Brissie*, Brisbane; *cozzie*, a swim-
suit; *mozzie*, a mosquito; *possie*, a position; *Tassie*, Tasmania; and
trizzie, a threepenny bit.

We have seen that many Americanisms have been purloined by
Australia and because of such influences as the cinema, television,

the American servicemen who were in Australia between 1941 and 1945, and the 10,000 or so Americans who migrated to Australia between 1945 and 1960, it would probably not seem extraordinary to outside observers if American pronunciation had also secured a strong place here. I have earlier quoted an official comment in 1854–1855 that we were tending, even at that stage, "to foster an Australian dialect which bids fair to surpass the American in disagreeableness." That view had remarkably little influence in curbing the development of the Australian accent.

With a few obvious concessions to dialectal influences from other English-speaking countries, Australian pronunciation today has strong characteristics of its own. It is not American and, for all the accusations of some critics, it is certainly not Cockney. If we look back over assorted comments on the subject toward the end of last century, our main impression will be their lack of unanimity. Some samples follow:

1852: S. Mossman, *Gold Regions of Australia:* "The Cockney drawl of the hucksters, selling fish and fruit, sounds so refreshing to the ear—so thoroughly English."

1859: R. H. Horne, *Australian Facts and Prospects,* alludes to "the colonial twang in the speech."

1873: J. A. Froude, *Oceania:* "In thought and manners, as in speech and pronunciation, they [Australians] are pure English and nothing else."

1881: Rolf Boldrewood, *Robbery Under Arms:* "Most of the natives [native-born Australians] have a sort of slow, sleepy way of talking."

1887: Samuel McBurney, reporting on a wide survey he made: "Why there should be a general tendency, as there undoubtedly is in Australia, to a Cockney pronunciation . . . is a mystery still to be explained."

1892: G. L. James, *Shall I Try Australia?:* "The English spoken in Australia is free from any distinguishing accent or provincialism to a marvellous extent."

Research in more recent times has confirmed the non-Cockney view. Dr. A. G. Mitchell, in *The Pronunciation of English in Australia* (1946), says: "No one familiar with the two types of speech would really fail to distinguish a Cockney from an Australian."

Mitchell is of the opinion that there are two well-defined types of speech in Australia, but that there are "many forms intermediate between the two." His two types are what he calls *Broad Australian* and *Educated Australian.*

Professor McLeod, however, has described three categories of Australian speech. He avoids suggesting a correlation between formal education and speech pattern by using different terminology: *Broad Australian* (characterized by diphthongal substitution, elision, sound substitution, and monotony of inflection and rhythm); *General Australian* (in which the characteristic substitution of (ʌɪ), (ɒɪ), (ʌu), (æu), and (iə) for the General American (eɪ), (aɪ), (ou), (au), and (ɪɚ) sounds is noticeable); and *Modified Australian,* which is the result of a deliberate effort to imitate what is thought to be standard Southern British pronunciation and which is often heard among people who have visited Britain and those who have taken elocution lessons.

My own findings largely coincide with these views and define three main types of Australian pronunciation: (1) the most slovenly form of our speech, (2) an improved version of this, and (3) educated Australian English.

In varying degree, these three types show a general Australian tendency to avoid using back vowels and low open vowels. Mitchell writes: "As a result, vowel sounds tend to be crowded upward and forward in the mouth and special emphasis is thereby imposed on frontal and mixed vowels, especially on those vowels in which the lips are half-closed." In Australian speech stress is more evenly distributed than in the English spoken in most other parts of the world.

In spite of the considerable size of Australia and the unequal population distribution, there are no local dialects, although some observers claim to be able to distinguish between the general speech habits of such geographically distant areas as far northern Queensland and Victoria, Western Australia and the East Coast, Darwin and Tasmania. Such alleged distinctions, however, have never been adequately illustrated. This is probably due to two main factors, the vast development of our communications networks (especially the influence of the Australian Broadcasting Commission), and the inveterate traveling of many Australians in their own country.

If we should pause to wonder how a nation with a "white" history dating only from 1788 and a population today of less than eleven million people should have developed so many recognizable features in its language, speech, and character, there is clearly no simple answer. But at least we can say this: for generations it has been clear that these things are strong enough and vital enough to survive all pressures that may seek to quench them.

BIBLIOGRAPHY

Baker, Sidney J. *Australia Speaks.* 1953.
——.*The Australian Language.* 1945.
——. *Australian Pronunciation.* 1947.
——. *Dictionary of Australian Slang.* 1941.
——. *The Drum.* 1959.
Crowe, Cornelius. *Australian Slang Dictionary.* 1895.
Downing, W. H. *Digger Dialects.* 1919.
Lentzner, Karl. *Wörterbuch der englischen Volkssprache australiens.* 1891.
Mitchell, A. G. *The Pronunciation of English in Australia.* 1946.
Morris, E. E. *Austral English Dictionary.* 1898.
Partridge, Eric. *Slang Today and Yesterday.* 1930.

PHILOSOPHY

JOHN A. PASSMORE

BETWEEN national image and cultural reality there is not uncommonly a discrepancy. The British, so the stereotype has it, are stolid and reserved, yet their culture is exceptionally rich in poetry; Americans are simple to the point of naïveté, yet America is the home of Melville, James, and Faulkner, perhaps the most complex of novelists; the French are logical, yet they have made little or no contribution to logical theory, and for a century or more their philosophy has been persuasive and rhetorical rather than closely analytic. Even allowing these precedents, it still comes as a surprise that Australia should have established its present reputation as a center of philosophical inquiry. For the image of Australia as a country devoted to physical achievement rather than to intellectual subtlety, blunt to the point of crudity, preferring rhetorical gestures to doctrine and either to rational discussion, is not only firmly established but largely true. And, on the face of it, this is not the sort of society in which the philosopher can expect to survive, let alone to flourish.

The facts, however, are indisputable. Although only in certain respects and at a certain level, the Australian contribution to philosophy is now a considerable one. The *Australasian Journal of Philosophy*—founded in 1923 as the *Australasian Journal of Psychology and Philosophy*—has established itself throughout the English-speaking world as a philosophical journal which maintains a high level of competence; Australian contributions to other philosophical periodicals and to anthologies are too numerous to arouse any special comment; and in recent years a considerable number of substantial books, diverse in authorship, in attitude, and in the direction of their interest, have been produced within Australian universities. These include Kurt Baier's *The Moral Point of View*, Q. B. Gibson's *The Logic of Social Enquiry*, C. B. Martin's *Religious Belief*, S. A. Grave's *The Scottish Philosophy of Common Sense*, D. M. Armstrong's *Berkeley's Theory of Vision* and *Perception and the Physical World*, my own *A Hundred Years of Philosophy* and *Philosophical Reasoning*. Nor is this a mere flash in the pan; other works have been accepted for publication, await a publisher's verdict, or are almost ready for submission.

This activity originates within notable university teaching departments and creates little or no interest outside them. Although undergraduate "pass" classes (for students who are not candidates for honors) in philosophy are very large, especially in Sydney and Melbourne, honors classes—as in the case of all liberal arts subjects—are extremely small, and only a small percentage of honors graduates go on to receive postgraduate degrees. There have to be large departments of philosophy in order to cope with the mass of undergraduates, but very few undergraduates have acquired a sufficient philosophical education to enable them to take a continuous interest in fresh developments in the subject—a difficulty accentuated by the increasingly "professional" and technical character of recent philosophy. The Australian philosopher, therefore, does not write for an Australian audience. He publishes his books and often his articles abroad; his books and the periodicals to which he contributes are rarely to be seen on the shelves of Australian bookstores; they are unlikely to be reviewed except in the *Australasian Journal of Philosophy* or in the rather recently established periodical, the *Australian Book Review*. Australian nontechnical periodicals concentrate their attention upon literature and politics rather than upon general ideas; such general ideas as appear in their pages tend to be pronouncements upon life and morality by poets rather than philosophical analyses.

Yet, in spite of the fact that his serious works are unlikely to attract the attention of Australian readers, the philosopher is by no means an inconspicuous constituent of Australian life. Many philosophers—men like A. C. Fox in Western Australia, E. Morris Miller in Tasmania, A. Boyce Gibson in Melbourne, Sir William Mitchell and J. McKellar Stewart in South Australia—have been exceptionally prominent in the universities to which they belong and in the wider life of the community because of their administrative gifts or force of personality. Others have become notorious as a result of their participation in religious, political, and educational controversies. This is certainly so in Sydney, where John Anderson and A. K. Stout are names familiar well beyond the bounds of the university; like Bertrand Russell in England and John Dewey in America, they have been admired or excoriated for their unorthodox opinions by thousands who have never read a philosophical book or consulted a philosophical journal. They have launched a thousand sermons and provoked newspaper correspondence of unprecedented dimensions.

The general atmosphere of illiberality in Australia provokes philosophers into public utterance who would most probably keep their unorthodox opinions to themselves in a more tolerant and easygoing intellectual atmosphere. This illiberality is not so powerful that its opponents are afraid to speak out against it, but not so weak that they can be wholly untroubled by it. The consequence is that there is a constant turmoil over such issues as academic freedom, censorship, and the government of universities, which are matters of life and death to philosophers. The present situation, therefore, is likely to continue: that almost nobody except professional philosophers reads their professional publications, but that many professional philosophers are nonetheless familiar public figures, the center of controversies which turn, not about their deliberate written words, but about their editor-truncated public utterances, from which, generally speaking, all the argumentation is omitted as being "of no interest to our readers."

In its concern with political, moral, and religious issues, Australian philosophy in the twentieth century is very like that in the nineteenth century; the difference is that Australian philosophy now somewhat resembles an iceberg, of which only a small segment lies in the public view, whereas in the nineteenth century it was almost entirely superficial, constituted by its public utterances. For until the end of the century, professional philosophy scarcely existed in Australia.

Professors like Charles Badham in Sydney taught philosophy along with the classics, but although his edition of Plato's *Philebus* (1878) is one of Australia's very rare contributions to classical philosophy, Badham's interests were not, in general, philosophical. Not until the 1880's was philosophy established as a separate department in Australian universities. Nor did Australia possess divines to match Jonathan Edwards; the Puritan-Cambridge Platonist movement of thought, which established philosophy in the American colonies, had lost its impetus before Australia was settled, and neither evangelical Protestantism nor Irish Catholicism, which were the main ingredients in Australian religious life, sympathized with the free play of ideas.

Yet, if they were not sympathetic to ideas, the clergy unwittingly encouraged their circulation; ideas came to Australia as weapons in the struggle against an exceptionally ignorant and bigoted clergy. As was naturally to be expected in a colonial culture, argument consisted for the most part in quotations from this or that English, or occasionally American, critic of the established orthodoxies. In his *Positivism and Nescience* (n.d.) the Reverend B. Boake complained that when "a Christian minister attempts to teach his congregation that to know God and Jesus Christ, whom He hath sent, is eternal life, he is at once met with the statement that Herbert Spencer has proved, and that Sir William Hamilton and Dean Mansel have admitted." Hamilton, Mansel, Spencer—these names constantly recur in the controversies of the period.

The name of a philosophically much more important figure—John Stuart Mill—also occurs frequently. But Mill's very great Australian reputation was not based on his most important philosophical work, *A System of Logic* (1843); what interested Australians were his views on morality, economics, politics, and religion. The reverence paid to Mill was, indeed, extraordinary. Sir Charles Gavan Duffy, prime minister of Victoria in 1871–1872, although a Roman Catholic, turned to Mill in 1866 when he was confronted by a question of public conscience: how far it is permissible to compromise on minor matters in order to gain a victory on a major issue. "I feel it a very high compliment," Mill replied, "that you should wish to know my opinion on a point of conscience, and still more so that you should think that belief likely to be of any assistance to you in the guidance of your own political conduct."[1]

The compliment was, indeed, a striking one; but in colonies concerned to establish their new dignity as representative governments, the name of Mill was naturally to the fore. Indeed, Mill was often embarrassed by the quoting of his opinion on matters on which he had come to change his mind—as when Judge Chapman, then prime minister of Victoria, used Mill's authority to support a proposal for the payment of members of parliament. The political concern in the Australian legislature was much more with such innovations in democratic procedure than with the deeper issues of political philosophy; Mill was esteemed as a political reformer rather than as a philosopher.

More philosophical issues arose as a result of the controversies provoked by the rise of free thought and, at a more respectable level, "humanistic Christianity." Although the freethinking movement of nineteenth-century Australia attracted very few adherents —as in England—those few were extremely vigorous publicists. "We are all really atheists now, although only some of us are aware of it," wrote one of the most uncompromising freethinking pamphleteers, H. K. Rusden; and he had sufficient company to provoke distinct clerical unease. The less radical conception of a "humanistic Christianity"—much influenced by Matthew Arnold and his niece, the novelist Mrs. Humphrey Ward—won wide support from those who wished to break with orthodoxy without ceasing to be Christians. The distinction between "true religion"—conceived as primarily ethical in character—and theology dates back to the relatively early days when Australians were looking for ways of circumventing the ambitions of the clergy or of side-stepping sectarian issues. But by about 1880 it took a more intellectual form. In Australia, as in England,

[1] *Letters*, ed. H. S. R. Elliott (London: Longmans, Green, 1910), II, 66.

They spoke of progress spiring round
And light, and Mrs. Humphrey Ward.

And if G. K. Chesterton's reaction to this situation,

I might have simply sat and snored;
I rose politely in the club
And said "I feel a little bored,
Will someone take me to a pub?"

was no doubt the common Australian one, still the periodicals of the time reveal the presence of an earnest and well-informed group to whom progress, light, and Mrs. Humphrey Ward were a natural trinity.

When, in 1885, the Hon. James Frazer, member of the Legislative Council, left in his will an endowment for a prize for an essay "in defence of the Christian Faith," the choice as the first subject of "Agnosticism from a Moral and Spiritual Point of View" was almost inevitable. The two victorious essays (1888) by H. T. Burgess and James Malone, both clergymen, are characteristic in their method: they set Martineau and Harrison against Spencer. The main argument is in quotations; the rest is Christian rhetoric. Like most of the quasi-philosophical periodical articles of the same period, these essays are well-informed; in that respect, as in their earnestness and seriousness, both essays and articles compare favorably with a good many of the contributions to the general-reader periodicals of our own time. In philosophical content, however, they are but pale shadows of pale originals, of interest only insofar as they throw some light on the intellectual preoccupations of well-educated nineteenth-century Australians.

The only substantial philosophical work to appear in nineteenth-century Australia, Barzillai Quaife's *The Intellectual Sciences* (1872), belongs in certain respects, although not all, to the Scottish tradition. ("Substantial," I say, but only in the sense in which on a broad, flat plain the lowest of hills appears to the grateful eye as a mountain.) *The Intellectual Sciences* is designed as an outline of psychology, metaphysics, moral philosophy, and logic. So that he "might not embarrass his students," Quaife writes in his prefatory remarks, he has "avoided even quotation and reference as much as possible," but where there are references they are almost wholly to Mansel, Hamilton,

McCosh, and Thomson, with an occasional secondhand mention of
Kant and Hegel. His approach, however, is more overtly theological
and anthropomorphic than the Scots allowed themselves to adopt.
"Man," Quaife begins, "is the chief being on this earth. For our
use are all the earth's provisions and arrangements." This leads him
to general metaphysical conclusions of a Leibnitzian sort. "All
truths are necessary," he writes. "In truth there is no contingency,
no dubiety"; this is because everything must be as it is, as being
created by an Absolute and Perfect Deity. "The Absoluteness, and
the consequently boundless Perfection of God are *necessary* characters of His nature; in that Absoluteness and Perfection are *necessarily* included His eternal and unbounded Energy and Wisdom: an
eternal and unbounded Energy must, *of necessity*, always work in
the best way." Thus Quaife's metaphysics is a full expression of
that conception of reality which, after Lovejoy, we have come to
think of as "the great Chain of Being"; to that extent, he writes in
the tradition of Continental metaphysics rather than British em-
piricism or Scottish common sense.

His moral philosophy, too, sets out from man's relation to God
rather than from man's relation to man, and in its details displays
the influence of evangelical standards of conduct. Work or the
pursuit of pleasure on the Sabbath day; adultery, which "ought to
be punished by life imprisonment"; gambling, which "contains the
whole essence of vice"; insolvency—"the law is immoral which encourages insolvencies"—these are the principal vices of humanity.
For Quaife, moral philosophy consists in condemning them as in-
fractions of Divine Regulations.

However, in his emphasis upon psychology and its details and in
his doctrine of "intuitions," Quaife largely follows Scottish masters.
So he does in his logic, which is much the least doctrinaire part of
his system, perhaps because evangelical pressures are not in logic
heavy and immediate. He accepts, in general terms, the sort of formal
logic Whateley and Hamilton had revived, but argues against a
great many of Hamilton's innovations. Quaife's logic is not only an
adequate introduction, but in some measure an independent contribution, to the elementary formal logic which prevailed in England in the first half of the nineteenth century—faint and relative
praise, no doubt, but it sets his work at a considerably higher level

than that of his Australian contemporaries. And his work as a whole, however unattractive its temper, displays a certain sober consistency; he tried, in some measure, to think his position out, although he lacked, of course, the stimulus of critical and informed discussion.

Quaife's work was not only the earliest, but the sole philosophical work to be published in nineteenth-century Australia. "The utilitarian spirit of the age, it must be confessed, is adverse to mental philosophy; and if this be the case in older countries, it is emphatically true in a colony such as ours, which has not yet emerged from its first youth." So wrote Henry Laurie (1838–1932) in the *Victorian Review* of November, 1881. But the situation was already changing. Laurie's article was entitled "A Plea for Philosophy," but he wrote in knowledge of the fact that the University of Melbourne had decided to institute a lectureship in logic and that moves were on foot—although against considerable opposition—to establish a chair of mental and moral philosophy.

The opposition came from two quarters: from those who argued that the progress of science had made philosophy obsolete, and from those who, like the Anglican Dean of Melbourne, feared that the teaching of philosophy would introduce an "unknown quantity" (which might be antagonistic to the Christian faith) into the intellectual life of the colony. The first group, Laurie argued, were themselves committed to philosophical creeds, to materialism, or to agnosticism, which they did not wish to have to defend; as for the Christians, they forgot that the colony had already felt the impact of the "doubting spirit of the nineteenth century." It was better for men to "fairly face their doubts"; as matters stood, in the absence of critical discussion, they were "quietly drifting into materialism." The choice was not between having, or not having, philosophy in the colony; the choice lay only between the critical discussion of philosophical issues and the mere acceptance of scientific or Christian dogma.

Laurie's article was scholarly, temperate, and thoughtful; not surprisingly, he was offered the new lectureship in logic and in 1886 was appointed to a professorship of mental and moral philosophy, which he held until 1911. On paper, his academic qualifications were not strong. He had attended the University of Edinburgh in 1856–1858, but ill health had prevented completion of his degree.

He was highly praised by his Edinburgh teachers, however, and had already made a considerable name for himself in Victoria—he arrived in the colony in 1864—as editor, journalist, and literary critic. He helped to train men like J. F. Archibald of the Sydney *Bulletin*, and in one way and another was intimately connected with the intellectual and literary life of both Victoria and New South Wales.

Of his Edinburgh teachers, the best known was A. Campbell Fraser, famous for his edition of Berkeley. Laurie, in most respects, stayed close to Fraser in doctrine and method. Like Fraser, he preferred to teach by critically expounding the works of some eminent philosopher rather than by the systematic exposition of his own views. Indeed, even those who were his pupils are unable to give a systematic account of his position. One of them, E. Morris Miller, professor of philosophy in the University of Tasmania from 1927 until 1952, reports:

In lack of a systematic presentation of his philosophical outlook, it is not easy to determine exactly what was Laurie's position in relation to the thought of his time. He seemed to be more anxious to give instruction in the philosophical theories of others, to interpret historical movements in philosophy, and to open the mind of the student to the ever-broadening expanses of thought than to set forth, in systematic form, his systematic predilections.

Laurie's major work, *Scottish Philosophy in Its National Development* (1902), typifies the general character of his teaching. It does not display the most erudite sort of scholarship, but it is a serious and fair-minded study of the Scottish philosophers from Hutcheson to Hamilton, in which criticism is interwoven with sympathetic exposition. Laurie's object, clearly, is to teach philosophy, not simply to describe the past; if he selects the Scottish philosophers for particular attention, this is not because he thought their work free from defects—he obviously was influenced by what he calls "the deeper speculations" of Germany—but because Reid and his successors concerned themselves "in a reverent spirit" with the great objects of speculation, "the human soul, the material world, and God," and in a way that insisted upon "the veracity of consciousness."

Although one cannot speak in detail of Laurie's system, its general intention is, nevertheless, clear. He set himself in opposition to the agnostic and secularist traditions of the new colony, which

139

his experience as editor had drawn forcibly to his attention. In his lectures, he dealt at length with Herbert Spencer. "At the time these lectures were given," writes Morris Miller,

the name of Spencer had a considerable vogue among young minds, and at popular assemblies and outdoor meetings of political reformers it was customary to hear effulgent commendations of the great English systema-tiser, so much so that his genius appeared to be of almost superhuman greatness to immature youths. . . . Many a thoughtful student entered Laurie's classes with an adoring attitude towards this cynosure of his philosophical firmament, and came out with a completely revised valua-tion of the permanence of Spencerian philosophy.[2]

Scottish philosophy went astray, as Laurie sees the matter, with Sir William Hamilton, who laid the foundation for modern ag-nosticism, and it went astray partly because there was, in the writings of the "common-sense" school, too little philosophical sophistica-tion. Like Campbell Fraser and A. S. Pringle-Pattison, Laurie hoped to retain the distinction between God, the individual mind, and nature, while at the same time subordinating mind and nature to God, and nature to mind. And, like them, he tried to achieve this end by grafting a quasi-Kantian idealism onto a Scottish common-sense stem.

Laurie's philosophical attitude and philosophical method were to dominate Australian philosophy, in most of its centers, for some fifty years. This is partly as a direct result of his influence. As we have already seen, one of his pupils, E. Morris Miller, became the first professor of philosophy at the University of Tasmania; another, J. McKellar Stewart, was appointed professor of philosophy at Adelaide in 1923. McKellar Stewart continued as professor of phi-losophy until 1949, Morris Miller until 1952. In Melbourne, Laurie was succeeded by a philosopher of much the same outlook; else-where in Australia the same general tendency of thought prevailed.

Philosophy was allied to literature and theology rather than to science, was committed to the defense of a liberal Christianity and to orthodox *mores*, and was Idealist in its metaphysical presumptions. It scarcely felt the influence of the newer philosophical tendencies

[2] "Henry Laurie and the Beginnings of Philosophy in Australia," *Australian Journal of Psychology and Philosophy*, VII (December, 1929), 247.

PHILOSOPHY

in England; it was not insular, but it looked to Scotland or Europe, not to Oxford or Cambridge. Most of the lecturers and professors had studied abroad, but not for the most part in English universities —which, indeed, had no provision for graduate students. In such philosophers as A. S. Pringle-Pattison and G. F. Stout, they recognized the continuators of Laurie's tradition, and they were interested, too, in the newer European Idealists—Eucken, Bergson, Husserl. Among American philosophers, James and Royce—the latter especially—attracted a great deal of attention; Royce's admirers included Australia's only philosophically minded prime minister, Alfred Deakin. Indeed, the Christian Idealists were interested in any philosopher who emphasized personality, moral action, and religion.

Some of them suggested that philosophies which laid the principal stress on the energetic expression of personality were natural to a young country. "During the first decade of the Commonwealth," wrote Morris Miller in an appreciation of McKellar Stewart,

the Australian-born graduates in philosophy were coming to the front in their own land. The more prominent among them, although they had been strongly influenced by the rational schools of thought in Europe, were ready to follow streams of tendency that fitted in with the energy and vigor characteristic of pioneering life in rural and urban Australia.

One suspects, however, that it was rather their moral and religious emphasis—and their rhetorical method—which attracted young Australians to philosophers like Royce and Eucken. Australian "energy and vigor," often enough, is the false energy of violence and rhetoric.

The Australian-born Idealists—several of whom had been trained as clergyman—thought of philosophy as an instrument of morality rather than as a rigorous or systematic discipline. Thus, for example, when Morris Miller turned his attention to Kant's ethics, as he did in a series of books of which the most substantial are *Kant's Doctrine of Freedom* (1913) and *Moral Law and the Highest Good* (1928), this was because he saw in Kant a writer whose "whole philosophy is a critical justification of the practical interests of man." In Laurie's manner, Miller's approach to Kant is not merely expository, but critical; Kant goes astray, he tries to show, by being insufficiently

141

idealist. The conclusion to *Kant's Doctrine of Freedom* will serve to summarize the point of view which characterized Australian philosophy:

If we recognize the ideal, not as something set over against us to be achieved, but as the rational end of our own being, for the realisation of which we are directly responsible, its expression in our life will not be separable from the divine order of the universe of which we form a part. For the reality of the whole fundamentally postulates a Moral Power as its guiding principle, comparable to our moral nature. To unfold this unity is the supreme task laid upon us in the conception of a moral ideal, and this deepening of the self in moral development, in which it becomes more and more self-sustained, reveals human freedom, not only as an indispensable condition of morality, but also as an achievement of the self's own activity.

In the same spirit, McKellar Stewart (1878–1953), the first Australian-born philosopher to be appointed professor of philosophy in an Australian university, wrote his *Critical Exposition of Bergson's Philosophy* (1911). He strongly criticizes the Bergsonian doctrine of "intuition" on the ground that it weakens the idea of an independent personality; he defends a Kantian conception of reason against Bergson's intuitionism. But he welcomes Bergson's rejection of the claims of science to "describe Reality."

A criticism of science in the interests of the "ideal," a defense of the self and of a personal God—these were the main concerns of Laurie and his followers. They stand sharply opposed, not only to any sort of naturalism, but quite as much to Bosanquet's Absolute Idealism. "Dr. Bosanquet," wrote Morris Miller, "reaches his position by disowning the reality of the individual in the sense in which it is known to us, and making it merely a phase of the life of the Absolute which for him conforms to the true type of individuality." For the followers of Laurie, the individual personality is the starting point for all philosophical analysis and must not be questioned in its outcome.

Laurie's influence was strengthened because his successor as professor of philosophy at the University of Melbourne, W. R. Boyce Gibson, stood in the same tradition. Did one not know otherwise, it would be natural to suppose that he had learned philosophy under Laurie. At Oxford, however, Gibson studied mathematics, not philosophy; so far as philosophy attracted him at this time, it was in the guise of the "scientific philosophy" of Herbert Spencer. After leaving the university he decided both that philosophy was his main interest and that the scientific way was not the only rational way of interpreting the universe. He worked under Eucken and Leibmann at Jena; then went to Paris where, with Boutroux, he studied Descartes; and finally moved to Glasgow, where Adamson and Henry Jones were his teachers.

Jones was a Hegelian, but he did not wean Gibson from allegiance to Eucken's and Boutroux's personalist philosophies. In 1902 Gibson contributed an essay, "The Problem of Freedom in Its Relation to Psychology," to the volume *Personal Idealism,* edited by Henry Sturt and designed as a declaration of revolt against the prevailing Absolute Idealism of Bradley and Bosanquet. He spent some years as a lecturer in the University of London and during that period turned out a surprising array of books, including *A Philosophical Introduction to Ethics* (1904), *Rudolph Eucken's Philosophy of Life* (1906), and *The Problem of Logic* (1908). In his Preface to *The Problem of Logic,* he wrote that "the Religious Idealism in which the author's own conviction culminates seems to him to call imperatively for a frank and fruitful cooperation between the Idealism of the Hegelian School on the one hand and the Psychologism of the Pragmatic and Genetic movements on the other." But in fact there is little or nothing of the Hegelian spirit in his work. The mere fact that he could write sympathetically of Eucken—Bosanquet had written that "there is in Eucken's immense literary output no really precise and serious contribution to philosophical science . . . free conjecture has been submerged by moralistic rhetoric"—is enough to show how remote he was from the British Hegelians. Significantly, *The Problem of Logic* is as devoid of references to Bradley as it is to Russell.

None of these works was written in Australia, but any of them might have been; Melbourne could scarcely have found, if continuity were sought, a more natural successor to Laurie than Boyce Gibson. "Personal Idealism, with *Man* as its starting-point, interprets its main position in equal opposition to Naturalism with *Nature* as its starting-point and Absolute Idealism with *God* as its starting-point"—this is Gibson speaking, in his *A Philosophical Introduction to Ethics;*

143

but the Idealism he thus describes was already characteristic of Australian philosophy.

Like Laurie, too, Boyce Gibson was a sympathetic expositor, alert to the appearance of fresh ideas with whose tenor he could wholly or partly sympathize. But he looked for them on the continent of Europe rather than in Scotland. Thus, although his energies in Melbourne were almost wholly devoted to his students—he was an enthusiastic and sympathetic teacher—he found time to translate Husserl's *Ideas* and to write articles on Husserl (*Mind*, 1925), on Melchior Palagyi (*Philosophy*, 1928), and on Nicolai Hartmann (*Australasian Journal of Psychology and Philosophy*, 1933–1935). These were substantial pieces of work, in which Gibson critically examined the new varieties of Continental Idealism in the light of his own views. His attitude toward Husserl is characteristic; he welcomed Husserl insofar as he could be read as insisting on the central importance of the knowing mind—as a subjective Idealist, in short—but condemned his abstract approach to the self as "an ideal nature or essence." Gibson, to sum up, was a cultivated representative of the Personal Idealist tradition, but he did not introduce a completely fresh note into Australian philosophy.

The differences within Australia were still differences between varieties of Idealism. The first professor of philosophy in the University of Sydney, Sir Francis Anderson, was trained at Glasgow, not at Edinburgh; there he came under the influence of Scottish Hegelianism, especially as that was exhibited in the work of Edward Caird. He took over the public-spiritedness of that Idealism and its concern with the social and political life of man; but logic and metaphysics were not the center of his interest. He first came to Australia as a liberal clergyman, and it was as a leader of liberal causes that he won his reputation. In certain respects he had a considerable influence, as in his criticisms of the New South Wales public educational system. But although he did much to encourage psychological and social inquiry, his contributions to philosophy were slight; his instincts were those of a reformer and a preacher rather than of a systematic philosopher. Nor was there anything in the character of what he advocated to disturb the Australian philosophical consensus. Although he had, in some quarters, the reputation of being a radical, his radicalism—so far as it existed—was not of the sort to disturb a Christian Idealist. When he criticized political and educational institutions it was from the standpoint of Christian Idealism; his emphasis, too, was on "personality." Sydney men went to Western Australia, where A. C. Fox has been a worthy representative of the public-spirited liberal-Idealist tradition, and later to Queensland, where under A. Scott Fletcher a strongly moral-religious tradition has been developed—Fletcher's background was theological—which has been carried on by Queensland-trained W. M. Kyle.

In the first quarter of the present century, there was only one systematic philosopher whose work is now of conceivable interest to anybody but the historian of Australian culture—Sir William Mitchell (1861–1962).[3] Mitchell's first important work, *The Structure and Growth of the Mind*, was published in 1907, some thirteen years after he had been appointed first Hughes Professor of Philosophy and Economics in the University of Adelaide. In 1925–1926 he gave the Gifford Lectures at the University of Aberdeen; the first volume of lectures was published as *The Place of Minds in the Modern World* (1933), but the second has not appeared.

Mitchell is one of the most difficult of writers. *The Place of Minds* is, indeed, almost impenetrable. Nor does he do anything to assist the reader. Such aids as an index are scorned, and Mitchell almost never ties his reflections to a specific philosophical controversy. *The Structure and Growth of the Mind* is rich in allusions to psychologists, *The Place of Minds* to theoretical physicists; but there is scarcely a reference in either book to Mitchell's fellow philosophers. Both books are, very obviously, the products of a solitary thinker. When Mitchell went to South Australia, contacts between Adelaide and the eastern states were rare, voyages to Europe or America even rarer. Few Australian philosophers so much as met Mitchell, and his influence in Australia has not been extensive. (The first professor of philosophy at the University of Queensland, Elton Mayo, worked under Mitchell as an undergraduate in Adelaide, but Mayo wrote little; what he did write lay in the field of political theory.)

The Structure and Growth of the Mind is designed as an introduction to psychology. But it introduces a psychology which is in turn an introduction to philosophy—a psychology which concerns itself

[3] Mitchell and John Anderson, whose work is discussed on subsequent pages, have died since this chapter was written.

with "the growth of the mind" as an introduction to an Idealist philosophy for which the mind is the central ontological conception. Mitchell's psychology is not a priori in the sense of ignoring experimental psychology; on the contrary, Mitchell writes with a constant eye on the English, European, and American psychological literature. But it is through-and-through philosophical in spirit, and its detail is exceptionally rich and concrete. The character of his thinking can be exemplified by his discussion of the mind-body problem.

He begins with a criticism of the traditional notion of "substance" —understood as an unknowable core to which attributes are attached. Mitchell rejects all doctrines of "unknowable cores," very largely on the same ground as the logical positivists were to reject them. "The question as to what a thing is in itself," he writes, "is unanswerable, not because the question is difficult, but because it is absurd"—if it means, that is, "what is a thing more than anyone, however searching and omniscient his senses, can ever possibly perceive it to be?" There is no such "core" in the case of the mind, any more than there is in the case of anything else. "Of the mind, as of other things, there is no saying what it is in itself apart from all its connections, because the question is in error. We know it, as we know other things, by what it does."

The parallelist supposes that brain and mind are parallel aspects of a single reality, this "reality" being the concern of the metaphysician, not of the psychologist or neurologist, who is interested only in the phenomena.

The reality itself, so the theory says, because it is reality and not phenomenon, is no affair of science whether of matter or of mind, but the problem of philosophy or metaphysics. At the same time, it is not thought that metaphysics can do anything with it except write poetry about it, and give it a name like substance, thing-in-itself, the absolute, the unknown and unknowable, or even matter. For it is thought that every theory about it must be beyond the reach of contradiction and verification. It is in this impossible quarter that the connection between brain and mind is supposed to lie.

But in fact, so Mitchell argues, "any serious theory of reality, whether called metaphysics or not . . . must reject a hypothesis that cannot be verified and ideas about an object defined as unknowable."

146

The traditional mind-body problems can be solved, according to Mitchell, only when it is realized that we are not dealing with two distinct sets of facts which have somehow to be correlated, "as if we had our experience by a kind of internal sense, and as if nature were literally mirrored by our external senses." His own conclusion he summarizes thus:

A mind and its experience are realities that are presentable to sense as the brain and its actions. In that respect the mind and experience are not parallel with nature, but part of it. And, on the other hand, the facts of nature, including the brain, whenever they are phenomena, are not parallel with mental phenomena, but part of them.

It is not surprising, then, that Bernard Bosanquet and his fellow Absolute Idealists greeted Mitchell's book with enthusiasm. More recently, the American philosopher Brand Blanshard has made extensive use of it in his *The Nature of Thought* (1939), in which, like Mitchell, he sets out to be at once a psychologist and an Idealist philosopher. Bosanquet was not pleased with every aspect of Mitchell's book: he thought it unduly pragmatic in its attitude to truth. But it was still very much in accordance with his own line of thought, insofar as Mitchell argued that the "individual" of everyday life is an abstraction, and as he saw in psychological and neurological inquiry alternative methods of explanation—the philosophical being the more "direct"—rather than attempts to describe entities of a different ontological order. Mitchell's work is unlikely ever to attract a great many readers, but now that there is a revival of interest in "philosophical psychology," it may well be consulted as an intelligent, if not always immediately intelligible, contribution to that form of inquiry, largely neglected for thirty years. It is interesting to compare, for example, what Mitchell has to say about our conviction that we know how to finish a poem or a sentence or to complete a mathematical series with Wittgenstein's treatment of the same topic in the *Philosophical Investigations*, as well as with William James's in his *Principles of Psychology*.

If *The Structure and Growth of the Mind* is a difficult book, *The Place of Minds in the World* carries obscurity to the point of outrage. Yet, once again, it is in certain respects quite notably concrete. Mitchell's reading in physical science is thorough and careful—very different from the perfunctory references to one or two "popular"

147

books to which, in metaphysical writings, we are only too accustomed. Nor does he, in the manner of the "personal Idealists" or their descendants, attempt to use modern physics in order to point to "gaps in Nature," loopholes for teleology, and indeterminism. For him, the idea of a gap is the very thing to be attacked. The crucial fact about modern science, as he sees it, is not that it "leaves room" for a freedom conceived as being in some sense supernatural; rather, it destroys the conception of a "Nature" to which human conduct and the human mind is alien or on which it is merely parasitic. "It is nature, nature proper," he finally concludes, "which refuses to confine the body of our mental life to the 'province packed up in two yards of skinne.' " For "nature, nature proper" turns out itself to be human. "Only last night," writes Mitchell, "I heard Eddington, constructive as he is, begin with the taste not being in the apple, and go on to the complete separation of the physical from the familiar world, which his chairman (Bertrand Russell) carried much further in the way of Socrates, after which, in thanking both, Professor Muirhead rescued Beauty. It might have been Athens come to Gower Street." Against "Athens" (understood as the spirit of separation), Mitchell sets the spirit of unification; and that, he thinks, still is and must continue to be the spirit of science. But although Mitchell's work was by no means in the tradition of Australian Christian Idealism, Mitchell, isolated in Adelaide and uninterested in philosophical controversy, did nothing to oppose it or to undermine its influence.

The situation in some measure changed when Sir Francis Anderson was succeeded as professor of philosophy in Sydney by Bernard Muscio (1887–1926). Muscio had studied in Cambridge; he introduced his students to the ideas that were circulating there. But his best-known work was in industrial psychology, of which he was one of the founders. Had he lived—he occupied the chair of philosophy for only five years—he would, no doubt, have modified the tone of Australian philosophizing, but scarcely in the cataclysmic manner of his successor, John Anderson (1893–1962), who took up the chair in 1927.

"Towards the close of the new decade," writes Morris Miller,

a new phenomenon appeared in the Australian philosophical sky. John Anderson came to Sydney in the form of a catalyst, and stirred up the

148

dovecote of rationalism; and facts, activities, events, occurrences as they happened, came forth in full splendour. . . . The old strongholds of idealism were put on the defensive. An era of critical evaluation dawned for the world of thought in Australia.

This is one of Laurie's men talking; and the violence of the metaphor displays something of the disturbance Anderson's arrival produced. For the next ten years Australian philosophy consisted for the most part in a controversy between Australian Idealists and the "Andersonians." (Anderson very quickly gathered around him in Sydney a large group of admirers and disciples, so that in Australia the phrase "an Andersonian" is a familiar descriptive expression.)

Anderson stood for everything to which the Christian Idealists had been opposed. That he was prepared to describe himself as a materialist, a positivist, an empiricist, a realist, was sufficiently startling, for in Australian academic philosophy these had been terms of abuse. But even more disconcerting was the fact that he did not fit into the picture which Australian idealists had constructed of their opponents—as in the fortress at Singapore, their guns were pointing in the wrong direction. Since he called himself an empiricist, they expected him to support the traditional empiricist epistemology; in fact, he turned out to be strongly opposed to it. He rejected sense data quite as firmly as he rejected the Idealist theory of judgment. Although he had learned much from William James, he was not a pragmatist. In logic, he did not accept, for the most part, Russell's innovations, but developed and extended the traditional logic. Expected to be on the side of reform and of innovations of every sort, he was in fact a firm defender of a traditional classical education. The "materialist" whom the Christian Idealists had been accustomed to describe to their students was either a utilitarian or else rejected ethics entirely; Anderson put forward what he called a "positive ethics" in opposition to any form of utilitarianism or subjectivism. When he quoted some philosopher in support of his own position it would as likely as not be Heraclitus, Plato, or Hegel, rather than Locke or Russell; he had none of that hostility to the history of philosophy which Idealists associated with the "realists." Not surprisingly, the criticisms to which he has been subjected have often rested on misunderstandings, deriving, in particular, from his description of himself as an "empiricist."

To make matters worse, his writings are quantitatively so sparse and qualitatively so concise as scarcely to be intelligible to those who have not heard his university lectures. Apart from a pamphlet, *Some Questions in Aesthetics* (1931), and a series of addresses published as *Education and Politics* (1932), he has written only articles and, since his arrival in Australia, has published only in Australian periodicals.[4] As a result, the philosophy of Anderson and of those deeply influenced by him has been in a somewhat special sense "Australian." The Christian Idealists were writing in a familiar tradition; the followers of Wittgenstein, who in recent years have played so conspicuous a part in the philosophical life of Australia, belong to an international movement of ideas. Anderson and his followers, in contrast, are familiar as a group only within the boundaries of Australia. This is the sense in which, as Professor A. N. Prior has put it, they constitute "the only indigenous philosophical school which Australia has yet produced."

Of course, it is not indigenous in its intellectual origins. For, like Laurie and Francis Anderson and Mitchell, Anderson could bear the label "made in Scotland." His original inclination was toward mathematics and physics, but when he turned to philosophy, his teachers were Glasgow Idealists. The difference is that he did not remain content with what they taught him; and although he did not study in England and has retained a Scot's suspicion of English ways and manners, he came strongly under the influence of philosophical ideas which had originated there.

As it happened, the main influence was that of an Australian-born philosopher, Samuel Alexander, who had been invited to give the Gifford Lectures in Glasgow in 1916–1918—the lectures later published as *Space Time and Deity* (1920). We Australians like to claim Alexander as our own; we can build up a more respectable intellectual record by laying claim both to men who were born in Australia and to those who came to live in Australia after being born and educated elsewhere. But Alexander left Australia at the age of eighteen, never to return, and although it is perhaps not entirely

[4] His articles, with some fresh material, have been brought together as *Studies in Empirical Philosophy* (1962). My own introduction to that volume—"John Anderson and Twentieth Century Philosophy"—approaches his work from a different, more technical, point of view than is for present purposes appropriate.

fanciful to detect in his metaphysics the influence of Australian egalitarianism, the fact remains that his philosophical education was entirely English. It is, all the same, a pleasant coincidence that John Anderson, a philosopher who was to exert so great an influence within Australia, should have been stimulated by the only Australian-born philosopher of any consequence.

Not that Anderson was a wholehearted follower of Alexander. He came to reject a great many of Alexander's most characteristic views: that space-time is a "stuff" as well as a medium, that matter, mind, and deity are at different levels on an evolutionary chain, that minds are "enjoyed" whereas objects are "contemplated." Nor was Alexander's the only influence that helped to shape Anderson's thought. G. E. Moore, Bertrand Russell, William James, Burnet, Freud, Marx, the economist Marshall, the "political pluralists," and Sorel all left their mark upon him. But the character of their influence was often unexpected, to say the least; like every creative thinker, Anderson partly created what influenced him.

The starting point of Anderson's philosophy is that when we make any assertion whatsoever we are taking things to go on in a certain way; and that only by experience can we discover *how* they go on. There are no ultimates; neither a system such that if we knew its principle of construction everything else would be clear to us, nor elements from which the total behavior of every complex is in principle deducible. Russell's "atomic propositions" and Bradley's Absolute share an error in common; Russell thought that *ultimately* there are "pure particulars," Bradley that *ultimately* there is a total system. But in fact, so Anderson argued, there are no "pure particulars"; and equally, there is no total system. To look for something "higher" or "lower" than complex states of affairs, complexly related, is to look in vain. Nor are there privileged forms of knowledge, which offer us irrefragable certainty, whether in the form of "first principles" or in the form of "sense data."

In the general cultural life of Australia, Anderson stands as the supreme example of nonconformity rather than as the exponent of a set of philosophical doctrines. He attacked almost everything which Australians were accustomed to take unreflectively for granted. In a sense, he reinstated the critical tradition of nineteenth-century Australian thought. But that tradition had faded almost into non-

151

existence in the prosperous, patriotic, hedonistic Australia of the first decades of the present century—it was represented only in an occasional disreputable Bohemian or obscure pamphleteer. Anderson's nonconformity came, for that reason, as a particular shock; his views were shocking in themselves, but it was even more shocking that they should be held by a professor of philosophy whose task, it had commonly been presumed, was to be a defender and expositor of traditional Christian doctrines and values.

For his students, in the stifling suburban atmosphere of Sydney, the effect was tonic; he was a fresh breeze from a larger world. Anderson's lectures were technical; they were anything but rhetorical in character; there was plenty to get one's teeth into. But at the same time they were free-ranging. A lecture might begin from a technical point in a Platonic dialogue, but it might end with some remarks on Freud, or Sorel, or Joyce, or Dostoievsky. Outside the lecture room, in a variety of student societies which developed under his influence, the range was even wider; the criticism of contemporary society, of its moral outlook and its religion, was more direct, vigorous, and outspoken—accessible to, if often badly misunderstood by, those who knew nothing of the close reasoning of the lecture room.

More than once efforts were made to have Anderson removed from his chair; he has been attacked as a "corruptor of the youth," censured by legislators, denounced by clerics and by Marxists alike. He has changed his mind over a good many questions, but whatever his views at a given time he has never been afraid to speak out. Yet he is not an "individualist" in the technical sense of that word, the sense in which the Christian Idealists are individualists; he thinks of himself not as *Athanasius contra mundum*, but as the spokesman for a tradition—the tradition of inquiry. And this reflects his metaphysical theory. For if things are distinct, he argues, they are nonetheless connected; this connection is no less real, no less ultimate, than their distinctness. When he calls himself a pluralist, this is not because he believes that there is a plurality of simple elements; on his view, every plurality is a plurality of pluralities, and a plurality in a plurality. A human being, as Anderson sees him, is not, then, an isolated center of activities; he is caught up by, and expresses, movements, "causes." If a man identifies himself with a cause, the identification is never complete: that is, persons do not vanish, as the Hegelians supposed, into some wider system. But neither are they simply "associated with" it, as something which remains wholly external to them.

Similarly, his political theory takes society to be a complex of interacting organizations, movements, institutions—each themselves complex—of which the State is one, but only one. The attempt to subordinate every form of social activity to the State, if Anderson is right, can never be more than partly successful; but insofar as it does succeed, it is at the cost of destroying what is most valuable in society. "The hidden harmony," so Heraclitus wrote, "is better than the open." The highest kind of civilization arises out of conflict and cooperation between a variety of institutions, not out of an attempt to impose a total plan on the whole nor, on the other side, to subordinate institutions to the service of individuals, as distinct from traditions. Thus, while Anderson has vigorously opposed State intervention in the affairs of universities, in internal university politics (to the bewilderment of those who identify opposition to the State with individualism) he has been insistent on the need for the maintenance of regular procedures, even when it leads to individual hardship.

For some years—until the early thirties—he would have described himself as a Communist. But this is because he saw in communism an attempt to bring about a wider distribution of enterprise throughout the community, to break down the barrier between an enterprising few and a servile mass. As soon as he became convinced that "the dictatorship of the proletariat" was not just a temporary expedient, and that in fact communism stood for rigid centralized control, censorship, secret police, and informing, he broke with it completely and has been its bitter enemy; if communism made no headway in the University of Sydney at times when it achieved its greatest influence over intellectuals elsewhere, this was largely a result of Anderson's influence. He came, indeed, to have more and more sympathy with certain varieties of conservatism, insofar as conservatism stands for the maintenance of independent traditions.

But not with Christianity, for Christianity, as Anderson interprets it, encourages, like communism and the welfare state, an attitude of servility. It draws a distinction between an omnipotent source of power—and ultimate source of benefit—and those whose destiny it is to serve and whose reward it is to receive; it distinguishes between guide and guided, between protector and protected. The idea of an omniscient, omnipotent, "necessary" being has in any case, Anderson argues, to be rejected on logical grounds; the idea of "knowing everything" is an unintelligible one, and so is the idea of a power which has no limits, and the idea of an entity which could not but exist. But unlike some other philosophical critics of Christianity, Anderson does not concede that, although Christian metaphysics is untenable, Christian morality is ideal. In certain of its forms, he will admit, Christianity has moral and intellectual advantages over a simple-minded, optimistic "humanism"; such a doctrine as that "man proposes, God disposes" recognizes the limited degree to which individual conduct and human history arise out of deliberate plans, the extent to which men are elevated or are destroyed by forces which they only very slightly understand. But these forces, in his view, are not supernatural; they are generated within human society.

It will by now be clear that Anderson was one of those relatively rare philosophers who have lit upon a mode of criticism, a method of explanation, which can be applied in a variety of situations. Certain key ideas recur. The idea of objectivity: the first question for Anderson is what things are in their own character, how they behave, how they are related to one another, as distinct from what use they are, how they affect me personally, how far they satisfy my longings. The idea of complexity: to understand anything is to see it as a complex of cooperating and conflicting tendencies; there is no "total description" of a situation; there are no simple entities, whether in the form of "pure particulars" or "pure universals." The idea of historicity: nothing is exempt from change, a thing's properties are its ways of behaving, its "nature" is the persistence over periods of time of regular patterns of change ("we step and do not step into the same river"). The idea of independence: nothing is constituted by its relations to something else, neither a mind by its objects, nor objects by the mind that serves them, nor a member of a system by its membership in that system, nor what is pursued by the fact that it is pursued, nor what is used for a certain purpose by the purpose for which it is used. ("The question

154

of independence," Anderson writes in "Realism and Some of Its Critics," "is the cardinal issue.") The idea of "a single way of being": there are not degrees or varieties of existence, higher or lower, necessary and contingent, potential and actual; to say of anything that "it exists" is to say that something happens in space-time. The idea of inquiry: nothing is sacred, above criticism, or ultimate, beyond further investigation.

Clearly, these key ideas are closely related one to another; they have, in a sense, to be taken together if we are to get a firm grasp of any one of them. They constitute a philosophical "system" insofar as they lay down a set of conditions which will have to be fulfilled by any satisfactory solution to any problem. "Realism," writes Anderson, "proposes as the provisional solution of any problem *the interaction of complex things*." But at the same time the ideas do not forestall, or act as a substitute for, detailed empirical inquiry.

Anderson's general conception of a problem and its solution have influenced Australian social theorists, literary critics, musicologists, jurisprudentialists, psychologists, anthropologists, and historians, even when they have not accepted Anderson's own special views about societies, books, minds, music, morals, educational practices, or historical periods. Anderson's great influence on his pupils partly derives from this fact: he leaves them plenty of room for independent work, and yet their work—even when he is hostile to it—gets its original impetus from his teaching. Of course, he has had "disciples" who have done no more than exchange one form of servility for another, who have undergone a change of sect rather than a change of heart. This was particularly so, perhaps, at a time when opposition to Anderson was so constant and unremitting that his followers closed their ranks. The sociologist interested in the study of sects could certainly find fruitful material in the history of "Andersonianism"; but for the historian of philosophy what matters is the character of Anderson's own teaching and its effects on such of his pupils, now a considerable number, as have engaged in inquiries which are not the less independent for being profoundly influenced by him.

During the 1930's a number of changes occurred in the Australian philosophical scene without fundamentally affecting the disposition of forces. In 1935 W. R. Boyce Gibson was succeeded as professor of philosophy in Melbourne by his son, Professor A. Boyce Gibson, best known as the author of *The Philosophy of Descartes* (1932). His father had been a close student of Descartes, and one of his father's ablest pupils, W. A. Merrylees, who retired from philosophy at an early age, wrote on the same theme, in his *Descartes* (1934). The younger Gibson, born in London in 1900, had been educated first at Melbourne and then at Balliol College, Oxford; in general terms, he has remained faithful to the philosophical tradition of his father, and where he has departed from his father's position it has been in the direction of Christian orthodoxy. He is now the main representative in Australia of Idealist metaphysics and would rank high among its contemporary exponents. His sympathies link him more closely with Scotland and with America than with England —he writes for the *Review of Metaphysics* rather than for *Mind*— and he has a considerably wider acquaintance with contemporary European philosophy than have most present-day British philosophers. In all this, as well as in the general character of his teaching, he conforms to what has been, until recently, the Australian tradition. He has devoted himself to building up a large and active philosophical department in the University of Melbourne; his publications, always well rounded, have not been considerable in number, nor, since his *Descartes*, large in scale. His interests lie mainly in the sphere of morals, politics, religion, and aesthetics, and in their interplay in the work of Plato.

In Sydney, a second professorship was established—in large part with the intention of providing a counter to Anderson's influence— and A. K. Stout was appointed to the chair of moral and political philosophy in 1939. His father, G. F. Stout, came to Australia with him, was interested in Anderson's ideas, and wrote a little on them and other topics; but he was then seventy-nine—not an age to play a prominent part in Australian philosophical life. A. K. Stout had been educated at Oriel College, Oxford. Before he came to Australia, he had written a number of articles on Descartes, but his recent work has been entirely on ethics. Prominent in Australian public life, he has carried on and extended the tradition of the public-spirited professor of philosophy. He has stood side by side with Anderson in a good many disputes on such questions as academic freedom and censorship, and has in some measure been influenced by Anderson's political and social ideas, but fundamentally he speaks for the British liberal tradition. As well, he has been prominent, as Anderson never has been, in a great variety of cultural and "liberal-reform" organizations. Philosophically, he has made less mark; his articles on ethics, although well received both in Australia and abroad, are few in number.

Anderson, then—with Gibson as his main critic—dominated Australian philosophical life in the thirties. Toward the end of that decade, however, an important new influence entered Australian philosophical life with the arrival of two of Wittgenstein's ablest pupils, George Paul and D. A. T. Gasking. Paul went straight to Melbourne, where he taught until he left Australia for Oxford in 1946; Gasking went first to Queensland, but later took up a Melbourne lectureship. So the University of Melbourne became one of the first important centers—perhaps *the* first—of Wittgenstein's ideas outside Cambridge.

Paul wrote nothing during his period in Melbourne and very little before or after it. But his personal influence there as a teacher was immense; not only undergraduates, but his fellow teachers were greatly influenced by his highly personal version of what he had learned at Cambridge. A writer in the Spring, 1961, issue of the *Melbourne University Magazine* sums up his influence thus:

George Paul was expounding with all-conquering charm the linguistic approach to philosophy which he had derived from the work of Wittgenstein and Wisdom. Paul's exposition was subtle, sophisticated, and wildly exciting. . . . Staff members from such diverse departments as English, History, Science and Commerce sat at his feet.

He had been educated at St. Andrews before he went to Cambridge, and he had a broader knowledge of, and a broader conception of, philosophy than purely Cambridge products sometimes possessed. Few men have exerted a greater influence on Australian philosophy than Paul—but that influence was almost wholly expressed in his teaching. It was, indeed, one aspect of his influence, deriving from Wittgenstein's theories and Moore's practice, that in Melbourne the emphasis was on personal discussion rather than on the written word and, so far as the written word is concerned, on the article rather than on the book. This is connected with the Cambridge emphasis on the "therapeutic" conception of philosophy; "treat-

157

ment," one might say, had to be directed at the individual, and it took the form of making him think more clearly on a particular issue rather than of introducing him to a systematic body of knowledge. In a sense, the Cambridge philosophers (and those Melbourne philosophers who were working in the same tradition) took themselves to be reinstating the Socratic conception of philosophy—as that is displayed in Plato's early dialogues—in opposition to the "system-making" of nineteenth-century metaphysicians.

Gasking has been scarcely more prolific than Paul. Occasional articles, of which the best known is his "Mathematics and the World," have made a mark outside as well as inside Australia; but they do not together add up to a substantial contribution to philosophy. Like Paul, he has been interested in, although critical of, Anderson's work, but his general point of view and method is that of the Cambridge of Moore, Wisdom, and Wittgenstein, interpreted, however, in an independent way. It is impossible to give any general account either of his or of Paul's philosophical opinions as the evidence is lacking; one is obliged to speak of them simply as exponents of Cambridge philosophy, although that is to understimate the independence of their thinking. That independence has recently been made clear, for example, in Gasking's article on "Clusters" (*Australasian Journal of Philosophy*, May, 1960), which reveals, among other things, that Gasking's approach is much more technical, metaphysical, and, in a way, formal, than the characteristic works of "everyday language" philosophy.

The decade 1940–1950 was not productive of philosophical publication, or even of discussion between universities. In part, the war was responsible for that fact, and after the war the great influx of undergraduates. But only in part. Discussion was difficult because the most influential figures at Sydney and Melbourne—during this decade the only philosophical centers which were at all in communication—only very imperfectly understood one another. Wittgenstein's newer ideas, those represented by Paul and Gasking, had not been published; it was obvious, too, that he did not care to have them described by others. And, as we said, the Melbourne emphasis was on discussion rather than on publication—as to some degree was also true of Sydney. Anderson had written little, and his former students did not feel it proper to do his writing for him. So nobody

158

in Australia outside Melbourne had any clear idea what was being taught there, and Melbourne was only slightly better acquainted with what was taught in Sydney.

There were other problems, too. Gibson and Anderson had at least a general understanding of one another's intentions and proceedings. Anderson, for all his innovations, was "in the tradition"; his conclusions might be unusual, but his manner of philosophizing was familiar. His teachers had been Idealists, and he had not lost all sympathy with them; he agreed with them, in particular, that philosophy must be systematic, and that it was best worked out by a method of continuous exposition. To the philosophical ideas of Wittgenstein, Anderson brought neither sympathy nor understanding. Writing of "the New Realism" and Absolute Idealism, he says: "Neither of these philosophies has any great support at the present time, but it may well be argued that each of them had much greater sweep and force than the piecemeal philosophies (or set of devices passing as philosophies) which nowadays almost monopolise the field." "Piecemeal philosophies"—this was his judgment on Wittgenstein and his followers. Anderson and many of his students disliked their method of discussion, perhaps even more than their doctrines, and the effect for a time was to disrupt philosophical communication in Australia. Philosophical congresses had always been hard-fought, but now they degenerated, often enough, into mere wrangles, as much over questions of procedure as over questions of doctrine.

In the last decade the situation has completely changed. The quality of discussion at philosophical congresses is high; the discussion is often fierce, but the atmosphere is not one of animosity. And even though many of Australia's ablest philosophers have still scarcely published, there has been, relatively speaking, a flood of new publications.

How has the change come about? In part, it is a result of general changes in Australian life; the situation of university teachers, intolerable for a period, has now in some measure improved as the result of Commonwealth grants. New universities have been set up, in which the day-to-day pressure of teaching is less intense. There has been a very large increase in the number of university teachers of philosophy: Sydney now has eighteen and Melbourne a comparable number. (In both universities the Philosophy Department for many years consisted of one professor and a lecturer, and even by 1940 it consisted of only three or four.) Universities are now relatively generous in subsidizing attendance at interstate conferences, and air travel has made rapid communication within Australia easier. Western Australia, for example, used to be cut off by sheer distance from Australian philosophical discussion, but in recent years that isolation has been at least partly overcome. At philosophical congresses—which are still small enough to be of real use—there is now represented a geographically much wider and a philosophically much more diversified range of opinion. The number of potential authors has greatly increased.

Then, too, the old barriers have in some measure broken down. In the last years of the occupancy of his chair in Sydney, Anderson's influence was less overwhelming than it had been in the thirties, partly because the tremendous postwar stresses in universities had drained his creative energies, partly because he did not come seriously to grips with the work of his younger philosophical contemporaries. Dissident groups sprang up in Sydney; they formed a halfway house between Sydney and Melbourne. As a result of the sharp increase in the number of traveling scholarships, too, many more of Anderson's best men went abroad for postgraduate studies, usually to Oxford, and although few, if any, of them were wholly converted to "ordinary language" philosophy, they came to understand it better and to appreciate its merits. The publication of such books as Gilbert Ryle's *The Concept of Mind* and Wittgenstein's *Philosophical Investigations* made it easier to come to grips with what was being taught at Melbourne. Wittgenstein's former pupils, for their part, felt freer to publish their own views, now that they were no longer obliged to begin by expounding those ideas of Wittgenstein which they took as their point of departure. They came, as well, to be more sympathetic toward traditional modes of philosophizing than they had been in the first flush of "the revolution in philosophy."

As it happens, however, many of the best-known products of the Melbourne philosophy school are no longer in Australia. Several of them had come to Australia as a result of the misfortunes of war rather than by inclination; their roots were elsewhere, and they were easily attracted to universities that offered them better posts. Others were Australians but preferred the wider opportunities offered by overseas universities. Gerd Buchdahl and Peter Herbst departed for Great Britain; Paul Edwards (an independently minded member of the Melbourne group), Michael Scriven, and Alan Donagan have all moved to the United States, as has likewise the only Melbourne-trained philosopher to have published a work of substantial proportions, Kurt Baier, whose *The Moral Point of View* was published in 1958.

When Baier first came to Australia he already had behind him a Viennese legal education; he went on to study philosophy, first at Melbourne and then at Oxford. In a number of articles, mostly but not entirely on ethical themes, he showed himself to be, in essentials, committed to the "ordinary language" approach to philosophy, but his *The Moral Point of View* has a considerable measure of independence. Reviewing *The Moral Point of View* in *Mind*, Bernard Mayo wrote of it that, "written in the style and idiom of Oxford Philosophy, it will appeal especially to those who feel that modern analytical ethics has not really come to grips with the fundamental ethical issues." Although in general terms it is a contribution to the "new rationalism" which has lately sprung up at Oxford, it is, in a way, more conservative than the younger Oxford moral philosophers have generally been and closer to the tradition of moral philosophy. Baier's main thesis is that an act is morally right if it has "the weight of moral reasons behind it." He has brought out very clearly, in the only book on ethics of any consequence yet to come out of Australia, the assumptions behind a good deal of conventional moral thinking. Other members of the Melbourne school, including Bruce Benjamin and A. C. Jackson (whose Australian reputation as teacher and critic stands very high and whom Oxford invited to give the John Locke Lectures), have still to publish on a major scale.

Many of Anderson's pupils have occupied university posts overseas, but, unlike the Melbourne men, their tendency is to return to, and settle in, Australia. For all that Anderson and his followers have been subjected to so much abuse in Australia and have not taken it lying down, there is certain harmony between Anderson's approach and manner—with its roots in the Scottish radical tradition—and Australian social habits, especially the habits of Sydney, as distinct from the "more English" habits of Melbourne academic life. Those who have come under Anderson's influence are seldom happy for long away from the rough-and-tumble of Australian political and academic life, its controversial belligerence, its sardonic rejection of any form of "uppishness." They tend to be not entirely at home in, however much they may temporarily enjoy, either the complex societies of Europe or the serious, ambitious atmosphere of a good American university.

Anderson, as I have said, sketched in outline a whole philosophical position; those who worked under him have generally gone on to concentrate in a specific field. Reading widely in their chosen field, studying it abroad, they have come under influences other than his. They have normally rejected at least a certain amount of what he taught, but at the same time they continue to work in a manner bearing the marks of his influence. And the conclusions they eventually come to are not infrequently very close to some of Anderson's own unorthodox conclusions.

Perhaps I can illustrate by my own case. Anderson is not, in any technical sense, a scholar; he is not widely read, as a scholar understands "wide reading," and he has a quite unscholarly tendency to rely upon some commentator who has seized his imagination without closely following the subsequent course of scholarly discussion. But it was his habit in lectures to expound his metaphysical and epistemological ideas through the medium of a critical commentary on the "classical philosophers." He thought of those philosophers not as historical curiosities, but as men struggling with philosophical problems and trying to solve them. In their character as critical commentaries, as well as in other respects, my *Ralph Cudworth* (1951) and *Hume's Intentions* (1952) both reveal his influence. So does my *A Hundred Years of Philosophy* (1957), although it is not explicitly critical, insofar as I try to discover what problems were agitating this or that philosopher rather than, simply, what conclusions he came to. (Anderson's lectures on the history of philosophy were never "outlines.") Yet Anderson neither could, nor would want to, write such books; they are too historical in character, too minutely documented. My *Philosophical Reasoning* (1961), similarly, grew very naturally out of Anderson's lectures. Even though it rejects views which he has held and maintains positions

162

which he would not at all accept, even though, too, it would never have been written had it not been for the work of Gilbert Ryle, it can still fairly be described as "Andersonian" in its general approach.

Also at the Australian National University, P. H. Partridge, now director of the Research School of Social Sciences, has concentrated on social and political philosophy. His recent work lies on the boundaries between social science, history, and philosophy; a good deal of it is not at all within the area of our present concern. But he has also interested himself in the question of how far philosophical inquiries are relevant to political science, as in his *Thinking about Politics* (1956). As Anderson did not, Partridge has read extensively, and he has been greatly influenced by what he has read. Yet, once more, he works in Anderson's tradition—in this case the tradition of political pluralism. And even his habit of ignoring the official boundaries between "subjects" is typical of Anderson's practice and precept; one of Anderson's constant themes has been the necessity for "following an argument where it leads," without paying any attention to 'no trespassing' signs.

Another, rather different, case is D. M. Armstrong. Different, because unlike Partridge and myself, he was taught by Anderson at a time when his influence was beginning to wane and Armstrong went on to do graduate work in Oxford at a relatively youthful age. Both his *Berkeley's Theory of Vision* (1960) and his *Perception and the Physical World* (1961) make it apparent that he has been in close contact with the methodical epistemology of H. H. Price. Furthermore, he has been teaching at the University of Melbourne and has felt the influence of Jackson and Gasking. Armstrong's epistemology is particularized, whereas Anderson's is a logical sketch. The fact remains that Armstrong's variety of realism is, in general terms, Anderson's, and a good many of his detailed arguments derive from that same source. Clear, detailed, fair-minded, his books take seriously, and try to reply to, a number of objections to realism which it has lately been fashionable to neglect.

Anderson's ethics, or at least the constructive part of it—his "positive" ethics, as distinct from his criticism of "moralism"—has not been generally accepted by his former students. But it plays an important part in Eugene Kamenka's *The Ethical Foundations of Marxism* (1962), in which the author, basing himself on a careful study of Marx's earlier writings, brings out the connection and distinction between Marxist and Andersonian ethics. Once more, Anderson's own work on Marx is, in comparison, only a sketch; Kamenka cannot be said merely to have filled in the details—his analysis of Marx's early thought is a quite independent contribution to scholarship—but the influence of Anderson's ethical theory has obviously been a powerful one.

Other pupils of Anderson's have been less active. Some of them have written only in the *Australasian Journal of Philosophy* and often enough in a manner scarcely intelligible to "outsiders." The best known of these article writers, perhaps—they have also published abroad—are A. J. Baker and J. L. Mackie, Anderson's successor as professor of philosophy at Sydney. Both studied at Oxford after taking their B.A. degrees at Sydney; Mackie before the war, in the days when Prichard and Price were the leading figures, Baker in the postwar Oxford of Ryle and Strawson and Austin. Mackie has latterly been particularly interested in logic, but has only just begun to publish in this area; once more, the influence of Anderson is marked, but Mackie concerns himself in detail with contemporary logic, as Anderson did not. The most discussed of his articles—"Evil and Omnipotence" (*Mind*, April, 1955)—is very much in Anderson's vein, although in "A Refutation of Morals" (*Australasian Journal of Philosophy*, May, 1946), he breaks entirely with Anderson by rejecting the idea of a "positive ethics." For the rest, journalists, jurisprudentialists, political theorists, psychologists—as in W. M. O'Neil's *Introduction to Method in Psychology* (1957)—have written in ways which display Anderson's influence, an influence sometimes exerted through his followers rather than directly from Anderson himself.

In 1927, only one professor of philosophy in Australia was not Australian-born and, as to his first degree, Australian-educated. In 1961, this was by no means the case. A. K. Stout, D. R. Grey, and L. Goddard were British-born, as was A. Boyce Gibson, although he had attended an Australian university; H. D. Monro and S. A. Grave came to Australia from New Zealand. Only in New South Wales and Canberra were there Australian-born professors. The situation in regard to subprofessorial faculty is rather different. The majority, perhaps, are Australian-born and Australian-educated, although Americans, Hungarians, Poles, Russians, and Germans have all been conspicuous in the recent philosophical life of Australia.

The new men—professors and lecturers alike—have greatly diversified the philosophical scene. Grey (who died in 1961 at the age of 42) was a scholar a great deal influenced in his general philosophical outlook by Oxford idealism, but known principally for his essays on Berkeley and Plato; Grave, too, is a scholar, and his *The Scottish Philosophy of Common Sense* (1961) is a meticulous study of the work of the Scottish School, much "closer" than Laurie's book on substantially the same theme; Monro, before coming to Australia, wrote a book on laughter and another on Godwin, but since his arrival has been mainly concerned with the critical study of contemporary moral philosophy; Goddard's interests lie particularly in the philosophy of mathematics.

The most conspicuous of the postwar arrivals is J. J. C. Smart, who has written an exceptionally large number of articles, many of which have established a place for themselves in contemporary philosophical literature. Although he has defended utilitarianism in his monograph *An Outline of Utilitarian Ethics* (1961), his main interest is in logic and, in a broad sense, metaphysics. For a time he was strongly under the influence of Gilbert Ryle and Oxford "ordinary language" philosophy, but he has now, in a sense, returned to his scientific beginnings. Contemporary philosophers, he complains, ignore or misunderstand not only specific scientific findings, but the whole tendency of science. Smart defends a variety of materialism—a "physicalism"—which takes for granted the criteria of plausibility and intelligibility commonly employed by the physical scientist. Smart's manner of reasoning is most clearly exemplified in his articles on "Sensations and Brain Processes" (*Philosophical Review*, April, 1959) and "Colours" (*Philosophy*, April and July, 1961), both of which reject the conventional contrast between sensations and brain processes. "An ultimate law," he argues in the second of these articles,

which would relate something which is itself perhaps simple, such as a sense-datum, and which has a determinate *quale*, to a very complicated and non-homogeneous process involving numbers of neurons . . . de-

165

pending on numerous negative feed-back mechanisms of complicated sorts, seems to me quite unbelievable. It is *so out of harmony with the whole tendency of modern science.*

It is an interesting fact that Smart is professor of philosophy at Adelaide, in the chair once occupied by Sir William Mitchell. For all the obvious differences in their doctrines and methods of approach, there is a clear sense in which Smart has inherited the Mitchell tradition, with the important difference that Smart is a very active participant in Australian philosophical life.

The other new arrivals strike a less individual, but still important, note. Some of them have contributed—as Smart has notably done himself—to that increased interest in the philosophy of science which has been a marked feature of Australian philosophy during the postwar years. Melbourne now has, in its Department of the History and Philosophy of Science, one of the few such departments in the British Commonwealth; in the University of New South Wales philosophy began as the philosophy of physical science. Most of the leading contributors to this field are younger men, and no large-scale work has yet come out of their activity. But the articles of C. L. Hamblin, C. F. Presley, G. Schlesinger, Brian Ellis, J. B. Thornton, and D. Stove, display that diversity of approach and readiness to put forward an unconventional or unfashionable point of view which is most typical of Australian philosophy. Some of these men are Sydney-trained, some Melbourne-trained, but both Presley and Schlesinger came to Australia from overseas. Their work is beginning to attract attention, and one can reasonably hope that it will develop to more extended proportions. Meanwhile, the philosophy of science is perhaps the most lively and controversial area within contemporary Australian philosophy.

There has been some interest, too, in the methodology of the social, as distinct from the physical, sciences. The main contribution so far has come from yet another member of that Gibson family which has played so striking a part in Australian philosophical history. Q. B. Gibson, however, does not work in the family tradition of Idealism; his postgraduate work at Oxford brought him under the influence of Cook Wilson's followers. *The Logic of Social Enquiry* (1960) approaches the social sciences from the standpoint of a basically "commonsensical" philosophy and concerns itself with the

166

purely philosophico-methodological problems raised by historical and social science investigation. Gibson teaches in the School of General Studies at the Australian National University in Canberra, and in that university interest in the methodology of social and historical inquiry is exceptionally strong. In the National University's Institute of Advanced Studies, J. C. Harsanyi, who has lately succumbed to the temptations of the United States, did important work on the theory of games in its application to social science. Harsanyi, however, stood alone in his interests; his mathematical talents took him beyond the point at which any but a very few of his Australian colleagues could follow him. That is still a serious difficulty in Australia—the specialist can seldom find a fellow specialist to talk to, and he is naturally attracted elsewhere. R. Brown, also of the Institute, has completed a detailed study of explanation in the social sciences. He is more intimately concerned than Gibson was with the detailed problems of social investigation, especially in sociology and anthropology. Add the essays of P. H. Partridge on methodological problems in political science and my own on the philosophy of history, and the total effect is one of a quite considerable center of inquiry into the philosophy of the social sciences.

Brown came to Australia from the United States, after graduate work in England; C. B. Martin of Adelaide followed that same pattern. But whereas Brown was trained in London, under Ayer, Martin went to Cambridge, and his *Religious Belief* (1959) belongs, in general terms, to the school of Wittgenstein. Only in general terms, however. Martin is not at all content with the view, which has recently flourished in Cambridge, that religious belief can be interpreted either as an aid to right conduct—in the spirit of the "true religion" of Matthew Arnold and his nineteenth-century Australian followers—or as a way of "drawing attention to certain features of the human situation." He takes religious beliefs in a much more literal way and brings a battery of sophisticated arguments to bear upon them—more particularly, upon the everyday doctrines of Christianity. His *Religious Belief* is a sober, philosophical analysis which proceeds by applying complex logical analyses of, for example, the distinction between proper names and descriptive phrases to the special case of religion.

It will by now be clear, at least, that the homogeneity of early

167

twentieth-century philosophy and, for practical purposes, the "two-school" atmosphere of the late thirties and the forties have both disappeared. Many different types of philosophizing are now represented in Australia, except that sympathy with European philosophy is at its lowest ebb; only Gibson pursues the older tradition of close contact with Europe. Recently, it is true, there have been intellectual stirrings among Australian Roman Catholics, who until the last few years—except for an occasional Jesuit—have largely restricted their philosophical activities to seminary teaching. But the main activity, even in that case, has come from philosophers who seek in some degree to reconcile the church to contemporary British philosophy, rather than from Thomists in the European manner. The only full expression of this point of view so far is to be found in M. J. Charlesworth's *Philosophy and Linguistic Analysis* (1959), in which a Louvain and a Melbourne training are conjoined. Charlesworth's standpoint, he says, "is one which might be called Thomist," but Charlesworth's "Thomism" takes contemporary philosophy seriously, as distinct from condemning it in an "external" way. Other Roman Catholic intellectuals would be less inclined to call themselves Thomists, and they stand closer to a purely Wittgensteinian position. Such contemporary European movements of thought as phenomenology and existentialism are not represented in Australia; nor does that depreciation of science which is characteristic of much European philosophy strike a responsive note in Australia. Medieval and classical scholarship, except for occasional articles on Plato and E. F. Osborn's *The Philosophy of Clement of Alexandria* (1957) have not been sufficiently cultivated, but in other areas of scholarship the record is a surprisingly good one.

The general picture is one of vigorous and lively thought, ranging over a wide variety of philosophical topics, more notable perhaps for forthrightness than for the more delicate forms of subtlety, but already productive and full of promise for the future. No great work has yet been produced in Australia, but great works in philosophy are very rare indeed. Competent work is rare enough; and it is at this level that Australia is beginning to establish itself within the world of philosophy.

BIBLIOGRAPHY

Anderson, John. *Studies in Empirical Philosophy.* 1962.

Armstrong, D. M. *Berkeley's Theory of Vision.* 1960.

——. *Perception and the Physical World.* 1961.

Baier, Kurt. *The Moral Point of View.* 1958.

Charlesworth, M. J. *Philosophy and Linguistic Analysis,* 1959.

Gibson, A. Boyce. *The Philosophy of Descartes.* 1932.

Gibson, W. R. Boyce. *A Philosophical Introduction to Ethics.* 1904.

Grave, S. A. *The Scottish Philosophy of Common Sense.* 1961.

Kamenka, Eugene. *The Ethical Foundations of Marxism.* 1962.

Laurie, Henry. *Scottish Philosophy in Its National Development.* 1902.

Martin, C. B. *Religious Belief.* 1959.

Miller, E. Morris. *Kant's Doctrine of Freedom.* 1913.

——. *Moral Law and the Highest Good.* 1928.

Mitchell, W. *The Structure and Growth of the Mind.* 1907.

——. *The Place of Minds in the Modern World.* 1933.

Passmore, John A. *Ralph Cudworth.* 1951.

——. *Hume's Intentions.* 1952.

——. *A Hundred Years of Philosophy.* 1957.

——. *Philosophical Reasoning.* 1961.

Quaife, Barzillai. *The Intellectual Sciences.* 1872

Smart, J. J. C. *An Outline of Utilitarian Ethics.* 1961.

Stewart, McKellar. *A Critical Exposition of Bergson's Philosophy.* 1911.

SCIENCE

SIR SAMUEL MACMAHON WADHAM

THE scientific development of any country at any given time is the result of many factors. It is influenced by the scientific institutions which the nation has supported and by the general standard of education, particularly at the secondary and tertiary (college) levels. The degree of prominence given to science in the universities and higher technical schools is important because these institutions must supply the teachers and research workers. In these days, the part played by governments in providing money for higher education and for the stimulation of research has become increasingly important. Behind all these factors is the force of public opinion which decides, to a considerable extent, the policies of governments in relation to science and influences the amount of government income to be spent on its development. The attitude of the man in the street is not readily changed; tradition plays an important part, and any changes which occur develop slowly. The historical approach seems especially desirable in studying Australian science because, until the last quarter of a century, the public mind has been largely

170

influenced by tradition and the realities of breaking in a new and difficult continent, a process in which endurance and strength rather than scientific knowledge seemed the most vital virtues.

Of particular importance is the growth of the scientific faculties in the universities. Originally the universities were dependent on the governments of the separate states for their funds, but they have gradually received a larger proportion of financial support from the Commonwealth government at Canberra.

Any claim of the Australian aborigines to scientific achievement must rest on the slender ground of their development of ways of living suitable to the arid and uncertain features of their country. It would be unrealistic to expect a people who had no written language to have any really scientific approach to problems, but they were empiricists of a high order in such matters as the development of weapons for killing animals for food; for example, the invention of the boomerang was quite an achievement. The woomera or throwing stick, a device for increasing the velocity of a spear, and the complicated fish spears used by some of the littoral tribes are other examples. The aborigines also evolved a system of restricting marriage by the subdivision of tribes into totemic groups, presumably as a result of observation of the unsatisfactory results of inbreeding.

The observation of natural phenomena is the background of all science, and the approach of the first European voyagers to the Australian coast was partly one of curiosity. The latter half of the eighteenth century was a time of world exploration, with Dutch, French, and British expeditions sailing far and wide in search of new lands and new types of plants and animals, some of which, it was hoped, would prove of general use. Captain James Cook, who sailed around Australia in 1770, was accompanied by the botanist Sir Joseph Banks, who collected, described, and studied many novel species. He, and others like him, were also empiricists, but they had the advantage of being able to place their observations on record and refer them to established schemes of classification. In this pre-Darwinian era, all classifications were designed for convenience and scarcely had a claim to be considered as "natural" systems.

After the beginning of British occupation in 1788, such science as existed was concerned with the further collection and description of the many new forms of animal and plant life offered by this newly discovered continent with its wide array of climates and soils. Many attempts were made at the introduction of species of plants useful for food and other purposes. Such attempts were very necessary to the early settlers in a land which had so few food plants. For many years societies set up for this purpose of acclimatization continued the work, which today is carried on by federal and state organizations, although, naturally, the methods nowadays have a sounder ecological basis.

The first decades of the nineteenth century saw the importation from other countries of the Merino and other races of sheep. These had been shown to have a capacity for using large tracts of land, of which Australia had much of no value for any other purpose. The expanding production of wool, the chief economic support for Australian development, led to the exploration of many parts of the continent and to gradual occupation except in regions where water was unobtainable and rainfall too uncertain.

The first exploitation of gold in the 1850's brought a large population and intensified interest in all aspects of geology. This decade also saw the foundation of the universities of Sydney and Melbourne —remarkable achievements in communities where most of the population consisted of tough types struggling to earn a precarious livelihood from the land, or spending their lives in hopes of "striking it lucky" in the diggings. But also in these jostling communities were families who had education and were steeped in the traditions of Europe and Britain, men and women who endeavored with considerable difficulty to advance human thought and knowledge in various ways. These individuals established several scientific societies, prominent among which were the Royal Societies in each of the colonies. The aims of these bodies were to foster the study of science and its application to the exploration and development of the states concerned. In those early days governments often looked to these societies for advice, for the organization of expeditions, and as media through which new knowledge could be collected. Thus, in the state of Victoria, the government gave the Royal Society £600 to be awarded for the best essays on the following subjects:

1) "The Origin and Distribution of Gold and Associated Minerals and the Approved Methods of Extracting Them."

172

2) "Water Collection—Its Storage and Use for Power, Mining and Irrigation."

3) "Agriculture—The Geology and Chemistry of Soils; the Rotation of Crops, and the Sources and Applications of Manures."

4) "The Use of Victorian Resources for Manufactures and for the Economic Development of the State."

This grant was symptomatic of the attitude of the times and an indication of the awakening of a scientific, if highly practical, approach to the problems of the new colonies. This approach was far from that of a backwoods community and doubtless was in part a distant result of the developing scientific surge in Britain at that time.

The growing communities in faraway Australia had an increasing need of professional men—surveyors, doctors, lawyers, botanists, geologists, engineers, architects, and builders—quite apart from the senior administrators who were officials from the Colonial Office in London. The local universities were not in a position to supply more than a few professional men, and most came from overseas, many of them in search of adventure or hoping to find a more satisfactory sort of life than that in Britain at the time. Some had been attracted by the lure of gold, but when they found that it was not as easily acquired as they had expected, they turned again to their professions as a means of livelihood. For many years the well-established pastoral families sent their children to British universities despite the existence of similar institutions in Australia.

The development of scientific studies in Australia was largely the result of the growth of the universities. These institutions were necessarily at first staffed by men from overseas. Gradually local graduates who had spent years in further study overseas were appointed in increasing numbers, but until about 1920 the majority of university professors were not Australian by birth. This dependence on other countries, chiefly Britain, for the leaders of scientific training in Australia meant that the state of scientific development was usually some years behind that of Europe.

The general progress of science in the Australian colonies may be gauged by the progress made by the several state universities that were founded from time to time. The universities have developed according to a common pattern, although the stage reached at any

173

time has been largely dependent on the age of the institution and the ability and readiness of the state government to provide the necessary finances. The actual dates of foundation of the universities were: University of Sydney, 1850; University of Melbourne, 1853; University of Adelaide, 1874; University of Tasmania, 1890; University of Queensland, 1909; University of Western Australia, 1911; Australian National University, 1946; University of New South Wales (Sydney), 1949; Newcastle University College, 1951; University of New England (Armidale), 1954; Townsville University College, 1960; Monash University (Melbourne), 1961.

The dates at which the various chairs in the scientific fields were founded at the University of Melbourne will indicate the general trend. The first professors at Melbourne were appointed in 1854; of these, one had the chair of mathematics and another the chair of natural science. The latter was Frederick McCoy, who came from Dublin and Cambridge universities to take charge of this subject which, even in his day, was showing signs of branching in numerous directions. He constructed a "system garden" at the university and built a national museum. Quarrels between the professors were frequent, and progress was slow. The range of McCoy's domain was restricted by the separation of biology in 1887. At that stage progress ceased for a time because the whole community suffered a severe setback through the economic depression which began in 1891 and lasted until the end of the century. McCoy died in 1899. His successor was a professor of biology. In 1900, the subject of geology was raised to a professorship. Botany and plant physiology were separated from biology in 1906, and when the professor of the latter resigned in 1919, the chair was designated as zoology.

A start had been made toward creating a faculty of medicine by the appointment in Melbourne in 1862 of a professor of physiology and histology. This faculty advanced a step with the addition of pathology in 1882. Bacteriology and biochemistry developed flourishing schools which serviced both the faculties of science and medicine, but chairs were not established until 1935 and 1938 respectively. A chair of obstetrics had been created in 1929.

The government of Victoria had long been interested in developing technical services in its Department of Agriculture and Public Health. It required its officers to be trained not only in general

174

scientific principles, but also in their application to the special conditions of the Australian environment. For this reason, the government provided specific funds for the foundation of the faculties of veterinary science (1908) and agriculture (1911).

The expansion of scientific knowledge after 1920, and the growing public appreciation of its importance in so many aspects of the life of the small nation trying to be modern brought some increased support for the universities from the state and federal treasuries and from private sources. This was accelerated by the foundation, in 1924, of the faculty of commerce. At that time the study of economics was regarded with some suspicion in certain quarters. The private endowment of the Ritchie Research Professorship in Economics in 1929 and the commanding personality and public service of its first occupant, Professor L. F. Giblin, did much to establish the subject in the eyes of the more thoughtful sections of the public.

When the Commonwealth of Australia was constituted in 1901, certain powers were reserved for the central administration; the states retained the remainder. Education was not a Commonwealth function; consequently, the government at Canberra could not readily be induced to provide money for university development in the states. But during the 1930's federal authorities began to be increasingly involved in various aspects of research, and the supply of personnel for their establishments became a matter of concern. On the side of the humanities, there was also a growing appreciation of the desirability of university training for those who occupied the higher administrative posts. This is particularly important in a public service of which the leaders are permanent and not political appointments. As the result of these pressures, the Commonwealth made, in 1938, a grant of £50,000 for research, to be distributed among the universities. It was hoped that this action would enable a larger number of students to remain at the universities for advanced scientific and humanistic study.

Other developments of this period were the establishment, in Melbourne, of a faculty of dental science in 1924. The study of metallurgy was stimulated by the mining companies that were interested in the lead, zinc, and silver ores at Broken Hill in New South Wales. The first professor of metallurgy was appointed in 1924. The faculty of engineering had started in 1882, but it did not have any professors other than the one in general engineering until after the Second World War. During the 1930's, progress was again halted by the economic depression which lasted most of the decade.

The war emphasized the great need for increased numbers of scientists in many fields, and the Commonwealth found it necessary to make grants to the states so that they could improve the desperate financial position of their universities.

The postwar period saw an immense expansion of university and technical development parallel to that which occurred in many other countries. The effect of this expansion on Melbourne can be gauged from the fact that the number of students increased from 4,010 in 1944 to 11,160 in 1960. During that period the faculty of engineering had new chairs in mechanical (1946), civil (1947), and electrical engineering (1948), and one in metallurgical research (1946).

In the medical sciences similar developments occurred; professors were appointed in experimental medicine (1944), pharmacology (1954), medicine (1955), surgery (1955), child health (1960), and experimental neurology (1961); the faculty of dentistry added chairs in conservative dentistry (1949) and dental prosthesis (1953). In addition, chairs have been established in psychology (1946), statistics (1955), and architecture (1947)—subjects which are borderline to the scientific faculties. Physical chemistry was added in 1960, atomic physics in 1961. During this same period the number of readers and associate professors increased from 10 to 57.

University expansion has become a matter of national policy, supported financially by the Commonwealth government with the consent of the states. This support has taken various forms. The foundation of the Australian National University at Canberra, which was originally devoted entirely to research in the natural and medical sciences, but has subsequently become responsible for undergraduate studies by absorbing the earlier-constituted Canberra University College, was one form of Commonwealth interest. In addition, grants have been made to the states to increase the allowances they make for the facilities and teaching and research personnel of their universities. The Commonwealth has also adopted the practice of giving studentships to selected candidates on the results of university matriculation examinations and has made considerable grants for research studentships. In these various ways it has gradually become deeply concerned in education at the tertiary and postgraduate levels.

By 1956 the Commonwealth government had become fully aware of the need for a careful examination of the position of the several universities and was anxious to put them on a satisfactory basis. On the one hand, it was pressed by academicians and those who were alive to scientific movements overseas; on the other, it had to overcome the die-hard conservatives who disliked higher taxation and the others whose sole ideas were either more bread and circuses or higher wages and shorter hours. Therefore, the government set up a Committee on Australian Universities, under the chairmanship of Sir Keith Murray, who had long experience with similar problems in Britain where he was chairman of the University Grants Committee.

This committee spent nine months in making a survey. Its report may be taken as an accurate summary of the situation, and the following are some of the salient points:

1) The demand for all university graduates is bound to increase in the liberal arts as well as in science and technology. One critical shortage is that of teachers.

2) The general weakness of honors work and postgraduate training and research work is disquieting.

3) Provision for the sciences, and particularly the technologies, presents one of the most urgent problems of Australian universities.

4) There is a general lack of university accommodation of all types.

5) In practically every university provision of equipment and materials for teaching and research is inadequate.

6) The problem of recruitment of academic staff presents another serious difficulty.

7) The number of scholarships should be increased at both undergraduate and postgraduate levels and the use of the means test should be reduced.

8) There are a number of problems yet to be solved in providing more people who can occupy positions between graduate engineers and applied scientists on the one hand and between technicians and craftsmen on the other.

9) The Commonwealth government should contribute toward the cost of providing the capital requirements of the universities.

10) The Commonwealth government needs a universities grants committee to provide continuous advice on the financial needs of the universities.

This report doubtless shocked a large number of people, but the government accepted it and set up an Australian Universities Commission to administer the scheme and recommend the allocation of money for new buildings and equipment. So far, despite the groans from the Treasury and doubts from the die-hards, the bill has been met. In September, 1961, the Commonwealth appointed a twelve-man committee "to consider the pattern of tertiary education in relation to the needs and resources of Australia and to make recommendations to the A.U.C. on the future development of tertiary education." The chairman of this committee is also the chairman of the Australian Universities Commission. This new policy of the Commonwealth government toward the state universities and toward higher education generally—especially in the scientific subjects—has been of the utmost importance. It is too early as yet to decide what the ultimate result will be, but the scientific faculties of the universities are extremely hopeful that in the future they will not have to struggle with all the difficulties which have confronted them in the past.

These recent developments have emphasized some of the disabilities under which Australian universities labored in the past and their fears as to their ability to cope with the increased number of students which must follow from the high birth rate in the 1940's and the migration of over a million people from overseas in the last ten years. The remarkable feature of scientific schools in the universities is the successes which their graduates have achieved with their very modest equipment, both in the limited research carried out in Australia and in universities and research institutions overseas, especially in Britain. This has been due, in part, to the intellectual quality of the students themselves and the opportunities which various traveling scholarships have afforded. But in part it has been due to the capacity of the men from the British Isles who were appointed to professorships in the Australian universities. Some of them stayed in Australia; others returned to Britain and there achieved scientific distinction in wider spheres.

178

The Commonwealth government has also been responsible for a direct stimulation of scientific research by creating, in 1926, an organization of its own to carry on this type of work. The Council for Scientific and Industrial Research (C.S.I.R.) was set up under an act of parliament in that year. Australians who were aware of the progress being made overseas, especially in adapting new scientific discoveries to the service of the farming industries, had influenced political leaders to establish this new organization. They knew that the universities had little money, that their staffs were overworked and incapable of doing much research, and that the efforts of state departments of agriculture to carry on research were often frustrated by the political pressure to transfer workers to lesser problems of immediate significance. The federal government acted on the advice of Sir Frank Heath, head of the Division of Scientific and Industrial Research in Britain. It was also aware of developments in the United States of America and of the large-scale enterprises created to assist the cattle industry of the Union of South Africa. The selection of the three executive officers of this new body was extremely sound: George Julius, an engineer who had already shown his genius in the invention of the totalizator or pari-mutuel machine for racecourses; Professor Sir David Rivett, an extremely able chemist with great capacity for making decisions; and Professor A. E. V. Richardson, an agriculturist well acquainted with both the intricacies of the Australian environment from the farming point of view and the most recent agricultural research in the United States and Britain.

This new body steadily set up research divisions to investigate problems of special interest. Some of the divisions took over and carried through work which was already in progress, but many new lines of activity were initiated. It was agreed from the outset that, in the main, the council would attack fundamental problems, leaving the local application of principles to the state departments. In general, this agreement has been honored, but naturally it has been difficult to draw a hard and fast line of classification of work on this basis. Although the scheme has worked well, it would be incorrect to suggest that there has been no friction, or that cooperation has invariably been perfect.

The early divisions of the organization were Plant Industry, Eco-

179

nomic Entomology, Animal Health, Soils, Forest Products, and Fisheries. It was decided that, as the work of the various divisions would naturally spread over the broad expanse of the continent, it would be politically significant if the headquarters of divisions were located in various states. Accordingly, Plant Industry and Economic Entomology were set up at Canberra, Animal Health and Soils at Adelaide, Forest Products at Melbourne, and Fisheries at Cronulla, near Sydney. In due course, laboratories of varying size were established at numerous other places by these divisions, while research stations have been constructed at centers in many of the more important climatic zones of the Commonwealth.

Politically, the organization was a new departure, and conservative interests greeted it with skepticism. However, one or two early successes—partly based on preexisting work—caught the public imagination. Prominent among these was the control of the prickly-pear cactus. This introduced plant was rendering certain grazing lands useless and was spreading at the rate of a million acres a year. An insect, *Cactoblastis cactorum*, was introduced and reduced the cactus to negligible proportions in the course of a few years. The control of the virus causing "bunchy top" in bananas and the explanation of "needle fusion" in pines were other successes. A new central bureau was set up for the introduction of species of plants from countries with climates similar to those in Australia, expeditions being sent abroad to search for plants likely to be suitable. In the veterinary sciences, work was carried out on pleuropneumonia of cattle and black disease of sheep; attempts were made to analyze the proteins of fodder plants with special reference to wool production. A long series of investigations was initiated into the life histories of the various species of flies which strike sheep, with a view to developing effective control measures.

The Division of Forest Products developed outstanding practical successes soon after its inception. The timber industry was at that time in a very primitive stage and, thanks to good public relations, the work of the new Division was soon accepted. It made detailed anatomical studies of the wood of all Australian trees and established authoritative descriptions of them. In conjunction with the paper industry it worked out methods for using eucalypt pulp in the manufacture of paper and fiberboards. Later it made intensive studies of the physical and chemical nature of cell walls, of the use of resins in making Australian plywoods, and of the suitability of various local timbers as replacements for imported types previously used for special purposes.

The Soils Division set about the gigantic task of assessing the great range of Australian soils in terms of the international classification and of constructing a detailed soil map of the continent. On the more applied side, it established the existence of manganese and copper deficiencies in certain areas and turned its attention to making detailed surveys of the soils of the irrigation districts, which were the most intensively used areas of land in the Commonwealth.

Apart from the description of species, no scientific approach had been made to the study of fish in Australian waters before the formation of the Division of Fisheries. Various fishing grounds had been recognized, but it had proved difficult to secure large catches with any regularity. The Division has studied the life cycles and growth rates of various useful species and has determined the appropriate minimum sizes to be retained for some species. The highly profitable oyster, crayfish, and prawn (shrimp) industries have been studied in the same way, and the value of the airplane for spotting the location of shoals of tuna and salmon has been demonstrated. During the war the production of agar was developed on a commercial basis.

Those of Australia's farming industries which produce perishable products have special problems to face in the length of the sea voyage to the main markets in Europe. A Division of Food Preservation and Transport was established in Sydney to study such matters as quality in frozen meat, the special problems of "chilled" beef, the export of apples, egg storage, vegetable dehydration, the preservation of fruit juices, and so forth. This Division has maintained close liaison with comparable research organizations in the United States and Britain, and in the course of its investigations it has frequently been confronted with fundamental problems in microbiology and biochemistry.

The gathering war clouds of the later 1930's induced the Commonwealth government to provide finance so that the C.S.I.R. could

181

widen the scope of its operations in various directions connected with secondary industries. The Division of Industrial Chemistry was founded, and it has expanded steadily. Much of its work has been in the direction of investigating the special features of Australian raw materials, but it has also done research into industrial problems and has some advisory work to its credit. The field of operations has been wide, including cement, ceramics, alkaloids, the chemical nature of wool wax, and a number of studies on metalliferous minerals. These investigations have usually had the ultimate objective of assisting in the foundation or development of industries, but they have inevitably been confronted by fundamental work requiring research of high grade.

A second development, in 1937, was the foundation of the National Standards Laboratory in Sydney. The work of this institution was of great importance during the war, when Australia was forced to start the manufacture of many new machines and materials owing to the impossibility of securing supplies from overseas. The laboratory has been organized in three sections, metrology, physics, and electrotechnology. It has endeavored to maintain a balance between applied work and research, so that staff members are stimulated to maintain the vigorous and fresh outlook which is apt to be deadened by routine work.

To this period, too, belongs the development of the Aeronautical Laboratory which was designed to assist the infant aircraft industry that was mainly centered in Melbourne. At the same time a chair of aeronautics was established at the University of Sydney—a curious division of effort, presumably rendered necessary by the exigencies of the political situation. After the war this laboratory was handed over to the Commonwealth Department of Supply because the C.S.I.R. did not wish to be responsible for the necessary security provisions. The most sensational development connected with the laboratory has been the Jindivick, a small pilotless aircraft which has been used in many countries.

The early days of the war saw the foundation of the C.S.I.R.'s Radiophysics Laboratory, which has been in the forefront of ground-to-air and air-to-ground communications of many types. It has also undertaken studies of radio transmission and fading which have carried its scientists into studies of the ionosphere and of the reflection of radio waves from bodies in outer space. In 1961 the Radiophysics Laboratory commissioned its giant radio telescope at Parkes, N.S.W., about two hundred miles west of Sydney. The telescope, which cost almost two million dollars to build, was financed in part by generous donations from the Rockefeller Foundation and the Carnegie Corporation. Through the two-hundred-foot instrument scientists can look ten times farther into the universe than through the world's largest and best optical telescope at Mount Palomar in California.

The new radio telescope can receive radio waves from five billion light-years away. It is rivaled only by the British radio telescope at Jodrell Bank, near Manchester, which is slightly larger. However, the Parkes radio telescope is considered superior to the Jodrell Bank instrument in surface accuracy. Its control system is especially sensitive.

With the two-hundred-foot radio telescope at Parkes and the new one hundred-inch optical telescope at the Mount Stromlo Observatory near Canberra, Australian astronomers and ionosphere researchers are now equipped more satisfactorily than ever before.

During the 1930's and 1940's, many advances of great value to the farming industries were made, partly as a result of local research and partly by adapting to Australian conditions the results of overseas work. Prominent among these was the introduction of "Strain 19" from the United States for the control of contagious abortion in dairy cattle. Mammitis, which had long been another curse of the dairy industry, had been studied in great detail in Australia, and when penicillin was discovered and rapidly became available owing to its local manufacture, veterinarians rapidly seized on its value for the control of this troublesome bacterium. Similarly, the myxomatosis virus (which sensationally reduced the menacing rabbit population) was discovered in South America and introduced to Australia via the Lister Institute in London. Considerable new knowledge of the effect of trace elements on plants and animals was acquired by the C.S.I.R. working in association with the University of Adelaide. This was of special significance to Australia in view of the large tracts of low-quality soils in the somewhat limited areas with high rainfall.

As a result of these developments, the general body of the public became aware of the value of science in furthering human welfare. The C.S.I.R. has gained enormous respect, and its ever-increasing budget seldom has been questioned. In fact, to the embarrassment of the Commonwealth Treasury, the demand became one for more research rather than for a reduction in research expenditure. At the same time, numerous industries began to make levies on their members so as to assist in the development of research which was carried out for the most part by C.S.I.R., but also to some extent by universities.

The research being undertaken became so wide in scope and involved so much expenditure that in 1951 the Commonwealth government passed a bill which turned the Council for Scientific and Industrial Research (C.S.I.R.) into the Commonwealth Scientific and Industrial Research Organization (C.S.I.R.O.). Theoretically, control had been through the council, which had an executive of three; in fact, the executive was really the dominant force and it satisfied the regulations by putting its actions and proposals before the Council, a body of wide interests, which met about twice a year. In the new organization there were to be three full-time and two part-time members of the controlling body and a council which would be purely advisory. The change was simple and realistic, but one of the part-time members was appointed from the staff of the Treasury; doubtless the intention was to keep a watchful eye on the mounting expenditure. Another new rule was that salaries of C.S.I.R.O. staff members should be kept more or less in line with those of branches of the public service which was controlled by the Public Service Board. Some observers regarded the change as the precursor of much tighter political control, but so far this has not been evident.

In 1959 the organization suffered a severe blow in the death of its chairman, Sir Ian Clunies Ross. The long illness of another member of its executive suggested that the load of responsibility was too heavy for three full-time and two part-time members, so the executive was increased to five full-time and four part-time members. By 1961 the organization's activities had been rearranged under twenty-eight divisions. The divisions and the locations of their head offices are as follows:

184

SCIENCE

Animal Genetics .... Sydney
Animal Health .... Melbourne
Animal Physiology .... Sydney
Biochemistry and General Nutrition .... Adelaide
Building Research .... Melbourne
Chemical Physics ⎤
Mineral Chemistry ⎟
Organic Chemistry ⎬ .... Melbourne
Physical Chemistry ⎦
Coal Research .... Sydney
Electrotechnology .... Sydney
Entomology .... Canberra
Fisheries and Oceanography .... Sydney
Food Preservation .... Sydney
Forest Products .... Melbourne
Land Research and Regional Survey .... Canberra
Mathematical Statistics .... Adelaide
Electrotechnology ⎤
Metrology ⎬ .... Sydney
Physics ⎦
Plant Industry .... Canberra
Protein Chemistry .... Melbourne
Radiophysics .... Sydney
Soils .... Adelaide
Textile Industry ⎤
Textile Physics ⎦ .... Geelong
Tribophysics .... Melbourne
Tropical Pastures .... Brisbane

In addition, there are many independent sections dealing with such matters as mineragraphy and upper atmosphere research, while two —the Agricultural Research Liaison and Industrial Liaison sections —arrange appropriate publicity for the results of research.

The organization has been able to construct numerous special pieces of equipment for detailed work, such as the large air-conditioned animal houses at Prospect, near Sydney, a phytotron at Canberra, and the radio telescope at Parkes. For the 1960–1961 biennium the C.S.I.R.O.'s expenditure was £10,618,060, of which only

£846,900 was for capital works and £9,603,960 for investigations. Of the total budget £8,192,295 came from the Treasury and £2,- 425,770 from sums provided by industries.

The extent of the activities of the C.S.I.R.O. and the great prestige which it has acquired in the community during the postwar period have had somewhat unfortunate tendencies in two directions. First, it has become the fashion to refer all matters requiring scientific investigation to the C.S.I.R.O. for solution. Second, the organization has tended to draw off a large proportion of the best young scientific workers as they finish their courses at the universities.

The executive has endeavored to counter the first of these tendencies by suggesting to the larger organizations that, where possible, they should develop their own research laboratories or, when this is not practicable, that the members of an industry should collectively form a research association to contribute a considerable part of the funds required for the maintenance of a special laboratory to serve the industry and investigate its problems. This has met with some success, but it would be idle to suggest that all Australian industries are conscious of their need for a scientific staff to investigate their problems. The Broken Hill Proprietary Steel organization, in which practically all iron and steel production in Australia is centered, has recently set up a research organization near Newcastle. The metal interests have recently done the same in the new Australian Mineral Development Laboratories at Adelaide. The Imperial Chemical Industries of Australia and New Zealand Limited, a big and wealthy organization affiliated with the one which exists in Britain, has large laboratories near Melbourne. Several pharmaceutical firms have followed suit. There is an Oenological Research Institute at Adelaide supported by the wine industry, but assisted by C.S.I.R.O., as are the Tobacco Research Station at Mareeba, Queensland, and the Bread Research Institute in Sydney.

The great increase in scientific work in Australia during the last fifteen years has inevitably meant a considerable drain on the pool of trained scientists from which government departments, the C.S.I.R.O., industry, and the universities must draw most of their personnel. The first result has been a great improvement in the remuneration offered to qualified men. Each branch of science has its professional organization, and these have been active in repre-

SCIENCE

senting to governments and to salary-fixing authorities the need for
increased salaries, so that science may be able to attract students of
suitable caliber. The problem has been accentuated by the general
monetary inflation which has taken place during the 1950's, but in
general the scientist now occupies a better status in the community
than he did before the Second World War.

As a result, many scientists have been attracted from overseas
countries to work in Australian laboratories where rates of pay and
conditions of work are now generally good. This influx has been
especially marked since 1955. Other scientific workers have transferred from state government departments and universities to
C.S.I.R.O. and industry. At the same time, there has been some movement in the opposite direction, and this would have been greater
if the transference of pension and superannuation benefits had been
easier. Naturally, this deterrent has been more potent in the case of
senior scientific personnel.

Although the C.S.I.R.O. occupies a dominant place in respect to
scientific work in Australia, numerous other government organizations, both federal and state, are also concerned with such matters.
The Commonwealth Department of Health maintains several scientific bureaus. The principal of these are the following:

Commonwealth Serum Laboratories. This organization was
founded in 1916 at Melbourne and is mainly concerned with the
preparation of prophylactic material for use in controlling human
and animal diseases. It undertook the early manufacture of penicillin
in Australia, and it was instrumental in devising local means of producing the Salk vaccine against poliomyelitis. It maintains regular
supplies of antivenins against the bites of Australian snakes; of the
less exciting but more important vaccines and inocula against such
troubles as smallpox, diphtheria, enteric fever, and the like in humans; and of vaccines against contagious abortion in cattle, pulpy
kidney in sheep, and other diseases of farm and domestic animals.
The maintenance of this service and the investigation of new diseases
and new control measures requires a large staff, and research is carried on in connection with the types of problems which are apposite
to its special functions. The director of the Serum Laboratories
represents the Commonwealth government on the World Health
Organization's Permanent Commission on Biological Standards.

187

Commonwealth Health Laboratories. These laboratories are situated at fourteen centers throughout the country. Their main function is the administration of the quarantine system, but they have also conducted research into problems of their districts. They have done work on leptospirosis and on a special form of endemic typhus which occurs in North Queensland. In South Australia lead poisoning has been investigated in the metal-smelting areas, and in Western Australia much attention has been given to silicosis among the miners of the Kalgoorlie region.

Commonwealth X-Ray and Radium Laboratory. This agency was established in Melbourne in 1929, when ten grams of radium were purchased as a basic stock. From this stock a service for the provision of randon needles to cancer clinics in all states has been developed. In addition, the laboratory is equipped for X-ray investigations, and in recent years it has organized the importation and supply of radioisotopes from overseas and from the Australian Atomic Energy Commission. These isotopes are used under license for medical, scientific, and industrial purposes. The investigation of radiation levels in buildings, and other similar problems, fall within the province of this laboratory.

The Commonwealth Department of Public Health also maintains a School of Public Health and Tropical Medicine in the University of Sydney, where specialized courses are provided and investigations made into health matters appropriate to its special purposes. The National Health and Medical Research Council acts for the Department in the allocation of funds for medical research to the universities and other capable institutions. During 1960 there were 160 of these allocations. The council originally sponsored the Acoustic Research Laboratory, which is now concerned principally with problems of noise in factories, but which has also studied general problems of deafness, including deafness in children due to rubella in mothers during pregnancy.

Research in nutrition is centered at the Australian Institute of Anatomy at Canberra. Astronomical observations and research are carried out at Mount Stromlo, a few miles from the federal capital.

The Australian Atomic Energy Commission was set up in 1952, with the primary objective of encouraging the production of uranium, and secondly to develop the practical uses of atomic energy.

This matter may be of great significance to some districts in Australia which are far removed from other usable sources of energy.

The Bureau of Mineral Resources, Geology and Geophysics was constituted soon after the Second World War in order to expedite exploration for minerals, including oil, in Australia. Its foundation was severely criticized by those who would have preferred a centralized geological survey, but in a land area as vast as Australia it seemed desirable to produce tangible results quickly by concentrating on areas where there were good prospects of success. This policy has proved successful, except in the search for oil.

Each of the states has its own Geological Survey and Mines Department which studies geological structures and produces new and revised geological maps of its territory. The states also have health organizations and laboratories which provide analytical services in respect to foods, minerals, soils, and water. Their agriculture and forestry departments have research stations and plantations of various types at which a considerable amount of scientific work is carried on in connection with the problems of local significance such as the breeding of races of crop and pasture plants, the fertilizer requirements of the various soil types, the control of fungus and virus diseases, of noxious weeds, and of insects and other pests.

From time to time gifts have been made and legacies left by private individuals to universities for research in special fields of study, quite apart from research which is subsidized directly by commercial organizations. Two of these benefactions are particularly noteworthy.

The Walter and Eliza Hall bequest placed a large sum of money in the hands of trustees who decided, after the First World War, to inaugurate a full-time institute for medical research. At first it took the form of a service laboratory for the Melbourne General Hospital, but by 1923 it had begun a program of research and is now entirely devoted to that end, although it is still located in a special part of the Royal Melbourne Hospital. It has also developed a clinical research unit with special facilities. The institute's outstanding work in recent years has been concerned with the detailed nature of virus diseases, and the method of using chick embryos as an incubation medium has been highly developed for the purpose. This virus research has been in the forefront of world knowledge on the

189

subject. The director of the Walter and Eliza Hall Institute, Professor Sir Macfarlane Burnet, was awarded the Nobel Prize in 1960 and the Order of Merit in recognition of his own contributions and his leadership of the group of research workers. Many other medical problems have been investigated in the institute over the years. The original endowment now forms only a small part of the sum needed to operate this institute. The remainder is provided by the Government of Victoria, the National Health and Medical Research Council, the University of Melbourne, and donations from private individuals and from the Rockefeller and other foundations.

Somewhat similar, but less well-known, research organizations are attached to other hospitals in Australia.

The Waite Agricultural Research Institute was founded in 1925 as the result of a bequest from Peter Waite, a pastorialist in South Australia. Other benefactors and the state government have increased the scope and effectiveness of this institution, the work of which is now widely known. It is associated with the University of Adelaide and has made many contributions to the sum of scientific knowledge, both pure and applied, with respect to the problems of the farming and pastoral industries. In particular, it has been associated with pasture plants and their ecology, soil microbiology, the physics and chemistry of soils, the chemistry of plant viruses, local entomological problems (especially the Australian locust), and in recent years has devoted increasing attention to biochemical research. It has the assistance of a staff of about forty specialists and is the center for academic courses in agriculture in South Australia.

Numerous other benefactions have been directly connected with the science schools in the universities, such as the McMaster endowment for veterinary research in the University of Sydney and the Winthrop Hackett bequest which endowed the chair of agriculture in the University of Western Australia.

Reference has already been made to the work of the Royal Societies in the various states. Each of these produces a publication principally devoted to the results of research which is of special local interest in its state. Authors whose work has been connected with more fundamental scientific studies usually prefer to send their contributions to overseas journals or to the principal scientific journals in Australia, which usually have a wider circulation. In recent years the great increase in the volume of scientific research in Australia has made additional channels of publication essential. The C.S.I.R.O., which previously had a small journal, expanded its publishing activities so that today it has its own printing establishment and is responsible for the production of no fewer than eight journals as well as special research bulletins and many other simpler publications. Most of the papers in these journals emanate from the organization's own workers, but research papers of suitable standard from other sources are also accepted now. This innovation has reduced the pressure on the capacity of the Royal Societies to print reports and papers, but it has not prevented them from maintaining their previous standards.

Another influence which has limited the significance of the Royal Societies in their scientific communities has been the establishment of institutes or other organizations whose membership is limited to persons qualified for some particular profession. The Royal Australian Chemical Institute; the Institution of Engineers, Australia; the Australian Institute of Agricultural Science; and the Australian Veterinary Association, are cases in point. As a result, the Royal Societies, while continuing as media for the presentation of specialized papers, have devoted more attention to the organization of high-grade public lectures and the discussion of borderline topics of interest to several scientific disciplines.

From time to time proposals have been advanced for the formation of an all-Australian scientific association, open only to a limited number of scientists of established prestige. A National Research Council endeavored to fill this function, but its membership was not large enough to provide the necessary funds for a permanent secretariat; on the other hand, it was too large to give sufficient academic prestige to its members. The situation changed with the increase in the appreciation of science in the community during the 1950's and with the foundation of the Australian National University primarily as a research institution. The Commonwealth government has now given financial support to an Australian Academy of Science, with headquarters in Canberra and open to a limited number of persons with high academic qualifications in some branch of natural science.

At a more popular level, the Australian and New Zealand Association for the Advancement of Science (A.N.Z.A.A.S.) was founded in 1878. It holds science congresses, usually attended by about 3,000 people, in each capital city in turn. The interval between meetings is normally about eighteen months. A congress has a presidential address, addresses by the presidents of its sections, and numerous memorial lectures, each apposite to the subject of the person it commemorates. The main work is conducted in the constituent subject sections. The advantage of these congresses is the opportunity which they afford for members from different states to meet one another for discussions, and also, in the case of biological and geological sciences, for those from other states to join in excursions to places of scientific interest in the host state. The Association also publishes the *Australian Journal of Science*.

In the foregoing sections an attempt has been made to sketch in outline the historical development and present position of science in Australia. Emphasis has necessarily been laid on the great expansion which has taken place in almost every subject since 1940. This expansion has occurred in the numbers engaged in scientific work and also in the intensity of the research effort. These advances are similar to those which have occurred in many other countries; they are not by any means unique.

For the universities, the period has been one of strain, owing to increased numbers; it has required resolute action on the part of faculties in their endeavor to maintain standards. It may justly be claimed that the standard of the first degree in science in most, if not all, Australian universities is comparable with similar degrees in universities of the higher grade in the United States and Britain although, in general, it does not cover such a wide range of subjects as is common in American institutions. (The pass B.Sc. degree course takes three years and the honors degree four, during which a student customarily studies only four or five subjects—all sciences.)

The output of research has increased markedly in recent years. Much of it has been local in character, but now and again workers have achieved results of world-wide significance. For instance, the Michell thrust-block system of power transmission greatly simplified the use of turbines and other machinery in ships. Some aspects of the flotation method of separating minerals have been of great significance, and the method is widely appreciated. Australian work on radio astronomy and on the physics of cloud formation, including artificial rainmaking, has been widely acclaimed. Some toxemia virus investigations have already been mentioned. The importance of many trace elements in the nutrition of plants and animals has been demonstrated under a variety of conditions. The relationship of cobalt to certain animal diseases has been very effectively proven. The discovery of the relation of copper and certain alkaloids to toxemic jaundice in sheep has been of outstanding value. Good work has also been done on the composition and physiological action of certain alkaloids and pharmacological products. In recent years great progress has been made in the knowledge of the detailed structure of wool fiber and of the tissues of some timbers. Put together, although these contributions to scientific knowledge are not very numerous, they seem a reasonable and commendable contribution from a country the population of which has only recently passed the ten-million mark.

BIBLIOGRAPHY

Books

Blainey, G. *Centenary History of the University of Melbourne.* 1958.
David, Sir T. W. Edgeworth. *The Geology of the Commonwealth of Australia.* 1950.
Tillyard, R. J. *The Insects of Australia and New Zealand.* 1926.
Wadham, Sir Samuel M., and Wood, G. L. *Land Utilization in Australia.* 1950.

Periodicals

Australian Forestry Journal. Monthly. 1918– .
Australian Journal of Agricultural Research. Bimonthly. 1935– .
Australian Journal of Applied Science. Quarterly. 1950– .
Australian Journal of Biological Sciences. Quarterly. 1948– .
Australian Journal of Chemistry. Bimonthly. 1953– .
Australian Journal of Experimental Biological and Medical Sciences. Bimonthly. 1924– .
Australian Journal of Physics. Quarterly. 1948– .
Australian Journal of Science. Monthly. 1938– .
Australian Journal of Zoology. Occasional. 1953– .

Australian Museum Magazine. Quarterly. 1921– .

Australian Veterinary Journal. Monthly. 1925– .

Australian Zoologist. Annual. 1914– .

Commonwealth Scientific and Industrial Research Organization. *Annual Reports.*

Medical Journal of Australia. Weekly. 1856– .

Waite Institute of Agricultural Research (University of Adelaide). *Annual Reports.*

Walter and Eliza Hall Institute of Medical Research (University of Melbourne). *Annual Reports.*

HISTORIOGRAPHY

JOHN M. WARD

"AUSTRALIA was the child of the American Revolution," wrote Professor Ernest Scott. It was the loss of the thirteen colonies that led the British government to found a settlement in New South Wales in 1788. After the War of Independence the United States of America could no longer be used as a dumping ground for British convicts sentenced to transportation. Surplus felons crowded the jails and prison hulks of the British Isles. An outlet for them could be found only in some new settlement, where there would be no free population to protest against the arrival of convicts. After many inquiries, the British government chose the eastern half of Australia as a suitable place for a penal settlement.

Australian historiography had more attractive beginnings than Australian history. When Captain Arthur Phillip was sent out to establish the convict colony, there was a bizarre quality about his expedition that stimulated commemoration. Several of his officers had interest and leisure during the eight months' voyage from England to write journals. Some of them continued to do so after their arrival in Sydney.

Two of these early historians, Watkin Tench and David Collins, both officers of the Marines, laid the foundations of Australian historiography. Tench's books [1] were not a formal narrative of the colony, but deeply humane sketches of the voyage to Australia and of life in early Sydney. Unlike some of his fellow officers, Tench wrote about convicts and aborigines as human beings, not as outcasts or savages. He felt the lure of the Australian bush, and his second book contained an account of his explorations.

In 1798, when Collins published the first volume of his *Account of the English Colony in New South Wales,* the British opponents of the settlement were still condemning it vociferously. Collins' work, which was a systematic history of the progress of the colony, was for many years the best unofficial information that the public of Britain had on conditions in New South Wales. As judge advocate (though ignorant of law) and secretary to the governor, Collins had unique opportunities to observe events. His first volume, founded on his own experiences in New South Wales, criticized the British authorities for their failure to plan and support the colony adequately. The second volume, published in 1802, was based on information sent to Collins from Sydney. For this reason, and perhaps also because he was out of employment, it was less critical of authority than its predecessor had been. Collins' work is the most important of the contemporary histories of early New South Wales.

The Blue Mountains that confined the Sydney settlement to the coast were crossed in 1813, and after that the exploration of the interior revealed vast territories for pastoral occupation. The journals of the explorers contained stirring accounts of great endeavors in an unknown and exhausting country. The most significant discoveries were those made by Captain Charles Sturt (1795–1869) in 1829, when he found the only large river system in the entire continent—the Murray and the Darling with their tributaries. In 1833 he published the story of his discoveries in a long and fascinating

---

[1] *A Narrative of the Expedition to Botany Bay: with an Account of New South Wales* (London: Debrett, 1789); and *A Complete Account of the Settlement at Port Jackson, in New South Wales, Including an Accurate Description of the Situation of the Colony* (London: Nicol, 1793).

work entitled *Two Expeditions into the Interior of Southern Australia*.

A stoic personality, weighed down with the cares of leadership, Sturt wrote unromantic observations in terse and readable prose. The irritability and melancholy of great exhaustion appeared rather often in descriptions that transferred to the country through which he was passing comments that were more appropriate to the states of mind of the explorers themselves: "It is quite impossible for me to describe the kind of country we were now traversing or the dreariness of the view it presented," or "Our route during the day was over as melancholy a tract as ever was travelled."

Later he made an expedition over country that truly was desolate, including the Simpson Desert. The plain prose of his *Narrative of an Expedition into Central Australia* (1849) matched well the country that he had to describe:

The stones, with which the ground was so thickly covered as to exclude vegetation, were of different lengths, from one inch to six, they had been rounded by attrition, were coated with oxide of iron, and evenly distributed. In going over this dreary waste the horses left no track, and that of the cart was only visible here and there.

Sir Thomas Mitchell (1792–1855), the temperamental, sometimes brilliant surveyor general of New South Wales, was another successful explorer who published his journals. He earned fame with an expedition across the Murray and through the western district of what is now Victoria. The story is told in his *Three Expeditions into the Interior of Eastern Australia* (1838). Mitchell wrote with a good eye both to country and to his own reputation. The book is said to have involved him in financial difficulties; it certainly earned rich dividends in other ways. *Blackwood's* declared in a review that "the kind of gentlemen who sit at home at ease . . . should follow this gallant soldier, man of science and man of accomplishment across the fiery sands of the Australian wilderness." The government rewarded him with a knighthood, and Oxford made him a Doctor of Civil Law. Back in Australia, he set out in 1845 to find a route from Sydney to the Gulf of Carpentaria. Perhaps with a view to repeating his earlier successes, he persuaded reluctant authority to grant him leave to visit England and publish a *Journal of an Expedition into the Interior of Tropical Australia, in Search of a Route from Sydney to the Gulf of Carpentaria* (1848). Less careful, less considered, and less impressive than his earlier work, it may be remembered for its humane reflections on the fate of the aborigines as white settlement extended.

Sturt and Mitchell had little time for one another, but they were both able explorers who performed deeds worth recording and set them down notably. They were among the greatest of the men who tracked the Australian loneliness and published journals to tell what they had found.

Where the explorers led, the sheepmen soon followed, looking not for glory but for grass. From 1820 to 1850 the major dynamic in the development of New South Wales was the growth of the wool industry beyond the mountains. Official policy was to blend the expanding pastoral economy with the objectives of the penal settlement. For a quarter of a century this uneasy association of near opposites produced political strain in the colony and weary perplexity in London. In New South Wales the great controversial questions were (1) how to receive emancipists in society and what political and legal rights to allow them, (2) how far to make the Legislative Council elective, (3) how much to depend on free as opposed to convict labor, and (4) whether to maintain, reform, or abandon convict transportation.

In Van Diemen's Land (Tasmania), where a colony had been founded in 1804, the necessities of the penal establishment were similarly at odds with economic development. The free settlers used convict labor and so profited from the working of the transportation system. But they became impatient with the autocracy of the governors of their penal farm and protested against policies that hindered their own progress and which they were powerless to change. The solution that some of them advocated was to grant a large measure of self-government.

None of these matters could be disposed of in Australia. All were questions for imperial decision in London. The best known of the second generation of Australian historians were able men of strong views, who wrote history in order to sway English opinion in their favor. Their books were addressed as much to members of the imperial Parliament and the Colonial Office in London as to readers in Australia.

198

William Charles Wentworth (1791–1872), one of the most ardent constitutional reformers, emerged during the 1830's as the leader of the emancipists. His only work of history, *Statistical, Historical and Political Description of New South Wales*, was first published in 1819 when he was in his late twenties. It called loudly for the establishment of free institutions that would open the gateway both to the political advancement of Wentworth himself and to the full realization of the emancipists' dreams of power, privilege, and wealth in their new country.

Wentworth's views were most strongly opposed by the "pure merinos," the wealthy settlers whose families were free of convict associations. Their leader in the thirties was James Macarthur, of the famous pastoral family. In 1837 he published in London *New South Wales: Its Present State and Future Prospects*, which was intended to influence the new constitution that the Colonial Office was drawing up for New South Wales. He wished to see the Legislative Council enlarged and given more power, but he also wished it to be kept the close preserve of men of his own class, admitting very few of the emancipists. Macarthur genuinely deplored the moral tone of what he thought of as a convict-ridden community, and he asked for improved administration of justice, stricter convict discipline, and more ample provision of schools and churches.

Macarthur was no mere reactionary. The Rev. John Dunmore Lang (1799–1878), a Presbyterian clergyman who later developed radical and republican views, agreed with him pretty well about the state of affairs in New South Wales in 1837. In that year Lang published both a second edition of his *Historical and Statistical Account of New South Wales* and a shorter work entitled *Transportation and Colonisation*. He favored the continuance of the convict system and a reform of the Legislative Council similar to that proposed by Macarthur. Although his sincerity cannot be doubted, Lang had taken up his pen in order to glorify himself as well as to advance his cause. What the *Westminster Review* said about his first edition could be applied fairly enough to the second: "A History of Dr. Lang, to which is added a History of New South Wales."

The point on which Lang, Macarthur, and Wentworth agreed in 1837 was that, in order to win in New South Wales, they had first to win in London. Knowing this, they wrote their works of history and observation for political purposes. They brought intelligence and literary vigor to their task, but they were too propagandist for their contributions to be regarded as good histories of New South Wales.

Their counterpart in Van Diemen's Land was Henry Melville (Wintle—1800–1873), proprietor and editor of the *Colonial Times* newspaper and author of *The History of the Island of Van Diemen's Land, 1824–1835* (1835). "The despotism . . . of the Chief authority is superior to the power of any prince in Christendom," he declared of the powers exercised by Governor George Arthur, whose native policy he thought absurd, his economic policy unwise, and his despotic rule both unjust and unnecessary. "The capability of the Colony to govern itself" was the theme of the book, which was clearly aimed at public opinion in England. Melville wrote it while languishing in Hobart Gaol, where he had been imprisoned for contempt of court. His incarceration was not rigid; the book was founded on official sources and newspapers as well as personal knowledge. It is a valuable contemporary record of how the problems of convictism affected the social, economic, and political growth of the colony. Melville's firm convictions led him into some errors of fact and some highly doubtful interpretations, but his history fully deserves to rank with the better-known works of Wentworth, Macarthur, and Lang.

Fifteen years after Melville's book was published, the convict system was producing the only really serious strain that has ever developed between Britain and Australia. At the height of the struggle over whether Australia should continue to receive British convicts against the wishes of most of the colonists, there appeared the best work of history written in Australia during the nineteenth century. This was the *History of Tasmania* (1852) by the Rev. John West (1809–1873), a Congregationalist minister at Launceston, in Tasmania. The second volume was a careful, but dramatic and utterly damning, survey of the convict system. West joined this magnificent indictment to what is still the best general history of early Tasmania and did so without imperiling the integrity of his scholarship. Only in dealing with the latest years of the convict story did his desire to prove the case for immediate abolition weaken the merits of his history.

200

West wrote with more eloquence than most historians of Australia have commanded. His description of the penal establishment for incorrigibles at Macquarie Harbour on the west coast of Tasmania is famous and not at all exaggerated:

The name of Macquarie Harbour is associated exclusively with remembrance of inexpressible depravity, degradation and woe. Sacred to the genius of torture, Nature concurred with the objects of its separation from the rest of the world to exhibit some notion of a perfect misery. . . . This region is lashed with tempests; the sky is cloudy and the rain falls more frequently than elsewhere. In its chill and humid climate, animal life is preserved with difficulty: half the goats died in one season, and sheep perish: vegetation, except in its coarsest and most massive forms is stunted and precarious. . . . The passage to this dreary dwelling place was tedious and often dangerous. The prisoners, confined in a narrow space, were tossed for weeks on an agitated sea. As they approached they beheld a narrow opening choked with a bar of sand and crossed with peril. This they called Hell's Gate—not less appropriate to the place than to the character and torment of the inhabitants: beyond they saw impenetrable forests, skirted with an impervious thicket; and beyond still enormous mountains covered with snow, which rose to the clouds like walls of adamant: every object wore the air of rigour, ferocity and sadness.

West joined together intellectual distinction, the craftsmanship of a scholar, and an overwhelming sense of mission. In the same year as his book was published the British government ended transportation to eastern Australia. The decision was taken before his powerful work had been received in London.

West was eminent both as historian and as advocate. The same compliment could not justly be paid to John Dunmore Lang, who (also in 1852) published a new book, *Freedom and Independence for the Golden Lands of Australia,* and brought out the third edition of his history of New South Wales. In each his new hatred of convict transportation, his bitter quarrels with the Colonial Office over immigration policy, and his dark suspicion that the British government was delaying the constitutional advance of the Australian colonies in order to keep them as penal settlements overflowed in pleas for independence. Lang looked forward to the time when the colonies would be separated peacefully from Britain and set themselves on the road to federation and national greatness according to the American model. He had visited the United States of

America and became one of its fervent admirers. In New South Wales, however, only a handful of people had any sympathy with his case for independence, except for a very short period at the climax of the movement against convict transportation. Australia has had few prominent advocates of either republicanism or the formal cutting of the ties with Britain, and they have never gained a significant following. The transition from colony to independent nationhood within the Commonwealth of Nations was altogether easier than Lang, preoccupied with the example of the United States, ever brought himself to expect.

The 1850's were a vital decade in Australian history. Convict transportation to eastern Australia ended; Victoria (1851) and Queensland (1859) were established as new colonies; responsible government was granted to all the colonies save Western Australia (founded in 1829) where the population was still very small. Rich discoveries of gold in New South Wales and Victoria brought wealth, population, and, perhaps, some speeding up of the processes by which government became more democratic. By 1859 four Australian colonies possessed manhood suffrage and four had the secret ballot. Political power was less democratically distributed than these institutional changes might suggest, for property still conferred political privilege. Unmistakably, however, the electorate had been greatly enlarged and the colonial legislatures had gained power over almost all internal questions.

Political conditions of this kind no longer encouraged the writing of Australian history. No one except Lang cherished the illusion that a good work of history, or even a cleverly persuasive one, might influence colonial electorates or colonial politicians. Political pamphlets were written, but the writing of history as propaganda very nearly died out for half a century save for Lang's restless pen.

Australia after the gold rushes and the gaining of self-government was so different from Australia before those climactic events that men did not think of the past as relevant to the present. In the decade after the discovery of gold, the population of Australia trebled; in Victoria numbers rose from 80,000 to 500,000. Most of the newcomers were more aware of British history and British politics than they were of Australian history.

Earning a living in a rapidly developing new country left little leisure for serious reading. The convict system, which had survived in eastern Australia down to the eve of responsible government, was a powerful barrier against the sort of "documania," or collecting of records and relics of every kind, that had swept across parts of the United States in the age of Andrew Jackson. The past had too many shameful associations for Australians to wish to recall it. Most of the history written between 1850 and 1880 was intended to interest the British peoples in the Australian colonies as valuable places for investment and immigration; it illuminated the present more than the past; it emphasized the British character of the colonies and was much concerned with how British customs and institutions had been preserved or modified in the antipodes.

The gold rushes naturally stirred up British interest in the wealth and possibilities of the colonies. Samuel Sidney's *Three Colonies of Australia: New South Wales, Victoria, South Australia* (1852) narrated Australian history from the beginnings to the gold discoveries and was intended to be useful to British immigrants. Its history was handbook style.

William Westgarth (1815–1889), first president of the Melbourne Chamber of Commerce, compiled four histories of Victoria. The earliest of them (in 1848) had advocated the separation of the Port Phillip District from New South Wales. In 1853, after separation had been achieved and the gold rushes had begun, he brought out a new version, *Victoria: Late Australia Felix,* which was an almost lyrical success story. Westgarth wanted to lure men and money to Victoria which, he declared, was "furnishing to Britain the envied possession of a second California, perhaps even more productive than the first and already assuming the position . . . of the first of British colonies." His two later books are different in subject matter, but similar in tone and purpose. From the middle fifties to the late eighties Victoria was the wealthiest and most developed of the Australian colonies. Westgarth gladly proclaimed its triumphs.

No such unabashed optimism emanated from New South Wales, where progress was slower than in Victoria and where politics were cantankerous and petty rather than exuberant and radical. Roderick J. Flanagan (1821–1861), a journalist of good standing, produced an industrious chronicle under the title *The History of New South Wales* (1862), adding to it a brief account of the other colonies. Hoping that his work would interest British readers, he set a theme that he did not pursue at all successfully: "The Australian colonies," he wrote in the Preface, "are, more than any other, an off-shoot of Great Britain, and the history of New South Wales is, to a considerable extent, the history of all Australia." His work was published posthumously and without the revisions that he might have planned. Intending to write the first good history of New South Wales since that by Collins, Flanagan labored hard in the official records and the newspapers to produce only a somewhat lifeless chronicle.

British readers found a more interesting work than Flanagan's in the two volumes of *Reminiscences of Thirty Years' Residence in New South Wales and Victoria* (1863) by Mr. Justice Roger Therry (1800–1874). An Irish lawyer who became a judge in Victoria and then in New South Wales, Therry on his retirement wrote a shrewd account of men and affairs in the colonies for the instruction and entertainment of readers in Britain. His observations on squatting, land tenure, the judicial system, the gold rushes, and the political and social history of the colonies were often contentious and always intelligent. There were two editions of his book, both in 1863. Judicial experience had not curbed a powerful flair for pungent characterization. The first edition was withdrawn immediately. The second corrected some errors of fact and modified the severe judgments originally passed on Governors Gipps, LaTrobe, and FitzRoy. Therry did not modify, however, his protest against the vehement prejudices and abusive polemics of his fellow colonist and fellow historian, John Dunmore Lang.

Sidney, Westgarth, Flanagan, and Therry all wrote for a British rather than a colonial public. Much later in the century, after the colonies had gained population and wealth, some of the politicians of Australia began to write history with an eye to local as much as to overseas readers.

One of the first to do so was Boyle Travers Finniss, first premier of South Australia. His *Constitutional History of South Australia* (1886), written during his retirement, was a political chronicle of the colony in which constitutional changes of importance were recorded. Finniss was a long-lived, well-meaning man who relied on memory, private sources, newspapers, and official documents to compile a history that was intended both for wide general reading and to save future historians of a federated Australia from labors in the archives of his colony. He achieved neither objective.

In political outlook, Finniss was a Benthamite who took sides often enough on matters of principle for his reminiscences to have had exceptionally great interest. For example, when reform of the constitution was being discussed in 1852, he had declined to support a property franchise that would have denied the vote to two-thirds of the colonists. In general, he had been quick to perceive the special interests of those who selfishly maneuvered for power in drawing up the new constitution. Unfortunately, he rarely set down what posterity would most like to know about the events in which he participated. The book is less interesting than the man because it excludes the man too much.

The same is certainly not true of *Fifty Years in the Making of Australian History* (1892) by Henry Parkes (1815–1896), the most outstanding and the most bewildering of the politicians of the nineteenth century. Writing at the age of seventy-seven, Parkes saw himself as the major figure in the making of Australian history. His book turned out to be a history of Henry Parkes—and a not very reliable one at that.

Parkes's history is good only where shrewd flashes of his political intuition illuminate some past controversy or junction of forces. Generally, he is better on his early years than on his maturity, where personal vanity obtrudes too much. His most famous judgment is that on the social and political forces that rallied to resist convict transportation in 1848–1852:

Nine out of ten of the immigrant classes had from the first joined the movement against the revival of transportation, and most of the merchants and shopkeepers, and the whole artisan body of the metropolis, gave breadth and force to the wave which in a short time swept all before it. On the one hand were ranged the large country employers—the men who, having obtained free grants of land and free assignments of convict servants, appeared to cherish as the one great end of life the ambition to found families, and, combined with them, the great officials who held their appointments direct from imperial authority in England, with a few aristocratic sympathisers about Sydney. On the other side were united all the independent elements of the population.

The later parts of the book rarely attained discernment to equal this. On publication it was well received in England as the political reminiscences of a distinguished colonial premier; in New South

Wales, where critics were both better informed and less well disposed, it attracted some highly unfavorable comments.

A briefer and more discriminating record of colonial politics was written by one of Parkes's contemporaries, Charles Gavan Duffy, the former Irish rebel who became premier of Victoria. Superior education, wider experience, and some sophistication in the literary graces gave Duffy advantages over Parkes as an author. His autobiography, *My Life in Two Hemispheres* (1898), is a well-written and valuable work on the history of Australia (and Ireland). No doubt it represents Duffy's own services to Victoria in an overly favorable light; it is the work of old age, published when he was in his eighties and living in retirement on the French Riviera. The thoughts that he chose to publish then may not have been the ones that motivated him forty years earlier.

In some ways the most useful parts of Duffy's chapters on Australia are those in which he records his mature impressions of his contemporaries. His description of George Higinbotham, fellow Irishman, fellow lawyer, fellow politician, and fellow advocate of greater colonial independence, is penetrating and might have served for Duffy himself: "A man of ability, principle and integrity, constantly embarrassed by honest prejudices and profoundly erroneous convictions."

W. B. Coote, who was active in Queensland politics for a short period, began a history of that colony that he apparently did not complete. Coote himself was a rolling stone, a journalist and architect, who migrated from England to Tasmania and then found his way north to Queensland. In 1882 he published Volume I of a history of Queensland. It traced the history of the colony down to 1859, when Queensland was separated from New South Wales. Volume II, which was to have covered the first twenty years or so of Queensland politics, was never published. Some chapters of it appeared in the Queensland newspaper *Week* in 1876. Coote was a careful historian, who used the official and published sources conscientiously, adding to them the political talk and reminiscences that he picked up in the colony.

The works of Finniss, Parkes, Duffy, and Coote, although varied in quality and range, are the best of the histories of Australian politics written from the inside during the nineteenth century. The picture that emerges of the contentious, provincially minded politics of the period is unprepossessing. Political history tended to be a dismal record of the "ins" and the "outs."

The absence from politics of more than a few men of first-rate ability and the persistent tendency to enmesh great questions of principle in a tangle of faction and personality were among the reasons for the poor quality of most of the political history written at the time. Between the fifties and the eighties the Australian colonies formulated their policies on such vital matters as constitutional reform, tariff policy, economic development, education, and land policy. But the men who wrote political histories churned out mere chronicles. The events of colonial history were often narrated under the names of successive governors, as if those Lilliputian sovereigns had been responsible for everything that happened in their terms of office. Among the exceptions to the general pattern of dull mediocrity was James Fenton's *History of Tasmania* (1884) which contained some fairly well-integrated political history and at least strove for order and proportion beyond mere chronology.

The most systematic political historian writing in the period was George William Rusden (1819–1903), who had been clerk of the Legislative Council of Victoria until his retirement in 1881. He wrote an ambitious *History of Australia* (1883) that was based on wide use of the sources and on personal knowledge. Rusden took great pains with his researches, and contemporaries were impressed with his learning. Unfortunately, he was inaccurate and tendentious. His three volumes were the most extensive contribution made to Australian history up to that time, but they were strongly prejudiced in favor of the conservative side. So thoroughly did they breathe the spirit of political faction that they have always lacked authority, despite the research on which they were based.

In the 1880's Australia experienced a vast boom. Rapid economic development was matched by a growing belief that in their new country the colonists might evolve a Utopia free from the ancient evils and cramping traditions of the older world. Two-thirds of the colonists had been born in Australia; the immigrant strain no longer predominated. The Australian-born majority sometimes thought that they were discovering for the first time the unique possibilities,

207

economically, politically, and socially, of the vast continent that British imperial policy had confided to their hands. Some of them began to evolve a self-consciously national literature and a national school of landscape painting. The 1880's were a period of optimism, emerging nationalism, bombast, excessive speculation, and incipient collapse.

The working classes began the eighties pretty generally satisfied with society as they found it. By 1890 they were becoming radical. In comparison with the violent conflicts of capital and labor that occurred in the United States about the same time, working-class radicalism in Australia was neither particularly passionate nor apt to make frontal assaults on the existing order of things. But it did have faith to move mountains. British and American influences helped to persuade wage earners that society was not functioning in their interest and that society, therefore, must be changed. The outcome of the "great strikes" and the depression of the nineties was to shake Australian confidence generally and to ease the way for the labor movement in working for reform by legislation.

Some of the early labor leaders wrote history in the service of their movement. W. G. Spence (1846–1926), the union leader and labor parliamentarian, published two works of history, *Australia's Awakening—Thirty Years in the Life of an Australian Agitator* (1909) and *History of the A.W.U.* (1911). The A.W.U. was the Australian Workers' Union, of which Spence was for many years the president. "The mildest-mannered man that ever ran a strike," Spence wrote in order to foster the growth of militant trade-unionism and the labor movement generally. *Australia's Awakening* eulogized the movement. Writing almost twenty years after the event, Spence declared that in 1890 the pastoral employers had "conceived the ambition of wiping out Australian unionism at one blow." But he himself in that year had been prepared to help employers organize themselves so that comprehensive agreements might be reached between masters and men. Even some labor historians have thought that Spence exaggerated the degree of "malice aforethought" on the part of employers and that he depicted the events of 1890 as more of a battleground than they really were.

Before Spence published his second book, George Black, a journalist and member of parliament, had brought out a *History of the*

New South Wales Labor Party (1910), partly founded on his own newspaper articles. It was essentially propaganda, significant mainly as a record of how Labor men thought of their movement. In the year that it appeared, New South Wales first had a Labor government.

The emergence of the labor movement, the growth of unionism, and the turmoil of the nineties were alarming to many Australians. A conservative historian appeared to represent them when Henry Gyles Turner (1831–1920), who had been manager of the Commercial Bank of Australia at the time of the bank crashes, wrote books in his retirement. Turner had always cultivated literary interests, and his *History of the Colony of Victoria* (1904), though full of resentment against his political opponents, was capably written. Turner wrote history to defend and explain the conservative position to the new generation of Victorians. At his best, he revealed the true conservative temper, valuing policies and institutions according to the way they worked and wary of ideas beyond his own experience. At the worst, he was so angry and prejudiced that he could not be either a useful or a convincing guide.

Labor was unenthusiastic about the federation movement, which received its decisive impetus from the depression of the nineties and came to its climax with the inauguration of the Commonwealth of Australia on January 1, 1901. The leaders of labor feared that a federal parliament would be reactionary and that it would find ways of undoing the reforms made by the state legislatures. Federation, so some members of the Labor party suspected, was desired by industrialists because it would provide the necessary political framework for a national market. The concomitant of a national market, they feared, would be the growth of monopolies and trusts, to the detriment of wage earners.

There is as yet no authoritative history of the federation movement in the nineties against which the accuracy of these opinions might be checked. But the beliefs and aspirations of those who led the federation movement are comparatively well known and they do not support the suspicion that federation was a conservative maneuver.

Many of the leaders of the federation movement were men of ability and distinction who recorded their own work and thought in excellent works of history and biography, some not published until much later. *Prosper the Commonwealth*, the gracious and fascinating autobiography of Robert Randolph Garran (1867–1957), solicitor general of Australia from 1917 to 1932, was published posthumously in 1958. Garran had died a little over a year before, when he was almost ninety. As a young man he had been a zealot of the federation cause, closely associated with Edmund Barton, who became the first prime minister of Australia. A large part of his book tells how federation was achieved. It is an unusual story. Australia was not federated because of any pressing external threat, such as war, nor any desire to promote independence of Britain. There were not even any urgent national problems of such magnitude that the dullest elector would be aware of them. There were economic and social arguments and defense arguments and administrative and political arguments in favor of federal union; there was also a powerful and well-reasoned case against federation. Garran's book records with much good humor and anecdote the labors of the men who worked like missionaries for federation because they believed in it with the dedicated faith of national vision.

In 1901 Garran collaborated with another zealot of federation, Sir John Quick, in publishing that monumental tome, *The Annotated Constitution of the Australian Commonwealth*, a remarkable record of the learning with which the federationists argued their case. Today it reads like a lawyer's introduction to the new constitution, commenting on it section by section and discussing American and other precedents with a wealth of detail.

The most perceptive of the political accounts of the federation movements written at the time was undoubtedly Alfred Deakin's *The Federal Story*, completed in 1900 and published in 1944. Deakin (1856–1919), three times prime minister of Australia, was one of the great intellects and orators of the federation movement. He was also a fine narrator with a keen sense of history. His first political experiences were in Victoria, and in 1900 he wrote a memoir of four eventful years in those times. Professors J. A. La Nauze and R. M. Crawford published it in 1957 as *The Crisis in Victorian Politics, 1879–1881*. Like the memoir on federation, it was intended to be material for historians in the future.

Deakin's work for federation in Victoria has been compared with the achievements in New South Wales of Edmund Barton. Deakin's record has the greater excellence, but in justice to Barton it must be remembered that he had the harder row to hoe. The special problems of the politicians of New South Wales, who resented the long-continued bumptiousness of Victoria in intercolonial matters and found differences over tariff policy a severe obstacle to federation, were a leading theme of B. R. Wise's *The Making of the Australian Commonwealth* (1913). A man of intellect and character, Wise thought that federation was more important than the rights and wrongs of tariff policy. His vehement prejudices against Sir George Reid, the free-trading premier of New South Wales from 1894 to 1899, are clearly exhibited in this book. Staunch federalists like Wise regarded Reid as fundamentally unsound on the great question; Reid's famous "Yes-No" speech of March 28, 1898, in which he declined to advise his followers about federation, was long quoted against him by those who had borne the brunt of the struggle.

Reid lived to become prime minister of Australia and later Australian high commissioner in the United Kingdom. His own good-tempered account of these affairs in *My Reminscences* (1917), treated his services to federation as though they had been consistent, purposive, and successful. In this respect, Reid has convinced a smaller portion of posterity than has Parkes, whose *Fifty Years in the Making of Australian History* contains a chapter on federation that has been accepted by his admirers as a just appraisal of his work for the cause.

Most of the Australian history written before the First World War was at least partly contemporary history. Most of it was the work of men who had shared in some of the events that they described. A very large proportion was either partisan or not much above the level of chronicle.

No historian seems to have been affected by the optimism of the eighties, although that decade might have been thought likely to stimulate belief in progress. The literary ebullitions of the late nineteenth century have no parallels in the writing of serious history. While the *Bulletin* was conscientiously striving to found an Australian literature, Australian historians were indifferent to nationalist sentiment. History in the eighties was written mainly by chroniclers or by politically minded observers—like Rusden—who looked

211

askance at the belief that Australia was a unique country where men would solve the social, economic, and political problems that had bewildered older nations. The truth about the relationship between Australian society and the literature and history of the eighties has still to be determined. The conspicuous lack of nationalist feeling in the early federation movements suggests that the historians were better identified with Australians as a whole than were the artists and creative writers. The noisy optimists declared that Australians would build a new Jerusalem, but the majority of their countrymen still assumed European superiority in anything that counted.

Before the twentieth century Australians lacked a firm conviction that the history of their own country was significant enough to justify sustained intellectual inquiry. Australia, in the words of Professor Douglas Pike, the author of its latest general history, has been the "quiet continent," untroubled by revolutions or civil wars and for much of its history small in population and highly conscious of imperial ties to Britain. It has not been either difficult or unreasonable for sensible men to believe that nothing happened in Australian history that did not happen more significantly elsewhere. There was not even any reason to believe that a knowledge of Australian history would help to solve Australian problems. Australia changed so much and so rapidly between 1851 and 1901 that a view of the past extending beyond five or ten years was liable to seem antiquarian.

Visitors to Australia had been reaching conclusions very different from these for some thirty years or more before the Australians themselves came to believe that their history might be significant. Anthony Trollope's *Australia and New Zealand* (1873), a shrewd and well-informed survey, was the best of several visitors' accounts published about that time.

The political and social experiments conducted in Australia from the eighties onward aroused discerning interest among observers overseas. W. Pember Reeves of New Zealand, a politician and an economist, wrote *State Experiments in Australia and New Zealand* (1902). This referred especially to social and industrial legislation and summed up incisively the experiences of both countries. Reeves was a firm believer in the compulsory arbitration of industrial disputes and introduced legislation to that end in New Zealand. A

French work, *Le Socialisme sans doctrines: La Question agraire et
la question ouvrière en Australie et Nouvelle-Zélande* (1901), by
A. Métin still stands as a perceptive and significant study of Australian attempts to legislate for economic equality along economic development. Like Reeves, Métin stressed the absence of doctrine in
the Australian labor movement. The American academic, V. S. Clark,
made a similar observation in his *Labor Movement in Australasia;
A Study in Social Democracy* (1906). There he shrewdly noted
that the Labor party had settled down to a course that was "liberal-
labor" rather than "socialist-labor." C. D. Allin, a Canadian-born
scholar who taught in the United States, was keenly interested in
the origins of Australian federalism. His *Early Federation Movement of Australia* (1907) was the first and until 1958 the only detailed account [2] of the abortive federation movements of 1846–1860.
In 1918 and 1929 Allin published useful works on Australian tariff
history which illuminated many of the controversies in the federation movements. His books were rather dull and suffered from a lack
of local knowledge, but they were founded on extensive research
and strikingly indicated the growth of overseas interest in Australian
history.

The colonial period in the writing of Australian history, which
these overseas writers helped to end, lingered on well into the twentieth century. While it lasted, most of the history written about
Australia was intended to influence British attitudes toward Australia
or to promote some political cause or ambition. Some of it, admittedly, had high scholarly standards. West was certainly conscious
of important intellectual affinities with Britain and the United States.
But even he wrote in order to change a policy and was as much in
the tradition of Wentworth, Macarthur, and Lang as of the great
overseas historians to whom he owed part of his inspiration.

The significance of the overseas contributors to historical writing
at about the beginning of the twentieth century was that they
demonstrated that Australian history and Australian institutions were
worthy of serious study for their own sake. In this way the works
of foreigners helped to begin the professional revolution that ended
the colonial period in the writing of Australian history and intro-

[2] See now J. M. Ward, *Earl Grey and the Australian Colonies, 1846–1857*
(Melbourne: Melbourne University Press, 1958).

213

duced standards, methods, and conceptions of inquiry resembling some of the scholarly history being written in other English-speaking countries.

While overseas writers were showing that Australian history could reward scholarly notice, great national events were stirring interest in Australian achievements. The financial and industrial troubles of the nineties, followed by Federation and the tremendous events of the First World War (in which Australia exerted all her strength and first attained a clear conviction of nationhood), all made Australian history seem more important than ever before.

Over the same period better formal provision was made for studying the nation's past. The universities established chairs of history. The sources were thrown open to research more extensively than before. Slowly, and with many false starts, historical societies were formed in one state after another to collect materials and help publish the results of research into Australian history.

In 1890 Sydney, the oldest of the Australian universities, established the Challis Chair of History. The next year it appointed George Arnold Wood (1865–1928), a young graduate of Oxford, to the new chair and so made him the first full-time professor of history in an Australian university. He remained in the chair until his death in 1928, writing relatively little but spreading his influence through his teaching and personal encouragement of research work. Late in life he published two books in Australian history, *The Discovery of Australia* (1922) and *The Voyage of the* Endeavour (1926), which narrated the story of Captain Cook's expedition on which the eastern coast of Australia was discovered in 1770. Wood planned a history of early New South Wales, but did not live to complete it. Only his articles in the *Journal and Proceedings of the Royal Australian Historical Society* survive as a published record of these researches.

No other professor so far has written quite so much Australian history as did Sir Ernest Scott (1867–1939), foundation professor of history in the University of Melbourne from 1913 to 1936. Scott was not a university graduate, but a journalist turned Hansard reporter whose writings won academic recognition. A man of wide culture, he possessed powers of inspiration and encouragement that

214

made his influence powerful in the study of Australian history. A significant proportion of the professors of history in Australian universities have been his students or students of his students. Of the ten books that Scott himself wrote, three testify to his deep interest in the history of Australian discovery and exploration.

Scott was Dominion advisor for the Australian volume of the *Cambridge History of the British Empire* (1933). This was a successful volume, summing up the main outlines of Australian history with a very sure touch. Much of it has not been replaced by any later treatment. Scott himself contributed several able chapters on early Australian history, exploration, and political conditions during the First World War. They are the most permanently useful of his writings in Australian history; in them his ability to sketch developments as a whole, leaving the more detailed researches of others to illuminate the details, had full play.

Most of the contributors to the *Cambridge History* volume probably wrote their chapters about the end of the 1920's. So substantial a study, founded on so much original research of lasting value, would not have been possible when Scott was appointed in 1913 and would have been almost inconceivable when Wood came to his chair in 1891. What the *Cambridge History* proved was that two of the lions in the path of Australian historical writing had been subdued rather effectively: the problem of sources and the problem of interesting historians in Australia's past.

The problem of the sources was solved in London before it was solved in Australia. The rich sources for Australian history in the Public Record Office and the government departments in London, in the papers of British statesmen, and in the great private collections were available (within limits) before there were Australian scholars to use them.

The sources in Great Britain were so much better preserved and better arranged than those in Australia that there was an early start to the long tradition of going overseas to write Australian history. Two graduates of the University of Melbourne, both before Scott's time, set the precedent. Marion Phillips (1881–1932) in 1909 published a pioneer study called *A Colonial Autocracy—New South Wales under Governor Macquarie*. In some ways it is still the best guide to Macquarie's economic policy. Six years later, R. C. Mills

215

(1886–1952), a law graduate, published *The Colonization of Australia (1829–42): The Wakefield Experiment in Empire Building*. This was a good, though too generous, account of the ideas of Edward Gibbon Wakefield, the most systematic of the English "colonial reformers," and of the importance of those ideas in the colonization of Australia.

Before Dr. Phillips had pioneered the professional revolution in the writing of Australian history, the government of New South Wales had attempted to solve the problem of the sources. The approach of the colony's first centenary stimulated interest in its past. Naturally, the government wished to have, for use in Australia, the excellent materials available in England. In 1887 the premier of New South Wales, Henry Parkes, appointed as government archivist James Bonwick (1817–1906), a schoolmaster, who had published some history and had a passion for using the sources. Bonwick was sent to London to transcribe the documents relevant to Australian history for the period 1769–1830. He was employed for nearly fifteen years, working on the records of British departments that had administered Australian affairs.

Bonwick's transcripts were a major influence on Australian historical writing. Although he was not a trained archivist in the modern sense, he had a good sense of values and genuine zeal. What he made available directed the attention of historians to the beginnings of Australian history and demonstrated the richness of the fields that awaited their reapers.

On Bonwick's labors was founded the *History of New South Wales from the Records* (1889–1892) by G. B. Barton and A. Britton. In 1891, when Wood was appointed Challis Professor of History, the government set up a History Board of which he was a member. It reported on the Barton project and recommended that the records themselves, not merely commentaries and extracts, should be published. As a result, the government of New South Wales published between 1893 and 1901 seven volumes of *Historical Records of New South Wales*, largely drawn from the Bonwick transcripts. Edited by F. M. Bladen, they covered only the period to 1811. The work stopped, apparently because the Hon. John Perry, minister of public instruction in the Lyne and See governments, feared that the zeal of the historians would overstrain the Treasury.

Bonwick's transcripts were used also for part of *Historical Records of Australia*, thirty-three volumes of which were published between 1914 and 1925 by the Library Committee of the Commonwealth parliament. Under the editorship of Dr. Frederick Watson, this was planned as a large venture in several series, to cover the whole of Australian history. Work ceased in 1925 with the project incomplete.

Although historians have criticized the selection of the documents used in *Historical Records of Australia*, there have been several moves to have publication resumed, perhaps on an amended basis. The prospects do not seem bright, at least until the present project [3] of microfilming all the sources of Australian history outside Australia has been completed.

The most important event in the bettering of conditions for the systematic study of Australian history was the opening of the Mitchell Library in Sydney in 1910. David Scott Mitchell was a collector endowed with scholarship, perseverance, and money. He brought together an incomparable collection of printed, manuscript, and pictorial materials relating to Australia, the South Pacific, and Antarctica. He gave it all, together with an endowment, to the trustees of the Public Library of New South Wales on condition that it be housed in a distinct wing of a national library, "quite separate in itself, but forming an integral part of the whole." The Mitchell Library is still the best single collection of material for the student of Australian history.

How many other benefactions throughout Australia have been inspired by the fruitful partnership of Mitchell and the library trustees in New South Wales is impossible to say. It is certain that the late Sir William Dixson was moved at least partly by what Mitchell had done to become a great benefactor himself. The William Dixson Galleries of historic pictures and the Dixson Library of books, manuscripts, and other materials now form (like the Mitchell Library) a most important special collection within the Public Library of New South Wales.

The opening of the sources to scholarly investigation and the beginnings of university interest in Australian history together brought about the professional revolution. Since the second decade of this century most of the notable contributions to the writing of

[3] Australian Joint Copying Scheme for Copying Australian Records Abroad.

Australian history have come from academic historians or from historians following the same standards.

Bonwick's transcripts, the printed records, the range of interest in some of the great collections, and a natural desire to begin at the beginning led many historians during the first stages of the professional revolution to write about the founding of the Australian colonies. Consider the historians already mentioned: Wood wrote about discovery and the early history of New South Wales; Scott was first a historian of exploration and discovery; Mills had chapters in his book on the founding of Western Australia and of South Australia; Marion Phillips chose a subject from the early history of New South Wales.

The trend continued. Dr. A. Grenfell Price published *The Foundation and Settlement of South Australia* (1924) and *Founders and Pioneers of South Australia* (1929). Dr. J. S. Battye, principal librarian of the Public Library in Perth, used the collections of which he had charge to write *Western Australia: A History from Its Discovery to the Inauguration of the Commonwealth* (1924). His interests were in discovery and foundations rather than in later developments; the book is still the best general history of early Western Australia. R. W. Giblin, author of *The Early History of Tasmania* (1928 and 1939), planned a three-volume history of Tasmania to the ending of convict transportation. Death interrupted him, and the second volume was published posthumously. Giblin was a careful scholar, and he cast his net particularly wide in searching both for material and for the factors that had shaped Tasmanian history.

In the 1930's two historians, who owed part of their training and inspiration to Wood, contributed significantly to the history of early New South Wales. They were Eris O'Brien and George Mackaness.

Eris O'Brien, now Roman Catholic Archbishop of Canberra and Goulburn, devoted his early books to the history of his church. *The Foundation of Catholicism in Australia* (1922) and *The Dawn of Catholicism in Australia* (1928) are both works of authority. In 1937 he published what is still the most important work on the establishment of New South Wales, *The Foundation of Australia, 1786–1800: A Study in Penal Colonisation*. In it he traced the origins

218

of the settlement in New South Wales to their roots in the British social system and the British penology of the eighteenth century. The second part of the book surveyed the operation of the system during the first twelve years of New South Wales history. O'Brien showed how the difficulties and weaknesses of the system were allowed to continue with little attempt at remedy. The convict problem continued in 1800 very much as it had when the colony was founded. Neither the convicts nor the methods of transportation were reformed.

George Mackaness (b. 1882), who was head of the Department of English in the Sydney Teachers College from 1924 to 1946, has contributed extensively to both literary and historical scholarship in Australia and is well known as an active editor and collector of Australiana. His major historical writings belong to the thirties. They commemorate three of the men who played important roles in New South Wales. His *The Life of Vice-Admiral Sir William Bligh* (1931) had an American edition in 1933 and a revised Australian edition in 1951. Mackaness planned a thorough and impartial study of a stormy and tempestuous career. Bligh suffered two famous revolts against his authority—the mutiny on the *Bounty* and the Rum Rebellion of 1808 when he was governor of New South Wales. The book set out the cases for and against Bligh and summed up strongly in his favor in both the mutiny and the rebellion. The concluding chapter exonerated Bligh from most of the personal charges brought against him and honored him as a conscientious officer, a fine seaman, a man of high ability and courage. Not all historians have found the case for Bligh so strong as Mackaness did.

In 1936 Mackaness published *Sir Joseph Banks, His Relations with Australia*. Banks, a wealthy amateur who was president of the Royal Society, had accompanied Cook on the *Endeavour* voyage during which the east coast of Australia was discovered. This experience early in life, together with his private fortune, strong character, and keen interest in Australia, made him the supreme unofficial arbiter in Britain of the destinies of New South Wales. Authority took his advice frequently. Mackaness' book, which is closely founded on various collections of Banks's papers, brought together a great deal of useful information.

A year after the appearance of *Banks*, Mackaness returned to biography again with *The Life of Admiral Arthur Phillip, R.N., Founder and First Governor of New South Wales* (1937). "In Australian history," he wrote in the Introduction, "Cook the discoverer will ever stand first, with Banks second. Phillip the founder must come next, with Macquarie the builder fourth in the hierarchy." Mackaness wished to ensure Phillip "a fame equal to that enjoyed by the other three." So far, nobody has challenged his very favorable verdict on Phillip.

While some historians explored the fascinations of early Australian history, others looked for the significant themes that would be fundamental to understanding the course of Australian history. Foremost among these was S. H. Roberts (b. 1901), one of Scott's students, who was Challis Professor of History in the University of Sydney from 1929 to 1947.[4] Roberts perceived the importance of land settlement as a key factor in Australian development. He planned his *History of Australian Land Settlement, 1788–1920* (1924) to reveal the main elements in a long and complicated story and so blaze the way for others to follow with more leisurely and detailed researches. So far, the work as a whole has not been replaced, although modifications of Roberts' views have been suggested.

Roberts returned to the theme of land settlement in 1935, when he published *The Squatting Age in Australia, 1835–47*. The best known of his many contributions to Australian history, this is a vivid and fascinating account of the life of the early pastoralists. The background of social, economic, and political conditions in New South Wales was depicted from the squatters' point of view. Roberts prefaced the book with a statement that it was a "preliminary monograph on a neglected period in Australian history." The period is no longer neglected, but the book stands as the best record of how the squatters lived and what they thought of themselves. There is reason to hope that Roberts may return to the writing of Australian history with another study of the social aspects of land settlement.

Roberts chose land settlement as the major theme of his research in Australian history both because of its importance and because so much of Australian land history has been unique. Myra Willard, one of Wood's students, chose a less massive but equally distinctive

[4] Now vice-chancellor and principal, University of Sydney.

theme when in 1919 she embarked on a study of free immigration. Her *History of the White Australia Policy* (1923), the first book published by Melbourne University Press, was part of her original study. Wood thought it "the best historical account of the central Australian idea." Miss Willard's account of how a new, small nation planned to keep a whole continent for itself as a free, white, and predominantly British country is still of the first importance.

Immigration, though almost as vital in Australian history as in American history, was slow to attract historians. The only other considerable work published on the subject before the Second World War was R. B. Madgwick's *Immigration into Eastern Australia, 1788–1851* (1935), which is particularly useful for the record of British official policy.

A theme that did attract considerable attention during the twenties and thirties was constitutional development. The record of how despotic institutions of the penal colonies gave way to self-government and of how the self-governing colonies were federated and emerged as independent members of the Commonwealth of Nations has fascinated many historians. The first task was to assemble the details of a story that was known only in the vaguest outline. Quick, Garran, Allin, and others, as we have seen, laid the foundations with their work on the history of the federation movements. E. V. Sweetman published two pioneering works in *The Constitutional Development of Victoria, 1851–56* (1920) and *Australian Constitutional Development* (1925). Both were useful surveys, but were narrow in approach.

The *Cambridge History of the British Empire* in this, as in so many other matters, first established the main pattern of the story. It contained excellent constitutional chapters by Associate Professor A. C. V. Melbourne of the University of Queensland, K. H. Bailey, then professor of public law in the University of Melbourne, Sir Robert Garran, and Sir Harrison Moore, formerly of the University of Melbourne. Together, these authors established a framework within which constitutional historians may still work to their satisfaction.

In 1934 Professor Melbourne published *Early Constitutional Development in Australia. New South Wales, 1788–1856*, intended as the first volume of a trilogy on the subject up to the beginnings of

221

responsible government. The remaining volumes did not appear, perhaps because Melbourne's interests shifted to the Far East. The work that he did accomplish in Australian constitutional history was eminently useful. As thorough a scholar as ever labored in the Public Record Office, Melbourne did as well as almost any scholar working alone thirty years ago could hope to do. Although he did not probe to the roots of the constitutional story, he did recognize that colonial politics and colonial economic and social changes, together with the course of British imperial policy, had all been important in fixing the pace and direction of constitutional change. He was not able to relate these elements sufficiently to one another and he altogether underestimated the significance of administrative history. Nevertheless, his work will stand as the best authority on the subject until there have been satisfactory assessments of colonial politics and administration and until imperial historians cease to be mesmerized by the famous report of Lord Durham in 1839 on British North America. Melbourne naturally had no exciting conclusions to present in 1934, and his work made little impact on his contemporaries. Few of them troubled to buy it. Most of the copies printed were destroyed by enemy action during the Second World War, so that this important book has become a rarity.

Much less academic than the pioneering studies just mentioned, but equally concerned with significant themes in Australian development, were the histories published for the Workers' Educational Association. The universities joined with this Association in providing tutorial classes for the general public. In this work they encountered a thirst for knowledge of Australian history, more particularly economic and social history and the Australian attempts to change economic and social conditions by legislation. None of the existing books slaked the thirst, and the Association commenced to publish on its own account; some of the books that it sponsored were partly historical.

The most famous was *A New Province for Law and Order* (1922), written by Mr. Justice H. B. Higgins, a High Court judge, who for fourteen years had been president of the Commonwealth Court of Conciliation and Arbitration. The book expounded eloquently the philosophy of industrial relations that had guided Higgins in his work as an industrial judge. He had sought to substitute for wage bargaining between employers and employees a system of reasoned awards of wages that would give men "certainty that their essential material needs will be met by honest work, and . . . release infinite stores of human energy for higher efforts, for nobler ideals."

Another important work in the same series was *History of Trade Unionism in Australia* (1921) by J. T. Sutcliffe, the director of the industrial and labor branch of the Commonwealth Bureau of Statistics. It is impartial, but neither detailed nor profound. No one has replaced it yet.

Sutcliffe's general ideas about labor and unionism were similar to those of Métin, Clark, and Pember Reeves. All four regarded the Australian labor movement as a means of orderly progress toward the welfare state. A more militant point of view was powerfully urged from the left wing when V. Gordon Childe [5] wrote *How Labour Governs* (1923). Disillusioned with the Australian Labor party, Childe, a Marxist, opposed the liberal-labor policies that in his eyes had beguiled the movement away from its correct objectives. His book is revealing about the tensions in the Labor party.

Dr. H. V. Evatt (b. 1894), lately Chief Justice of New South Wales, was a judge of the High Court of Australia when he made his principal contributions to the writing of Australian history. A former Labor member of the Legislative Assembly of New South Wales and later a prominent member of Australia's Labor government during the Second World War, Evatt wrote works of history and law that touched on two significant themes in Australian history. These were the relations between British law and Australian development and the emergency of the labor movement.

The King and His Dominion Governors: A Study of the Reserve Powers of the Crown in Great Britain and the Dominions (1936) was almost as interesting to historians as to lawyers. Some of its chapters referred at length to critical events in Australian constitutional development, such as the dismissal of J. T. Lang, Labor premier of New South Wales, by Governor Sir Phillip Game in

[5] The famous archaeologist, author of *The Dawn of European Civilisation* (1925), *Man Makes Himself* (1937), and many other works. An Australian, Childe held a chair at the University of Edinburgh from 1927 to 1946 and at the University of London from 1946 to 1956. He met his death in tragic circumstances while visiting Australia in 1958.

1932. *Injustice within the Law: A Study of the Case of the Dorchester Labourers* (1937) discussed the famous Tolpuddle martyrs, condemned in 1834 to transportation to Australia for having formed a union. Their crime lay in the secret oaths and ritual of their organization. *Rum Rebellion: A study of the Overthrow of Governor Bligh by John Macarthur and the New South Wales Corps* (1938) analyzed the significant court cases of the Bligh period and suggested several new points to consider in understanding the rebellion. Like Mackaness, Evatt summed up strongly in favor of Governor Bligh.

His next book in Australian history took him away from the early period and reflected his deep interest in the Australian Labor party. *Australian Labour Leader: The Story of W. A. Holman and the Labour Movement* (1940) traced the career of one of the founders of the Labor party, who was premier of New South Wales from 1913 to 1920. Evatt's treatment was sensitive to the problems of leadership in the Labor party but was not definitive on either Holman or labor.

Scholarly assessments of the whole course of Australian history, as distinct from monographs and attempts to explore particular themes, were slow to appear. Historians do not usually relish large-scale guesswork, and they had to await the results of fundamental researches.

The first academic study of the whole of Australian history was Scott's *Short History of Australia* (1916), orderly and coherent, but not really interpretative. Two years afterwards, Sir Timothy Augustine Coghlan, the agent-general of New South Wales in London, published his monumental study, *Labour and Industry in Australia from the First Settlement in 1788 to the Establishment of the Commonwealth in 1901*. Despite its errors and misinterpretations, this book was certainly a useful study of economic and social developments in the nineteenth century. But it was not in any sense a key to the understanding of Australian history. Moreover, Coghlan, whose researches were almost certainly extensive, wrote without footnotes or other apparatus to disclose his sources, so that his massively detailed account has to be treated with special caution.

At the end of the 1920's there were three memorable attempts to survey Australian history as a whole. The Australian volume of the *Cambridge History of the British Empire* (not published until 1933) has already been mentioned. The other two were W. Keith Hancock's *Australia* (1930) and E. O. G. Shann's *An Economic History of Australia* (1930).

Hancock's book turned out to be one of the most influential studies of Australian development. Belonging to H. A. L. Fisher's series "The Modern World," which surveyed political, economic, and social tendencies in several countries, it was only in part formally historical. It contained so many general ideas about Australia that other historians have often been content to follow up the hints and hypotheses that Hancock threw out in profusion.

Writing over thirty years ago, Hancock stressed the themes of nationalism and democracy in Australian history. He thought that both had had their beginnings before the gold rushes of the 1850's. Moreover, nationalism and democracy in Australia, he considered, had been closely associated with one another. "Australian nationalism took definite form in the class struggle between the landless majority and the land-monopolizing squatters." The landless had felt themselves to be liberty-loving Australians, rooted to their country, long before the richer classes had given up thinking of themselves as mere temporary settlers who would go home to England when they had made their fortunes. "It would, nevertheless," Hancock warned, "be erroneous to dismiss Australian nationalism as nothing more than an aspect of Australian democracy." Pride of (British) race, love of country, and a vaunting colonial ambition to see Australia rule the whole South Pacific were also among its roots. He recognized that the protests against British rule and the British connection had rarely been important in stimulating nationalism in Australia. The colonists had become "independent Australian Britons" almost without a struggle. "Since the Mother-Country was so placid, so impotent, what occasion was there for that mutinous defiance proper to adolescent, independent daughters? The posture of rebellion would be ridiculous."

Hancock showed that Australians had soon convinced themselves that the state was "a vast public utility, whose duty it is to provide the greatest happiness for the greatest numbers." Although he recognized that the political parties did not differ much among themselves on this principle, he found reasons for contrasting the Labor party

225

with what he called the "parties of resistance." When Australia was entering the depression and bright hopes of economic and social betterment had been dashed, he suggested that "perhaps the auguries will brighten once more for Labour and for democracy when they begin to understand that their triumph is not predestined."

Hancock's task was to explain the tendencies of Australian development as he saw them. Shann's book was designed, he advised in the Introduction, to "keep in the forefront the private activities by which British settlers in Australia have transformed a prison-yard and hunting-ground of savages into a productive annexe to Europe and Asia." Many of the tendencies that Hancock elucidated Shann forthrightly condemned. He looked unfavorably on the growth in Australia of governmental participation in business. He disapproved of the protective tariff. He suspected that the economic activities of the state were being manipulated by private interests for their own profit. Shann was a liberal free trader of the old school who denounced what he disliked.

As a historian, he had the vital gifts of integrity, style, and vision, but not of deep learning nor of profound research. His best chapters were those in which straightforward narrative raced easily ahead, as when he wrote on pastoral pioneering or the gold rushes or the land boom. Both his *Economic History* and his smaller study *Cattle Chosen* (1926), a history of early settlement written from a set of family papers, are still widely read. His political preferences were stated so honestly that his conclusions are referred to again and again by those who seek a corrective to the equally strong political views of left-wing historians.

The works of Brian Fitzpatrick differed radically in outlook from others that attempted to sum up the course of Australian history. Fitzpatrick wrote under the impact of the great depression of the 1930's. It determined his approach; it sharpened his political convictions. A graduate of the University of Melbourne, he published two major studies of Australian economic history—*British Imperialism and Australia, 1783–1833* (1939) and *The British Empire in Australia: An Economic History 1834–1939* (1941). Between these important books he brought out *A Short History of the Australian Labor Movement* (1940). The Introduction to this book contains a statement fundamental to understanding the position from which Fitzpatrick writes history. In Australia, he declared, there has been a "struggle between the organized rich and the organized poor" for political and economic power that both sides wish to seize and exercise in their own interests. "I suppose," he added, "no sensible person, whether of the Right or the Left, will quarrel with me on that score." How many historians does he regard as "sensible"?

Fitzpatrick's political principles have been clear and consistent throughout all his writings. His economic histories were the first significant application to Australia's past of a left-wing interpretation of history. *British Imperialism and Australia* asserted that the British government had intended from the first that New South Wales should be both a penal colony and a peasant-proprietor colony. It was established in order to receive the "redundant poor" of Great Britain, whether convicts or not. British policy varied afterwards according to the economic and social needs pressing on the imperial authorities in London and took regard of local conditions only when the emergency of the pastoral economy offered the British splendid opportunities of investment and wealthy immigration in addition to the pouring out of convicts and paupers. *The British Empire in Australia* concluded that state policy throughout Australian history had always been to help capital, "including much English capital," to earn a high average dividend. "The reservoir of Australian labour and industry," wrote Fitzpatrick, "has never failed to provide a stream tributary to the broad river of English wealth."

Fitzpatrick's analysis was partly in terms of class interests, and his books were vigorously argued. It is not surprising that some of his conclusions have been treated as controversial even when they contain much with which nearly all historians would agree. A. G. L. Shaw, whose own *Economic Development of Australia* (1944) steered a middle course between the opposing views of Shann and Fitzpatrick, mildly described Fitzpatrick's histories as "somewhat partisan in outlook." Shaw gave him full credit for the extent of his researches and the significance of his contribution to Australian economic history. S. J. Butlin, whose *Foundations of the Australian Monetary System* (1953) pointed to errors in Fitzpatrick's major works, and who disagreed with many of his interpretations, concluded nevertheless that "his two volumes are the most substantial economic history of Australia yet available."

Writing in the *Journal and Proceedings* of the Royal Australian Historical Society in 1945, Eris O'Brien claimed that "the contemporary may justly be described as the scientific period in Australian historical writing . . . a period which, I believe, reaches maturity in the publication of the Ferguson *Bibliography*." Sir John Ferguson's *Bibliography of Australia*, which O'Brien praised so highly, was a project of the first importance begun many years before. While still a judge of the Industrial Commission of New South Wales, Mr. Justice Ferguson, as he then was, undertook the tremendous labor of compiling a bibliography of every publication relating to Australia printed anywhere in the world and also of every imprint made in Australia. The first volume, covering the formative years of 1784–1838, was planned to be ready for the sesquicentenary of Australia in 1938, but was not published until 1941. It was modeled on Evans' well-known *American Bibliography* and Hocken's *Bibliography of the Literature Relating to New Zealand*. Sir John Ferguson, as he now is, has brought his erudite work down to 1850 in four volumes. For the period from 1850 to 1900 the work will be selective. Historians of Australia are deeply indebted to his dedicated scholarship.

O'Brien welcomed [6] Ferguson's second volume as evidence that the new trends in Australian historical writing had come to stay. He traced Australian historiography from Collins and Tench to Scott, Wood, Roberts, Melbourne, and their scholarly contemporaries. He welcomed what he called the new "scientific" (or academic) history and noted how well its precision and standards were served by the researches of Ferguson. He referred also to the foundation of a new journal with high scholarly aims. This was *Historical Studies Australia and New Zealand*, which had been launched successfully by the University of Melbourne in the early part of the Second World War.

By "maturity" O'Brien meant ripeness of scholarship. He was correct in thinking that by 1945 good academic standards had been

[6] E. O'Brien, "Maturity in Australian Historical Scholarship," *Journal and Proceedings of the Royal Australian Historical Society*, XXXI (1945), 154 ff.

firmly established in the writing of Australian history. He would also have been right if he had said that Australian historians were well on the way to establishing their own traditions, discovering the distinctive elements in their country's history, and not being content merely to find in it the patterns of development that had been observed in other lands.

Perhaps the Australians had already gone too far in that direction and become too conscious of the unique elements in Australian history to be able to learn, for example, from the progress made in interpreting the American or the Canadian past. Certainly, it was not easy for Australian historians to profit from the work of scholars in other countries whose histories had comparable features. So many vast tracts of Australian history had still not been explored, or had been pioneered only roughly, that comparisons with developments elsewhere could not be well enough founded to satisfy a scholar's conscience. Most of the good books published before 1945 were the first substantial contributions in the fields to which they were devoted.

Since the Second World War, Australians have awakened to the fascination of their own past. More works of Australian history have been published since 1945 than ever before. The professional revolution has continued. The universities have accepted Australian history as a respectable academic subject for undergraduates and have set hundreds of graduate students to work on research in Australian history. The neighboring social sciences—such as economics, politics, and law—have often been historically minded. Scholars trained primarily as economists or as political scientists have made some of the most significant contributions to Australian history in the last ten years.

The academic standards of the professionals have influenced most historical writing, but have not set the pace along the whole of the moving frontiers of knowledge. A strong sense of nationhood, coupled with the excitement of a period of rapid economic growth, has produced an insatiable public appetite for all sorts of Australian history. Scholarly monographs, local histories, schoolbooks, reprints of valuable family papers, and lurid accounts of notorious episodes and periods have abounded.

Unfortunately, the standards of academic reviewing have not

been as firm or as steady as they should have been. Probably because so many parts of Australian history are not well known, reviewers have tended to overpraise books that were merely useful or painstakingly recondite. Similarly, they have been constrained by their own ignorance to assess the significance of new work in only vague, general terms. Sometimes they have missed the main themes of scholarly works and merely picked the bones that they could identify. There are, however, signs that these defects will be remedied as greater numbers of competent scholars enter the various fields of Australian history. Really learned reviewing, which is the just desert of the many good books published, may be the general rule before the end of the 1960's.

Help in surmounting the perils of ignorance is now forthcoming to a degree that would have amazed the pioneers in the prewar days. The Social Science Research Council of Australia and the Australian Humanities Research Council have powerfully encouraged the writing of Australian history. The universities have helped with grants for research by their staffs. Library facilities have improved tremendously, a notable development being the growth of the Australian National Library in Canberra. Bibliography has flourished as never before.

Generally, throughout Australia the position of the public archives is now better than it has ever been, with the Commonwealth and all the states taking an active interest. The losses and depredations of the past cannot be made good, however, and constant vigilance is needed now to ensure that records are preserved, organized properly, and made available to historians. Business archives are becoming available also. Corporations have their own preferences in approving repositories for their records. At present, most of the principal research libraries, the Business Archives Council, and several of the archives departments in the universities are all reporting accessions of valuable business records.

Several new journals have been founded since the war. Professor Gordon Greenwood of the University of Queensland was the moving spirit behind the foundation of the *Australian Journal of Politics and History* in 1955; it has already acquired a considerable standing both in Australia and overseas. B. E. Mansfield and some of his colleagues in the History Department of the University of Sydney took the lead in forming an association that publishes the *Journal of Religious History*. First issued in June, 1960, the new journal has surmounted the perils of infancy and has been widely welcomed. Neither of these periodicals is confined to Australian history or to the writings of Australian historians.[7]

The new maturity of Australian historical scholarship that is reflected in these developments flourishes on a general desire to know the ways by which Australia grew to its present nationhood. Inevitably, the two decades since the war have been a time of monographs in which scholars have probed and analyzed particular problems, exploring in detail one small area of a vast tract of country known as a whole only imperfectly. The day of the brilliant pioneers, who took quick looks at large subjects and reported their findings in general terms, has given way to the day of the meticulous scholar who has to guard against the dangers of myopia while patiently seeking for truth, accurately determined and precisely stated. History written under these conditions will attain obvious brilliance only rarely; some of it is bound to be dull, except to the erudite minority of scholars qualified to perceive its significance. Fortunately, from the standpoint of the general reader, biography has come into its own as part of the age of the monograph; and biography, whether of persons or of families, has often been attractive as well as good.

One of the most exasperating barriers to research in Australian history has been the lack of knowledge about people. In a country where so many of the inhabitants were new settlers or moved freely from one state to another, the task of identifying even the members of legislatures has been difficult. A. W. Martin and P. Wardle set a good example of how to remedy part of the problem when they compiled their handbook, *Members of the Legislative Assembly of New South Wales: 1856–1901*, which was a list with biographical notes. The Australian National University, which published this useful tool for research, has given the lead in two larger projects of the greatest value. One is a national register of Australians, a work

[7] Other new publications include *University Studies in History and Economics* (University of Western Australia), the *Papers and Proceedings* of the Tasmanian Historical Research Association, the monographs and occasional papers of the Australian Humanities Research Council, and the *Bulletin* of the Business Archives Council of Australia (N.S.W. and Victorian Branches).

231

long needed, that under the leadership of Sir Keith Hancock, who returned to Australia in 1957 and became professor of History in the Australian National University, has become a cooperative effort among scholars throughout the country. The register, which will be a list of materials (including portraits) held all over Australia, will be compiled in Canberra and copied for use elsewhere. Hancock and the Australian National University have also made possible another project that had long been under discussion—a really comprehensive biographical dictionary. Australia has had many biographical dictionaries, the best being Percival Serle's *Dictionary of Australian Biography* (1949). These have all been the work of single authors and therefore have necessarily been limited in scope and authority. The new *Australian Encyclopaedia* (1958), edited by A. H. Chisholm, which contained over two thousand biographies, was the work of many authors, but it was not the great work comparable to the British *Dictionary of National Biography* that scholars needed. Under Hancock's leadership the *Australian Dictionary of Biography* has been planned federally (with central responsibility taken by the Australian National University) and is the first large project ever undertaken jointly in the writing of Australian history.

Hitherto, Australian biography has not much attracted the professional historians. Impelled by their need as teachers to throw light on little-known periods in Australian history, the academics have given priority in their research work to periods and problems and have tended to neglect persons. Given the state of ignorance about most periods in Australian history, their view had reasons other than the merely pedagogical to support it. One mark of a good biography is the ability to put a life in context; how can that be done until the context has become known? In deciding whether history comes before, with, or after biography, the professionals for long went one way and the amateurs another.

There are, however, signs of change, partly because of the rapid growth of knowledge concerning Australian history, partly because the demands of the *Australian Dictionary of Biography* will persuade nearly every professional historian writing Australian history to try his hand at biography. Some may develop a taste for it; all will be influenced by the *Dictionary* when it begins to appear within the next two or three years.

Among the professionals who have already written biographies are two women, Associate Professor Kathleen Fitzpatrick and the late Margaret Kiddle, both of the University of Melbourne. Mrs. Fitzpatrick's book, *Sir John Franklin in Tasmania* (1949), was partly intended to revise the unfavorable judgments that contemporaries and posterity have passed on the governorship of Franklin. Although a beautifully written study, it does not prove the whole of the author's case for Franklin. His principles, honesty, and manliness are strikingly vindicated; whether the same can be said for his wisdom and skill as an administrator is doubtful. One difficulty is in accepting Mrs. Fitzpatrick's view of Tasmania and the convict system while Franklin was governor; another lies in the obvious warmth of her admiration for Franklin and his circle and her severe attitude toward his enemies.

In 1950 Margaret Kiddle published *Caroline Chisholm*, a readable life of the philanthropist who labored to improve the conditions of immigrant women in Australia. It is better as history than as biography, but succeeds in presenting Mrs. Chisholm as a strong and dedicated character.

Ben Chifley (1961) by Professor L. F. Crisp, of the Australian National University, is a political biography of Joseph Benedict Chifley, prime minister of Australia from 1945 to 1949. "This study," wrote Crisp, "is the work of a political scientist, a former civil servant and an active Labor Party member who (in both official and party capacities) served Chifley through the latter's great decade." Glowing with admiration for Chifley as a man of character, ideals, and intellect, it narrates his party's history as well as his own and covers the years during which he acquired political experience and suffered political misfortune as well as the years of his ascendancy when he was Labor leader, Commonwealth treasurer, and prime minister.

The next few years should see a succession of good biographies by professional historians. Among works to be expected are Professor J. A. La Nauze's study of Alfred Deakin and the early Commonwealth, L. F. Fitzhardinge's life of William Morris Hughes, F. K. Crowley's study of John Forrest (the Western Australian statesman), and B. E. Mansfield's political biography of E. W. O'Sullivan, a prominent reformer in New South Wales politics at the turn of the century.

Notable as the contributions of the professionals have been in writing Australian biographies, they have been quite outdistanced by the amateurs. Unrestrained by any responsibility to teach over the whole range of Australian history, the amateurs have been free to write about people. They have tended to choose subjects in periods and places that do not raise really formidable problems of context and background.

The only really notable exceptions to this tendency are both placed mainly in the late federation movements and the early Commonwealth, which have the unity of a well-defined historical era. Nettie Palmer's memoir of her uncle, *Henry Bournes Higgins* (1931), had merits both as history and as literature. It told the story of a great man and of the society and politics in which he moved. *Edmund Barton* (1948) by John Reynolds lacked the warmth and intimacy of Mrs. Palmer's book and was on a much more difficult theme. It sketched Barton's role in the politics of New South Wales, in the making of federal union, as prime minister of the Commonwealth, and as a High Court judge.

Most biographers have preferred subjects whose historical background is less complicated and extensive than that of Barton or Higgins. M. H. Ellis (b. 1890), the best known of Australian biographers, has published three major works, all from the early period of Australian history. His *Lachlan Macquarie* (1947), *Francis Greenway* (1949), and *John Macarthur* (1955) are by far the greatest single contribution of any individual author to Australian biography. They extend little past the 1820's. William Charles Wentworth, whose life Ellis is now writing, remained important in the political life of New South Wales down to 1862 or later. It will be interesting to see how a scholar as thorough as Ellis, accustomed to fit each life deeply into the context of the times, copes with the problem of depicting Wentworth's role throughout a long period many of whose major developments are still obscure.

Ellis' gifts as a biographer are obvious. He has steeped himself in the sources of early Australian history. He keeps in his mind a lively, detailed picture of the turbulent, brawling colonies that were early New South Wales and Tasmania. He knows the geography of early Sydney, the idiosyncrasies of its inhabitants, and the vagaries of its weather; he forgets neither the farmers in the country nor the powerful authorities in distant London. His characters move

234

almost visibly round a scene that seems as familiar to him as does Sydney today. He goes with them as they move, noting the minutiae of their nature and existence as well as the decisions and actions of which historians usually make the stuff of their narrative.

These are fortunate qualities in a biographer; there are, however, weaknesses. In his two best books, *Macquarie* and *Macarthur*, Ellis, like many other sympathetic biographers, identified himself with his subjects. He fought their battles over again; he liked their friends and hated their enemies. In *Macarthur* he poured contempt and ridicule on Governor Bligh, the archopponent of his subject. Mackaness and Evatt found reason to defend Bligh and even to praise him. Ellis wrote him off as a "Sea Monster," a "noisy son of Boreas, twin brother to King Borea Bunglee-boo," a man "vain, mean-souled, naked of principle." Bligh's assistants in the colony certainly included men of depraved mind and low reputation, but Ellis condemned them in terms so strong that the reader's sympathies are almost enlisted on the opposite side. According to Macarthur, Judge-Advocate Atkins cherished against him "a rancorous inveteracy." Ellis represented Atkins as a "disreputable old remittance man so deeply pickled in piety and spruce beer" that he discharged his duties in "an alcohol-scented twilight of confusion"; after the departure of his wife and son, he found his comforts in his "brandy bottle, his concubine, and his increasing gaggle of illegitimate daughters."

Ellis' views on Macarthur changed between 1947 when he published the first edition of *Macquarie* and 1955 when he presented Macarthur as the subject of an able biography. In the earlier book Macarthur, who had troubled most of the governors including Macquarie, was described as "ringleader of all the Colony's mischiefs." He confronted Macquarie with "purposeful hatred"; he was not the great innovator of the pastoral industry, but "primarily and at all times by nature an exploiter of other people's notions." This troublesome person became something of a hero when his own biography was written, although a hero in whom weaknesses were were very properly admitted to exist. Ellis then found in Macarthur a founder of the Australian wool industry, a man of stern rectitude and strong passions whose taste for controversy and rather self-righteous contempt for others produced unpopularity in his own day and unreasonable condemnation afterwards. There can be little doubt that Ellis was right about Macquarie in the first book and right about Macarthur in the other.[8]

Ellis' achievements as a biographer are obviously significant. He has pronounced informed—although not always persuasive—judgments on very many of the people important in the early history of New South Wales. His books taken together present a well-integrated picture of the colony as a whole.

Another amateur biographer who has put students of Australian history in his debt is Mr. Justice J. V. Barry of the Supreme Court of Victoria. His *Alexander Maconochie of Norfolk Island* (1958) is a really good study of a pioneer of penal reform. Maconochie was one of the few administrators of convict transportation enlightened enough to attempt to salvage the men in his care and to develop theories of penology. After going out to Van Diemen's Land with Sir John Franklin, he devoted his life to penal reform. In Barry's book the scene moves from England to Tasmania, to Norfolk Island, and then back to England again for a short term as governor of Birmingham Prison. Barry has altogether relieved Maconochie of the calumnies heaped upon him in his lifetime. Moreover, Maconochie's intellectual relationships with the Italian positivist school of criminology (especially Lombroso, Garofalo, and Ferri) have been revealed with learning and skill.

Barry's book stands high, both as history and as biography, an excellent contribution to knowledge of the convict period and a judicious assessment of a reformer who labored hard to establish a "scientific and sensible approach to the complex problem of criminal punishment."

There have been many biographies of explorers, who have a fascination peculiarly their own and do not usually have to be depicted

[8] Ellis himself commented on his change of opinion on Macarthur in the Preface to the later biography. There he remarked on the importance of the new material that had not been available when *Macquarie* was written. No one could doubt the fundamental importance of the new material in question (the Macarthur Papers), but it may be noted that in 1933 Professor Ernest Scott, without the benefit of any unpublished Macarthur papers, published conclusions on John Macarthur's character not unlike those reached by Ellis in 1955 (*Cambridge History of the British Empire* [Cambridge: Cambridge University Press, 1929–34], VII, 104).

against a complicated background of political or economic development. Dr. K. M. Bowden's *George Bass* (1952) is one of the best biographies of an Australian explorer, a very worth-while study of the brief and high-spirited life of the discoverer after whom Bass Strait is named. Dr. J. H. L. Cumpston wrote biographies of *Charles Sturt* (1951) and *Thomas Mitchell* (1954), the two famous explorers who own writings have been mentioned in this chapter. Cumpston's books are more useful as narratives of exploration than as studies of personality or circumstance. The second edition of A. H. Chisholm's *Strange New World* (1951) was a readable account of some of the journeyings of John Gilbert, the naturalist, and Ludwig Leichhardt, the explorer who was lost in the Australian wilderness in 1848. Chisholm condemned Leichhardt as a poor leader, incompetent, slovenly, morose, and obstinate. He summed up Gilbert with the line, "There was ever more in him to be praised than pardoned." Kathleen Fitzpatrick's *Australian Explorers* (1958) mentioned Chisholm's judgment of Leichhardt, but did not comment on it. The book contains a lucid introduction to the story of Australian discovery by land and well-chosen selections from explorers' writings.

The pioneering settlers, who followed (or even preceded) the explorers, have also provided fascinating opportunities for biographical studies, mostly on the family scale. Marnie Bassett's *The Hentys: An Australian Colonial Tapestry* (1954) is a fine example of such work. Vividly narrating the story of an English family that was important in the Swan River Settlement, in Van Diemen's Land, and in Victoria, this unpretentious, gracefully written book manages to be convincing about the Hentys and their problems and full of interesting glimpses of the colonies. It is social history as much as biography. Margaret Kiddle's *Men of Yesterday*, published posthumously in 1961 with the editorial assistance of J. A. La Nauze, is a fascinating narrative of the squatting families of western Victoria from 1834 to 1890. Founded partly on papers that Miss Kiddle herself had collected, it is good social history that will help to reinterpret the role of "aristocracy" in Australian history.

Think of Stephen (1954) by Ruth Bedford did for a family of city dwellers what Marnie Bassett and Margaret Kiddle did for pioneers and pastoralists. Sir Alfred Stephen was Chief Justice of New South Wales for twenty-eight years. Miss Bedford, his granddaughter,

237

covered nearly the whole of his long life in this book, drawing on his letters and memoirs and on the diaries of his second wife, Eleanor. Without being biographical in form, the book is partly biographical in achievement, for it presents very clear pictures of the judge (off the bench), his wife and family, and the circles in which they moved.

Australian biography has progressed tremendously in the last twenty years and is sure to develop rapidly in the near future. The main advances in historical knowledge, however, are still being made not in biography, but in the writings of historians who have analyzed particular problems and periods. There have, indeed, been so many works of fundamental research that the task of assimilating their conclusions into broad studies of Australian development is lagging badly.

Economic historians have been particularly active. Books like *The Australian Wheat-Growing Industry* (1956) by Edgars Dunsdorfs and Alan Barnard's *Australian Wool Market* (1958) are very welcome additions to historical knowledge that should be required reading for political historians as well as economic and social historians. Dunsdorfs has traced the whole history of wheat growing in Australia down to 1945, perhaps too much in isolation from the rest of the economy, but with a good eye to official policy and technical knowledge. Barnard's book covers the period 1840–1900 during which Australia became the "world's largest exporter of merino wool and a dominant force in the world wool markets." He has shown how the growth of the wool industry encouraged the development of transport, personal services, banks, and marketing agencies. Some of these topics reappeared in Barnard's latest book, *Visions and Profits: Studies in the Business Career of Thomas Sutcliffe Mort* (1961). A successful entrepreneur of enduring reputation, Mort sought "not only profit, but also prestige" and believed "that religion and ethics imposed an obligation to serve his neighbours." Barnard has used some of the sources to write well about Mort's participation in the wool industry and other ventures and has tried to discover the secrets of his success.

J. A. La Nauze's *Political Economy in Australia—Historical Studies* (1949), which is generally recognized as one of the best works of Australian scholarship, was the first important contribution to the history of economic thought in Australia. The major figures

238

in the book were William Edward Hearn ("economic optimism" and free trade) and David Syme (protection). A brief chapter on W. S. Jevons in Sydney was described by the author as "a biographical contribution to the history of English political economy."

The most prolific of the economic historians has been S. J. Butlin, professor of economics and dean of the faculty of economics in the University of Sydney. In eight years he has published three major works. The first and best known, *Foundations of the Australian Monetary System, 1788–1851*, appeared in 1953. Although in some ways a demandingly technical study, it immediately attracted a wider audience than the title might invite because it corrected at some point or other every economic history (and most of the political histories) touching on the period. For example, Butlin's views about the economic slump of 1841–1843, although described as tentative, were sufficiently well formed to rebut Fitzpatrick's emphasis on a decline in British investment and a fall in the value of wool. Butlin thought that Fitzpatrick and other historians had not sufficiently regarded the effects on the pastoral industry of the "apparent exhaustion of opportunities for profitable expansion into new areas." The University of Cambridge recognized the merits of this book by awarding its author the degree of Doctor of Letters.

Butlin's volume in the *Official History of Australia in the War of 1939–1945*, on war economy between 1939 and 1942, was a clear, competent account of a difficult subject; he is to write also a second volume on economic history, 1942–1945. His latest book, *Australian and New Zealand Bank* (1961), is really good business history, showing keen awareness of economic developments and founded on a very wide range of sources. Historians will be especially grateful for his clear, penetrating account of the position of the banks in the depression of the nineties and at other times of stress.

Another good banking history was *The Growth of a Central Bank* (1951) by the late Professor L. F. Giblin. It recorded the central banking functions of the Commonwealth Bank of Australia up to 1945, when amending legislation came into force. As a member of the Bank Board, Giblin had intimate knowledge of financial policy during the depression and of the roles played by some of the leading men involved. His book was recognized at once as a standard authority for the period.

Unlike the works of Butlin and Giblin, *Gold and Paper* (1959), the story of the National Bank of Australasia by Geoffrey Blainey, was not economists' history. Blainey wrote a sound general history that emphasized the role of the bank in promoting economic expansion and in saving the fruits of expansion during times of stringency.

Blainey had already made a name for himself with an interesting piece of industrial history, *Peaks of Lyell* (1954), whose scene was the difficult West Coast region of Tasmania. Tin, silver, gold, and copper were the lures that led prospectors and companies to try their fortunes in an area where terrain and climate alike balked their efforts. The book successfully integrated problems of pioneering, mining, and metallurgy, together with much company and trade-union history. In 1957 Blainey published *A Centenary History of the University of Melbourne*, in which the story of the university was told largely through the histories of its professors and councilors. Witty, candid, and sympathetic, it has been recognized as both a complement and a supplement to Scott's history of the university published in 1936.

Business and institutional histories are a new field of Australian historians. So is educational history, which has acquired quite a large band of practitioners. The outstanding book so far has been *Catholic Education in Australia* (1959) by Brother Ronald Fogarty, F.M.S. Religious questions have persistently complicated Australian views on education, and the place of Catholic education has often been discussed as a subject of general public importance. Brother Fogarty has written a history of the years from 1806 to 1950 that exhibits learning, good judgment, and sound scholarship. Whether or not he understands correctly the position of some of those who have disagreed with his church over the place of religion in education, he has written of them with moderation and charity. His is a highly important book, based on profound researches, that has set good standards for the writing of Australian educational history. A. G. Austin's *Australian Education, 1788–1900* (1961) is less massive than Fogarty's work, but wider in scope. The subtitle, *Church, State and Public Education in Australia*, indicates the theme. It traces objectively the stormy processes by which state-maintained primary education in Australia became predominantly secular, while the churches (especially the Roman Catholic Church) maintained schools of their own.

The stream of good books now appearing on special topics in Australian history is likely both to fascinate and to bewilder the "general" historians. No one has yet produced a synoptic view of Australian history, according to which the discoveries of scholars could be set in proportion with one another. There are no schools of interpretation of Australian history because the interpretations that have been determined are of limited developments and have had time to acquire neither a following nor a concerted band of opponents.

The so-called "Whig" interpretation of Australian history is an example of such limited interpretations, useful and contentious in themselves, but not providing a theme for Australian history comparable with Frederick Jackson Turner's frontier thesis in the United States. The "Whig" interpretation is not "Whig" at all; the name derives from a fancied resemblance to the Whig version of British history. No one book embodies it completely. Russel Ward's *The Australian Legend* (1958) and R. A. Gollan's *Radical and Working Class Politics: A Study of Eastern Australia, 1850–1910* (1960) do, however, if read together, come near to presenting the "Whig" view as understood by some of their contemporaries.[9] Russel Ward, a contributor to this volume, is a well-known historian of Australian society and social attitudes. Gollan is prominent among those studying Australian labor history.

Russel Ward's book makes extensive use of literary sources, including ballads, in order to argue that a specifically Australian outlook first grew up among the bush workers of the pastoral industry and that this group's attitude had a disproportionately large influence on the social and political attitudes of the whole Australian community. This is a beguiling thesis, but Ward has not really established its truth. His major premise about the Australian legend is itself doubtful; do Australians really and distinctively think of themselves as practical men, rough and ready, quick to decry affectation, willing to improvise, unwilling to work hard without good

[9] See, for example, the review of Gollan's book by A. W. Martin in *Economic Record*, XXXVII (March, 1961), 118–119.

cause, and so on? Unless he is right about what the Australian legend is, his arguments about the ideals of bush workers have diminished relevance. Some critics have wondered whether his "legend" existed even among them. Even if he were right on these points, he has not shown satisfactorily—and perhaps nobody could do so—how those ideas gained acceptance elsewhere in the community (assuming that they did). For all the doubts that may be expressed about its arguments and evidence, however, Ward's book is undoubtedly both stimulating and significant. In 1961 it shared the Ernest Scott Prize of the University of Melbourne for published work in Australian and imperial history.

The essence of the "Whig" interpretation becomes apparent if Gollan's book is added to Russel Ward's. Gollan has written about radical and working-class attitudes in the second half of the nineteenth century, during which Australia had a striking record of democratic political and social advance. There were two bites at democracy in Australia, one in the fifties and another in the eighties and later. The first is supposed to have been accomplished by middle-class liberals and radicals who took power from the former oligarchy of pastoralists and officials in the early years of responsible government. The second bite at democracy is attributed to an increasingly articulate working class. The trade-unions, inspired sometimes by radical and collectivist ideas from overseas and enlivened by the social ideals of the indigenous rural proletariat (Dr. Ward's bush workers), were the motive power behind the later move toward political democracy and social reform. Labor, in other words, provided the architects of Australian democracy that was at once egalitarian and national.

Obviously, this interpretation—set down here with rather crude brevity—is related (if only distantly) to the views that Hancock expressed thirty years ago about Australian nationalism and Australian democracy. It is not an interpretation that every Australian historian will accept. More needs to be known about the middle classes and the non-Labor parties; the emphasis on the ideas of the pastoral workers is hard to understand, as they were only a small minority in a continent dominated by its large cities; the attitudes of the electorate as a whole toward unionism and social and political reform will also need to be known before the "Whig" view is accepted. Similarly, the approach used by Dr. George Nadel in *Australia's Colonial Culture* (1957), a study of ideas, men, and institutions between 1830 and 1860, should be tried for the later period also. Nadel's conclusions on colonial culture in 1860, based mainly on records of urban life, do not march well with the views of either Russel Ward or Gollan.

In their search for general views on Australian history, a few scholars have applied Turner's frontier thesis to Australian conditions. Professor F. Alexander, whose interests are less in Australian history than in other fields of historical study, produced a provocative essay called *Moving Frontiers: An American Theme and Its Application to Australian History* (1947). He has admitted since to having written it somewhat tongue-in-cheek to stimulate colleagues who were producing impressive specialist tomes on particular topics of local history. Alexander certainly provoked them, but not to the point of substantial publication. It was left to a visiting English scholar, Professor H. C. Allen of London, to write a comparative study of the Turner frontier thesis in Australia and the United States, *Bush and Backwoods* (1959). Australian historians who have written on the frontier thesis as applied to their own country include Associate Professor N. D. Harper, who contributed a chapter on the subject to *Australia in World Affairs, 1956–58* (1961) and Russel Ward (in the last chapter of his *Australian Legend*). Neither Turner's views nor any other form of frontier thesis has much influenced the course of Australian historical writing.

The absence of accepted views about significant themes in Australian history causes difficulties for authors and editors of general histories. The most substantial history of Australia attempted in recent years has been *Australia: A Political and Social History* (1955), edited by Professor Gordon Greenwood. He proposed to bring out a political and social history of Australian society which would show the many-sided nature of its development at any given time. Although the book was welcomed by the reviewers, not one of them thought that Greenwood and his contributors had managed to achieve their difficult objective. In the state of knowledge that existed seven years ago, some periods were closed books so far as their social developments were concerned; only some of the recent periods were at all well charted for their politics. The situation

243

today is better, but the materials for the synoptic view that Greenwood would have liked to present are still scattered and incomplete.

Several other general histories have been published during the last twenty years. C. Hartley Grattan's *Introducing Australia* (1942) lived up to its title well, not least because it presented some interesting, brief summaries of Australian history. The United Nations volume, *Australia* (1947), that Grattan edited, had several workmanlike chapters of history. Inevitably, they summed up a state of knowledge that was already being undermined by postwar research. Professor R. M. Crawford's *Australia* (1952) belonged to the series of British Empire histories edited by Sir Reginald Coupland. Crawford was especially interested in the growth of Australian democracy, nationalism, and culture. His conclusions on the last were reflected in the judgment that Australia "has still to forge an intellectual and artistic culture at least as responsive to its present industrial society as to its pastoral past."

The Story of Australia (1955) by A. G. L. Shaw is the best general introduction to Australian history for those who come new to the subject. Shaw's book was remarkably successful in striking a balance of political, economic, and social factors. Its interpretations were middle of the road, unromantic, sensible, illuminating, and persuasive. The most detailed of the short histories, it managed to sum up the Australian experience with simple brevity.

State history is ever a source of trouble to the general historian of Australia. The myth that everything significant in Australian history happened in either New South Wales or Victoria died hard. What killed it was the fact that the other states, which have the smallest numbers of people, proved to be the most tractable for historical research and in consequence have long had the best colonial and state histories. Professor Pike's *Paradise of Dissent* (1957) was a history of South Australia from 1829 to 1857, unusual in that it put religion first. South Australian history certainly justified such an approach, for the religious aspirations of some of its promoters and settlers were constantly important in its early history. *Australia's Western Third* (1960) by Dr. F. K. Crowley was a detailed, scholarly history of Western Australia from the first settlement to modern times. It both complemented and supplemented the work of Battye published thirty-six years before. Crowley was especially interested in the economic development of Western Australia and tended to play down both politics and people.

In some senses, state history is the oldest form of Australian historical writing—for the works of Tench and Collins are justly claimed in Sydney as the first histories of New South Wales—but it does not rank high among the interests of the country's historians. Periods, problems, and people are more rewarding to historians than the record of what chanced to happen within any particular set of arbitrarily drawn state boundaries. During the last two or three decades, historians have entered freely into fields opened up by the growth of Australia's national interests and problems.

Many books have attested the growth of interest in external affairs and in Australia's trusteeship responsibilities in New Guinea. Gordon Greenwood's *Early American-Australian Relations* (1944) recorded the contacts between Australia and the whole of North and South America up to about 1830. J. M. Ward's *British Policy in the South Pacific* (1948) noted the influence of Australian and New Zealand interests in the South Pacific on decisions taken in London. *Australian Colonial Policy* (1956), a survey of native administration and European development in Papua by Professor J. D. Legge, and *Australians in New Guinea, 1914–21* (1958) by C. D. Rowley were both valuable contributions to Australian history. There are few studies of Australian foreign policy. *Australia in World Affairs, 1950–1955* (1957) and its sequel (1961), both edited by Gordon Greenwood and N. D. Harper, were contemporary comment rather than history. N. D. Mansergh's two *Surveys of British Commonwealth Affairs* (1953 and 1958) offered searching analyses of Australia's external relations between 1931 and 1952. C. Hartley Grattan made a useful, if contentious, summing up of Australian foreign policy, especially since the Second World War, in his *The United States and the Southwest Pacific* (1961).

The problems of the federal system have interested historians and political scientists as well as lawyers. Gordon Greenwood's *The Future of Australian Federalism* (1946) was not at all legalistic; mainly historical, it contained some trenchant political judgments such as: "Concentration of political power in the hands of the central parliament has become essential in Australia because unification of economic life has already taken place." Among lawyers' books that historians have found useful is *Australian Federal Politics and Law* (1956) by Professor Geoffrey Sawyer of the Australian National University. This described the constitutional foundation and structure of the Commonwealth parliaments and recorded their activities from 1901 to 1929. *Parliamentary Government of the Commonwealth of Australia* (1949) by L. F. Crisp was a historical and descriptive survey of the political parties, the public service, and the High Court as well as of parliament and cabinet. Crisp has written also *The Australian Federal Labour Party* (1955), a history of the organization and policies of the party from 1901 to 1951. Professor Louise Overacker's *The Australian Party System* (1952) was an American contribution—a valuable detailed analysis, partly historical, but rather uncritical of some of the Australian sources. The most profound work on Australian politics may be the late Sir Frederic Eggleston's *Reflections of an Australian Liberal* (1953). It is an evaluation of the Australian political achievement, based on long personal experience in Australian public life. Scholar, lawyer, diplomat, soldier, and politician, Eggleston left his countrymen a fine political testament. Although critical, even acid in tone, it was fundamentally constructive in principle. Everyone who wishes to relate Australian politics to Australian development should read it.

Reinterpretations of Australian history have been involved in most of the books published since 1945 and in quite a few before that year. But works that challenge widely accepted theses about Australia's past have not been large in number. Some of the writings of N. G. Butlin, C. H. Currey, C. M. H. Clark, R. M. Crawford, and J. M. Ward belong to this class.

N. G. Butlin, of the Australian National University, has begun to offer a basic reinterpretation of Australian economic history since about 1860. Two articles published in the *Economic Record*[10] and some papers issued by his university have indicated some of his conclusions. Butlin's researches have been highly technical in method, resting heavily on analyses of statistics, corrected by necessary study of other sources. Significantly, one of his articles opened with the

[10] N. G. Butlin, "The Shape of the Australian Economy, 1861–1900," *Economic Record*, XXXIV (April, 1958), 10–29; and "Some Structural Features of Australian Capital Formation, 1861 to 1938–39," *ibid.*, XXXV (December, 1959), 389–415.

sentence, "Australia is, perhaps, the only country in the world whose entire career is documented in detail with statistics of wide coverage and reasonable accuracy." So endowed, Butlin has already presented a formidable case for a new view of Australian history in the period 1860–1900.

The most revolutionary of Butlin's conclusions—especially for economic historians—is that economic development in the years 1860–1900 was largely a story of urbanization; the leaders in the expansion of the period were the manufacturing, building, and transport industries. A large part of Australian resources were used to build cities. Housing absorbed a much higher proportion of capital investment than historians have recognized. Railway construction and personal services also developed remarkably. Until the depression of the last decade of the century, the period was mainly one of steady growth—a "generation during which children grew to middle age without personal experience of economic depression." Growth rested on rapid increases of population and of capital equipment, both of which depended heavily on inflow from Britain. The depression itself was less prolonged and recovery by 1900 more complete than most historians have believed.

Butlin's reinterpretation, which has been merely illustrated here, may be as important to social and political historians as to economic historians. His emphasis on the growth of cities, it may be suggested, will require some large readjustments of view. First, it should end glib talk about the long continuation of the old pastoral ascendancy. Second, it is a useful reminder that some of the most important developments of economic and social history are often little discussed by those who participate in them. Australian literature in the second half of the nineteenth century failed to reflect—or even refer to adequately—the tremendous urbanization of that period. Historians who use Australian literature as evidence for social history and social attitudes may find that both their methods and their conclusions will need revision.

The Irish at Eureka (1954) by C. H. Currey, legal scholar and historian, was by far the best of the many books, pamphlets, and articles published at the centenary of the Eureka Stockade incident. Currey suggested two new views—or views to which insufficient attention had been given. He showed that some of the problems that delayed the redress of the gold miners' grievances were due, not to authoritarian obstinacy in Victoria, but to the inescapable requirements of British statutes that had ceased to be appropriate to the time and place. He provided another welcome corrective to the political nonsense so often uttered about Eureka when he emphasized the role of the Irish in the affair. "It is the Irish strand in the affair," he concluded, "that lends particular significance to the *emeute*, and gives coherence to the drama in which it was the central act." This reinterpretation must be read along with his firm opinion that "more forebearance . . . on both sides of the stockade would have rendered unnecessary the monument that now crowns it."

Most of Professor C. M. H. Clark's reinterpretations of Australian history are foreshadowed rather than actually stated. He is writing singlehanded a history of Australia to appear in several volumes. Partly to prepare for it, partly to fill a pedagogical need, he published three volumes of documents in Australian history,[11] and the comments that introduce the selections are the principal evidence of where his thoughts are tending.

The first volume had little editorial comment and in its emphasis reflected the secondary works most widely in use. The second volume broke new ground: "Academic history," Clark declared, "is little more than hasty selections of what is available in the main libraries." In the same paragraph he justified his own reluctance to use unprinted material in his selections by protesting against "the manuscript mystery cult" that led historians, so he asserted, to believe that manuscripts were the "keys to great truths."

Other comments contain glimpses of what may be important new insights into Australian history. He has suggested, for example, that the political democracy of the second half of the nineteenth century was not a triumph for the radicals but, rather, evidence of their weakness. He has several anticipations of illuminating treatments of social attitudes. At many places he has suggested new views of Australian history in which men's religious beliefs would be found significant. "Men, we are assured," he wrote, "do not live by bread alone; they also have their faiths." Even on secular topics, his com-

---

[11] *Select Documents in Australian History, 1788–1850* (Sydney: Angus and Robertson, 1950); *Select Documents in Australian History, 1851–1900* (Sydney: Angus and Robertson, 1955); *Sources of Australian History* (London: Oxford University Press, 1957).

ments may have ecclesiastical tones, as when the pompous prose of the third Earl Grey was generously described as "Prayer-Book" in style and when a section of documents on the gold discoveries opened with a reminder that "the love of money is the root of all evil." Clark may place more emphasis on religious factors than almost any other writer of a general Australian history has done so far.[12]

Professor R. M. Crawford's latest work, *An Australian Perspective* (1960), which was founded on Knaplund Lectures that he delivered at the University of Wisconsin in 1958, sketched some of the groundwork for two reinterpretations of Australian history. Crawford protested rightly against the altogether excessive tendency among Australians to draw "attention away from a component in Australian history which is not democratic but aristocratic." And he attacked rightly the "dead-level" interpretations of Australia, according to which egalitarian democracy has caused cultural mediocrity. It is to be hoped that Crawford will return to these themes, developing them at the length that their importance warrants.

J. M. Ward's *Earl Grey and the Australian Colonies, 1846–57* (1958) reached conclusions about the early federation movements that conflicted at nearly every point with those put forward fifty years earlier by C. D. Allin and followed by most later historians. According to Ward, the impetus to the federation of Australia between 1840 and 1860 came, not from the colonies, as Allin had thought, but from Britain. In Ward's view, imperial initiative (as distinct from colonial agitation) was not only at the root of the abortive federation movements, but also was significantly responsible for the important changes that were made in the Australian constitutions between 1850 and 1856. The mother country rather than the colonies set the pace in many sectors of the move toward greater colonial self-government.

During the next decade Australian historians will propose many more challenges to views now generally held. A period of reinterpretation is beginning. Recent work suggests that the new views will arise from a reassessment (both in Australia and overseas) of

[12] Since the above was written, Professor Clark has published Volume I of *The History of Australia* (Melbourne: Melbourne University Press, 1962). It covers Australian history from the earliest times through the period of Governor Macquarie, its main theme being the coming of European civilization to Australia. The interpretation is largely in terms of religious beliefs and the lack of them.

British imperial policy, from definitive studies of subjects like convict transportation and general administrative history—which are
not nearly well enough known—from revised ideas about the origins
and nature of Australian nationalism, from less "present-minded"
and less aggressively democratic interpretations of Australian society and politics in the nineteenth century than those now current,
and from greater attention than before to urban life, the "middle"
classes, business history, religion, and social attitudes.

As new concepts of Australian history are evolved in the next ten
years, scholars will certainly seek for larger views of the continuity
of Australian history than they have been able to discover so far.
The story of the prison colonies and other isolated settlements that
grew into a united, independent nation, holding to the Commonwealth of Nations, occupying an entire continent, and enjoying
high levels of culture and material achievement according to the
standards of the western world is not yet understood with clarity
or assurance. Perhaps the scholars of today (through no fault of their
own) are seeing too much of the trees and to little of the wood.
Most of them have technical competence; many have genuine originality; few of them, however, experience as historians the satisfaction that their achievements might be expected to win for them.
They know both too much and too little. Knowing what they do,
they cannot easily indulge in the bold hypotheses that lent brilliance
and distinction to the works of predecessors less encumbered by
other men's researches. Knowing more than they do now, they might
have the materials and the confidence for enlightened judgments of
real scope and authority. The most vigorous historians of Australia
today believe that the time is rapidly approaching when they will
see their country's history clearly and wholly as no one has ever
seen it before.

BIBLIOGRAPHY

Books

The following are authoritative studies of several aspects of Australian
history not covered by books listed in the bibliographies of the other
chapters in this volume, or general studies of particular merit.

HISTORIOGRAPHY

Butlin, S. J. *Foundations of the Australian Monetary System, 1788–1851.* 1953.

Deakin, Alfred. *The Federal Story.* 1944.

Ellis, M. H. *Lachlan Macquarie.* 1947.

Fitzpatrick, Brian. *British Imperialism and Australia, 1783–1833: An Economic History of Australia.* 1939.

Greenwood, G., ed. *Australia: A Political and Social History.* 1955.

Hancock, W. K. *Australia.* 1930.

La Nauze, J. A. *Political Economy in Australia.* 1949.

Mackaness, George. *The Life of Vice-Admiral Sir William Bligh.* 1931.

Mills, R. C. *The Colonization of Australia (1829–42): The Wakefield Experiment in Empire Building.* 1915.

O'Brien, Eris. *The Foundation of Australia, 1786–1800: A Study in Penal Colonisation.* 1937.

Phillips, Marion. *A Colonial Autocracy—New South Wales under Governor Macquarie.* 1909.

Roberts, S. H. *History of Australian Land Settlement.* 1923.

——. *The Squatting Age in Australia, 1835–47.* 1935.

Shann, E. O. G. *An Economic History of Australia.* 1948.

Shaw, A. G. L. *The Story of Australia.* 1955.

Sutcliffe, J. T. *History of Trade Unionism in Australia.* 1921.

Ward, J. M. *British Policy in the South Pacific, 1786–1893.* 1948.

——. *Earl Grey and the Australian Colonies, 1846–57.* 1958.

Willard, Myra. *History of the White Australia Policy.* 1923.

Articles

Alexander, F. "Survey of Recent Research: Australia," *International Studies* (Delhi), II (April, 1961), 425–445.

Crawford, R. M. "History," in A. Grenfell Price, ed., *The Humanities in Australia* (1959), pp. 148–162.

Heaton, H. "The Progress of Historical Studies in Australia," *Journal of Modern History,* XV (Dec., 1943), 303–310.

La Nauze, J. A. "The Study of Australian History, 1929–1959," *The Australian Journal of Science,* XXII (Dec., 1959), 227–234.

MacKirdy, K. A. "Clio's Australian Accent: Main Trends of Recent Historical Writing in Australia," *The Canadian Historical Association Report, 1958,* pp. 77–98.

LAW

D. J. MACDOUGALL

THE Australian attitude to law is equivocal. On one hand, there is a tendency to regard law and legal institutions as unnecessary and unproductive superstructures that interfere with the real business of life. Of course, this attitude is found in all countries, but it is particularly common in Australia where it represents a lasting inheritance from the tough original settlers. Australians are no longer a race of hardy pioneers, but the pioneering traditions did not die and are fading away slowly. Moreover, Australia is remarkably free from internal instability and serious crime, which are two of the principal reasons why other nations have welcomed strong central government and comprehensive legal regulation.

On the other hand, the demands of twentieth-century social life are reflected in increasing clamor for sophisticated legal regulation in certain fields—especially industrial and commercial matters. At the same time, the complexity of life in a modern society and the high standard of education are contributing to a breakdown in the traditional attitude. Nevertheless, it is rare to find an Australian who is not affected by both of these competing attitudes to law.

LAW

The Commonwealth of Australia came into existence on January 1, 1901, when a federal government was formed to unite the six original, independent colonies of New South Wales, Victoria, Queensland, South Australia, Western Australia, and Tasmania, which became the six states of the new federation.

In form, the Commonwealth of Australia is created by an act of the United Kingdom Parliament—the Commonwealth of Australia Constitution Act, 1900—passed in response to the wishes of the Australian people, as evidenced by the results of a referendum, and presented to the British authorities by a special delegation from the federating colonies.

The Commonwealth Constitution creates a federal parliament, executive, and judiciary. The Commonwealth parliament exercises legislative authority over the six original states and also over the federal territories, which include the internal territories called the Northern Territory and the Australian Capital Territory as well as the external territories of Papua, various Pacific and Indian Ocean islands, the Australian Antarctic Territory, and the trust territories of Nauru and New Guinea. Insofar as the Commonwealth parliament legislates for the federal territories, it has an unlimited power; insofar as it legislates for the residents of the states, it is limited to those matters specified in the Constitution. Some of these matters (for example, excise duties, the Commonwealth Public Service, and, in effect, control of naval and military forces) are within the "exclusive" jurisdiction of the Commonwealth parliament, so that the various state governments have no legislative power in these areas. Other matters (taxation, banking, insurance, divorce and matrimonial causes) are within the "concurrent" jurisdiction of the Commonwealth parliament. On these matters both the Commonwealth and the state parliaments may legislate. If there is any inconsistency between a law of the Commonwealth and a law of a state, Section 109 of the Constitution provides that the Commonwealth law is to prevail. In fact, most of the matters on which the Commonwealth may legislate are matters within the "concurrent" jurisdiction of the Commonwealth and the states. Questions of inconsistency arise frequently, and the High Court of Australia has given Section 109 a wide operation.

First, although a "law of the Commonwealth" does not include an award made by somebody under the legislative authority of the Commonwealth parliament (such as an industrial tribunal), any state law which is inconsistent with the award will be held to be invalid because it will be inconsistent with the Commonwealth legislation which authorized the subordinate body to determine the matter.

Secondly, "inconsistency" is said to exist not merely where it is impossible to give effect to both laws, but also where the law of the Commonwealth demonstrates that the Commonwealth parliament intended to express completely and exhaustively the law governing a certain subject matter—or, as it is aptly, if less accurately, stated, "to cover the field."

However, the Commonwealth parliament is a parliament of specific or enumerated legislative powers. Those powers which are not given expressly to the Commonwealth remain with the states. In this respect the Australian Constitution follows the American, rather than the Canadian, model.

It would be misleading to leave the question of Commonwealth legislative power at this point because a method has, in fact, been discovered by which the Commonwealth parliament may extend its influence over matters which are theoretically beyond its competence. The Commonwealth parliament exacts a tax which imposes a high rate of income tax and will raise sufficient revenue to cover essential Commonwealth expenditure and grants-in-aid to the states. Then, under Section 96 of the Constitution, the parliament may grant financial assistance to the states "on such terms and conditions as the parliament thinks fit." Naturally, these conditions may include a condition that the assisted state should accept Commonwealth policy in the use of that financial aid. In this way the federal parliament has extended its influence over matters such as education and road construction which are not expressly given to it in the Constitution. True, the state government may reject the Commonwealth grant, but it could only do so in any important matter if it were prepared to impose taxation at such a high level that the cumulative effect of federal and state taxation would result in a severe burden on the taxpayer. In the present Australian political climate this would be a suicidal policy for any state government to adopt. Although

LAW

Australia is a federation in legal theory, in fact the majority of Australians are nationalist rather than federalist in sympathies, and there are few who would give energetic support to a demand for more protection of states' rights.

Despairing of any hope of confining Commonwealth activities by political pressure, the states have on two occasions asked the High Court to strike down a series of Commonwealth taxation acts as a "legislative scheme" to effect an unconstitutional extension of Commonwealth legislative power; but on both occasions this argument was rejected.

Although this indirect Commonwealth influence over the states through the control of the purse should not be overlooked, it is equally true that it should not be exaggerated. Whatever the potential of the Commonwealth's power may be, in fact it has been used sparingly. Consequently, the states still have effective control over most domestic matters.

For many years it was a characteristic of Australian law that it was copied law. Major legislative changes generally followed comparable developments overseas—particularly in the United Kingdom—although the translation of the foreign legislation into the Australian legal systems occasionally involved extensive modifications. In recent years an increasing number of legislative reforms have been initiated within Australia. Most of these reforms have been concerned with problems that do not arise in the United Kingdom, because they arise from the federal structure of government within Australia. Certainly American lawyers will appreciate the uncertainties that result from (1) variations in the laws of sister states; (2) doubts about the legislative competency of governments possessing limited legislative power; and (3) attempted evasions of policies enforced in some states but not in others. Although Australian lawyers became fully conscious of these problems only recently, it is significant that already there has been a considerable —and, indeed, an amazing—progress toward the solution of many difficult and controversial problems of this character.

Two of the most significant experiments in Australian law have been in the fields of industrial law and family law.

In Australia, industrial disputes are subject to compulsory arbitration before a complex system of government agencies. Few other countries possess such a highly developed system of arbitration, and it is common for overseas experts in industrial relations to refer to the Australian experience whenever any system of compulsory industrial arbitration is considered. Nevertheless, it must be acknowledged that Australian law is itself indebted to the law developed in New Zealand.

Industrial disputes within Australia may come within the legislative competence of either the Commonwealth government or a state government. As a result of generous judicial interpretation of the Constitution, however, the Commonwealth power has become very extensive.

Nevertheless, there is a very significant limitation on Commonwealth power. Generally speaking, the Commonwealth parliament has no power to legislate directly on industrial conditions or disputes. The principal source of Commonwealth power is *placitum* (xxxv) of Section 51 of the Constitution, which gives the Commonwealth parliament power to legislate with respect to "conciliation and arbitration for the prevention and settlement of industrial disputes extending beyond the limits of any one State." Under this *placitum* the Commonwealth power is limited to the provision of tribunals or other means of conciliation and arbitration.

This has the odd consequence that tribunals may be created which are dependent on Commonwealth legislation for their existence and jurisdiction, but which are independent of the Commonwealth government in the decisions they reach on wages and industrial conditions. Consequently, these tribunals may deal with matters that affect the fundamental economic policies of the Commonwealth government, yet that government may be powerless to direct a tribunal's conclusion or to alter its decision. It might be thought that this is a legal fiction and that the Commonwealth government may achieve indirectly what it cannot achieve directly. It is true that the Commonwealth government can exercise considerable influence on these industrial tribunals. However, it is equally true that a considerable body of public opinion supports the view that these tribunals should be free from direction by the Commonwealth government, and this furnishes an effective political check on governmental interference with the tribunals. The result is that, in fact as well as in legal theory, the Commonwealth industrial tribunals constitute a semiautonomous organization with jurisdiction to settle industrial disputes.

The foundation for these tribunals was laid in the 1890's, when a series of disastrous strikes in the maritime, mining, and pastoral industries had a serious effect on the development of the eastern colonies. Unable to achieve their objectives by direct action, the unions supported plans to give official tribunals compulsive powers to fix hours of work, wages, and conditions of employment. By 1904 each state had introduced some such system.

It is possible that when *placitum* (xxxv) was added to the Constitution it was intended to apply only to nomadic workers, such as shearers and seamen. These were two of the principal groups in the strikes of the preceding decade, and it was essential that some tribunal should exist with jurisdiction to settle their disputes. Such disputes extended beyond the geographical limits of any one state, and only a federal tribunal could prove adequate.

The terms of *placitum* (xxxv) still require proof that a dispute has an interstate character, but this is a burden easily discharged. If in at least two states employees in a particular industry simultaneously make demands on their respective employers, there is an interstate dispute, even though none of the employers has a business which extends to more than one state. With the development of national associations of employers and employees most major industries are subject to the control of the Commonwealth tribunals.

The tribunals established by Commonwealth legislation have taken various forms. The original act of 1904 created a Commonwealth Court of Conciliation and Arbitration, which was endowed with part of the judicial power of the Commonwealth as well as conciliative and arbitral powers. However, the members of this court were appointed for a term of years, not for life. In 1918 it was decided in the *Alexander* case [1] that the judicial power of the Commonwealth could be exercised only by a court which fulfilled the

[1] *Waterside Workers' Federation of Australia v. J. W. Alexander Ltd.*, (1918) 25 Commonwealth Law Reports 434.

conditions specified in Chapter III of the Constitution. One of the provisions of Chapter III—Section 72—has been interpreted as requiring courts exercising judicial power of the Commonwealth to be constituted by judges with life tenure. Consequently, the Court of Conciliation and Arbitration, as then constituted, could not exercise any of the Commonwealth judicial power.

In an effort to cure this defect, legislation passed in 1926 conferred life tenure on the judges of the Conciliation and Arbitration Court and also introduced concilation commissioners. At first these officers had a very limited power. Their function was to conduct preliminary informal discussion with the disputants in an effort to settle the dispute. In 1930 they were given limited arbitral powers as well as conciliative powers, and in 1947 their arbitral powers were extended even further. The 1947 reorganization was intended to ensure that the court concentrated on major questions of policy, such as standard hours of work and the basic wage, while the commissioners settled the minor disputes by conciliation or arbitration. To avoid inconsistencies among the commissioners or between the policies of the court and the commissioners, it was intended that there should be frequent conferences between the commissioners, and the court and that a bureau should be established to provide relevant economic and statistical information. Partly because of continued dispute about the "proper" relationship between the court and the commissioners, these plans never materialized.

In any event, the next decade witnessed the system-shattering decision in the *Boilermakers'* case.[2] This case is an extension of the *Alexander* case, and it determines that none of the judicial power of the Commonwealth can be exercised by a tribunal with significant nonjudicial functions even though that tribunal is composed of members enjoying life appointments. As the Court of Conciliation and Arbitration was principally concerned with the nonjudicial functions of conciliation and arbitration, it could not exercise any of the judicial power of the Commonwealth. As a result of this decision, the Commonwealth industrial tribunals were reconstituted and comprise:

1) *The Commonwealth Industrial Court*, which exercises a judicial function over matters arising under the Commonwealth Con-

[2] *R. v. Kirby ex. p. Boilermakers' Society of Australia*, (1955–56) 94 C.L.R. 254.

ciliation and Arbitration Acts (for example, the enforcement of awards made by the following organization).

2) *The Commonwealth Conciliation and Arbitration Commission*, which exercises the nonjudicial powers of conciliation and arbitration formerly exercised by the court and the conciliation commissioners. The Commission consists of three presidential members, at least six commissioners, and an indefinite number of conciliators. Although the titles are altered, the pattern existing before the *Boilermakers'* case is preserved, and matters of basic policy are reserved for the Commission sitting in presidential session while other matters are referred to a conciliator (if agreement between the disputants is likely), or to a commissioner (if agreement is unlikely).

Although the states have industrial tribunals of varying types, they usually follow the trend of decisions in the Commonwealth tribunals. In general terms, it would seem that the United States and some other countries emphasize conciliation in their treatment of industrial disputes whereas Australia insists on compulsory arbitration by an independent third party if conciliation proves unsuccessful. Conciliation has not proved an over-all success in Australia. Powerful industrial groups are reluctant to grant concessions lest they be taken as a sign of weakness, and even where an agreement is reached it may take undue time and effort as the operation of the collective bargaining system in the United States demonstrates. Consequently, whatever the theoretical advantages of conciliation, compulsory arbitration is the standard solution for most serious industrial disputes in Australia.

Could the Australian system succeed in other countries, or would the compulsive powers attract insurmountable resentment from either the employers' organizations or the unions? This is a difficult question to answer. Admittedly, the arbitration system was introduced into Australia at a most opportune time; but that is not an adequate explanation of its success and subsequent expansion. Credit for the later development of the system must be given to the judges and commissioners whose integrity commanded general respect and whose worldly wisdom led to decisions which proved to be practical solutions of industrial disputes. In short, an arbitration system in the

259

contentious industrial world will last as long as it commands the respect of the disputants—and no longer.

Recently, significant developments occurred in the field of family law in Australia. Generally speaking, at Federation the states retained their legislative competence to deal with marriage, divorce, adoption, and the multiplicity of personal relationships conveniently subsumed under the title of "family law." Many of these matters arise in the shadowland between law and morality, and even where there is general agreement that legal regulation is required to protect some public interest, there will certainly be controversy concerning the scope and content of those regulations. In Australia, as in the United States, the states enforced policies and legislation which varied significantly from state to state. This inevitably led to attempts to evade certain legislation and to doubts concerning the status of various persons, such as adopted children. Quite apart from these and similar problems of a technical character, the differences in state legislation could be used to support a cynical attack on marriage and family life generally, and on the law of any one state in particular.

Australia is fortunate in that those who drafted the Constitution were conscious of the problems in the field of family law. Consequently, the Commonwealth parliament was given power to legislate with respect to "marriage" (Section 51 [xxi]) and "divorce and matrimonial causes; and in relation thereto, parental rights, and the custody and guardianship of infants" (Section 51 [xxii]).

These provisions do not give the Commonwealth an exhaustive power over family law. It is doubtful whether the Commonwealth has any power to legislate with respect to custody of children generally, as the Constitutional provision seems to limit Commonwealth jurisdiction to cases where questions of custody arise incidentally in proceedings for divorce or other matrimonial relief. Moreover, the Constitutional provisions do not give the Commonwealth power to alter the law with respect to property rights within the family. These limits on Commonwealth power may lead to complications in the future, but the Commonwealth has ample powers over marriage and the dissolution of marriage to deal with any problems that arise in those areas.

The Commonwealth powers lay dormant until quite recently.

260

After the Second World War the Commonwealth enacted certain limited legislation dealing with technical questions of jurisdiction in matrimonial causes. Then the tree which was planted at Federation bore more substantial fruit, and the Matrimonial Causes Act 1959 and the Marriage Act 1961 were enacted by the Commonwealth parliament. At the same time, proposals for uniform state legislation on adoption, guardianship, and the custody of infants received a welcome stimulus.

It may seem strange that the Commonwealth did not exploit its powers generally for more than fifty years. The reason is obvious. There was considerable opposition. No one suggested that the variations in the state laws could be justified by local circumstances, but there was considerable controversy concerning the content of any proposed Australian law.

In the Matrimonial Causes Act 1959 the draftsmen attempted to do two things—to overcome the problems arising from a diversity of state laws by replacing them with a uniform federal law, and to draft the most effective legislation possible to maintain the family unit. This has led to some interesting innovations.

For instance, the act provides for subsidies to be paid to marriage guidance agencies which conform to minimum standards approved by the attorney general. The hope has been expressed that this financial assistance will encourage suitable people to make careers as counselors and will permit standard courses of training to be introduced. To encourge efforts at reconciliation, the new legislation provides that statements made in the course of an attempted reconciliation are privileged and may not be used as evidence in any subsequent proceedings or otherwise made public. Even where the parties have reached the stage of actual litigation, the judge is charged with an obligation to effect reconciliation if possible; to carry out this obligation he is given power to adjourn the proceedings and to discuss the matter with the parties informally in his private chambers.

If reconciliation is impossible, and a case for a decree of divorce has been demonstrated, the court must not declare the marriage dissolved unless it is satisfied that proper provision has been made for any children of the marriage or that special circumstances justify the order even though such provision has not been made. This represents a significant change in emphasis. Until recently the decisive force behind the divorce law was a maudlin sympathy for the parties to the unsuccessful marriage. Although Australians have a deep love of children, any consideration for the children in divorce proceedings was largely accidental. Undoubtedly there are practical limits on any scheme to give legal protection to the children of unsuccessful marriages, but it is refreshing to see that attempts are being made to ensure that these innocents suffer as little as possible for the wickedness or folly of their parents.

Generally speaking, the grounds on which a decree of divorce may be granted are similar to those that previously existed in the laws of the various states. Most of these cases require the petitioner to prove a matrimonial offense by the other party to the marriage. However, the new Commonwealth legislation permits a divorce in some cases where no matrimonial offense can be proved; and at least one of these cases represents an innovation and a considerable extension of the law existing before the new legislation. A divorce may be granted where one party to the marriage has been of unsound mind for six years, or where a spouse has disappeared and is presumed to be dead. Moreover, it is now possible for a marriage to be dissolved where the parties have lived separately for five years and there is no likelihood of cohabitation being resumed. This ground is separate from the ground of desertion. Desertion for two years gives the innocent party good grounds for a petition. Consequently, this new provision is intended to cover cases of voluntary separation and of petitions by the deserting spouse where the deserted spouse has not taken proceedings for divorce. As such, it represents the admission of divorce by consent, but the requirement of five years' separation should ensure that it will be used only where the marriage has failed utterly.

Naturally, these provisions excited considerable discussion. Certain religious groups opposed the legislation because it widened, in some respects, the grounds on which a divorce could be decreed. Lawyers complained that the legislation made legal proceedings for divorce more complex and expensive. (This was largely the result of the provisions designed to achieve a reconciliation which, it was said, were impractical.)

The Marriage Act 1961 did not provoke as much controversy.

The provisions which led to the widest discussion were the provisions fixing the age at which children may marry. The marriageable age for males is fixed at eighteen years and for females at sixteen years. However, males at the age of sixteen and females at the age of fourteen may apply to a judge or magistrate for authority to marry even though they have not reached the marriageable age. In any event, all persons under twenty-one must have the consent of the parents or a court to the marriage.

It is clear that the force of this drive for reform in the field of family law has not been spent. There are proposals for a uniform law dealing with the adoption, custody, and guardianship of infants. However, these matters appear to be outside the powers of the Commonwealth parliament, so that the various states must agree on the terms of any proposed uniform law. Nevertheless, the general acceptance of the controversial Matrimonial Causes Act 1959 raises hopes that agreement can be reached on these less controversial matters where the problems are of a technical, rather than an ethical, character.

The constitutions of many other countries include a comprehensive set of provisions designed to protect fundamental human rights. This is not true of the Australian Constitution. The principal check on government is not a formal set of constitutional prohibitions, but the popular vote expressed in democratic elections. It would be easy to explain this in terms of a deep faith in democratic government, and undoubtedly this is a partial explanation for the omission of a "Bill of Rights." However, a more decisive reason for the omission is a deep-seated skepticism about the efficacy of such provisions, which often delay needed reforms and rarely stop a government determined to control the matter apparently protected by the constitutional guarantee.

Of course, the mere existence of the federation and the consequent division of legislative power leads to the result that legislation by either the Commonwealth parliament or one of the state parliaments may be beyond the legislative competence of the government concerned, and therefore be invalid. The idea of a limited sovereignty is strange to English legal thought, although it is a practical working concept for Australian lawyers. This has led to some difficulties, because Australia has retained a general right of appeal to the Privy Council in London, and the learned members of that tribunal have found it difficult on occasion to forget the political dogma of their own country when the legal validity of an act of Parliament is called in question.

Some exceptional provisions do protect basic liberties. Thus, Section 116 of the Constitution prohibits the Commonwealth from making any law for establishing any religion or for prohibiting the free exercise of any religion, and Sections 99 and 117 prohibit discrimination against the resident of any state if the discrimination is based on his residence in that state. However, these are far removed from the comprehensive provisions of the United States Constitution.

Yet there is another famous, or notorious, provision in the Australian Constitution which has been invoked frequently to protect individual liberties. Section 92 provides that "on the imposition of uniform duties of customs, trade, commerce and intercourse among the States, whether by means of internal carriage or ocean navigation, shall be absolutely free." No lawyer can look at the words "trade, commerce and intercourse . . . shall be absolutely free" without asking the inevitable question: "What does it mean?" because it is obvious that the words cannot be accepted at their face value. Interstate businesses must comply with reasonable registration provisions and pay ordinary taxes on their profits. Interstate haulers must obey the ordinary traffic regulations. The literal meaning must be qualified if chaos is to be avoided.

It will come as no surprise that the phrasing of the section was suggested by a person without legal training, and the section was approved despite the protests of some able lawyers that fantastic problems of interpretation would arise unless it were rephrased. This "little bit of layman's language" has provoked a considerable amount of litigation.

It seems clear that those who drafted Section 92 were concerned to strike down interstate tariff walls, and several commentators have suggested that the section should be limited so as to invalidate only legislation imposing fiscal burdens on interstate trade. But it seems equally clear that the draftsmen of Section 92 might have rejected the more sophisticated practices of state marketing controls as well as the use of the crude economic instruments of tariffs. It must be

264

presumed that the policy was not to be evaded by alterations in the form of the restrictive state legislation, and that the section was adaptable to invalidate modern forms of protective economic legislation. Consequently, attempts to limit Section 92 in terms of its alleged historical origin have never commanded significant support.[3]

At first it was considered that Section 92 bound the states, but not the Commonwealth. However, in 1936 this solution was rejected by the Privy Council in *James v. Commonwealth*.[4] With this decision the courts seemed to reach the position that the section gave a constitutional guarantee of laissez-faire economic policies in interstate trade. Inevitably this involved a more precise delineation of the operation of the section. Nevertheless, it is not easy to give an accurate summary of the present law.

Some members of the High Court of Australia require a distinction to be drawn between things or acts which are an essential or an inseverable part of interstate commerce and things or acts which are merely incidental to interstate commerce. The essential element in the concept of interstate commerce is the movement of goods or persons from one state to another, but the premises occupied by an interstate trader, the equipment carried on his vehicles, and the gasoline used by them are incidental to his trade.

Obviously, the distinction drawn is a formal rather than a real one, as the matters characterized as incidental can be incorporated into some broader concept of interstate trade. Consequently, the definition of the essential or inseverable parts of interstate trade must be effected by stipulative definition with the members of the various federal courts, and the High Court in particular, exercising the powers of definition.

Nevertheless, once the distinction is conceded, it has been determined that any law which imposes a real burden or liability on

[3] See F. R. Beasley, "Commonwealth Constitution: Section 92," (1948–50) 1 *University of Western Australia Annual Law Review* 97–111, 273–88, 433–40.

Many views have been expressed concerning the intentions of those who framed the Constitution. It seems clear that tariffs prompted the introduction of Section 92, and some writers have implied that an interpretation which extends the section beyond tariffs is improper. This view seems particularly naïve. Those who drafted the Constitution did not foresee modern protective control of industry, but it is reasonable to suppose that other restrictions on interstate trade, as well as tariffs, would have been considered unfavorably.

[4] (1936) 55 C.L.R. 1; (1936) Appeal Cases 578.

an essential attribute of interstate trade will be unconstitutional. To determine whether the law imposes a real burden it is necessary to consider the operation of the law. If it prohibits some essential attribute of interstate trade, it will impose a liability except in unusual cases. However, regulation (as distinct from prohibition) is consistent with the freedom guaranteed by Section 92, provided that the regulation does not impose a real burden on interstate trade. Insofar as the law deals with incidentals of interstate trade, it will be valid unless it operates so as to impose a real burden on interstate trade.

It might be said that the legal rules merely obscure the fact that the basic problem is as much political, social, or economic as it is legal. There is some truth in this criticism. The only difference between the "essentials" and "incidents" of interstate trade is a difference of degree, and the courts have not provided a precise test to distinguish the two classes. Moreover, references to "regulation" and "real" burdens are indeterminate until the terms are objectively defined.

The courts are aware of these criticisms and the limited effectiveness of the rules they have established. But the responsibility for determining constitutional issues rests uneasily on their shoulders, and cases in which Section 92 have been invoked frequently involve live political issues. The legal rules represent an attempt to demonstate that a court, bound to determine whether Section 92 invalidates a certain law, answers the question in terms of traditional legal techniques and not on some broader political basis.

The success of the rules has been limited. At least in part, they are self-defeating, because where a distinction is drawn which is to some extent illusory, a skilled draftsman can turn the distinction to his own advantage. Consequently, unless the broader political and economic questions are incorporated into the legal rules, Section 92 could become a dead hand of the law grasping only those few matters which it had controlled before life left it.

Generally speaking, Section 92 has been the bane of socialist economists. It has been used to thwart attempts to create government monopolies in interstate air transport and banking. Marketing schemes and legislation designed to penalize road hauliers competing with the state railways have to be limited within the area permitted by Section 92. Nevertheless, it is quite wrong to regard Section 92 as a constitutional guarantee of free enterprise. Clearly it does not purport to have, nor does it have, such a wide operation. However, it has been adapted to meet new forms of restrictive economic legislation, and it can be predicted that the present interpretation represents merely one stage in a continual evolutionary adjustment in which the section is interpreted to give effect to the basic economic and political convictions of the time.

In Australia, as in the United States, the courts exercise two jurisdictions. Firstly, there is the inherent general jurisdiction which belongs to each of the states. This state jurisdiction existed before Federation, and it continues to exist except insofar as it has been affected by the Commonwealth Constitution or by legislation passed under it. Secondly, there is a federal jurisdiction superimposed on the basic state jurisdiction. This federal jurisdiction covers matters arising under Commonwealth legislation and a few other matters. American lawyers are familiar with this distinction between federal and state jurisdiction, but it must be emphasized that there is a vast difference between the court systems in the United States and Australia.

In Australia, unlike the United States, there is only one system of courts. The Australian state courts have been invested with federal jurisdiction in general terms in addition to their inherent state jurisdiction. The High Court of Australia, the supreme federal court, is a general appellate court over the state supreme courts even where the dispute concerns a matter within the original state jurisdiction.

The Australian courts form a single pyramid. At the apex is the Judicial Committee of the Privy Council, sitting in England. Australia is one of the few countries in the British Commonwealth which has preserved the right of appeal to this old, imperial tribunal, and there is a steady flow of appeals to the Privy Council. Even constitutional matters, such as the correct interpretation of Section 92, may be taken to the Privy Council. The chief limitation is a practical one—the expense of an appeal. However, Section 74 of the Constitution expressly limits the right of appeal to the Privy Council where the dispute concerns a so-called *inter se* question.

Such a question arises whenever the case involves the limits *inter se* of the Constitutional powers of the Commonwealth and those of any state or states, or the limits *inter se* of the Constitutional powers of any two or more states. In such a case no appeal can be taken to the Privy Council without a certificate from the High Court; and the High Court habitually refuses to grant the required certificate. This practice has been explained as follows:

Questions characteristic of federalism should *prima facie* be decided finally in this Court, habituated as it is to the conceptions and considerations governing such questions, conceptions and considerations peculiar to Federal systems and appearing strange and exotic to those who have enjoyed only a unitary form of government.[5]

The odd decisions that the Privy Council has reached in some constitutional cases justify the explanation. However, questions "characteristic of federalism" may arise under other provisions of the Constitution besides Section 74, and it may be questioned whether any constitutional issues should be dealt with by the Privy Council.[6]

Although the High Court of Australia is theoretically subordinate to the Privy Council, it is by far the most significant court for lawyers in Australia. Most of its work is appellate, although it has a limited original jurisdiction. At the present time there are seven justices of the High Court, and it frequently sits in divisions of three justices. However, Section 79 of the Judiciary Act provides that at least three justices must concur upon a decision "affecting the constitutional powers of the Commonwealth"; and where such a decision can be foreseen, the High Court will take the precaution to constitute itself with at least five members.

The very flexibility of the High Court has its dangers. It is conceivable that two differently constituted divisions of the High Court might give inconsistent decisions, although this problem is less likely in constitutional cases where the majority of the Court

[5] *Nelungaloo Pty. Ltd. v. Commonwealth*, (1952) 85 C.L.R. 545 at p. 570 *per* Dixon, J.

[6] It is quite clear that the Commonwealth government could abolish appeals to the Privy Council. The only question is whether it should. The opposing views are canvassed by F. R. Beasley, "Appeals to the Judicial Committee: The Case for Abolition," (1957) 7 *Res Judicatae* 399 and E. G. Coppel, "Appeals to the Judicial Committee—A Reply," (1957) 1 *Melbourne University Law Review* 76.

sit in every case. This theoretical problem has not proved a significant difficulty in practice, and the division of the Court has enabled it to deal with an increasing amount of work.

In each state there is a superior court known as the supreme court. It has a general jurisdiction, civil and criminal, original and appellate.[7] In addition to the supreme court, each state has a number of inferior courts with limited jurisdictions which are either predominantly civil or predominantly criminal in character. The various states have different systems of inferior courts, so that it is impossible to make accurate generalizations about them; but we may take the courts in New South Wales as an illustration.

In this state the inferior civil courts are called district courts and courts of petty sessions. District courts have a general civil jurisdiction over matters involving £3,000 or less. There are some exceptions to this rule. On one hand, the parties may consent to trial in the district court even though the dispute involves a sum greater than £3,000. On the other hand, certain cases may be transferred to the supreme court even though less than £3,000 is involved (for example, cases concerning title to land). District courts are constituted by a judge, who must have professional experience, and a jury—where this is appropriate to the case. Courts of petty sessions have a summary jurisdiction over minor civil matters, and they may be constituted by a stipendiary magistrate, two justices of the peace, or a single justice of the peace. The jurisdiction of courts of petty sessions depends on its members, but in general no court of petty sessions may determine a matter involving more than £150. Stipendiary magistrates are paid, and justices of the peace are not; but professional qualifications are not required for appointment in either case. Generally speaking, the stipendiary magistrate is replacing the justice of the peace; and as the courts of petty sessions have more technical questions committed to their jurisdiction, it can be assumed that there will be a growing demand that these magistrates should have a formal legal education.

---

[7] Five states have copied the Judicature Act system introduced in England in the late nineteenth century. In New South Wales, however, common law and equity are still administered as separate jurisdictions. This separation is an anachronism found in few, if any, states outside New South Wales. Attempts to facilitate the transfer of actions from one jurisdiction to the other have not proved successful, and it seems that only the traditional conservatism of the legal mind postpones the adoption of the Judicature Act system.

The inferior criminal courts in New South Wales are the courts of quarter sessions and the courts of petty sessions. Courts of quarter sessions have jurisdiction over all crimes committed in the state except those punishable with death before the Crimes Act 1955 and the few remaining capital offenses.[8] In addition, they have an appellate jurisdiction over decisions of courts of petty sessions. The chairman of quarter sessions is a district court judge, and he constitutes the court together with a jury in the more serious criminal cases. Courts of petty sessions have a jurisdiction over all offenses declared to be punishable summarily. Generally speaking, the court of petty sessions must be constituted by a stipendiary magistrate except in country districts where a justice of the peace may serve.

The integration of the state and federal courts was dictated by a prudent desire for economy in judicial personnel because an elaborate system of subordinate federal courts could not have been justified in Australia as it existed sixty years ago. However, the integration of the two jurisdictions has produced some important consequences for law in Australia. As the High Court of Australia is a general appellate court from the states, there is not the same diversity among the common-law rules of the various states as there is in the United States. If a state supreme court declares a common-law rule which is incompatible with a common-law rule formulated by the supreme court of another state, the apparent conflict can be resolved by an appeal to the supreme federal court. Naturally, this type of court organization contributes to a national rather than a parochial view of legal principle, and this may explain the success of proposals to introduce national law on such controversial topics as marriage and divorce.

Admittedly the system has its complications. Courts of petty

---

[8] The major exceptions to the jurisdiction of courts of quarter sessions are the crimes of murder, rape, piracy, and treason. In 1955 the death penalty for murder, rape, and related offences was abolished in New South Wales. Because the jurisdiction of courts of quarter sessions was defined in terms of the punishments these courts could inflict, the restriction of capital punishment brought murder and rape within the jurisdiction of quarter sessions. This was criticized, and in 1957 the legislation provided that these crimes should be tried in the supreme court even though the death penalty could no longer be inflicted.

sessions have been invested with federal jurisdiction, subject to the proviso that the court must be constituted by a magistrate sitting alone. In some cases there may be doubt whether the matter arises within the scope of the state or federal jurisdiction. There may be questions where the two jurisdictions overlap. The obvious difficulty is that a court may exercise federal jurisdiction without considering whether it is properly constituted to do so. Moreover, if there are cases where a double jurisdiction exists, how can it be determined whether the court was exercising state or federal jurisdiction? These technical mysteries could be solved by remedial legislation, and it is rather surprising that the Commonwealth parliament has let the doubts linger so long. The reason may be that the judicial organization has operated so satisfactorily that no one has felt a pressing urgency to overcome the few technical difficulties.

Nevertheless, the days of this idyllic system may be numbered. The dual function of the High Court as the supreme federal court and as a general court of appeal from the various states results in a tremendous quantity of appellate work. The division of the High Court into separate tribunals is a partial solution only, and an increasing number of rules have been introduced to check appeals to the High Court. The immediate consequence may be an increase in the relative importance of the state supreme courts. The ultimate result may be changes and extensions to the Commonwealth court structure.

If it is difficult to select aspects of Australian law that reflect the peoples' attitude to law, it may be easier to convey the native character by considering how Australians treat those who are concerned with law enforcement.

Few people in the community are given the respect given to judges. The judiciary has maintained the highest standards of scholarship and integrity. Traditional in their attitude, Australian judges consider that there is a substantial body of authoritative law. Within such established legal principle, the judge may create law interstitially; but his lawmaking powers are strictly limited. Nevertheless, the High Court will overrule one of its earlier decisions if it is considered incorrect. One of Australia's great judges, Sir Isaac Isaacs, put his view in these words:

If, then, we find the law to be plainly in conflict with what we or any of our predecessors erroneously thought it to be, we have, as I conceive, no right to choose between giving effect to the law and maintaining an incorrect interpretation. It is not, in my opinion, better that the Court should be persistently wrong than that it should be ultimately right.[9]

Thus the High Court applies a principle akin to that applied by the United States Supreme Court and contrary to that applied by the British House of Lords which, theoretically, is bound to follow its own previous decisions.

Although judicial appointments are made on the recommendation of the appropriate government, a vigilant profession backed by an insistent public has frustrated the few injudicious attempts to make political appointments. Undoubtedly, this is one of the secrets of the success of the industrial arbitration system. For some time economists have argued that they are better equipped to deal with industrial disputes. They have argued unsuccessfully. There seem to be two basic reasons for their failure: the first is that the decisions made by the industrial tribunals are not decisions on matters exclusively within the realm of economics; the second is the fact that the Australian people have more faith in the impartiality and objectivity of the judiciary as a class than they have in economists as a class.

The public respect for the judiciary explains the customary selection of a judge to conduct a royal commission. A royal commission is an inquiry designed to elicit as much information as possible about a designated subject. The subject investigated may be selected simply because it merits a long and searching inquiry. Thus there have been royal commissions concerned with the basic wage and the monetary or banking systems. However, a royal commission has become the accepted procedure for conducting an inquiry into allegations of graft and corruption in public life, and two of the more sensational royal commissions disclosed serious corruption by a minister of lands in New South Wales and within the council of the city of Sydney. A royal commission is the Australian equivalent of the congressional investigation bodies in the United States. The commissioner completes a report on his investigations,

[9] *Australian Agricultural Co. v. Federated Engine-Drivers and Firemen's Association of Australasia,* (1913) 17 C.L.R. 261 at 278.

and this furnishes a basis for appropriate action in the legislature or the courts. While anyone may be appointed a royal commissioner, more often than not a judge is appointed; and where there is any suggestion of graft or malpractice, it is almost certain that a judge will be appointed.

Although Australians pay a wholesome respect to the judiciary, they are surprisingly uncooperative with, and even contemptuous of, the police. This attitude is difficult to explain because the Australian police forces have inherited the British traditions of service and integrity, and generally they have preserved those traditions untarnished. Yet it is not uncommon to hear of a crowd watching a fight between a policeman and some minor criminal and intervening only to obstruct the police and allow the criminal to escape. Some commentators regard this sorry state of affairs as a survival of an Irish resentment of authority, but it seems strange that the Irish influence in Australia should be so permanent and widespread. Perhaps the unpopularity of the police is partly due to the fact that their principal function in Australia is to enforce laws against speeding, "sly grog" (illegal sales of liquor), two-up, and other trivial offenses. It may be that the price of enforcement of an expanding list of minor offenses against generally law-abiding citizens is an increasing resentment against those who are charged with the enforcement of the law.

Unfortunately, the magistrates are classified with the police rather than with the judiciary. For some years the stipendiary magistrates were known as police magistrates, and the change of title has not elevated them in public opinion. Generally speaking, the training these magistrates receive tends to link them with the police rather than to set them apart, and it cannot be expected that the aura surrounding the judiciary will encompass them until their training and practice follows the pattern required of the judiciary.

The attitude of the public to the legal profession is just as equivocal as the attitude to law itself. The Australian is usually critical of those who merely provide services. Where work results in nothing tangible, he is likely to conclude that it has resulted in nothing valuable to the community. Certainly the lawyer in Australia has been described in harsh and unkind words on many occasions. Yet the legal profession enjoys a preeminent position in politics

273

and public life, and this is striking evidence that the community regards many members of the profession as men who are capable and wise in the ways of the world.

Each state has a different system of legal education and professional organization. The Australian lawyer may be either a barrister or a solicitor. The barrister is a specialist, intimately involved in litigation as a skilled counsel or advocate, and he is selected by the solicitor. The solicitor is a general practitioner, competent to handle the day-to-day business of legal practice, but obliged to seek the skilled assistance of a barrister whenever an unusual question arises. In several states the two professions are amalgamated, but in New South Wales, Victoria, and Queensland there is a strict division of the profession either by law or by customary practice. Where the separation of the profession exists, cases involving difficult legal questions are conducted more skillfully; but the price that must be paid for this increased skill is increased expense.

Throughout Australia most lawyers qualify for their profession by passing a university degree in law combined with some practical experience in a legal office or the chambers of a barrister. In some states it is still possible for a person to become qualified to practice without obtaining a university degree in law, but an increasing public concern with the standards of professional men will make a university degree in law an essential qualification within the foreseeable future. At present the glamour of science is attracting many able students into scientific careers, and an increasing percentage of poor students are attempting a career in law. These facts are reflected in the number who fail to pass the examinations prescribed for admission to the legal profession. However, law has a glamour of its own, and it continues to attract those idealists cynical enough to realize that an effective and just legal system provides the fertile ground in which other skills may grow and prosper.

274

LAW

BIBLIOGRAPHY

Books

Baalman, J. *Outline of Law in Australia.* 1955.
Cowen, Z., and Mendes da Costa, D. *Matrimonial Causes Jurisdiction.* 1961.
Davis, S. R., ed. *The Government of the Australian States.* 1960.
Foenander, O. de R. *Industrial Conciliation and Arbitration in Australia.* 1959.
Joske, P. E. *Marriage and Divorce.* 1961.
Mitchell, R. E., ed. *Essays on the Australian Constitution.* 1961.
Paton, Sir George W., ed. *The Commonwealth of Australia,* Vol. II of *The British Commonwealth: The Development of Its Laws and Institutions.* 1952.
Portus, J. H. *The Development of Australian Trade Union Law.* 1958.
Sykes, E. I. *Strike Law in Australia.* 1960.
Wynes, W. A. *Legislative and Executive Powers in Australia.* 1956.

Articles

Barwick, Sir Garfield. "Some Aspects of the New Matrimonial Causes Act." (1961) 3 *Sydney Law Review* 409.
Menzies, R. G. "The Challenge to Federalism." (1961) 3 *Melbourne University Law Review* 1.

EDUCATION

G. W. BASSETT

IT is sometimes said that countries have the educational systems that they deserve. This way of stating the relationship between the characteristics of a social institution and the quality of aspiration of a nation is usually intended as a criticism of those whose educational system is defective. It could be just as equally intended as praise for those whose educational system is effective and progressive. Yet in neither case is it an adequate principle of social analysis. One might as well claim that an individual has the physique that he deserves, as though his level of aspiration toward a particular objective were the only measure of his attaining it.

An educational system is a unique cultural product. Ideals of social progress, expressed politically, are a part of this product, probably the part most closely aligned to the idea of getting what one deserves. But social institutions, like people, are shaped by factors other than convictions as to a desired form. Some of these factors determine, fairly definitely, the limits within which ambition may move.

276

EDUCATION

The moderate economic prosperity of Australia, based until quite recently mainly on primary industry and a small population set in a vast area, must be kept in mind in assessing its educational development. So, too, must other parts of its social history.

If an Englishman at the end of the eighteenth century gave any thought at all to the educational system of a remote penal settlement, he would have surmised that education in the colony of New South Wales was conducted by various voluntary agencies such as churches. He would not have been surprised if a large number of children of socially inferior groups were not being educated at all. His predictions would have been quite correct. There was a chaplain with the first fleet to Sydney, but no schoolmaster; this chaplain and the other clergy who came to the colony in its early years were responsible for the creation of the country's first schools. In spite of the admirable efforts of these men, Governor Macquarie, soon after his arrival in the colony in 1809, claimed that he had "seen a number of children about the town of Sydney who appear to be wholly neglected in their education and morals."

Within eighty years the educational system in New South Wales had changed so much in its administrative aspects as to be almost unrecognizable as English in origin; and in the other Australian states as they were formed, the same general structure as in New South Wales emerged.

The great difference that appeared between the educational systems in Australia and in the mother country lay in the different roles adopted by government in its relation to the church. The first public funds for education in England were provided by the British government in 1833, yet in 1800 Governor King of New South Wales, impressed by "the vicious and wretched state" of many orphaned and abandoned children among the convict population, had established a public fund to provide schools. A school for orphan girls, opened in 1801, was a fully public institution established and maintained out of public funds. This pattern of direct public activity in setting up schools and in assisting schools established by private venture was extended by later governors of the colony. Governor Macquarie, who was responsible for a great deal of the early developmental work in the colony, extended and consolidated the educational fund and increased government assistance to communities for the erection of schools. The virtually despotic nature of government in the foundation years of the colony, the unusual nature of the population and its dependence on government action for any amelioration of its condition, and the reliance of outlying frontier communities on the administration at Sydney all help to explain the state-centralized scheme that ultimately emerged.

The steps by which this plan came to finality in New South Wales and the detailed variations that occurred in the development of the other states cannot be traced in a brief statement of this kind. The major outline of development in New South Wales only will be given.

In 1824 a Church and Schools Corporation was established under charter from the British government for the control and development of both churches and schools in the colony. This British pattern of control ignored both the Australian government's interest in education and the interests of religious denominations other than Anglican; and despite the undoubted advances it brought to educational provision in New South Wales, it was doomed to failure. The advantage that it conferred on the Anglican Church was bitterly resented and opposed by other church authorities. In 1833 the Corporation was dissolved.

The religious controversy that centered on the Church and Schools Corporation is the prevailing theme of the years succeeding its dissolution. Governor Bourke sought to fill the vacuum created by the withdrawal of control from the Church and Schools Corporation with a system along the lines of the Irish national school system. Support in the Legislative Council for denominational schools was strong enough, however, to secure, in 1836, the passing of a Church Act which committed the state to a general system of aiding denominational schools on a pound for pound basis with no limit of subsidy specified. A national system of education seemed further off than ever. The anomalies of this system soon became apparent. In larger communities needless duplication of schools occurred; in smaller communities the basic minimum to attract subsidy could not be raised. Governor Gipps, who campaigned unsuccessfully for a national system, claimed that "if this country was still to be deprived of a comprehensive system of education—if the present imperfect, partial, ineffective, expensive and wasteful mode of conducting schools was to be continued, it behoved him at least to show to the people that the fault does not rest with him."

An uneasy solution to the problem of maintaining existing denominational schools and setting up and extending national schools came in 1848, when a dual system was introduced with the appointment of two boards to control the national and denominational schools respectively. The schools of the National Schools Board prospered; those of the Denominational Schools Board languished through rivalry between constituent churches. It was clear that the dual system was not succeeding, and public opinion was swinging in favor of a single national system. A figure influential in directing public opinion toward this solution was Sir Henry Parkes, newspaper editor and politician. His articles in the *Empire* did much to secure the appointment in 1854 of a commission on education to inquire into the state of education in the colony. The chairman of this four-man commission was Parkes himself. The report that was presented was a documentation of appalling inefficiency in educational provision. It recommended that the dual system give way to a single system. This report set the scene for the climax of the educational drama. Following the defeat in 1859 and again in 1863 of legislation to set up a public system of education, Parkes in 1866 steered to a narrow victory a Public Schools Act which replaced the two boards with a single Council of Education.

The Public Schools Act was a compromise piece of legislation. It retained the principle of state aid to denominational schools, but increased public control over them by requiring that they meet certain conditions to qualify for state aid. Religious teaching in the public schools was restricted to "general religious teaching as distinct from dogmatical and polemical theology." This restriction was quite unacceptable to the Roman Catholic Church, and it strove to retain its separate denominational schools. In 1879 the archbishop and bishops of the Roman Catholic Church launched a spirited attack on the legislation of 1866. They attacked the public schools as "godless" and as "seedplots of future immorality, infidelity and lawlessness." Parkes's own words express the political reaction to these attacks:

279

What the secularists had failed to do by their many motions in Parliament, the archbishop and his associate bishops contrived to do by one rash, blind move. I felt that the time had come when the field in which I had labored and patiently watched for fourteen years must be resurveyed. I felt, in common with tens of thousands of my fellow colonists, that a wanton and libellous attack had been made upon our schools.

The result of the resurvey was the Public Instruction Act of 1880, which abolished all aid to denominational schools and set up a system of free, compulsory, and secular education under centralized state control.

The main provisions of this Act have governed the development of education in New South Wales for the last eighty-odd years. Whether they will continue to do so for the next eighty years, it would be idle to prophesy. The need for centralized control may pass, and the breach between state and church in education may be healed.

But the systems described in the following sections are the product of this history, whether we deserve them or not.

There is no articulated body of ideas and beliefs that one could call an Australian philosophy of education. The combination of youth and smallness of population is not a likely one for producing such a philosophy.

The ideas that guide our practice are eclectic, mainly a compound of British and American ideas. Because of our British origin and our continuing strong affinity with British thought, it is to be expected that our ideas about what education should aim at and the methods by which these aims should be realized would be largely derived from Britain. An American observer would probably see this more clearly than we can, because for him the contrasts with his own system are sharper.

He would see the emphasis on a blend of intellectual and character training which inspires so much of British effort in education. The evidence of concern with intellectual training is seen in the predominantly selective organizational schemes we adopt which guide the more able children into academic courses or schools, the great prestige we give to academic courses compared with alternative vocational courses, and the relatively low statutory minimum leaving age (14 or 15 years) which encourages the less academic children to seek early employment.

The curriculums and teaching methods employed are influenced by this intellectualist aim.

Academic courses are largely prescriptive. They include the foundation studies, such as English, mathematics, science, foreign languages, history, and geography, and are arranged so that each subject is studied sequentially through the various years of the secondary school. The content of syllabuses in each year is not rigidly prescribed, but the external examination, which is taken at the end of the course and on which matriculation to the universities is based, has the effect of determining fairly rigidly the content of courses.

The methods used by teachers reflect the serious intent to reach prescribed standards of achievement—exposition, explanation, set homework, tests, and guided study of texts are the usual methods. There is little disposition to experiment in the teaching of academic courses because examination results are too important for both teacher and student.

The goal of character training lies behind a good deal of what the teacher does and is a test (although often implicit) of his success. This character training takes many forms; probably the most general is the interpretation that the Australian teacher places on discipline. Discipline, to most Australian teachers, is the maintenance of a proper relationship of authority and control between himself and his students. On the whole, it is not unkindly or harshly sustained, but it does assume adult authority and the child's obedience to that authority. In the intellectual affairs of the school teachers who have learned, on a theoretical level, to distrust the efficacy of formal discipline proceed in practice as though their distrust is half-hearted. In character training the submission of children to authority appears to be valued for the general strengthening of character that it is believed to provide.

This authoritarian attitude to child upbringing appears to be giving way in Australian homes to a more permissive approach. To borrow William James's expressive words "tender" and "tough" from the context in which he used them, it could be said that the attitude to discipline in schools, as compared with that in homes, is "tough" rather than "tender."

Another expression of this goal of character formation is the value placed on sport, particularly on team games. Cooperation with teammates, doing one's best for the institution represented, and sportsmanship in success and defeat are stressed as generalized character traits.

The stress on moral training is seen in its most direct form in church-controlled schools (which, as will be shown later in the chapter, play an important part in Australian education). One of the avowed purposes of these schools is to influence character development through cultivating religious observance. In government-controlled schools a similar effect is aimed at by appeal to moral principles without invoking religious beliefs.

American influences have been superimposed on this basic British pattern. American books on education are widely read in Australia. A scrutiny of reading lists for courses in education in colleges and universities would give ready proof of this statement. Australian educationists also visit the United States in considerable numbers, often aided by American funds to do so. The Australian educator is commonly an interested and informed observer of the American educational scene.

The structure of American education in its administrative aspects has had little influence on Australian education. As will be shown later, Australia has state-centralized systems of education and is likely to be committed to them for a long time to come.

American ideas about teaching methods and curriculums have been more influential. Emphasis on interest in learning has tempered more formal (and forceful) methods of stimulating effort in the children, and a wider range of subjects (with departures from traditional content) is now offered. A more permissive atmosphere is more common in classrooms, and group methods of teaching—aided by sociometric and psychological studies—are gaining a little ground.

The more informal classroom climate and the more experimental approach to content and method are more likely to be found in the lowest levels of the school, in kindergartens and infants' classes. The progress through primary and secondary school is usually marked by an increasing degree of formality as the sterner realities of scholastic achievement are grappled with.

The impact of these predominantly British and American influences has produced both a blend and a dichotomy. Our ideas are undoubtedly different because of the double influence than they would be if only one or the other were operative. At the same time, these influences have produced adherents who face one another with some antagonism. Most issues which get ventilated in the public press could be classified broadly in two opposing attitudes to education. The one expresses concern for standards of scholarship and is rather intolerant about "child-centered" schools, modern methods ("soft pedagogy"), and "newfangled" studies; the other professes itself to be more concerned about the well-being of children and the quality of the society they will live in. Both are fundamentally interested in the same outcome, but each has a different view of how it might be achieved.

Australian educational practice, then, is animated by adopted ideas which produce an uneasy kind of equilibrium. It is a curious blend of conservatism and liberalism. It has no clear idea where it is heading, but in this it would not be greatly different from most western democracies.

One ideal that has guided its progress is not an educational aim at all: this is the objective of equality of educational opportunity which stems from the social philosophy of the country. This article of democratic faith, which has been fulfilling itself in many ways in the twentieth century, has influenced the development of education strongly. Compared with that of England, the pace of development has been fast. With approximately the same point of origin (about 1870) for the establishment of a system of free public education, the Australian states created a superstructure on the elementary system providing opportunities for all adolescents to take advantage of secondary education much earlier than did England. The achievements of the 1944 Education Act in England would be looked at a little wonderingly by an Australian who might ask what all the fuss was about. It provided opportunities for academically talented children to pass through the school system to the university entirely without cost; opportunities for less academically talented children to profit from secondary education through types of courses alternative to the academic ones; and opportunities for children to specialize in technical education at secondary level. Australia had all of these after the First World War.

The more resistant social stratification in England, as compared with Australia, suggests why the same dynamic forces of education in both countries worked themselves out in different ways.

This is not to say that Australia has no class divisions or that Australians are not aware of these divisions. There *are* class divisions, and Australians *are* aware of them. But mobility is easier. The prestige hierarchy can be described with almost complete accuracy in terms of types of employment engaged in, from the leading professions to unskilled work. Because of this, one's "class" depends on one's capacity to take advantage of educational opportunities. What one's father does (or the class to which he belongs) is no barrier to what his child may become. The capacity of the child to take advantage of the educational system embraces both intellectual and financial features. A bright child might be deterred from a long period of schooling because of economic necessity in the home. However, most parents in a low-income group, if they were sufficiently ambitious for their children, could support a child through school and university. An able child from a poor home would be assisted at the school level by various forms of bursaries and scholarships offered by the state authority and by scholarships, cadetships, and the like at the university level offered by the Commonwealth government.

Accordingly, the public education system becomes a vast sorting machine redistributing many of the children of one generation from the lives their homes have made for them into lives their new vocations will make for them.

For the professional educationist, education is intellectual and moral discipline; for most of the parents, it is an escalator for their children to preferred types of employment. In practice, these two divergent views work out fairly harmoniously. For the teacher, the well-established subjects are the ones that produce the best mental disciplines; for the parents, the well-established subjects are the ones that lead to the professions.

The most-publicized feature of Australian education, both within and outside of Australia, is the degree of centralization of administration. The pattern of local authorities or school boards of education carrying on the work of schooling under national or state supervision cannot be found anywhere in Australia. In fact, there are only six public authorities for education: the governments of the six states of the Commonwealth. In each state the responsibility for education rests with a cabinet minister who, through his Department of Education, carries on all the activities of the whole state.

284

In discharging this responsibility, the ministers for education, in ways that differ somewhat from state to state, have to take account of other governmental departments or statutory bodies, such as a purchasing authority, a works department, a state architect's department, a government auditor, a public service board, and an arbitration court or special tribunal concerned with teachers' salaries. To a degree, the power of a minister for education is controlled not only by government and parliament, but by powers and responsibilities of other governmental and statutory authorities.

Judgments about the degree of centralized control in education vary somewhat with the criteria adopted. Some critics of the Australian systems base their criticisms on the size of these systems, determined by the number of teachers employed and the burden of head office administration. Against this, it can be pointed out that local authorities in large cities in England and the United States are larger on these counts than the system in the state of Victoria and very much larger than in Tasmania and Western Australia, whose populations are relatively small.

The comparison takes a different turn, however, when the size of the systems is considered in terms of geographic area. The largest cities in England and the United States have an area of a few hundred square miles. The state of Victoria has an area of approximately 90,000 square miles, and it is one of the smallest states. New South Wales, the fourth-largest state, is three and one-third times the area of Britain, and its head office for education in Sydney is as far from its most distant school as Rome is from London. Western Australia, the largest state, is over six times the area of California.

It is in this geographic factor, this remoteness of the governed from the seat of government, that the reason for centralization of administration lies. In spite of their size of population, large cities are something of a community. Their people live close together, have broadly common vocational interests, and share common recreational and other facilities. In no comparable sense is an Australian state a community, although its government assumes responsibility for many of the community services usually carried out in some overseas countries by local government or *ad hoc* authority.

Australian education actually is not as centralized as it could be. Complete centralization would be a national system of education controlled by the federal government. There are movements in Australia to secure special appropriations of funds for education from the federal government, and pressures are put on it to survey the needs of education in the country as a whole. But even the most ardent of these petitioners would not suggest, or wish, that the federal government should administer education. The sovereignty of the states in the field of education was well established before the Commonwealth of Australia came into existence in 1901 and is guaranteed by that Constitution. It is unlikely, whatever assistance the federal government may decide to give to the states, that there will be any move to disturb the present arrangement of state responsibility.

The Commonwealth government plays a specialized but important role in education. It provides educational facilities in its own territories—the Australian Capital Territory, Northern Territory, Papua, New Guinea, Nauru, Norfolk Island, Cocos Island, and Christmas Island—and in the armed services. This provision is made either directly, as in wholly financing the Australian National University in Canberra, or by meeting the expenses of other authorities, usually states, that carry out the schooling. An Office of Education is maintained to advise the Commonwealth government on educational matters, undertake educational research, and maintain a liaison with state authorities.

In Australia's overseas commitments for education, the Commonwealth government is responsible. These commitments include responsibilities as a member state of UNESCO and responsibilities under the Colombo Plan's Technical Cooperation Scheme which has provided specialized training of various kinds for many thousands of Asian students. The special educational measures taken to assist in the assimilation of migrants who have come to Australia under the Commonwealth's postwar immigration policy are also financed by the federal government.

The major form of federal assistance to education within the states is by financial assistance to students undertaking higher education and to educational institutions.

The scheme of assistance to students arose out of the rehabilitation of ex-service personal after the Second World War. In 1951, this specific purpose gave way to the more general one of assisting able students to undertake courses of higher education in universities and other approved institutions. At present four thousand scholarships are awarded annually on a competitive basis. These exempt the recipients from payment of fees and, in cases of financial hardship, provide living allowances as well. The most successful university students are encouraged by postgraduate Commonwealth scholarships to undertake postgraduate study.

The major direct financial assistance to educational institutions is given to the universities, both for recurrent expenditure and for capital building programs. On a very much smaller scale, financial assistance is given to the Australian Pre-School Association, the Commonwealth Council for National Fitness, the Australian Council for Educational Research, and the Departments of Indonesian and Malayan Studies at the Universities of Melbourne and Sydney.

One further form of aid to education provided by the Commonwealth government is worthy of mention. It is the indirect aid that comes from allowing as an income tax deduction certain approved expenditures by parents on the education of their children. The total amount allowable is not great, but it is an appreciable form of assistance to parents.

There is considerable interest in Australia in decentralization. In the main, this interest expresses itself in statements of alarm at the concentrations of population and secondary industry in a handful of centers and the weakness of this position from the point of view of national defense. There are also expressions of dissatisfaction on the part of rural areas at alleged domination by city interests and at the "talent erosion" which occurs when the able young men and women move off to the cities to take advantage of better vocational opportunities. In Queensland and New South Wales there are fairly active movements toward the formation of new states in order to overcome the centralization of power in a remote capital city. In none of these movements, however, is the decentralization of education a very significant consideration, although, of course, it is assumed that control of education would pass to any new state created.

Departments of Education, particularly in the larger states, are concerned about the high degree of centralization of administration, and two of them have introduced a measure of change. In 1948 Queensland was divided, for educational purposes, into five regions:

each was placed under the control of a director of education. This officer is answerable to the director general of education in the capital city, but is empowered to deal with many regional matters which previously would have been referred to the central administration. A similar development has taken place in New South Wales.

The area organization has reduced the cumbersomeness of the state-wide administration and accelerated action on matters within the competence of the regional directors.

These area divisions are in no sense comparable with English local authorities or American local school boards, for no forms of lay control are associated with them. Because there is a senior official of the Department of Education resident in the area, head office policy is brought closer to the people in the area. This is a distinct gain, because as confidence in these regional education officers grows, the people of the area look to them for leadership and they, being identified with an area and its development, can more effectively press the claims of the area for educational services. Politically, however, the claims of the area are in no stronger position than they were before the area was established. Being departmental officials, these regional directors must communicate via the administrative head of the whole state system. The claims of the people of an area for political action are still through parliamentary representatives in the state government.

It is possible that, with greater experience in the operation of regional offices, Education Departments may seek to develop something akin to local regional school boards with limited powers under state legislation. But the idea is so strange to the tradition of Australian education that it appears unlikely that this will happen. On the present evidence, it would not be incautious to predict that no new authorities for education will be created in Australia in the foreseeable future except by the creation of new states; and the early creation of new states is by no means likely.

The centralized character of Australian systems gives rise to a fairly high degree of mobility among teachers. Teachers are state government employees and accept the whole state as their sphere of work. They may be appointed to any school in the state (although their wishes are considered) and transferred from it to meet the needs of the Department of Education. A teacher seeking promotion is committed to fairly frequent transfers, since a post of added responsibility is often to be found only at another school. Teachers are regarded in a town as birds of passage. It would not be uncommon to find that the majority of a country high-school staff considered their homes to be elsewhere.

These teachers may adjust themselves quite rapidly to the town in which they find themselves and make a significant contribution to its life (as they often do), yet the itinerant nature of their life is unsettling to themselves, the school, and the community. Some teachers, having reached a position of moderate status, settle in a town congenial to them and forego further advancement.

The incidence of this mobility has been mitigated to some extent by reduction in the grading of schools, thereby reducing the necessity of teachers to seek advancement by moving to another school. Another modification in Queensland and New South Wales, where the area organization exists, is a greater degree of movement within the area rather than to distant parts of the state. A relatively high degree of mobility, however, seems to be inherent in the system. There are so many isolated and unfavorable areas that it would be unreasonable to keep a teacher too long in one of them. Whereas, in some local systems, the unfavorable district gets a second-best teacher, in Australia it always gets a fully trained teacher; but he serves there for only a few years and then moves on to something more to his liking.

It is interesting to note that the movement of teachers is within not between states. The absence of reciprocal arrangements for transfer of seniority and pension rights probably accounts for this.

Centralized systems of education are prone to excite less public interest in education than do decentralized systems, and to this generalization Australia presents no marked exception. It is, of course, difficult to make accurate assessments of public interest in and support for education. Possible criteria are the community relations of individual schools, expression in the press and other forms of mass communication, and the concern with educational issues at election time. None of these, when examined, would suggest that the level of public involvement is high.

There is usually an association of parents and other citizens linked with each school. Considering the number of parents with children at a particular school, effective membership of these associations is small. These small bands of parents often perform prodigious feats in arranging activities to assist the school. The form of assistance is nearly always directed toward providing equipment and other amenities. There is sometimes a closer contact with educational programs of the school when some educational matter is discussed at a meeting or when the school is thrown open to parents to see the children at work. When the children perform at a concert, it is easy to fill every seat in a large hall—provided sufficient children participate in the program. No doubt in any country parental interest in education is closely related to parental interest in their children. In Australia, interest in their own children is very much the larger part of parents' interest in education. The work of the school is regarded as the school's business. Criticism of it is not often invited or always welcomed when it is offered.

Concern with educational issues in the metropolitan and country newspapers and on radio and television programs varies somewhat from place to place. It would be fair to say, though, that unless some major educational change is proposed or some major problem is raised, education is not regarded as having good news value. When secondary education is to be altered; when universities are overcrowded, and public interest is aroused by restriction of entry or by the proposal to create an additional university; when some notables attack the universities or the schools for corrupting the young in some way that they believe they have detected; or when some religious issue comes up, the mass media of communication show some interest. Apart from such crises the work of the educational system goes on in the background of public interest.

It is a similar story when governments go to the people at election time. Political campaigns are usually waged on domestic issues such as economic policies, housing, employment. Rarely are educational issues raised as a means of belittling an opponent or programs advanced as a means of gaining support.

There has grown up among educational administrators and teachers the view that the provision of schooling is a matter for experts. The public generally seems to feel that, although this is not necessarily the whole truth, there is little they can do about it. The local school is staffed by teachers who report there at the behest of a distant authority; it follows a curriculum and syllabuses of study prepared by a distant authority. The needs of the area in which the school is set may be adequately met, but this again is attributable to the wisdom of the distant authority who thinks for the local area or to the approval of the distant authority following the petition of the local area. Education in Australia is very much an official matter. Its growth and development derive mainly from the initiative of its own officers.

The level of interest generated internally by official stimulation, as judged by the attendance of teachers at professional conferences, refresher courses, and the like, is moderately high. The emphasis of these activities is more on "keeping up to date" than on "trying something new." It seems hard to create an adventurous outlook on educational procedures in a large system where most of the initiative for professional activity comes from the top. The tendency for top-level administrators is to secure acceptance throughout the system for some course of action judged to be worthy of introduction, rather than to encourage spontaneity of action at lower levels. The stimulus to change that comes from the influence of a diversity of practices—possible when education is decentralized—is less apparent in the Australian systems. One advantage of this is that ill-considered innovations are not experimented with, but the price of this advantage, in terms of responsiveness to desirable change, may be high.

Even the severest critics of Australian educational administration, however, will concede that the control of public education in the whole of each state by a single authority results in an equalization of opportunity for schooling for rural and urban children that would be difficult, if not impossible, to achieve under any other system. J. B. Conant (a recent friendly critic of Australian education) has this to say: "The whole subject of rural education, including a survey of the state scholarships for bringing talented boys and girls to city schools, represents a field of education in which Australia and New Zealand lead the world." The methods adopted to secure this equalization of schooling for rural children is dealt with more fully later in this essay.

Having stated the objectives of Australian education and described the administrative scheme, we may now examine the various edu-

291

cational institutions which these objectives and this administration sustain.

It will be profitable to begin with the universities, for in them it is to be expected that educational aims will be expressed in their purest form. Particularly is this likely when the major educational objective is intellectual discipline. Such an aim, which produces all kinds of difficulties in work with younger children of highly variable intellectual talents and interests, can be pursued with singleness of purpose in an institution whose students have been selected for their fitness and readiness to undergo such discipline.

It has been stated earlier that Australian educational aims could be said to be intellectual discipline and moral discipline and that these derive principally from British influence. At the university level, intellectual discipline is held to be the primary objective, although reference is made from time to time by university leaders to the sense of social responsibility which the university should inspire in its graduates.

Dedication to high standards of scholarship and the disinterested spirit of inquiry which underlies them can be found in all the universities of Australia. In a significant sense, Australian university tradition is continuous with British tradition and is jealously protected by university people when it is threatened. Requirements for graduation in all liberal arts schools (usually there are separate schools of arts and sciences) demand that the student concentrate in depth on relatively few subjects.[1] The standard of achievement reached by successful students is high. The failure rate is also high. Of the 1951 intake of students into six Australian universities only 35 per cent graduated in minimum time and only 58 per cent were expected to graduate at all.

It is difficult to say how widely among their student bodies universities manage to inspire the same love of truth and intellectual curiosity that are found among their faculties. Perhaps scholars of this kind are few in any educational system, and Australian universi-

---

[1] In contrast to United States educational practice where the B.A. is a first degree, providing both general education and some preparation in a special field, and is followed by the professional degrees in dentistry, law, theology, medicine, and so on, the Australian B.A. is a specialized degree, and professional degrees are alternatives.

292

ties have at least produced replacements of their own ranks. Whether they will be able to do so in the future period of expansion is not so certain.

Yet this intellectual tradition, when viewed against the background of the public which lies behind the university and from whom it recruits its students, is only thinly held. To the public at large the university is, par excellence, the institution which can provide for greater vocational opportunities. For them it is the gateway to the professions. They listen politely to the university spokesmen who praise learning and research, they pay lip service to the idea that the university is the guardian of intellectual freedom, and they are impressed on ceremonial occasions with the medieval splendor of its academic processions. But what is real for them is the prestige of its professional training. For them, the university is the rung of the educational ladder that leads to positions of leadership, good remuneration, and social prestige. For an occupation to improve its standing in the community, the surest method is for it to be accepted into the university fold.

The strong pressure on Australian universities to provide more and more vocational courses has altered markedly their traditional life and character. They are increasingly becoming high-level training institutions. Courses in pharmacy, forestry, surveying, physiotherapy, social work, town planning, agricultural economics, radiography, and many other new subjects have appeared on the scene to swell the number of university students and create new professions where only occupations existed before.

If the criticism of the university as an ivory tower for academics, pursuing their studies in a leisurely and detached way, was ever true, it is not true today. Universities are busy places where young people are taught to take a position in the contemporary world.

Some university people think (with Wordsworth) that the world is too much with them and that there is a danger of academic myopia developing.

The swing to vocational courses is accompanied, and to some extent supported, by another movement—a pressure toward scientific and technological studies. University departments concerned with pure and applied science and professions based on science are expanding and subdividing and absorbing increasing proportions of

293

money available for universities. Their equipment is expensive to a degree that scarcely entered into the conception of university financing a few decades ago.

Whereas at other times in our educational history the ideal of the scholar who reached his fullest development in the universities was the rhetorician, the philosopher, the man of letters, today in Australia the scholar is rapidly becoming identified with the scientist. Thomas Huxley and other eloquent nineteenth-century advocates of a place for science in the education of youth would be astonished at how complete the revolution has been.

A sample count of the staff of one large university, not specialized in science and applied science, yields a percentage of 75 for staff employed on scientific courses and professional courses based on science. The university of New South Wales, established in Sydney in 1949, has almost completely specialized in the basic and applied sciences, and it may well be the precursor of other similar institutions. In this university professors strange to the accustomed Australian university scene have appeared, teaching such disciplines as highway engineering, traffic engineering, and wool technology.

The scientific academics are frequently reminding the public that the increased attention to science in the universities has not gone nearly far enough, but vastly increased expenditure on staff and equipment is needed, as well as more and better-prepared students. On the whole, these claims are received sympathetically by the public, and the greater readiness shown by governments in recent years to assist the universities more generously is in part an expression of this public opinion. The man in the street, like the man in the university, believes that an education in science is one of the prime needs of Australians today.

There is another view, less frequently and less strongly urged, that recognizes the importance of science in relation to questions with which it concerns itself, but which doubts whether these questions should be taking precedence over others. To people who hold this view, the questions to which a larger proportion of our young people should be addressing themselves are ones concerned with human and social values. Indeed, they would claim that the transformation of social life which science and its technologies have accelerated accentuates the need in our day for humanistic and social studies. Training the most able of our youth for leadership in a profession or some specialization in science is not enough, they say, and in the long run Australia will suffer.

Such opinions and predictions are listened to, but scarcely seem to alter the course of events. To borrow a figure from science itself, it could be said that an intelligent being from outer space, surveying our educational activity, particularly at its highest level in the universities, would probably come to the conclusion that we were a people primarily interested in satisfying our scientific curiosity and increasing our standards of material well-being and industrial power, and that because we display such little evidence of the most developed form of intellectual curiosity (what could be called "philosophic inquiry"), we seem less concerned with the cultivation of wisdom. It probably wouldn't make much difference to the judgment of our hypothetical man from outer space into which of the more highly educationally developed countries his landing on Earth happened to bring him.

The increasing popularity of universities, for whatever reason students are drawn to them, is a statistical fact gratifying to those who value an increased span of education for youth, and yet disturbing to those charged with the responsibility of providing it. In 1951 there were 27,000 university students in Australia, or 3.8 per cent of the population aged 17 to 22 years. In 1959 this figure had risen to nearly 47,000, or 5.8 per cent of the population in the same age group.[2] In short, enrollments have increased disproportionately to the population from which they are drawn. The predicted enrollments for 1966 are 95,000, three times those of 1951.

[2] In the United States in the same year 29 per cent of the population in this age group was attending some type of college. But these statistics, without annotation, are somewhat misleading. The Australian statistics of university student numbers do not include those students attending technical, agricultural, theological, military, and teachers' colleges, whereas American statistics of "college" student numbers include the figures for these other types of institution and for junior colleges as well. Accordingly, if the numbers of students attending all types of post-high-school institutions in Australia were aggregated, the total might be as high as 100,000, or about 12 per cent of the 17 to 22 age group. Further, it should be noted that few students enter United States colleges before age 18 (because of the longer high-school course) and many of those who graduate with a B.A. or B.S. degree continue their studies toward a professional degree.

To assist the country to cope with such an alarming expansion, an Australian Universities Commission was established in 1959 to inform and advise the prime minister on the necessity for financial assistance to the states in relation to universities and to coordinate the balanced development of universities. Following the agreement by the Australian states to their heavy financial commitments under the plan proposed by the commission a new era of expansion in university education was inaugurated.

There are at present ten universities and three university colleges in Australia. New South Wales has three universities and two university colleges, Melbourne has two universities, Queensland has one university and one university college, and the other states and the Australian Capital Territory each have one university. The Australian National University at Canberra, the federal capital, was established as a postgraduate institution, but has recently been amalgamated with the Canberra University College and now provides undergraduate teaching as well.

The current scene at all of these institutions is one of bustling activity, and the activity is likely to continue for years to come. New buildings are appearing on all campuses, and committees and conferences are earnestly and anxiously considering and debating how expected enrollment increases can be met, how staff can be recruited, and how the efficiency of instruction can be improved. It is abundantly clear that the present institutions, in spite of the expansion that is occurring within them, cannot cope with the number of students to be cared for in the next decade. Whether multiplication of universities will continue, or whether new types of institutions will be created, will become clearer as the findings of both state and federal committees set up to examine this problem become known.

The newly created Australian Universities Commission has the extraordinarily difficult task of trying to steer the universities through this period of explosive growth, having regard to the Commonwealth government (which has accepted responsibility for assisting university development voluntarily and not because of any constitutional obligation), to the state governments which are constitutionally responsible, and to the universities—each of which is autonomous. If this task can be achieved without infringing the

296

autonomy of the separate universities and the sovereignty of the states, it will be a remarkable achievement.

Australian universities are largely financed out of public funds. They could not exist without assistance and are completely dependent on such funds. It remains to be seen whether the price of this greater scale of financial assistance will be an increased bureaucratic management of universities. This is something that only time and the wisdom of governments can determine.

The public-school systems of the six states of the Commonwealth are sufficiently similar to allow of their being dealt with in a generalized statement. Where distinctive features of importance do occur, reference will be made to them.

The state systems provide free education from the age of five, when children commonly enter infants' schools or infants' classes, to the end of secondary school which is usually reached by about the age of seventeen.

This education is sometimes described as secular as well as free, because denominational religious teaching by the school authority is not permitted. This feature of the public system does not express any hostility to religious teaching, but was intended to provide a solution to the interchurch rivalry at the time the public systems were established. In fact, provision is made in the parliamentary acts controlling educational practice for the clergy of the various churches to give religious instruction in schooltime. The Roman Catholic Church takes least advantage of this provision, preferring to provide separate schools for Roman Catholic children, but the clergy of other churches visit schools regularly for religious instruction.

The years of schooling are divided into three stages—infant, primary, and secondary—with the break between the second and third stages more clearly defined than that between the first and second. The typical age for transfer from infants' to primary is the eighth year, and for transfer from primary to secondary, the twelfth year. In Queensland, the period of primary schooling is longer (with a correspondingly shorter period of secondary schooling), and transfer usually occurs there in the fourteenth year.[3] Since the minimum

[3] Commencing in 1964, transfer from primary to secondary schools is to be made one year earlier.

statutory school-leaving age in Queensland is also fourteen, it is legally possible in this state to leave at about the end of the primary school. Three other states (Victoria, South Australia, and Western Australia) have a minimum leaving age of fourteen years, one (New South Wales) fifteen years, and one (Tasmania) sixteen years. Since the secondary stage of education for all these five states begins in the twelfth year, it can be seen that each of them prescribes some years of secondary schooling. The minimum age of leaving is not an expected age of leaving. Increasingly, children are voluntarily staying on beyond this stage.

In spite of the tendency for children to stay longer at school than previously, there is a serious falling out of pupils before the full secondary course is completed. Some figures for the most populous state, New South Wales, illustrate this wastage from the school system: of every hundred students who entered the secondary schools in 1952, 55.5 were still in attendance by 1954 and only 16.1 in 1956, when they would have completed the secondary course. The reasons for this fall out are no doubt complex and are certainly not known in any precise way. Economic factors would weigh with some, lack of interest in schoolwork with others. Underlying all the particular reasons is the widespread uncertainty about the need for an extended period of schooling for everyone. Some express this openly and unequivocally and say that secondary education is suitable only for the academically able children. The remaining children, they claim, would be better served by terminating their full-time schooling at fourteen or fifteen and seeking employment. For those who hold this view, the falling off in attendance does not represent "wastage," except in cases of children of superior intelligence.

State Education Departments, on the whole, have expressed a belief in the value of all children staying at school beyond the minimum leaving age by trying to adapt the curricula of secondary schools to the varying needs of the children. Although some of the courses alternative to the academic ones are very good from the educational viewpoint, they have not been valued as they should be by a considerable number of parents.

The belief of the State Departments of Education that primary and secondary school should form two necessary stages in the child's

298

education is given practical expression in the ease of transfer from the primary to the secondary schools.

The elimination of examination hurdles at this transfer point has created a need for guidance to aid children and parents to make wise choices of the secondary courses available. This need has been met by the establishment of efficient guidance services. These consist usually of a guidance section in the head office of the Department of Education, suitably staffed with psychologically trained personnel and with either itinerant or resident officers in various parts of the school system. In some states guidance services are associated with the educational research service. During the primary stage of education, ability and other tests are administered, so that by the time the secondary stage is reached, considerable educational data on each child are usually available.

A guidance service may be thought of as existing to assist the education authority determining the child's educational future, or to offer guidance to the children and parents who must elect among a number of alternative courses of action. Australian school guidance services have functioned in both of these ways. As types of courses available to secondary-school students become more diversified, as is happening, the trend in guidance programs is toward advising students and parents in situations which are genuinely ones of choice for them. Educational guidance services are usually supplemented by more specialized units dealing with vocational guidance and by clinics concerned with behavior problems and speech disorders, some of which are maintained by authorities outside the Education Departments. State Departments of Health administer school medical and dental services, ensuring that children in need of minor treatment receive it. Aid to physical fitness is rendered by the Commonwealth Council for National Fitness, which assists school authorities to promote activities designed to raise the level of physical fitness in the nation.

The problem of providing education in country districts presents such special problems that it will be convenient to give separate descriptions of country and urban education.

In a country town one would find a primary school and a secondary school. If the town were too small to justify a separate secondary school, the two would be united.

The typical country high school is coeducational and multilateral, offering a variety of courses such as academic, home science, technical, commercial, and agricultural.

As one moves out from these town centers to the more sparsely settled areas, regular secondary-school work disappears, and the primary schools become smaller. In some, one would find two teachers at work, with the children divided into upper and lower divisions. In some cases a single teacher would operate the whole school of perhaps fifteen or twenty children. The one-teacher school, in fact, is the most common type in Australia. These tiny outposts of culture perform a very important function. As well as giving boys and girls in remote areas a good start in life, they provide an educational and recreational center for the scattered rural community. Social functions involving the children and their parents are usually high lights of the year.

The teachers in these schools are specially trained in techniques of teaching grouped classes and in the sociology of the small rural community. The experience that Australian educational authorities have had with this type of school has brought its methods to a high pitch of efficiency. In spite of the excellence of the work done under obvious difficulties, many educationists believe that these schools cannot offer the same advantages as a larger school. Where consolidation is possible by transporting children to a larger school, the small schools have tended to close, often not without protest by the local community. The state education authorities subsidize or meet the cost of the transportation involved. Another factor that has influenced the closing of some one-teacher schools has been the movement of people away from farms and station properties as increasing mechanization and improved methods have reduced the demand for labor. In spite of this trend toward greater consolidation of schools, the little "bush schoolhouse" is likely to remain a permanent feature of the Australian educational scene.

The one-teacher school itself represents a degree of consolidation, in that many children, to attend it, have to ride bicycles or horses or be transported by car. Beyond these small communities lies an even more sparsely settled outback where a mustering of even twelve to fifteen children is not possible. For these children in the lonely places of Australia the correspondence schools and the schools of the air have been created.

EDUCATION

The correspondence school in each state, or the "school in the mailbag" as it has been called, makes an admirable contribution to Australian education. The teachers work in the capital cities, preparing work for each pupil enrolled and correcting work submitted to them. Their pupils may be hundreds of miles away, but so skillfully do they carry out their task that a genuine teacher-pupil relationship is quite evident. The arrival of the mailman (perhaps weekly) at some isolated rural property, bearing lessons and corrected work for the children, is an exciting event, and the children talk about their teacher as though he were personally known to them. Correspondence tuition needs the assistance of someone on the spot to supervise the children's work and give any help needed. Usually the mother of the family does this. A great deal has been written in praise of the "women of the outback" for their part in pioneering work, and it is well merited. Insufficient recognition has been given to them for the part they have played in cooperating with the correspondence school in the education of their own children.

This correspondence tuition is not restricted to the primary level of schooling. It is possible to progress through the whole span of secondary education by correspondence, and many children do this. Indeed, some of the universities have introduced correspondence courses leading to a degree and have had notable success. Teaching by correspondence, whatever its shortcomings, is an imaginative answer in Australia to the problems created by vast distances and small populations. Through it a person can be educated from the kindergarten to the university.

A valuable supplement to correspondence education is the use of radio, and increasing use is being made of this. In 1950, the first school of the air was established at Alice Springs in the very heart of Australia, and by making use of the two-way radio equipment developed by the Royal Flying Doctor Service, teacher and children, separated by hundreds of miles, are welded into a "class." Three other such schools have been established, and the four teach children who are scattered over an area of almost a million square miles.

The Australian Broadcasting Commission, through its school broadcasting program, also supplements the work of the correspondence school in a valuable way. The programs arranged by the Broad-

301

casting Commission cater, of course, to children in regular schools as well as those in isolated areas. Its "Kindergarten of the Air," broadcast on six mornings of the week, is brilliantly conceived and executed and has brought joy and profit to many thousands of young children.

In spite of all these provisions for the education of children in remote rural areas, it could fairly be said that these children are at a disadvantage as compared with those in urban areas. This is particularly so for those of secondary-school age. Correspondence tuition at secondary-school level is probably less effective than at primary or college level. The increasing difficulty of the work and the decreasing assistance possible from many parents whose children are at an educational level higher than their own account for this decrease in effectiveness. The students pursuing studies at university level are generally a more restricted and selected group and have had appropriate prior educational experience that enables them to study independently.

The parents of these children of secondary-school age are faced with the alternatives of allowing them to proceed somewhat uncertainly by correspondence or of sending them away from home to urban centers. Some go to hostels attached to state high schools, some to private boarding schools. Limited financial assistance is available to some of these children, but on the whole parents are faced with a heavy financial burden. Australian educational authorities have done a great deal to equalize educational opportunities for rural and urban children, but the gap is not quite closed.

In the towns and cities the typical primary school is a large institution of a thousand pupils or more, divided into an infants' department and a primary department. This primary department may be divided into separate girls' and boys' departments or maintained on a coeducational basis. The public systems of education show a general preference for a coeducational arrangement. Where boys and girls are separated for schooling, it usually is done rather for administrative convenience than because of opposition to the principle of coeducation.

Metropolitan secondary schools are more diversified than those in the country. The omnibus-type high school of the country town can be found, but it is much less common. The usual pattern is of

302

separate schools offering traditional academic courses, technical and industrial training, or home science and commercial education.

Wherever the children receive their secondary education, standards of achievement for most of them are measured by a written examination set and graded by an external authority—an examinations board, state Department of Education, or university. The actual practices vary from state to state. With the exception of Tasmania, an examination is held at a point approximately midway through the secondary school (variously called junior or intermediate examination). In three of the five states conducting this type of examination, it is fully external; in two, the schools' examinations are recognized by the public authority. Since this examination is taken at an age which approximates the statutory minimum leaving age, or is a little beyond it, the examination serves as an exit certificate for many children seeking employment or wishing to satisfy entrance qualifications of various vocational institutions. For others, it serves as a demonstration of fitness to proceed to the senior work of the secondary school.

In all states except Tasmania and Victoria, an external examination called leaving certificate or senior certificate is held at the end of the secondary-school course. This examination is accepted by the universities for matriculation purposes, provided that the student has the required grouping of subjects. The possession of a leaving certificate is required for entry to some positions in industry and commerce, for more advanced types of work in the public service, and for admission to the teachers' colleges. Greater numbers of employers are requiring the leaving certificate as a qualification for employment.

Tasmania has a slightly different arrangement, placing the leaving certificate (schools board examination) one year before the final school year (and conducting it in part by accreditation), with provision for a final school year designed for students who are progressing to the universities. In Victoria the leaving certificate precedes university matriculation by two years. New South Wales has recently adopted a somewhat similar arrangement.

These differences in examining procedures draw attention to the rather serious problem of how schools are to prepare students well for the particular demands of university study, at the same time preparing well the majority who do not proceed to the university —assuming, as many do, that the needs of these two groups are not identical. In practice, the requirements of university matriculation tend to influence both the many students not destined for the university and the education of secondary-school students years before the actual point of matriculation. Separation of the leaving certificate from the matriculation examination is an attempt to deal with this problem.

A description of the public provision for education could not fairly be concluded without reference to the steps taken to educate those unfortunate handicapped children for whom the general educational service is unsuitable. The special institutions that exist present a varied pattern. One striking feature is the cooperation of public and private charitable organizations. An arrangement whereby a voluntary agency establishes and administers an institution and receives substantial government assistance (generally in the form of provision of staff) is quite common. The crippled, the spastic, the deaf, the blind, and the mentally subnormal are provided for by either public or private institutions.

The University of Queensland's faculty of education has taken a special interest in the educational problems of backward and subnormal children and has set up a Remedial Education Center where it works with retarded children, conducts research into problems of educational retardation, and trains teachers in diagnostic testing and remedial teaching. It also publishes a journal, *The Slow-learning Child*, which has a wide circulation.

The foregoing survey presents a picture of moderately developed public systems of education organized to serve country and urban, normal, gifted, and handicapped children; to prepare children for the university and other institutions and for a varied range of occupations; and to create a general level of competence in the future citizens of the country. They are democratically conceived systems, offering reasonable opportunity for all.

Attendance at school is compulsory in Australia, but need not be at a public school. A variety of schools are approved by the state authorities, but are independent of them. They are variously called "independent schools," "public schools" (in the English sense), or "church schools." The extent of private education in Australia in

EDUCATION

1957 (the most recent year for which statistics are available) can be seen clearly from Table 1.

Table 1. Public and Private Education in Australia

State	Schools		Pupils	
	State	Private	State	Private
New South Wales	2,551	789	539,981	175,021
Victoria	2,132	521	360,576	139,901
Queensland	1,577	286	214,301	62,838
South Australia	663	163	143,635	31,145
Western Australia	501	183	105,585	33,742
Tasmania	279	52	59,048	11,332
Totals	7,703	1,994	1,425,126	453,979

In summary, approximately one-fifth of the schools in Australia are private and are attended by almost one-third of the school population. The role of the private school is even more significant than these total figures suggest: at the upper end of the primary school (within the span of compulsory schooling), public-school enrollments greatly outnumber private-school enrollments, but by the final years of the secondary stage, the enrollments are approximately equal. The output from each system, private and public, of students who have completed secondary school is about the same. In fact, in the majority of states the output of the private schools is greater. In New South Wales, however, the public high schools educate many more students than private high schools.

This shift in the proportion of pupils attending state and private schools is due mainly to two factors, the relative importance of which it would be difficult to assess—the transfer of pupils at about twelve years of age from a state primary school to a private secondary school, and the greater holding power of the private school beyond the compulsory attendance age.

An explanation of the transfer of pupils from a state primary school to a private secondary school is that many of the private secondary schools were well established before the state entered this field. Public secondary education is a twentieth-century development and is still regarded by many as something of a newcomer. The private school, on the whole, has high social status, not

305

necessarily in a snobbish sense, although snobbery is a factor with some parents. For country parents it solves the boarding problem for their children, since most of these schools are either wholly residential or have a nucleus of boarders. With few exceptions state high schools are day schools only. Since most private schools have some church affiliation, they have an added attraction for those parents who wish their children to be educated in a religious atmosphere. The scholastic standards for most of these schools is quite high, certainly as high as the state secondary schools.

The private schools have greater holding power because their students—in the main—come from homes where there is not only a high level of aspiration for the children, but also the financial means to delay the child's earning for an extended period.

Of the private schools, the great majority are controlled by church authorities, and of this majority the greater numbers are conducted by the Roman Catholic Church. No less than three-quarters of all the children attending private schools are enrolled at Roman Catholic schools. Whereas the Anglican and other Protestant churches have restricted their educational activity mainly to secondary education, the Roman Catholic Church has established a complete system of education with primary and secondary schools and other educational agencies. (There is no Roman Catholic university in Australia although moves have been made in the past to establish one.) This system cares for nearly 19 per cent of all the children enrolled in schools in Australia. In few other countries has the Roman Catholic Church been able to establish such an extensive system without government aid.

The non-Roman Catholic secondary schools are largely a British importation. In fact, it is not uncommon practice to secure headmasters for these schools from England and to encourage ambitious masters to seek experience in English public schools. The Australian counterpart of the English public school differs somewhat from its prototype in being far more largely a day school, but in its stress on games, its student self-government through a prefect system, and in the significance of the school chapel, it is a faithful imitator.

Foreign observers of Australian education, with their knowledge of socialist trends in Australian political thought, are somewhat surprised at the dual system of education that they find. In Australia, however, it is not regarded as a public issue. At the universities where students from both private and public schools mingle, there appear to be no problems resulting from this dual system.

To judge from American writings on education, the typical American teacher is a woman. The pronoun used is nearly always "she." In Australia the appropriate pronoun is "he," for teaching is as much a career for men as for women. Of the approximately 56,000 public-school teachers recorded in the statistics of the six state Departments of Education in 1959, almost exactly half were men, and in three states there was a decided excess of men over women teachers. Since teaching is an occupation that can be regarded as being equally open to men and women, it would probably not be incautious to suggest that its holding power for men reveals a reasonably favorable attitude to it as a career.

Arrangements for the training of teachers vary somewhat from state to state. Typically, primary-school teachers are prepared in two-year courses at teachers' colleges administered by the state Departments of Education, and secondary-school teachers are trained in universities where they graduate in divisions appropriate to the subjects that they will teach and then undergo one year of professional training for teaching, for which they are awarded a Diploma in Education.

To give greater accuracy to this general statement, the following facts should be noted. First, in addition to the form of training described for primary teachers, three of the states, Tasmania, Western Australia, and New South Wales, offer a B.Ed. degree for primary-school teachers. Few students, however, avail themselves of it.

Second, some prospective secondary teachers, being prepared for specialist subjects such as art, shorthand, industrial arts, and music, receive their preliminary training in subuniversity institutions where these subjects are taught (technical colleges, agricultural colleges, conservatoria of music, and the like) and then proceed to professional teacher training in a teachers' college or university.

Third, because in recent years expansion in secondary education has outrun the supply of university-trained teachers, many persons trained for only two years in teachers' colleges have been employed in secondary schools. At present this "dilution" of the secondary teaching force is going on apace and is expected by many to lead to a lowering in standards of achievement in secondary schools. The situation may correct itself when the current stresses on secondary education, due to a sharply increased birth rate in the early postwar period, have been lessened.

Fourth, many infants' and kindergarten teachers are trained in nongovernment colleges. The course in these colleges is usually three years in duration.

In the two-year course of the teachers' college an attempt is made to continue the general education of the student beyond that attained in school, to give him professional courses in education, psychology, and methods of teaching, and to afford him adequate opportunity for practical teaching so that he can be appointed to a full-time teaching position with a reasonable degree of competence. To do all these things in so short a time is difficult. To do them well is impossible. There is a good deal of agitation among teachers'-college people and in the profession itself to extend this period of training to three or four years. Present conditions of staffing difficulty give little promise that this desirable step will be taken in the immediate future.

The initial training, whether given in teachers' colleges or in universities, does not equip the teacher to continue indefinitely in his profession. Considerable attention has been given in recent years to the problem of the professional growth of the teacher. State Departments of Education have emphasized more the supervisory function of the inspector of schools and have used him as an agent advising individual teachers on more effective methods of instruction and conducting short refresher courses and demonstrations. The Departments have also made provision for vacation, part-time, and correspondence courses with the same object. Teachers' colleges and universities have done likewise, and the school principal has been encouraged to accept as an important part of his responsibility the guidance and enlivening of his staff.

Most students in training in teachers' colleges and universities are financially assisted by the state Departments of Education and are bound, in return for this assistance, to teach for a number of years. The financial assistance varies from state to state, but on the whole it is generous, enabling a student, by careful handling of his money, to manage independently of help from home. This assistance has undoubtedly enabled many students to enter teaching who otherwise would have been prevented from doing so for financial reasons. The system of scholarship awards (with a pledge to teach) also has had the advantage of regulating the flow of recruits into training.

The bonding system comes under attack from time to time from various quarters. One criticism is that it forces the student to make a decision about his employment too early. This applies particularly to those who proceed to the university for a relatively long course and discover new interests as they progress. Another criticism of a more serious kind is that the existence of a bonding system suggests that teachers have to be held in the profession against their will, and this has an adverse effect on the public's estimation of the status and attractiveness of teaching. Whether or not teachers *have* to be held in their position by the obligation they have entered into is difficult to say. The answer would only be known with certainty if the bonding system were discontinued. It could be said, however, that defections from the teaching service after the period of obligatory service is over (generally three to five years) are not greater than one would expect in any occupation in which almost half the employees were women. It is the writer's opinion that removal of the pledge to teach would not affect greatly the supply position and might improve the recruitment position.

The favorable financial conditions under which teachers may prepare for their profession probably account (or help to account) for the fact that teachers are recruited in large numbers from lower-middle-class and working-class homes. Some speak of teaching as a "bridge" profession enabling the grandchildren of a low-income family to rise to positions in the well-established and more highly remunerative professions.

It is certainly true that teaching occupies a position in social esteem between the skilled trades and the professions.

Teachers are showing an increased concern for the status of their position. Professional literature shows an increasing volume of articles dealing with different aspects of the question. The most common claims are that salaries should be increased, conditions of work should be improved, courses of training for primary-school teachers should be lengthened, and the universities should participate more in the training of all kinds of teachers.

The most powerful weapon in the teacher's hands in trying to improve his lot is his professional association or union. These unions exist in all states and are federated into an Australia-wide body. Since the federal government is not directly concerned with the provision of education, it is at the state level that these unions are most effective. The union negotiates salary agreements with the wage-fixing authority, whether it be a court, tribunal, or public service board.

The main activities of these unions have been in seeking to secure better salaries and conditions of work for teachers. Their success has been moderate, at least managing to keep teachers' salaries in line with the inflationary trends that have been apparent since the Second World War. In some instances they have managed to better the relative position of teachers in the wage structure of the state. The professional activities of the unions have been less marked, by comparison with well-established professional associations overseas. It is likely, as the material gains for teachers aimed at are won, that greater concern with professional issues will emerge.

In practically all that has been expressed in this section, it is the teacher as civil servant in the public schools that the writer has had in mind. Since approximately one-fifth of the teachers in the country teach outside the public system, reference to them is merited.

The private-school teachers outside the Roman Catholic Church could well be considered as a group. These teachers have been prepared for their work in private training colleges or in the universities. Their salaries and conditions of work, by the competitive influence of the state systems, would approximate those of teachers in the state systems. Those in prestige private schools would probably enjoy a higher social status than that accorded to state schoolteachers. This would occur mainly through their association with the more wealthy families that patronize the private schools.

The teachers in the Roman Catholic school system are generally members of teaching orders although, with increased pressure of enrollments, greater numbers of lay teachers are being employed. The Catholic Church provides its own training establishments and makes considerable use of the universities for the academic preparation of its secondary-school teachers.

The total picture of the teaching profession in Australia is a highly heterogeneous one. Within the public system, by type of training and by professional interest, teachers are divided into infants', primary, and secondary. Outside the public system they are divided by religious denominations as well as by educational level. Each group is primarily concerned with its own affairs and rarely meets other groups to deliberate on common problems. This weakens the conception of a single profession based on teaching, at whatever level and under whatever authority it occurs.

A notable move to mitigate, or remove, this disunity has occurred recently in the formation of the Australian College of Education. The move to set up such a body was made initially by a group of educationists from independent schools, but it was readily taken up by representatives of state school systems. In 1959 the College was founded. It had its inaugural meeting in Sydney in 1960. It is now an established professional body with a federal council and chapters in each state of the Commonwealth, uniting within its membership educational leaders from every kind and stage of education in Australia. In such a body where university, primary, and secondary teachers meet, where public-school teachers meet with private- and church-school teachers, a concern with teaching as such can be expressed. It is believed that, as the College grows in strength and influence, it can do much to raise the status of the profession and will be able to speak for the profession to the public and in high places with an authority and a united voice that it has never had before.

BIBLIOGRAPHY

Anchen, J. O. *Frank Tate and His Work for Education.* 1956.

Austin, A. G. *Australian Education 1788–1900: Church, State and Public Education in Colonial Australia.* 1961.

Bean, C. E. W. *Here, My Son: An Account of the Independent and Other Corporate Boys' Schools in Australia.* 1950.

Butts, R. F. *Assumptions Underlying Australian Education.* 1957.

Crane, A. R., and Walker, W. G. *Peter Board: His Contribution to the Development of Education in New South Wales.* 1957.

Department of Education, Tasmania. *The Tasmanian Area School.* 1942.

Fogarty, T. P. *Catholic Education in Australia.* 1959.

McDonnell, R. M., Radford, W. C., and Staurenghi, P. M. *Review of Education in Australia 1948–1954.* 1956.

Radford, W. C. *The Nongovernment Schools of Australia.* 1953.

Report of the Australian Universities Commission on Australian Universities 1958–1963. 1960.

Report of the Committee Appointed to Survey Secondary Education in New South Wales (Wyndham Report). 1957.

Report of the Committee on Australian Universities (Murray Report). 1957.

Report of the Committee on State Education in Victoria (Ramsay Report). 1960.

Turner, I. S. *The Training of Teachers in Australia.* 1943.

UNESCO. *Compulsory Education in Australia.* 1953.

Wyeth, E. R. *Education in Queensland.* 1955.

Valuable statistical information regarding the various aspects of Australian education is published in the annual reports of the ministers of education in the several states and in the bulletins and research studies issued by the Commonwealth Office of Education and the Australian Council for Educational Research.

THEATRE

A. L. MCLEOD

OF the public interpretative arts, the theatre is the least developed, least encouraged, and yet most pertinacious in Australia, just as its literary counterpart, the drama, is the most jejune of the creative arts. It is, perhaps, inevitable that if the drama is neglected or unmastered by a country's writers, the theatres will be shunned or unappreciated by its public, and vice versa. However that may be, it is readily to be observed that in the story of Australia's cultural development the theatre arts have struggled against an unenthusiastic public that has regarded those associated with the theatre with disdain, against an avuncular attitude of government and society, and, in the present century, against a not wholly benign association of commercial theatre enterprises. There has been neither the governmental support nor the private endowment that has permitted the establishment of great art theatres abroad, and there has been a singular lack of that initiative on the part of the commercial managements that has created the theatres of London, New York, Boston, Toronto, and Paris. The amateur theatre, too, should accept

313

at least part of the responsibility for the state of the theatre in Australia. For too long it has led, by apparent choice, an eremitical existence in dingy quarters in the cities during the winter months and has never seriously tried to establish a local equivalent of summer stock—that grass-roots foundation of the legitimate theatre in North America.

Whether the changes in attitude to and support of the theatre that have been discerned in the past decade augur well for the future remains to be seen. The several governments have overtly encouraged writers, painters, and musicians by the provision of fellowships, prizes, and awards and by the construction and maintenance of art schools, conservatoria of music, symphony orchestras, art galleries, and libraries. But there has been no expenditure of public moneys —until the present decade—in support of the drama and theatre, except insofar as it was unavoidable, could provide inexpensive programming for the national broadcasting networks, or seemed a judicious and economical means of allowing school children to witness some form of semiprofessional theatre. New Zealand has its National Theatre, England has its British Council, Canada, its Canada Council—but there is no permanent government body charged with the encouragement and development of the arts, including those of the theatre, in Australia.

Art and music have long been recognized academic subjects in the Australian educational system from kindergarten up; but theatre remains profane, allowed to show itself only occasionally—and then as an adjunct to English literature.

The history of the theatre in Australia is such that most individuals interested in or contemplating a theatrical career in this country would instantly be discouraged upon becoming apprised of it. It is the distressing story—with few ameliorating incidents— of discouragement, of protean struggle against apathy (even antipathy), and of long-sustained hardship leading inexorably to failure and despair. It is the story of amateur theatricals—in the most derogatory connotation—frequently motivated by the dictum of "for fun and funds" and only occasionally by a sustaining desire to perform the great classics of the European stage, and of closely coordinated commercial managements noticeably reluctant to stimulate theatrical appreciation and talent by even the occasional production of avant-garde, experimental, philosophical, artistic, or "cultural" theatre. There has been no Ibsen, no Camus, no Ionesco, no Brecht performed commercially; but Gilbert and Sullivan, the Shakespeare plays that are being studied by school examination classes, and the inevitable London and New York light-comedy successes are common.

Notwithstanding the vicissitudes of the theatre in Australia, one can see ample evidence of the herculean efforts, the noble causes espoused, the unrequited enthusiasms that have traditionally been associated with, and happily been the pride of, the devotees of Thespis.

The colonial period of Australian history was the period of the foundations of an identifiably Australian culture. At first, of course, it was merely a transplanted British culture, but it inevitably shook off much of the old and developed its present idiosyncrasies.

The first theatre in Australia, as in Canada, was garrison theatre. On June 4, 1789, a little more than a year after the arrival of the first fleet at Sydney Cove, George Farquhar's roisterous comedy, *The Recruiting Officer*, which had not long before been revived with acclaim on the London stage, was performed by a cast of eleven convicts as a King's Birthday entertainment for the governor, Captain Arthur Phillip, and an audience of some sixty persons. Captain Watkin Tench, one of the audience, has described the theatre as "a mud hut, fitted for the occasion." Admission was in kind, and rum, tobacco, wine, poultry, corn, and wheat to the value of £20 were taken at the door; since admission to the London theatres of the time could be obtained for a shilling, it must be allowed that the audience for *The Recruting Officer* was either particularly generous or most eager to witness a stage performance. Apparently the performance was up to expectations, for Tench reports that "some of the actors acquitted themselves with great spirit and received the praises of the audience."

Whether theatrical entertainments became frequent divertisements, we do not know. Two chroniclers of the Australian theatre, L. L. Woolacott and Paul Maguire, feel that this initial performance was not followed up, since there are no extant records of others. But it could hardly be thought likely that the governor would approve the building of the infant colony's first—though primitive—

315

theatre during 1795, at a time when more utilitarian edifices were most pressingly required, if there had been no theatrical activity since 1789.

Meanwhile, in 1793, in the convict-punishment settlement on Norfolk Island, off the coast of New South Wales, Captain P. G. King, the commandant, authorized the performance of plays at monthly intervals and on public holidays—which he would be most unlikely to do if, in fact, no plays were being performed in the principal settlement in Sydney. After a riot at one of the performances in January, 1794, King felt obliged to inter his fledgling theatre.

In 1795, Robert Sidaway, a former convict "of the more decent class" who had become Sydney's first baker, sought and was granted official permission to organize a theatrical company and to build a theatre in what is now Bligh Street; this, it is interesting to note, before there was even a public general store in the colony. Whether Sidaway was one of the cast of *The Recruiting Officer* is uncertain, but his enthusiasm for the Theatre—or the Playhouse, as his building was sometimes called—was considerable. There is no known sketch of the theatre.

Under the management of John Sparrow, the theatre opened on January 16, 1796, with a performance of Edward Young's *The Revenge* and a farce, *The Hotel*. Lieutenant Colonel David Collins commented thus on the new venture:

They had fitted up the house with more theatrical propriety than could have been expected, and their performance was far above contempt. Their motto was modest and well-chosen: "We cannot command success, but we will endeavour to deserve it."

At the licensing of this exhibition, they were informed that the slightest impropriety would be noticed and a repetition punished by the banishment of their company to the other settlements; there was, however, more danger of improprieties being committed by some of the audience than by the players themselves. A seat in their gallery, which was by far the largest part of the house, as likely to be the most resorted to, was to be procured for one shilling; and as much flour, or as much meat or spirits as the management would take for that sum, was often paid at the gallery door. It was feared that this, like gambling, would furnish another inducement to rob; and some of the worst convicts, ever on the watch for opportunities, looked on the playhouse as a certain harvest for them, not by picking the pockets of the audience, but by breaking into their houses while the family might be enjoying themselves at the theatre.[1]

On February 4, Nicholas Rowe's *The Fair Penitent* was performed as a benefit for Mrs. Eales, a soldier's widow, and realized £12. For the next two years there was a regular procession of Restoration and early eighteenth-century plays and farces, but in 1798 the new governor, John Hunter, ordered the demolition of the theatre, ostensibly because a determined playgoer killed an officer's greyhound and sold its meat as kangaroo flesh at 9d. a pound in order to finance his admission. The real reason for the closing was probably adumbrated by Colonel Collins. Furthermore, it is almost certain that the playhouse was closed rather than demolished, for Hunter was no fool and would hardly have been instrumental in razing one of the few substantial buildings of which the colony could boast. And in 1800 Sidaway was again granted permission to present plays, presumably in the same playhouse. He opened his new season with the old favorite, *The Recruiting Officer*, and a farce, *The Virgin Unmasked*. A month later he offered truncated versions of *Henry IV* (Parts I and II) and *The Irish Widow*. The leading actor of the time seems to have been W. Smith, for he played Captain Plume in the Farquhar comedy and the Prince of Wales in *Henry IV*. Whether by fiat of the governor or by choice dictated by financial problems, Sidaway closed his playhouse again in 1800, and theatre in Australia virtually came to a standstill for more than a generation.

In 1826, during the administration of Governor Darling, "the Debtors' Room of the Sydney Gaol was turned into a Temple of Thespis" wherein "persons of the highest standing in the town were not ashamed to witness the crude representations of dramatic enthusiasts," Joseph Fowles wrote some thirty years later. Darling's sympathies toward the theatre extended to permitting performances at the convict settlements at Emu Plains and in the soldiers' barracks in Sydney. On the visit of the ships *Crocodile* and *Zebra* in 1830, the officers performed *Agnes; or The Bleeding Nun* and *The Miller and His Men* in a tent at Farm Cove for the edification of the colonists.

[1] David Collins, *An Account of the English Colony in New South Wales* (London: Cadill and Davies, 1804) pp. 319–320.

Barnett Levey, owner of the Royal Hotel, Sydney, advertised in 1828 the sale of two hundred shares, at £5 each, in a theatre that he proposed to erect at the rear of his premises in George Street. The *Sydney Gazette*, ever alert to its high responsibility as guardian of the public morality, commented on the proposal on June 26:

> We very much question the policy of such a species of amusement being as yet introduced among us. However laudable and spirited it may be in individuals to contemplate and enter upon such a subject, yet we are decidedly of opinion—not that we are in any way desirous of affecting the interests of any party who may have embarked in such an under-taking—that the state of colonial society is as yet unfitted, and wholly unprepared, for the establishment of a theatre. . . . We judge it high time, for the sake of all interested in such an enterprise, to institute the inquiry . . . whether a theatre will be allowed?

Permission to build was delayed, but eventually was granted. Before the new premises were ready for occupancy, Levey—often re-garded as the patriarch of theatre in Australia—presented, under the guise of "At Homes," entertainments at his hotel, in which he regaled his audiences with songs such as "My Love Is Gone to Botany Bay."

Eventually, on October 5, 1833, Levey's Theatre Royal (soon to become a ubiquitous name in Australian theatre), accommodating a capacity audience of almost a thousand, including the governor, Sir Richard Bourke, opened with the popular melodrama, *The Miller and His Men,* and the farce, *The Irishman in London.* According to the *Sydney Monitor* of October 9, the governor "considered it politic, no doubt, to patronize this intellectual, civilizing and conse-quently most useful and patriotic of all public amusements." The paper then continued in puritanical, hortatory vein with the follow-ing admonition:

> We exhort all ministers of religion, in and out of the establishment, catholic included, to be kind and courteous to those thoughtless but generally kind-hearted beings, the sons and daughters of Thespis; and in lieu of thinking of and looking up at them with visages of un-Christian scorn, to regard them with kindness, praising their agreeable talent to amuse, and deprecating their faults with parental meekness and sympa-thizing regard for their temporal and spiritual welfare. By this means, the playhouse will be a college of moral exhibition and the play enactors a moral—though we are afraid, never a very wise—generation.

Subsequently, Levey produced a number of those contemporary farces and melodramas that marked the low ebb of British drama in the nineteenth century. From time to time he re-presented the old successes of earlier years. But there was little daring, and he appears to have been guided rather by concern to amuse than by desire to educate. Before long he was badgered by his audiences and, unable to control their enthusiasms or behavior, found himself excoriated by the *Sydney Gazette* for permitting a "half-tipsy, half-strumpet" audience and for maintaining a company of actors that was in continual disaffection. Levey bowed out of the theatre for a year and was succeeded by Joseph Simmons as manager for a syndicate of businessmen. In 1836 he returned to the Royal, but within the year he died, at the age of thirty-nine. After his wife unsuccessfully tried to carry on the playhouse and its company, the Theatre Royal closed in March, 1838, and burned down just two years later. Thus, in ignominy, ended the first real attempt at commercial theatre in Australia.

Four days after the Royal closed, Joseph Wyatt's Royal Victoria Theatre opened. Designed by Henry Robertson and with a stage of grandiose proportions (47 feet wide, 100 feet deep), the Royal Victoria accommodated almost two thousand people and was, as the *Australian* observed, "at least equal to, if not superior to, any of the second-rate London theatres."

What had happened during these first fifty years in Sydney was repeated, *mutatis mutandis*, elsewhere in Australia. In Hobart, Kotzebue's *The Stranger*, together with an inevitable farce, presented at the Freemasons' Tavern by Samson Cameron's company, was the earliest professional performance in Tasmania. Cameron also played in *Romeo and Juliet* in Hobart. When he departed a Mrs. Clarke—who went to London to recruit actors and even trained a few local residents—established a short-lived company. Her offerings, *The Vampire, Love, Law and Physic*, and similar pieces, although offered thrice weekly, were unable to prosper where Kotzebue and Shakespeare had failed to flourish. After a short, comatose existence, her theatre quietly succumbed. In Launceston, on the north coast of Tasmania, George Coppin—who eventually had associations with almost every legitimate theatre in Australia—vainly struggled to maintain his Olympic Theatre. He soon transferred his efforts to Adelaide, Melbourne, and other mainland cities.

In Adelaide, an upper room of the Adelaide Tavern was euphemistically entitled the Theatre Royal in 1838 and was the locale of several "entertainments" of a nondescript nature before George Coppin arrived. Coppin's fortunes in Adelaide were hardly more auspicious than those in Launceston, for the economic depression of 1841–1842 forced the closing of his theatre. Undaunted, he returned in 1846 to open his New Queen's Theatre and resume his remarkable career on the stage.

Melbourne's first recorded theatrical performance was held in 1842 in a wooden pavilion identified by the distinguished name Theatre Royal. The usual fare was offered, though in 1843 Samson Cameron—who peregrinated from city to city—offered *Othello*, and in 1845 Francis Nesbitt, an actor from Sydney, presented a Shakespearean season before the theatre closed. Just three nights before the demise of the Royal, George Coppin and his wife opened their Queen's Theatre Royal, another theatrical venture that contributed to his early insolvency.

In Western Australia, no play was performed before 1839; in Queensland, none till 1850; but on August 24, 1839, the crews of the *Britomart* and *Beagle,* two Royal Navy survey ships, performed *Cheap Living* for the minuscule settlement at Port Essington. The larger provincial towns, such as Ballarat and Bendigo, saw itinerant theatrical companies sporadically.

Of the players of this period, little need be said: each company was recruited by an actor-manager who, like Coppin, Cameron, Levey, Clarke, or Wyatt, was also the star performer. The only outstanding actress was Elizabeth Winstanley, who for ten years was the cynosure of the Australian stage. She eventually went to England and played in Manchester and London before appearing, by Royal command, before Queen Victoria at Windsor Castle as Mrs. Malaprop, Mrs. Subtle, Lady Franklin, and Lady Freelove. In addition, she acted in New York and Philadelphia before returning to Australia for a brief stay during the 1860's and then forsaking the theatre for literature. Her *novellas* appeared in *Bow Bells,* and her autobiographical *Shifting Scenes in Theatrical Life* (1859) was the first personal account of theatre in Australia.

320

THEATRE

The economic development of the post-gold rush period of the 1850's proved to be of immeasurable value in helping the nascent theatre in Australia to become viable. Defunct acting companies were reorganized, new ones were recruited, theatres were opened in Bathurst, Newcastle, Maitland, Geelong, and other country centers, and both local and overseas actors toured the "frontiers." The endorsement of the theatre by Queen Victoria and Prince Albert elevated it in the eyes of the general public and seemed to pave the way to undreamed of prosperity and repute. But, as late as 1858, the Launceston *Examiner* felt obliged to caution its bucolic readership by castigating the theatre as "the synagogue of Satan." Notwithstanding this, the theatre revived both in Tasmania and on the mainland.

Between 1850 and 1900 Melbourne claimed preeminence as the cultural center of Australia. George Coppin, always adventurous, became an impresario and brought Gustav Vaughan Brooke, a Dubliner and an experienced Shakespearean actor, to Melbourne under contract to give two hundred performances. Brooke took the leading roles in the standard Shakespearean repertoire and in *A New Way to Pay Old Debts*, *Rob Roy*, and *The Bride of Lammermoor*. That Brooke's performances were unsurpassed is evident; the august and prestigious Melbourne *Argus* commented that Brooke's Othello was "a performance such as, on leaving our English home, we never expected again to witness."

The irrepressible Coppin, undoubtedly elated by his fortuitous success, opened a second theatre in Melbourne in 1855—the Olympic, better known by the sobriquet the Iron Pot, since it had been prefabricated in Manchester. Within the year he had opened a third, and by 1860 he was managing no fewer than six theatres in the same city.

After five years in Australia Brooke returned to England, reputedly some £50,000 the richer for his visit. On his way back to Australia in 1866, he was drowned when the *London* foundered in the Bay of Biscay.

Coppin was a versatile entrepreneur and impresario. Following the success of Brooke's tour, he brought to Australia the famous American actors Joseph Jefferson, Edwin Booth, and McKean Buchanan, the renowned English actors the Keans, and the inimitable and almost legendary Lola Montez—whose love affairs with the King of Bavaria had recently made her into the very personification of the *femme fatale*. With success crowning success, Coppin met all his long-standing debts and paid creditors in full.

The outstanding feature of Australian theatre in the 1860's was the apparently insatiable appetite for Shakespeare: sometimes two or even three plays would be offered simultaneously in the principal cities and towns. But coeval with this was its antithesis—crude melodrama and vaudeville. Lavishly staged, but devoid of art, vaudeville and pantomime (as distinct from true mime) are still vastly popular in Australia and are standard fare for children and their parents at Christmas time. Originally the legacy of Elizabethan and Restoration theatrical divertisements, vaudeville soon became a major force in Australian theatre. What Signor Dalle Casse, the Italian acrobat, introduced in the 1840's by importing Brazilian jugglers and Ethiopian "eccentrics" has continued unabated.

From 1870 to 1900, Australian theatre developed under the aegis of a small coterie of actor-entrepreneurs: J. C. Williamson, Alfred Dampier, and George Rignold. James Cassius Williamson, born in Mercer, Pennsylvania, in 1845, went to California as an actor and there met Margaret Virginia Sullivan ("Maggie Moore"). In 1874 they went to Australia to act in Coppin's theatres and to present their *Struck Oil*, a play that Williamson had bought from an old Californian miner and had altered somewhat. The play, with its quasi-Pennsylvania Dutch dialect, was immensely popular and was the basis of Williamson's fortunes. *Struck Oil* ran for an unprecedented eighty nights in Melbourne; it was hardly less successful elsewhere in Australia and in India, England, and the United States where Williamson presented it before returning in 1879 with sole rights for Australian performances of the new operetta, *H.M.S. Pinafore*, and for all succeeding operas that Gilbert and Sullivan should write.

Williamson later formed his Comic Opera Company on a permanent basis and toured the main cities with the constantly growing Gilbert and Sullivan repertoire. Nellie Stewart, subsequently a favorite of the London stage, was the Australian star of *Patience*, *Iolanthe*, and *Princess Ida*.

For the next eighty years J. C. Williamson Ltd., the successor company to the founder, zealously guarded its rights to Gilbert and Sullivan operettas, and largely through them became an uncommonly successful enterprise, at the same time stifling the arts or crafts of theatre costume and set design, since sets, scripts, and costumes were rented out in package deals.

In 1885 Williamson engaged Dion Boucicault's entire company to perform a series of Irish comedies in Australia. After a year, the elder Boucicault proceeded to the United States, while his son Dion and daughter Nina, together with Florence and Robert Brough, remained and comprised the nucleus of a company that has seldom been equaled in Australian theatrical annals. Their repertoire, almost none of which had been performed in Australia beforehand, included *The School for Scandal, She Stoops to Conquer, Caste, Lady Windermere's Fan,* and *The Second Mrs. Tanqueray.*

For a number of years Williamson had worked in partnership with Arthur Garner and George Musgrove, but in 1904 he withdrew from the partnership and established a proprietary company, J. C. Williamson Theatres Ltd., known to the Australian theatre public as "The Firm." On Williamson's death in Paris in 1913, the Tait brothers—who had been responsible for the highly successful tours of Harry Lauder and *Peg o' My Heart*—expressed interest in amalgamating with the Williamson organization. This consolidation was effected in 1920, since when the Taits—Sir Frank in Melbourne and J. Nevin in London—have controlled the largest professional theatre organization in Australia.

From 1870 until 1900, Alfred Dampier provided Australian audiences with highly praised Shakespearean productions, widely lauded melodramas and imaginative and artistic adaptations of Australian novels; his stage versions of *For the Term of His Natural Life* and *Robbery under Arms* are two of the more interesting Australian excursions into dramaturgy. But the public's taste for melodrama exceeded its appetite for Shakespeare, and Dampier was obliged to play five nights of the former to support one night of the Bard. Few of the melodramas appear to have been written locally; there were, in fact, few Australian plays produced—although it would seem that some adequate ones were available. As one manager explained in 1909: "You can't blame me for importing my plays. I don't say they are all good, or even as good as some I have had offered to me in Australia, but . . . I have the verdict of an English or American audience to help me, while with an Australian-made play I have to play a lone hand." Unfortunately, this attitude seems to have become and remained endemic among Australian managers and producers. Notwithstanding, there have been locally written successes: *Collitt's Inn, Seagulls over Sorento, The Drovers, Rusty Bugles,* and *The Summer of the Seventeenth Doll* readily come to mind.

Dampier was obliged to struggle against an unenlightened and undiscriminating public taste: his audiences' appetite for melodrama must have seemed unassuageable, just as their behavior must have seemed, to the oldest members of the community, little improved during the course of the century. James A. Froude, that perspicacious peripatetic of the Victorian era, took pains to record his impressions of a Melbourne variety audience for readers of his *Oceana* (1886):

The audience was English to the heart. There were the English cat-calls from the gallery, the English delight in animal fun which can be understood without effort. Two monsters pulling each other's noses in the background while the chief actors in the play were discoursing in front of the stage brought down the house. Clown and harlequin tumbled over pantaloon, knocked down the policeman, robbed the shops, jumped in and out of windows—all in the approved style. Satisfaction turned to exuberant delight when one or the other was thrown on his back. It was English with a difference. Some improvised singing, with allusions to local politics, was good-natured and well received. The Governor came in for his share of wit-pellets and laughed as loud as anyone.[2]

It surely must have taxed Dampier's adaptability to have had to contend with this type of audience five nights a week in order to command the attention of a Shakespearean audience on the sixth; to have been transported with hebdomadal regularity from the nadir to the zenith.

George Rignold, also an experienced English actor, contributed largely to the development of the Australian theatre. After successful tours in 1876 and 1883, he returned to Australia in 1887 and until about 1900 directed a small group of playhouses. Schooled in the grand tradition, he was particularly fond of Shakespearean

[2] Quoted in Paul Maguire, *The Australian Theatre* (Melbourne: Oxford University Press, 1948), p. 149.

roles, and his *Henry V*, often performed, was regarded as a truly fine and artistic interpretation.

The theatre of the 1890's gradually became more sophisticated. Overseas actors toured the main Australian towns and cities and brought with them many of the newer "realistic" dramas. Kyrle Bellow appeared in Sardou's *La Tosca*, Janet Achurch played Nora in *A Doll's House*, Olga Nethersole and Charles Cartwright appeared in Ouida's *Moths*, and the ineffable Sarah Bernhardt played in *Camille* and *Fedora*. (In Sydney, perhaps as indication of the city's catholicity of taste—perhaps as proof of its two levels of taste —Bernhardt was followed at Her Majesty's Theatre by the former pugilist, John L. Sullivan, in a play especially written for him, *Honest Hearts and Willing Hands*.) Other overseas artists who braved the insouciance of antipodean audiences were Wilson Barrett (*The Sign of the Cross*), Edward Terry, Edith Crane, and Reuben Fox.

The Australian theatre in the pre-Federation period was at least alive: it provided for three levels of public culture. Dampier and Rignold tried to limit their efforts, as far as feasible, to quality theatre; Williamson devoted his most concerted labors to surfeiting the "middlebrows"—although he did not eschew the theatre's greatest attainments and its greatest practitioners. To satisfy the other end of the spectrum was the ambition of Harry Rickards, a former English music hall entertainer. In 1893 Rickards took an eight-year lease of the Garrick Theatre in Sydney, renamed it the Tivoli, and gradually built up a vaudeville circuit with properties in all Australian states and in New Zealand. For twenty-five years Rickards annually went to Europe and the United States to sign up new acts for his theatres, offering fees second only to those obtaining in London. Under his management almost all the great vaudeville and music hall artists of the periods—including W. C. Fields—played in Australia. On his death in 1911, Rickards personally owned the largest theatre combine in the world. For twenty years after Rickards' death his vaudeville empire languished—as is often the case when such large enterprises have been managed for a long period by a lone proprietor. The First World War and the depression intervened before Mike Connors, Queenie Paul, George Dickinson, and Bert Boland (aided by Roy "Mo" Rene and Jim Gerald as principal comedians) reestablished variety in 1931 with the creation of what is now known as the Tivoli Circuit. From 1944 until 1958 the Tivoli Circuit was run by David N. Martin, who maintained the old Rickards policy of engaging the world's top variety artists: Chico Marx, Ben Blue, Katherine Dunham, George Formby, Gracie Fields, Arthur Askey, and Tommy Trinder.

Writing of this period, Paul Maguire comments: "The Australian stage of the 'eighties and 'nineties was rich in plays and players. It reflected the upsurge of vigour in Australia at large and the high optimism which have since strangely declined in the theatre and the wider scene."[3] There followed a period of prolonged somnolence, misdiagnosed by some of the less sanguine contemporary observers of the cultural scene as *rigor mortis*.

Soon after the turn of the century, the development of the theatre in Australia which had been evident from about 1850, but most noteworthy from about 1880, came to an end. Prototype films, infant radio, world war, and economic depression appeared of such proportions as to jeopardize the very continuance of the theatre as a public art institution. But, as the professional or commercial theatre gradually restricted its activities, a vital new force in Australian theatre, the little theatres, developed into significant enterprises.

The problems associated with ensuring the success of the new Commonwealth, with averting world war and depression, and their internal consequences apparently dictated an end to the performance of serious drama, for from 1900 until 1935 tragedies were less frequently performed. The commercial theatres produced, almost exclusively, those lighter entertainments that are the bane of the theatre, that result in the denigration of the theatre professions, and that impair the development of cultivated tastes.

As if in despair of the state of theatre in Sydney in 1903, William Anderson attempted to stage *Cyrano de Bergerac* with the American actor, Henry Lee, and Eugenie Duggan in the leading roles. But he was met by a derisive first-night audience and the play was, perforce, withdrawn. In the following year an elaborate production of *A Midsummer Night's Dream*, staged by George Musgrove, was quite well received, but its success was—at least in part—attributable to the type of production, which approximated a modern extrava-

[3] *Ibid.*, p. 145.

ganza. By 1911, it seems, audiences were somewhat more sedate and more appreciative; in that year H. B. Irving, the son of the distinguished Sir Henry Irving, toured Australia in *Hamlet*—and a number of melodramas—while Gregan McMahan was able to stage *Arms and the Man*.

A little before the outbreak of the First World War put a temporary halt to much theatrical activity, Oscar Asche, then one of the few internationally famous Australian actors, returned on tour. Asche had studied at the famous Bjornsterne Drama School in Bergen, Norway, where he acted in Ibsen's plays and was highly praised by that dramatist himself. On Ibsen's advice, Asche went to England, met and acted with Ellen Terry and Beerbohm Tree, and within a few years had played in over two hundred Shakespearean roles. On his Australian tour, Asche and his wife, Lily Brayton, starred in a Shakespearean festival and in *Chu Chin Chou*, with which he achieved further fame and considerable fortune.

One of the most enterprising and indefatigable Shakespeareans to visit Australia was Allan Wilkie who, with his wife, Frediswyde Hunter-Watts, labored to establish a genuine appreciation for the Stratford plays. Wilkie visited Australia first in 1915 and, working at times under disheartening conditions, presented over a period of twelve years some twenty-five of Shakespeare's plays in almost every theatre in Australia and New Zealand. From 1920 he had a permanent Shakespeare company which became, in addition, the first competent drama school in the country. In 1925 he was created a Commander of the Order of the British Empire in recognition of his contribution to the theatre in Australia. A year later, while he was playing in Geelong, Victoria, fire consumed his entire wardrobe. Since he played with almost no properties and with the simplest of backdrops, the loss of his costume wardrobe was an exceptional blow —one from which he never recovered. Later that year Wilkie left Australia, played in the United States for a while, and finally settled in England. His departure created a lacuna that has not yet been adequately filled.

The depression years which followed so soon after the First World War caused further curtailment of professional theatre in Australia, and the times seemed to call for light domestic and musical comedies. Accordingly, J. C. Williamson Ltd. revived the old war horses, *The Maid of the Mountains* (which since 1914 had starred Gladys Moncrieff), *White Horse Inn* (the personal property, it seems, of Strella Wilson for twenty-five years), and the full repertoire of Gilbert and Sullivan. To these were added the more recent successes of Sigmund Romberg. It was the perennial revival of this somewhat limited and stereotyped programming that earned for the J. W. Williamson company the displeasure of many theatre people; yet, under the existing economic circumstances, it could hardly be expected that a commercial enterprise would court disaster by the more exciting though fiscally less sound policy of staging exclusively the plays of Odets, Shaw, Galsworthy, Yeats, Maugham, Molnar, and the "social realists" of the period. Maguire and others blame the extension of entertainment tax to legitimate theatre tickets for the generally sad state of the theatre from 1930 to 1950; some see the J. C. Williamson policy as the cause. Both parties seem oblivious to the fact that the commercial theatre suffered an almost universal slump during that period, Broadway musicals excepted.

Overseas artists who toured Australia during the late thirties included Irene Vanbrugh and Dion Boucicault, Guy Bates Post, Sybil Thorndike and Lewis Casson (in *Saint Joan*), and Fay Compton (in *Victoria Regina*); their brief yet satisfying visits were a credit to the commercial theatre managements who engaged them.

In 1940 Kathleen Robinson inaugurated a new theatre group in Sydney, Whitehall Productions, to present plays in a new building, the Minerva, located out of the city proper, at King's Cross. For ten years the Minerva presented recent London and New York plays, but with uneven success. In 1950 the Minerva closed, and the theatre was then used for movies. Some critics saw this failure as proof that an "independent" professional theatre was not feasible in Australia. A second unsuccessful attempt lasted a year.

After the Second World War—the demise of the Minerva notwithstanding—there was a revival of interest in the live theatre in Australia, and at two levels: in amateur groups and in the best overseas actors and companies on tour. In the past fifteen years the theatre has been rejuvenated periodically by the visits of Robert Morley, Madge Elliott, and Cyril Ritchard (expatriates), Cicely Courtneidge, Noel Coward, Judith Anderson (still an Australian citizen, though she has lived in the United States since she was eighteen), and Elizabeth Bergner. The 1948 tour of the Old Vic Company, led by Sir Laurence Olivier and Vivien Leigh (*The School for Scandal, Richard III*, and *The Skin of Our Teeth*) the visits of the Shakespeare Memorial Theatre Company, led by Anthony Quayle and Diana Wynyard in 1950 (*Much Ado About Nothing* and *Macbeth*) and 1953 (*As You Like It, Henry IV, Part I*, and *Othello*) and of the Old Vic Company with Vivien Leigh and Robert Helpmann in 1961, however, must be regarded as the undoubted high lights.

Meanwhile, the Broadway musicals—often five and six years after their heralded openings—have replaced those of Gilbert and Sullivan, which are now in the public domain and are therefore more than ever the staple of community musical and dramatic groups.

Australia has never been able to claim any considerable number of truly repertory theatres, although the Union Theatre in Melbourne might be considered the nearest to the repertory type. It has, however, a vast array of amateur and semiprofessional groups which range in competency from one extreme to the other. These groups perform from one to five or ten nights at a time and customarily present from two to five or six plays a year. When organized on a permanent basis, these amateur groups provide the training experience upon which most Australians are dependent for their knowledge of the theatre arts.

The earliest effort to establish an Australian repertory theatre was made by Leon Brodsky, who in 1904 formed the Australian Theatre Society (later the Playgoers' Society) in Melbourne. It was Brodsky's purpose to produce both Australian and serious plays from the whole of Western drama that would not otherwise be staged in Australia. Writing in *The Lone Hand* in 1908, Brodsky lamented: "Most of us are almost in despair when we see how little relation the theatre in Australia has to the national life of the country." In the following year Brodsky was obliged to discontinue his enterprise, but two years later Gregan McMahon started his Melbourne Repertory Theatre which, operating as a semiprofessional company, produced fifty-seven plays before it closed in 1918, having somehow survived the war years. McMahon moved to Sydney and, aided by the Taits, established the Sydney Repertory Theatre Society, which produced six or seven plays a year using both amateur and professional actors—this before Actors' Equity prohibited such amalgams. After seven years and almost fifty productions, McMahon left Sydney to resume his work in Melbourne, continuing there until his death in 1941.

After the disbanding of the Sydney Repertory Theatre Society, Doris Fitton (who had been trained by McMahon) worked to establish a successor theatre. In 1930 she launched a cooperative venture, the Independent Theatre, in a converted garage in North Sydney. After thirty years the Independent is still flourishing—though it has seen difficult times and has had to weather those vicissitudes encountered in all theatrical enterprises, but found at their greatest strength, it often seems, in Australian theatre. The productions of the Independent Theatre have generally been of erratic standards, but they have often been the only Sydney productions of Wesker, Pinter, Miller, and Williams. Today the Independent operates a drama school with a faculty of six, has a workshop group, does play readings regularly, offers a children's theatre on Saturdays, and presents two plays weekly. Almost all Sydney actors have appeared at the Independent. For her work for the Australian theatre Doris Fitton recently has been decorated.

Also working in Sydney, May Hollinworth has devoted over twenty-five years of her remarkable energy and ability to the amateur theatre. In 1928 she became director of the Sydney University Dramatic Society, but after a disagreement on policy she established her Metropolitan Theatre in 1942 and directed its activities until her semiretirement in 1952. Always eschewing the meretricious and ephemeral, May Hollinworth has done more, perhaps, than any other person in Sydney to inculcate a taste and appreciation for the best that the theatre can offer: her standards and her expectations of actors and technicians alike are high, and her results are distinguished.

Of the other little theatres, perhaps the most successful have been the Adelaide Repertory Theatre, established in 1910 by Bryceson Treharne, an American, the Perth Playhouse (now called the National Theatre), and the New Theatre League in Sydney. From its inception, the Adelaide Repertory Theatre has been in continuous operation and has introduced to its audiences the plays of Synge, Shaw, Ibsen, Lady Gregory, Molnar, Strindberg, and Galsworthy long before other theatres. It has kept close to its stated aim: "to produce plays of literary or artistic value . . . poetic and symbolic dramas, plays bearing directly on the actual problems of life." The New Theatre, a liberal Sydney group, has given particular attention to political and sociological drama: its *Of Mice and Men, The Quare Fellow* (Australian premiere), and *The Crucible*, in recent years, have maintained the high standards of imaginative and resourceful production that have come to be expected in its work—the effect, in no uncertain way, of its relentless program of training its members in all aspects of theatre work. It is interesting to note that the press has, for almost two decades, steadfastly refused to recognize the New Theatre's existence by reviewing its productions.

The Ensemble Theatre, which was organized in 1958, is a small yet vigorous addition to Sydney's little theatres. Started by Hayes Gordon, a former United States actor and college theatre teacher who played the leading role in the Australian professional production of *Kismet*, the Ensemble has become the center of method acting in Australia. Gordon's theatre-in-the-round productions of Williams' *20 Wagons Full of Cotton* and *Orpheus Descending*, of *Boy Meets Girl*, and of Dinelli's *The Man* quickly achieved deserved applause.

At present, amateur theatre groups are to be found in all the cities and in many of the smaller country towns, as well as in the universities and teachers' colleges. The university dramatic societies—especially since the introduction of the Universities' Drama Festival a few years ago—achieve very high standards. By contrast, the teachers' colleges' dramatic productions are uniformly lamentable.

With such an equable climate as Australia enjoys, it is remarkable that there has never been any serious attempt to introduce summer stock, that vital, necessary, and popular branch of American and Canadian theatre that is so much a part of the North American cultural scene. Although universities are on long vacation during the summer months, and although most of the population has its vacation then and spends it regularly at a few well-known locations, there are no summer theatres in Australia. It is especially noticeable that there is no counterpart of the Chautauqua, New York, program or of the Stratford (Connecticut and Ontario) drama festivals.

In the past four or five years there have been signs of a possible renaissance of the theatre in Australia, and the largest cities can offer a considerable choice of entertainments, albeit many of them light and few of them of the type of drama that the Adelaide Repertory Theatre and others have long thought the most significant. Below is a list of the theatre offerings in Sydney during one recent week: [4]

PLAYS

Arts Council of Australia	*Under Milk Wood* [5]	Dylan Tomas
Ensemble Theatre	*The Seven-Year Itch*	George Axelrod
Independent Theatre	*The Aspern Papers*	Michael Redgrave– Henry James
Minerva Theatre	*The World of Suzie Wong*	Richard Mason
Pocket Theatre	*Dinner with the Family*	Jean Anouilh
Sydney Theatre Club	*Playboy of the Western World*	J. M. Synge
Sydney University Players	*'Tis Pity She's a Whore*	John Ford
Theatre Royal	*The Constant Wife*	W. Somerset Maugham
Waterside Workers' Federation	*The Drums of Father Ned*	Sean O'Casey

MUSICALS

Elizabethan Theatre	*The King and I*
Her Majesty's Theatre	*My Fair Lady*
Mosman Musical Society	*White Horse Inn*
Palace Theatre	*Lock Up Your Daughters*
Tivoli Theatre	*The Student Prince*

REVUES

Ballet Theatre	*Contrast*
Capitol Theatre	*The Crazy Gang Variety Revue*
Phillip Street Theatre	*Stop Press!*

BALLETS

[None]

[4] The capacity of the Ensemble, Pocket, Waterside Workers', Sydney University Players', and Arts Council theatres combined is less than 1,000. The Pocket Theatre seats 60, the Ensemble 90.

[5] Presented as a one-man reading.

The fact that the university dramatic societies regularly attain a high standard of performance is not adventitious; all those associated with them are very devoted to the theatre. But, in all except one university—the new University of New South Wales—there is no formal instruction in the drama such as is to be found at Cape Town, Durban, Bristol, and almost all Canadian and American universities. In fact, it is important, when attempting to assess the position and achievement of the theatre in Australia, to understand the attitude of educational authorities and institutions toward theatre.

The state Departments of Education have, until three or four years ago, never had any officers directly responsible for the teaching of speech and drama—although, it must be allowed, these areas have been officially encouraged, especially drama, since it is an important means of raising funds for school treasuries. Few of those persons now in charge of drama have had academic or professional theatre training. The general attitude toward theatre in schools can be summed up in the not inappropriate epithet "for fun and funds." Each high school is expected to hold a play day each year—a pernicious practice that compels school populations to watch class plays (poorly rehearsed, shoddily costumed, horrendously produced) on one day of the school year from 9 A.M. until 3 P.M. Recent recommendations that one or two one-act plays should be presented at monthly intervals (in the interest of minimal dislocation of school routine, improved production standards, and the development of an appreciation for the theatre) have been disregarded. Over recent years the numerous high schools all seem to have made their selection from about a dozen well-known one-act plays; visits to a small number of play days therefore become harrowingly repetitious experiences. Teachers of English or others with a penchant for the theatre are usually expected to supervise play days, but they are given no course of training in theatre practice. There are few auditoriums in high schools, and those that exist appear to have been constructed without any thought for the needs of stage productions: generally, there are no lighting panels, no wings, no property or dressing rooms, no raked floors.

In recent years, some teachers have studied the theories of Jacob Moreno, whose sociodrama is now largely discredited overseas. This interest in sociodrama is perhaps an attempt to stimulate dramatic

333

activities in schools that have neither the money nor the facilities for true theatre experiences.

Ten years or so ago the University of Melbourne established a Diploma in Dramatic Arts curriculum, somewhat after the fashion of the University of London's course in drama, and assisted the student union in equipping its theatre to professional standards. At first, the number of students was encouraging, but because of insufficient support the diploma course was allowed to lapse. In 1958 the University of New South Wales, in Sydney, decided to accommodate the newly formed National Institute of Dramatic Arts, a cooperative venture of the university, the Elizabethan Theatre Trust, and the New South Wales government, and to promote a two-year diploma course. Response has been good, and the classes—limited to thirty students a year—have been filled. Good though it is to find some university interest in the theatre, it is to be regretted that the arrangement between the university and the National Institute is so irregular. Technically, the diploma offered is not a university diploma; the faculty (with the exception of Associate Professor Robert Quentin, the director of the Institute and a member of the university's School of English) are not members of the university teaching staff; the course of instruction is so vocational that it would not be approved in a university in the United States. Diplomates will probably find that it will be difficult for them to pursue higher studies in the dramatic arts. It is to be hoped that the University of New South Wales will, in due time, establish a full department of speech and theatre arts and approve a regular degree course. Although the state government was instrumental in the arrangement whereby the university and the Institute cooperated, it must seem ironic that, in order to obtain an auditorium for the Institute's use, the university was obliged to justify a "science lecture theatre." If the University of New South Wales should ever incorporate the State Conservatorium of Music and the National Art School in Sydney, it would be possible for it to offer instruction in the full range of theatre arts, including opera, costume, and scene design. At present, these ancillary arts are to be learned only in the little theatre groups.

In 1949 the British Council, with the support of the Chifley Labor government, invited the distinguished British producer-director,

Tyrone Guthrie, to visit Australia to report on the theatre and to recommend ways by which it might be developed and controlled. Guthrie claimed, *inter alia*, that private enterprise was not producing the type of theatre that Australia should have. (This same observation, made over the years by Australians, had been discredited as the product of particularly jaundiced minds.) Further, Guthrie reported, a national theatre might be able to provide what was missing and necessary if it were established as a permanent theatre company and not just as an imposing edifice. He believed that only in London could properly trained Australian actors, designers, managers, producers, and technicians be found, and that therefore such a national theatre company should be established first in London—as was the Research School of Medicine of the Australian National University. But what the country thought appropriate for a university faculty it did not consider proper for a theatre company.

By 1952 the Australian authorities had taken no action on Dr. Guthrie's report and its recommendations, and when he was invited to assume the directorship of the Stratford, Ontario, Shakespeare Festival Theatre, Guthrie accepted with alacrity. He mustered the best acting talent in Canada, augmented it with talent from Britain (Alec Guinness, James Mason, Irene Worth, Douglas Campbell, Siobhan McKenna, and Anthony Quayle) and—on a free form Elizabethan stage designed by Tanya Moiseiwitsch—commenced operations in a temporary, commodious tent in isolated Stratford. By 1956 the Stratford Players had become world famous and had stormed Broadway and been acclaimed at the Edinburgh Festival. What Dr. Guthrie accomplished in Canada he had wanted the opportunity to do in Australia.

In 1954, when the visit of Queen Elizabeth to Australia was to take place, Dr. H. C. Coombs, governor of the Commonwealth Bank of Australia, who had disagreed with Dr. Guthrie's findings, announced plans for an Australian Elizabethan Theatre Trust, so named that the Trust could be considered a memorial of the Queen's visit. The committee behind the Elizabethan—as it has come to be known—was a polyglot one, few members of which had had any association with the performing arts. The Trust, in resplendently chauvinistic through imitative rhetoric, proposed to provide a "theatre of Australians, by Australians, for Australians." Its achievements have been principally in the third part of its policy, though it has certainly tried to implement all.

The Trust appealed for public subscriptions for an endowment of £100,000 and received £90,000—a poor omen. To this sum the federal government added a paltry £30,000, and on this shoestring capital—which no Broadway or London producer would consider adequate for a single production of even the most unambitious nature—the Trust proposed to establish its national theatre. One of the first acts of the Trust was to engage Hugh Hunt, an English producer known for his *Julius Caesar*, as manager; then they obtained the services of a number of minor English actors and commenced operations in a dilapidated movie house in Newtown, one of the least salubrious of the older semi-industrialized inner suburbs of Sydney, with a production, under commercial management, of Terence Rattigan's *The Sleeping Prince*.

The Elizabethan Theatre Trust's stated aims are commendable:

To promote drama, opera, ballet and any arts of the theatre in Australia in any way whatever; and in particular, and without limiting the generality of the foregoing,
  (i) to promote the writing of plays, operas, ballets and other works for theatrical performance in any way whatever;
  (ii) to promote the training of producers, players, musicians, singers, dancers and other theatre personnel in any way whatever;
  (iii) to assist with the presentation of drama, opera, ballet and any other art of the theatre in Australia by lending or giving money, by acting as surety, or in any other way whatever;
  (iv) to provide or assist to provide theatres and appurtenances of theatres.[6]

In order to subsidize its own productions of "high standard drama and opera" by presenting "a percentage of thoroughly popular entertainment"—sound enough policy for commercial managements—the Elizabethan has courted disaster. There has never been a dearth of "thoroughly popular entertainment" in Australian theatre; but there has never been sufficient "high standard drama and opera." What, in effect, the Elizabethan proposed to do was merely to provide more of the theatrical fare that Australia was already getting. It was a far cry from the national theatre envisioned by Tyrone Guthrie

[6] The Elizabethan Theatre Trust, *Memorandum of Association*, Sec. 2.

and most of the theatre lovers of Australia. The "percentage of thoroughly popular entertainment" has tended, inexorably, to increase. A few Australian actors from overseas—including Grant Taylor and Ron Haddrick—joined the Elizabethan's permanent company before it was disbanded in 1961; but few actors, producers, writers, or dancers have found permanent or challenging new opportunities. Some people claim Ray Lawler's *Summer of the Seventeenth Doll* as an achievement of the Elizabethan; but it must be remembered that the play was given its first production at the Melbourne Union Theatre. It could not be claimed that the Elizabethan's activities have either elevated public taste in the theatre or encouraged significant new developments; its first eight years' achievements are insubstantial.

The Arts Council of Australia, with branches in each state, has since its inception (as the Council for the Encouragement of Music and the Arts) encouraged the theatre by supporting companies which play (often just one-night stands) in distant country towns. The Council is dependent for a critical part of its operating budget on grants from the state governments. According to the political situation it can fare well or find itself almost without sufficient funds to operate. Mostly it finds itself in the latter condition. The Arts Council's companies of semiprofessional actors travel in semitrailers loaded with wardrobes and minimal properties; both the Council and the actors are to be commended for their efforts to take serious drama (often in abridged versions for country school children) to the most remote parts of the continent. But it is sad that its work is not more adequately recognized by the various governments—and it is still a moot question whether poor, emasculated productions are, after all, better than none.

In the theatre arts other than acting and producing, some Australians have made distinguished contributions, though most of those who have done so were obliged to gain their experience overseas. After serving their apprenticeships in London, Paris, or New York, the majority have chosen to remain expatriates, visiting Australia infrequently. With most little theatres producing a play for a matter of nights rather than weeks, months, or years, as overseas, the practice has been for all except the largest and most affluent companies to rent costumes and sets from the commercial theatre managements; the result is a generally depressing uniformity of shabby, inappropriate, ill-fitting, and often anachronistic costumes in amateur productions.

In scene design, however, there have been several competent, imaginative artists. Frank Hinder, William Constable, and Kenneth Rowell are worthy of individual mention. Hinder painted very interesting backdrops for the Sydney productions of Anthony Coburn's *The Bastard Country* and Richard Beynon's *The Shifting Heart;* William Constable, F.R.S.A., has created unusual, imaginative, and impressive sets for Douglas Stewart's verse drama *Shipwreck* (produced by May Hollinworth's Metropolitan Theatre) and for a whole series of ballets, in both Australia and England; Rowell has designed for the Ballet Rambert and the Royal Ballet in England as well as for the Australian stage. In addition, the work of Robin Lovejoy (a skillful theatrical factotum) and of Loudon Sainthill should be commended. During recent years Lovejoy, Sainthill, Amie Kingston, and Ann Church have given some attention to the design of stage costumes—though the quality of their work has often passed unnoticed and they have had insufficient opportunities. Apart from the work of these few artists, Australian theatre design is at its best mediocre and at times incredibly inappropriate and inartistic.

Stage lighting is as yet not regarded as an exacting art in the Australian theatre. Outside the commercial theatres there is little modern equipment; that used by most amateur groups is, of necessity, both archaic and crudely utilitarian. No individual has gained a reputation for his mastery of stage lighting.

From the turn of the century until quite recently, no legitimate theatre in Australia was performing in an edifice constructed for that purpose. The older theatres of the nineteenth century were gradually condemned and razed. Then, with the advent of motion pictures and the apparent eclipse of the live theatre, it undoubtedly seemed judicious to build theatres primarily as movie houses—making provision for a stage in case a lecture or other assembly might need to be accommodated. As a result, when in the past decade there was a growing demand for premises for legitimate theatre, the former movie houses (now closed as a result of the introduction of television) were pressed into service. In most cases these vast, cavernous premises are unsuitable for the drama. Many of the little theatre groups perform in converted garages, church halls, basements, boat sheds, and attics. Such locations add an element of Bohemianism to theatregoing, but contribute little to the joys of the actors or the advancement of theatre arts.

When the University of Sydney student union rebuilt its theatre recently and announced that it was now a "modern, well-equipped home for the arts of stage and cinema," further proof was given that theatre architecture is apparently an unknown subject in Australia still. The auditorium is merely a presentable version of the standard cinema architecture of the 1930's: narrowly rectangular, with seats slightly raked and parellel to an imposing proscenium arch, it has no boxes or balconies, little space for properties, staff, or preparation, and none of the appurtenances now regarded as standard in contemporary theatres. There is, unfortunately, no provision for arena theatre, none for Elizabethan-style staging, and none for any but the simplest ventures into experimental production techniques, musical drama, or ballet. Again, an exceptional opportunity has passed unutilized, and expectation has been disappointed by performance. With little extra cost it would have been possible to engage the services of experienced theatre architects overseas, but chauvinism dies hard, and the possibility of an Australian university theatre of the caliber of those at Queen's College, Hofstra College, the University of Oregon, or Stanford University has, lamentably, passed. The newly established University Union Repertory Theatre Company—which planned to present Australian plays, Brecht and Giraudoux, but which was forced to disband through lack of patronage—soon found the restrictions that such architecture imposes upon performances.

Whereas the technical theatre arts and crafts are not highly developed in Australia, dramatic criticism is even less satisfactory. There has never been any long-lived theatre journal. Persons who supply the newspapers and journals with comments on theatrical productions are, of course, legion. But their observations reveal little perspicacity. Most write noncommital and virtually useless reviews of a few hundred words or rejoice in petulent criticisms; many just do not know what they are writing about, suffering as they do from a stultified knowledge of the drama, from restricted familiarity with the conventions, techniques, and achievements of the theatre, and from an apparent inability to write meaningful prose

339

of reasonable literary elegance. No critic has established a reputation for discernment, for unusually penetrating observation, for helpful, valuable criticism, for that rare insight into the purpose of the theatre to be found in the dramatic criticism of Shaw or—in our own time—Howard Taubman and Brooks Atkinson of the *New York Times*. The very fact that newspaper theatre critics are so undistinguished probably accounts for their not being taken seriously by playgoers and for the little value placed on their services by the newspaper proprietors themselves, who commonly allow neophyte reporters to review plays as part of their duties. A recent correspondent in *Nation*, a national fortnightly journal, wrote: "Critics in Australia give the impression of suffering from too many clarets before the show, faulty spectacles, bad memory, indigestion, the university cafeteria, second nights and Eric Bentley." The poor theatre criticism that is published testifies to the hegemony of a truculent band of reviewers of insular outlook who regard disagreement as contumely and to whom the onerous responsibilities of serious criticism are either alien or anathema. The poet Roland Robinson, who formerly danced with the Kirsova Ballet, should be exculpated: his criticisms of the ballet and of dance recitals, written for the *Sydney Morning Herald*, reveal at once an understanding of the dance, an uncompromising set of standards, and the ability to write meaningful prose.

The Australian film industry was one of the world's earliest. *The Kelly Gang*, a full-length feature, was made by theatre impresarios J. and N. Tait in 1905, just a short time after *The Great Train Robbery* created such a sensation in the United States.

Most of the early films featured popular stage personalities and were of the then stock adventure format: *Captain Midnight, The Bushwhackers, The Bushranger*. The First World War inspired a number of patriotic films, among which were *For Australia* and *How We Beat the* Emden, and was hardly over before Australian studios issued *The Martyrdom of Nurse Cavell, The Mutiny on the* Bounty, and *For the Term of His Natural Life*.

Charles Chauvel and Ken G. Hall are the most prominent of Australia's few film producers. Chauvel's most ambitious films were *In the Wake of the* Bounty (1933) which starred Errol Flynn, the young actor from Tasmania, in his first film; *40,000 Horsemen* (1941), a story of the Palestine campaign of the First World War which introduced the now well-known actor "Chips" Rafferty; *The Rats of Tobruk* (1944); *Sons of Matthew* (1949), released overseas as *The Fighting O'Riordans;* and *Jedda* (1954), the story of an aboriginal girl, filmed in color. Hall's interests have been directed principally to the newsreel, the documentary, and the feature film, though his film biography of Australian aviator Sir Charles Kingsford-Smith, *Smithy* (1946), was highly regarded in Australia.

In recent years several British and American producers have made films in Australia, but they have used few Australian actors in important parts. Some of these films are *On the Beach, The Overlanders, Kangaroo, Bush Christmas,* and *The Sundowners.* The reasons for not using Australian actors in leading roles are doubtless multifarious, but some are obvious: local actors have no box-office drawing force overseas; their accents are seldom eliminated; except in rare cases, they cannot simulate British or American dialects convincingly; and they are often awkward and gangling, since they have had little opportunity to act before cameras and have seldom had any considerable experience in the theatre. Under the circumstances, there has been little incentive for Australian actors to aspire to careers in the film industry, though some—Merle Oberon, Peter Finch, Errol Flynn, Cecil Kellaway, Ron Randell, "Chips" Rafferty, and Victoria Shaw—have achieved eminence in Hollywood.

The introduction of television in Australia in 1958 raised some hopes for new avenues for theatre personnel, but the networks—conscious of costs and the distinct, expressed public preference for overseas programs, regardless of their quality or inanity—have given little encouragement to local actors and little time to local productions. The few programs that have been produced in Australia, mainly by the Artransa company, are so patently amateurish in camera work and general production standards that they have not been readily marketable overseas. Without the opportunity to work frequently within the stringent demands of television, it cannot be expected that actors will find this a significant aspect of the theatre in Australia as it has become overseas.

341

PATTERN OF AUSTRALIAN CULTURE

The dance, as a theatre art, has always been found in Australia, as elsewhere; but it has never attained a popular following (except tap dancing, which presented immediate opportunities in variety and vaudeville) and can hardly be said to have established for itself a very significant niche in public culture. The small segment of the population who could claim to have attended a classical ballet form the hard core of enthusiasts on whom the success of any season of ballet is dependent. Sadly, the ballet has always been considered too effeminate a concern for Australian males, and interest in it has been thought an indication of cultural pretensions or an abberation of European immigrants. It has, therefore, been tolerated rather than encouraged.

Not until the 1880's did Australian audiences witness ballet, though they had had entertainments by exotic dancers—Signor Dalle Casse's Brazilian tightrope dancers, Scottish and Polish folk dance groups, and Tomato the Three-Legged Dancer—during the preceding years. Such dance as had appeared before the 1880's was incidental to variety entertainments, and it was not until after 1855, when Lola Montez visited the country, that a full program of dance was offered.

A definite attempt to establish ballet was made in 1899 when J. C. Williamson employed Marie Reddell, formerly of the Gaiety Theatre in London, to train a small company of dancers in Melbourne. Of Williamson's group of eight dancers, Minnie Everett, Frances Scully, Minnie Hooper, and Jennie Brenan later opened their own dancing academies. But they often devoted their efforts to teaching uninterested youngsters the basic mechanics of song-and-dance routines or tap dancing rather than the techniques of the ballet or modern, expressionist dance.

Modern dance, both ballet and interpretative, has been promoted largely through the efforts of Gertrude Bodenweiser, a former professor of dance and choreography at the State Conservatory of Music and Dramatic Arts in Vienna. After a tour of Australia in 1940, Madame Bodenweiser remained in Sydney and established a school of dance. Through those of her early students who are themselves now teachers, she pioneered and promoted modern interpretative dance in Australia. Her company has toured all states, New Zealand, Britain, India, and South Africa.

The Americans, Katherine Dunham, Ted Shawn, and Jan Veen

342

(of the Boston Conservatory), the Indians, Shivaram and Pryagopal, and the Spanish dancer, La Joselita, have presented recitals of the dance in Australia in recent years, but the effect of their art is yet to be determined.

Classical ballet in Australia is the direct effect of visiting companies, in particular, of Colonel de Basil's Ballet Russe and Ballet de Monte Carlo, which toured in 1936 and 1939–1940, respectively.

Before de Basil, Australian audiences had seen Adeline Genee and the Imperial Russian Ballet in 1913, Anna Pavlova and Laurent Novikoff in 1926, Pavlova and Pierre Vladimiroff in 1929, and Victor Dande (Pavlova's husband), Olga Spessiva, and Anatol Vilzak in 1934. But these were not complete companies, and their effect was more like that of a visit to an art gallery than the purchase of a palette and colors.

In 1936 J. C. Williamson Ltd. arranged for a tour of Colonel de Basil's secondary company—the first was on tour in the United States. There were forty-five dancers in the company, and they presented twenty-two ballets, many with choreography by Massine, Balanchine, Fokine, and Nijinsky. Later, in 1938 and again in 1939–1940, the principal de Basil company, the Covent Garden Russian Ballet, visited Australia. On this 1939–1940 tour, Colonel de Basil himself directed the world premiere of Lichine's *Graduation Ball*.

Although Mischa Burlakov remained in Sydney to teach ballet after the Pavlova season of 1929, his influence was not great, notwithstanding his founding (with Louise Lightfoot) of the First Australian Ballet, which gave stimulating student performances of *Swan Lake*, *Petrouchka*, and *Scheherazade* long before they were professionally staged in the country.

The real growth of ballet in Australia was the result of the efforts of three dancers from de Basil's companies who decided to remain after the conclusion of their tours: Helene Kirsova, Edouard Borovansky, and Raissa Koussnetzova. Borovansky settled in Melbourne, and his ballet company—after several reorganizations—has had a close association with the J. C. Williamson management, playing seasons in its theatres on an infrequent yet somewhat predictable schedule.

Between 1940 and 1945, when it disbanded, the Kirsova Ballet presented some highly praised performances in Sydney.

343

Madame Koussnetzova's Polish-American Ballet, also located in Sydney, has performed in most of the capital cities and larger country towns; in 1951 it presented *Coppelia* with mimes and tableaux—the first occasion on which the complete ballet had been presented in Australia.

A handful of Australian dancers are now internationally known. Robert Helpmann, who was born in Adelaide, is perhaps the *doyen* of the group. Helpmann, as a student dancer, toured with the Pavlova company, joined the Sadler's Wells Ballet in 1933, and rose to become one of the distinguished members of that ballet. He has since acted in a number of films, done the choreography for several new ballets, and achieved fame by his dancing in the film *The Red Shoes*. Elaine Fifield, a leading danseuse of the Sadler's Wells company, and Henry Legerton have appeared in British and European ballets; Phillipe Perrottet has gained the distinction of becoming ballet master of the Norwegian State Ballet. Another Australian—now, like the others, a permanent expatriate—has been conductor of the Sadler's Wells and Covent Garden Ballet orchestras: he is Charles Mackerras, former oboist in the Sydney Symphony Orchestra.

Several ballets have originated in Australia; of them the most original in conception and choreography is undoubtedly Rex Reid's *Corroboree* (1950), based on music by John Antill, the dean of Australian composers. Of the remainder of Australian ballets, few have had more than an occasional performance or received more than perfunctory, fulsome applause for their slight merits.

The tours of the Ballet Rambert (1948), the Royal Ballet (1956) with Dame Margot Fonteyn and Michael Soames, the Bolshoi Ballet (1960), the Maly Ballet and the New York City Ballet (1961), and the American Dance Theatre (1962) have further stimulated interest in the dance. But Australians still, in general, regard the ballet as an art form that ceased to develop after Pavlova. As one recent critic described the situation, "Australia has never seen a really modern ballet. . . . We in Australia still prefer to wallow in the atmosphere of the Russian and French high society of a century ago. We imitate them on a rather funny provincial scale."

Hugh P. Hall's *Ballet in Australia from Pavlova to Rambert* (1948) is an extraordinarily impressive record of the ballet in the form of photographs taken during actual performances.

THEATRE

In Australia the theatre has always been the stepchild of the arts; its best talent—actors, designers, producers, dancers—have inevitably gravitated overseas, motivated by both the desire for experience at the highest professional levels and the desire to make a career in the theatre.[7]

There has never been the same attitude by government to the theatre as to the other arts, and although some might demur (seeing some change in the past decade), it seems unlikely that any considerable change will be witnessed in the foreseeable future.

It has been claimed that there has been a renaissance of interest in the theatre arts in Australia in the last few years and that great achievements are imminent; but this is not easily supported and smacks of unjustified optimism.[8] The record shows merely a decline in the number of premises used for films and the use of some of them for vaudeville, variety, Broadway musicals, and light, situational comedies. The little theatres are still bearing the burden of responsibility for producing a steady diet of serious drama.

Partisans would claim for the Elizabethan Theatre Trust all manner of miraculous achievements in the past eight years; but its contribution to Australian theatre has surely been overstated. There seems little doubt that, had Tyrone Guthrie's recommendations of 1950 been implemented, Australia would now have been able to support perhaps two professional national theatre companies and a ballet, and their contribution to the nurturing of a genuine and cultivated appreciation of the theatre arts would be immeasurable. Meanwhile, the little provincial town of Stratford, Ontario, has

[7] Recently Zoe Caldwell, an Australian actress who has achieved some distinction at Stratford-on-Avon, Stratford, Ontario, and the Royal Court Theatre, London, returned to Australia. Lois Hunter, writing in the *Bulletin* (Sydney), felt compelled to ask: "What will Miss Caldwell do next? She wants to stay here and do an Australian play, and in order to do so has relinquished the role of Titania in Tony Richardson's film version of *A Midsummer Night's Dream*. But now we have a problem. When we have an actor or actress in Australia who has made good, and is prepared to sacrifice both prestige and money to stay here, what have we got to offer? It is a hard question to answer."

[8] Much was made, for instance, of the announcement that Tennessee Williams' new play, *The Milk Train Doesn't Stop Here Any More*, based on his short story, "Man, Bring This up Road," was to have its tryout in Australia. The locale for the tryout was decided, it appears, merely because the author of the play had never visited Australia; eventually, however, the play was given its tryout in Spoleto, Italy.

345

gained an international reputation for its Shakespeare Festival Theatre which, under different circumstances, might have brought culture and fame to Canberra, Melbourne, or Sydney.

To date, Australia's principal contribution to the theatre has been in supplying talented individuals to overseas theatres. It is hoped that this will change and that oral interpretation, the theatre, and the ballet will become so significant in Australian culture as to merit international acclaim and emulation.

BIBLIOGRAPHY

Aldous, Allan. *Theatre in Australia.* 1947.

Australian Drama and Theatre. Current Affairs Bulletin (University of Sydney), XXII (July 28, 1958).

Australian Elizabethan Theatre Trust. *Australian Theatre Year Book.* 1958– .

Brewer, Frank. *Drama and Music in New South Wales.* 1892.

Garling, J. *Australian Notes on the Ballet.* 1950.

Hall, Hugh. *Ballet in Australia from Pavlova to Rambert.* 1948.

Kardoss, J. *A Brief History of the Australian Theatre.* 1955.

Kirsova, Helen. *Australian Ballet.* 1944.

——. *Pioneering Ballet in Australia.* 1945.

Macgeorge, N. *Borovansky Ballet in Australia and New Zealand.* 1946.

Maguire, Paul. *The Australian Theatre.* 1948.

Palmer, Vance. *Louis Esson and the Australian Theatre.* 1948.

ART

DANIEL THOMAS

TODAY, for the first time in Australia's history, there is a foreign audience for the country's painting. Sculpture, architecture, and design do not create such interest, in spite of some good work being done.

Understandably for a Commonwealth country, the center of this outside interest is in London, although Sidney Nolan and—to a lesser extent—Albert Tucker are known in the United States and Europe. Nolan's inclusion in the Brussels World Fair Exhibition, "Fifty Years of Modern Art" and representation in the Museum of Modern Art, New York, and in the Tate Gallery, London, add up to the most considerable overseas success achieved by any Australian painter.

To Australians this success can sometimes be disquieting. Overseas admiration of Australian art is often expressed in terms of delight in an exotic landscape, deserts, strange beasts, and bushrangers, rather than in terms of the undoubted artistic merit of a work. The equal artistic merit of a near-academic painter such as William Dobell or of abstract painters such as Ian Fairweather and John Olsen goes largely unremarked and is given less opportunity to be remarked.

The present wave of interest probably began when Sir Kenneth Clark visited Australia in 1949 and encountered the work of Russell Drysdale and Sidney Nolan. He encouraged Drysdale to exhibit his outback landscapes at the Leicester Galleries the following year; one was bought by the Tate. In 1951, Nolan first exhibited with the Redfern Gallery, and his work was again bought for the Tate. Two years later, he left Australia permanently (only an occasional week has been spent here since then), and in 1957 he was given a major retrospective show by the Whitechapel Art Gallery, London.

By then curiosity about what else Australia had to offer was aroused. Drysdale's second London exhibition in 1958 received much more attention than that of eight years earlier. In 1961 the popular response to a large survey of contemporary Australian painting at Whitechapel came close to rapture, very different from the boredom caused by the previous surveys of 1953 (a small Arts Council exhibition), 1923 (Royal Academy), and 1898 (Grafton Gallery).

An even larger official exhibition, discussed haphazardly for nearly ten years, will probably be shown at the Tate Gallery in 1963. A tentative version of this proposed exhibition was seen at the 1962 Adelaide Festival of Arts. Its emphasis was on the contemporary artists, but two other periods were also selected for inclusion: the "colonial" and the "impressionist." It will be reasonable to follow this scheme, but although the first half of the twentieth century produced little of interest, it nourished some influential painters and some avant-garde ones who will be mentioned briefly.

Colonial art consists of a number of isolated figures of varying merit working from 1788 to about 1860, by which time all the six colonies had become self-governing. Nearly all these first painters were immigrant Englishmen; some were convicts.

The earliest surviving Australian oil painting is "View of Sydney Cove" (Dixson Galleries, Sydney) painted in 1794 by the convict Thomas Watling. It is a typical application of the formula for picturesque landscape deriving ultimately from Claude Lorrain. Graceful trees, which do not appear in Watling's factual drawing for the picture, have been added to frame the view. The serpentine curve of the horizon has been improved, a foreground building is emphasized, and a cluster of aborigines introduced to remind the spectator that the small settlement is in a strange new country.

Such picturesque landscapes remained the most common kind of painting in Australia for many years. More recent and more nationalistic generations have condemned them for failing to render the true appearance of the native Australian gum tree (the eucalyptus) or the characteristic Australian light. Such condemnation forgets that naturalism was not then part of any normal artistic program, and it also forgets that less consciously artistic painters, making purely topographical records, did succeed at least with the form of the landscape and vegetation, if not with the color. J. W. Lewin, who arrived in Sydney in 1800, after Watling's departure, had by 1808 turned from natural history draftsmanship to the painting of accurate views.

Augustus Earle, a nephew of the American painter Ralph Earle, was in Australia from 1825 to 1828 in search of places as yet unvisited by professional artists. He sent views for a panorama back to London, painted portraits of the local gentry, published lithographic views, and executed many watercolors before moving on to Madras. He was the first artist of merit to visit Australia.

Later, in 1838, he sent a fascinating and elaborate subject picture to the Royal Academy, "A Bivouac of Travellers in Australia in a Cabbage-Tree Forest" (Nan Kivell Collection). It showed frontiersmen and aborigines in precisely painted vegetation, dense and exotic. The exotic landscape, vegetation, and curiosities of the South Seas had had to be portrayed for an English audience from the time of Cook's voyages. By the 1830's this necessity had done much to break down pictorial stereotypes. Dr. Bernard Smith's *European Vision and the South Pacific* (1961) provides a full account of how on the one hand artistic formulas affected the earlier scientific records of South Sea exploration—aborigines appearing as neoclassical noble savages—and how on the other hand the requirements of scientific geography contributed to the development of naturalism in art.

John Glover (1767–1849) was the next important painter to arrive, and unlike Earle he came to settle. At the age of sixty-three he left England in 1830 to take up land for his family in Tasmania. He was retiring to a farm after an extremely successful career devoted to somewhat facile landscapes and to teaching, but his paintings of Tasmania are nevertheless numerous. There is little doubt that the challenge of a new landscape, and perhaps the necessity of documenting it for prospective immigrants, caused him deliberately to modify his style. The composition is sometimes Italianate, but the details are authentically Australian, and the subject matter a genuinely felt pastoral Arcadia. His are the first professional paintings with a real feeling for Australia instead of a display of picturesque curiosities.

Tasmania in Glover's time had rather more artistic activity than the other Australian colonies. In the 1840's, two skillful practitioners of the early English watercolor were in Hobart—John Skinner Prout and Simpkinson de Wesselow. Thomas Griffiths Wainewright, a poisoner, dandy, and artist, spent the last ten years of his life as a convict in Hobart, where he executed a number of mannered portraits in crayon or watercolor. Another convict-painter, W. B. Gould, who arrived in Tasmania in 1827, has left many naïve but charming still lifes of flowers and fruit.

The best-known artist of the colonial period is Conrad Martens (1801–1878). A pupil of Copley Fielding, he arrived in Sydney in 1835, where he remained until his death. Unlike Glover, a pastoralist who painted for the English market, or Augustus Earle, a passing visitor, he lived by his art alone. He was the first to do so in Australia. Watercolor landscapes, a few oils, lithographs, and teaching provided a modest livelihood. Since he was painting for an Australian market, his picturesque landscapes did not dwell insistently on curiosities or topography; instead, they tended toward a gentle romanticism. He occupied himself principally with the enchantments of Sydney and its harbor and with portraits of country houses. Weather and atmosphere could stir him, and in some of his dark, stormy landscapes there is real drama.

The last painter to be mentioned from the colonial period is S. T. Gill (1818–1880), who arrived in Adelaide from Plymouth, with London experience, in 1839. He seems to have been entirely a watercolorist, but unlike Martens and Glover he was more of a genre than a landscape painter. From the 1840's there are some lyrical sketches of farming activities in the Adelaide hills and some street scenes. However, he is primarily associated with the gold fields of Victoria, whose exuberant population he recorded with the gusto and humor of a Rowlandson. At times he can seem the most Australian of all artists.

It was during the administration of Governor Lachlan Macquarie that Australian buildings first saw the effect of professional architectural supervision. Macquarie appointed Francis Greenway (1777–1837), an architect who had been transported for a fourteen-year sentence, as government architect of New South Wales. Greenway's contribution was considerable: he planned and supervised the building of the hospital, the barracks, and St. James's Church in Queen's Square at the heart of early Sydney (these elegant buildings are still in use) and St. Matthew's Church at Windsor. Commissioner J. T. Bigge, who was sent in 1819 to report on Macquarie's administration of the colony for the British government, reported adversely on the elegance of the public works being undertaken, yet felt justified in commenting: "Mr. Greenway's architectural skill has been the means of introducing into the buildings of the colony greater celerity and better taste than had previously prevailed." When Macquarie was recalled, Greenway was displaced by an "engineer," as recommended by Bigge, and he completed his life in total obscurity. The elegance of his designs is much admired today, and it is generally agreed that Bigge's recommendation of Greenway's dismissal was ill-advised. After Macquarie's administration architecture was not given any considerable attention for half a century.

Gold was discovered in 1851—most of it in Victoria. In consequence, Melbourne became—within four or five years—the largest Australian city and remained so for the rest of the century. It also became the center of Australian art. The first public art collection was founded there in 1861. An Austrian artist, Eugen von Guerard was chosen as curator; he had arrived in 1853.

There were some new English arrivals at this time: William Strutt working in the fifties and William Ford in the seventies, but Continental artists dominated the mid-Victorian period. Nicholas Chevalier, a Swiss painter, was in Melbourne from 1855 to 1867; but another Swiss, Louis Buvelot (1814–1888), undoubtedly led the development of Australian art after his arrival in 1865. Buvelot had studied in Paris and spent eighteen years in Brazil before settling in Melbourne. His work is very close to the Barbizon school in mood

351

and subject matter. Suburban farms and settled countryside were almost his sole preoccupation, not the cities, the mountains (very popular in the seventies), nor the deserts. Nor was he a plein-air painter, although he sketched extensively in the open. His compositions retain a degree of formality, but nevertheless his academic realism has a delicate freshness unlike Von Guerard's, or Chevalier's, or indeed that of Piguenit, an Australian-born artist who began painting grandiose mountain scenes in the 1870's. Buvelot understood Australian vegetation well enough, and he was interested in light and atmosphere, with a preference for the gentle light of dusk.

It was Buvelot's sincerity and his merit, as well as his limited Australianism, which the generation of the eighties revered. His presence in Melbourne set a standard for the first truly Australian school to follow. This school, which emerged in the eighties, has a very special place in Australia's affection. Tom Roberts (1856–1931), Arthur Streeton (1867–1943), and Charles Conder (1868–1909) are the three leading members. Although only Streeton was Australian-born, the other two began their painting here; although Conder left Australia in 1890, when he was twenty-one, his contribution was real. In fact, there were only two years, 1888–1890, when the group was together. These two years were remembered by all three with the greatest nostalgia, especially their painting and teaching camps at Heidelberg and other villages near Melbourne. Here they were young, they were well supplied with girls, they danced under the trees on summer nights, and they were excited by the new artistic program which Tom Roberts had brought back in 1885 from a study period in London.

Sometimes these artists are called the Heidelberg school, sometimes the Australian impressionists. It is true that the big event of the Heidelberg years was their exhibition, in 1889, of "9 x 5 Impressions." With Frederick McCubbin (1855–1917), a close associate, and others, they exhibited 182 small sketches on cigar-box lids, each 9 by 5 inches. The title page of the exhibition catalogue carried the following quotation: " 'When you draw, form is the important thing; but in painting the *first* thing to look for is the *general impression* of colour'—Gerome." This was followed by a statement:

To the public: An effect is only momentary: so an impressionist tries to find his place. Two half-hours are never alike, and he who tries to paint

352

a sunset on two successive evenings must be more or less painting from memory. So, in these works, it has been the object of the artists to render faithfully, and thus obtain first records of effects widely differing, and often of very fleeting character.

This sounds like impressionism, and the exhibition certainly caused some scandal in Melbourne. But the paintings do not look very much like what we understand as French impressionism today. They were plein-air painters, but there was no color analysis, no division into pure color, seldom a colored shadow. What seemed scandalous to Melbourne was the lack of finish, the spontaneity, and the sketchiness. This was seldom carried so far in their larger paintings, and Roberts especially, with his years at the Royal Academy schools in London, could paint large, elaborated figure compositions, though even these retain great sensitivity of touch. Besides freer handling, tonal accuracy is characteristic of their work, and this indeed is an important aspect of impressionism.

One or two of their paintings look very Whistlerian; some have Whistlerian titles. Tonal subtlety and rejection of finish would connect them as closely with Whistler as with the French impressionists; today we are inclined to forget that Whistler stood for the English avant-garde in the eighties and that he was called an impressionist. Conder in particular, the same artist who later became a celebrated painter of fans in Paris and London, already in his Australian youth showed a special gift, akin to Whistler's Japonaiserie, for decorative placing.

Besides Whistler's impressionism, that of Bastien-Lepage, a then famous popularizer of sentimental open-air genre, must surely have influenced them. McCubbin especially, with his anecdotes set in dusky landscapes, demonstrates it, and so do Roberts' earlier subject pictures.

In spite of the quality of their painting, none of this would be enough to establish these artists so firmly in our affections. But their interest in truth of tone had made them able to paint the first high-keyed, brightly sunlit Australian landscapes; Tom Roberts' "Bourke Street, Melbourne" (1885–1886) was perhaps the first. There was a feeling that light and heat were typical of Australia, and to render this effectively was the achievement of these men.

The other significant change was a conscious shift in subject matter, perhaps consequent on the centennial celebrations of 1888 and on the emergent nationalism of the period.

From around 1890, just before Roberts and Streeton moved to Sydney, the heroic pastoral paintings begin. In "The Golden Fleece," "Shearing the Rams," and "The Breakaway," Roberts presents ordinary events in a style of considerable grandeur and nobility; in "Fire's On!" and "The Purple Noon's Transparent Might," Streeton makes the landscape itself heroic. Blazing heat and dust, the dangers of pioneering and from bushrangers, the frenzy of thirst (all by then receding into a romantic past)—these themes prefigure the present-day cult of the desert, which was so successful at Whitechapel in 1961. These themes do occur earlier—with Strutt in the fifties, for instance—but from an outsider's viewpoint and with more melodrama.

Perhaps already in the 1890's an urban population, readers of the *Bulletin,* welcomed the myth that the typical Australian is an outback pioneer, not a townsman or a small farmer. Yet there is little doubt that the artists of the Heidelberg school had a passionate interest in the actual appearances of Australia and sincerely sought a typically Australian subject matter. Unlike the isolated colonial painters, they make a coherent group, and they led the first Australian-born or -trained generation of artists. Since this generation (which coincided with a period of political and literary nationalism) was also the first to be passionately concerned with Australian subject matter, they can be called the founders of an Australian school of painting. But not, of course, of an Australian style.

The trouble was that Streeton's landscape style was eventually imposed as an orthodoxy: it was promoted as the only true Australian style. This did not happen, however, until he returned after the First World War from twenty relatively unsuccessful years in England.

It was during this period that black-and-white drawing established itself as a significant aspect of popular art in Australia. Livingston Hopkins ("Hop"), an American artist, joined the *Bulletin* staff as an illustrator; he soon raised cartooning to an artistic level, and within a decade most important Australian artists were engaged in drawing political cartoons for the *Bulletin.* Phil May, David Souter, Norman Lindsay, and G. W. Lambert drew for the *Bulletin;* George Finey drew for *Smith's Weekly* after it was established in 1919 and continued drawing for the Sydney press until a few years ago. But the two artists whose work was most successful were Will Dyson and David Low. Low is now internationally famous and regarded as perhaps the most powerful political cartoonist in England.

There are still some artists whose work is of a high standard; among these should be included George Molnar (a lecturer in architecture at the University of Sydney) and Emile Mercier.

The Heidelberg "impressionists" soon scattered. In the 1890's Streeton and Roberts moved to Sydney, where the latter painted a number of delightful female portraits as well as his "national" pictures; both were in England during the Edwardian years. Neither contributed much more of value, though Roberts never lost his integrity in the way that Streeton did.

A true impressionism was developed by a Sydney painter, John Russell (1858–1931), who had left for Europe in 1881 with Tom Roberts on his first study trip. Russell gained most from Paris, not London. He studied at Cormon's, where he knew Toulouse-Lautrec and was an intimate of Van Gogh. He was wealthy, did not exhibit much, and his work is little known in Australia or elsewhere. His house on Belle-Isle was much visited by French artists in the later nineties; Monet knew him, and the young Matisse stayed there. Russell returned to Sydney in the 1920's, but his work remains virtually unknown.

Two other Melbourne painters who went to France had some success with their Salon impressionism. Consequently, they did not return to their native land or did so too late to affect Australian art. The first to go was Rupert Bunny (1864–1947), who left in 1884, sent paintings and whole exhibitions back now and then, and returned, an old man, in 1933. His Belle Epoque impressionism and his decorative allegories of the 1920's were beginning to be justly admired shortly before his death.

The other successful expatriate was Phillips Fox (1865–1915), whose contact with Australia remained more fruitful. After study in Paris from 1887, he was back in Melbourne by 1892, where he stayed for ten years and conducted an art school. His "The Art Students" (1895) is a large, low-toned impressionist figure composition of great subtlety, carried out on a scale seldom attempted successfully by the more nationalistic landscape artists. An exhibition sent to Australia in 1913 contained paintings in strong, pure divisionist color, which helped inspire Roland Wakelin to Sydney's first postimpressionist experiments.

Walter Withers (1854–1914) had also studied in Paris in the late 1880's and was an associate of Fox in Melbourne the next decade. David Davies (1862–1939) was another to return to Melbourne from Paris in the nineties, but for only five years. These two, Davies and Withers, introduced a more poetic note, sometimes akin to, but surely unconnected with, Wilson Steer's early work. It leads easily into the pure *art nouveau* of Sydney Long (1872–1955) who, in 1897 and 1898, painted "The Spirit of the Plains" and "Pan," in which mauve and peacock landscapes of attenuated gum trees are populated by slender *fin-de-siècle* nudes and Australian animals. The style may have come only from reproductions in *The Studio;* certainly it was a passing phase, which soon gave way to repetitive but still painterly landscapes whose sinuous trees always kept an *art nouveau* flavor.

Long's early pictures belong to the nationalist impulse in Australian art. Whereas Roberts set about endowing the daily life with nobility, Long intended to provide the empty landscape of a new country with some sort of mythology. The intention has been more adequately fulfilled in recent years by the bushrangers and explorers of Nolan and Tucker.

Sydney Long's paintings and the aesthetic watercolors of Blamire Young (1862–1935)—an Englishman who had worked with the Beggarstaff brothers in the nineties—are probably the most interesting work from the Edwardian years, for apart from McCubbin, nearly all the well-known artists were then abroad. Hans Heysen (b. 1877) began his gum-tree portraits at this period. They remain the best of their kind and are indeed very good, but unfortunately they are surrounded by a body of immensely popular but stale imitators.

Streeton's return, to dominate Australian landscape between the wars, has been mentioned. Max Meldrum (1875–1955) was a scholarship winner who returned to Melbourne in 1913 with a tonalist method of painting, easily taught, which still infects official portraiture. Velasquez, popular everywhere around 1900, would have been one of his sources; the method's appeal lay in its insistence on being scientific and in its dismissal of the need for imagination. Meldrum's own work is, in spite of his theory, often excellent, in the manner of an overblown early Corot. His followers have been an extremely reactionary force.

G. W. Lambert (1873–1930) painted the last of the heroic pictures of national life, "Across the Blacksoil Plains," in 1899. The following year he won a student scholarship and in 1921 returned to dominate Sydney for the next decade as a smart portrait painter. His flashy style is close to Orpen's. Brilliant, academic drawing was his specialty, and he was the joy of the art schools, where he is still remembered piously. His influence in Sydney was healthier than Streeton's and Meldrum's in Melbourne, and he did sympathize with the modern movement. In 1926 he lent his authority to a group which became known as the "Contemporary Group." Its innovatory members were Roland Wakelin, Roy de Maistre, and Grace Cossington Smith.

These artists were products of Dattilo Rubbo's studio. Here in 1913 were seen the first reproductions of postimpressionist and cubist art in Australia, brought out by an attractive girl, Norah Simpson, who had studied with the English postimpressionists, Gilman, Gore, and Ginner. A strength of design and vitality of color, new to Australian art, came into their work, which passingly reflected the influence of Seurat, Matisse, Van Gogh; but in the case of Wakelin and Smith it settled down to Cézanne in the twenties.

Before this Wakelin and De Maistre had held, in 1919, an exhibition of "Color Music"—paintings investigating the relation of color to music, with titles like "Synchromy in Red Major" or "Caprice in Blue Minor." This led them into abstraction, and theirs would be the first nonfigurative pictures produced in Australia. It was, however, only an isolated experiment, probably due to reading Willard Huntington Wright's *Modern Painting*, with its chapter on American synchromism. Wakelin returned to Cézanne, and De Maistre, abroad on a scholarship from 1923 to 1926, finally left Australia permanently in 1930. His work became cubist, and he now holds a high place among contemporary English artists.

In Melbourne Arnold Shore and William Frater also began, in the mid-twenties, to exhibit paintings showing the influence of postimpressionism.

357

Perhaps the best artist of the twenties was Margaret Preston (b. 1883). She had studied in Paris and London before the First World War and afterward settled in Sydney, where she still works. There is always an easy—but not superficial—decorative quality in her work, always strong design and beautiful color. It is very pure painting, concerned primarily with fresh expression of her formal gifts. The subject matter, naturally enough, is usually still life; and there are some landscapes. She has never stood still, however; she has employed various print media, notably woodcut and monotype. In 1926 and 1927 she briefly expressed the current machine aesthetic in almost colorless still lifes of kitchen implements. She is almost the only artist to incorporate elements of Australian aboriginal style successfully into her work. This began about 1940, although fifteen years earlier she had been one of the first to take an interest in aboriginal art from an aesthetic point of view.

One of her "aboriginal" landscapes is at Yale. It arrived there when the Carnegie Corporation circulated a large exhibition, "Art of Australia 1788 to 1941," among twenty-nine American and Canadian cities between 1941 and 1945. In New York it was shown at the Metropolitan. It must have been a dull exhibition; ten years later something much better would have been possible.

The 1930's are rather uninteresting in a consideration of art in Australia. A Contemporary Group was formed in Melbourne in 1932, where Eric Thake's work showed the first intimations of surrealism. Later, Frank Hinder returned to Sydney from America with an elegant and quite efficient brand of cubism. The teaching of George Bell in Melbourne also propagated a kind of postimpressionism related to early Derain and to Modigliani.

Art politics rather than the paintings themselves is exciting in a study of the art of the thirties. The immediate prewar years were the noisiest phase in the acceptance of modern art. The present prime minister, R. G. Menzies, then attorney general, supported the formation of an Australia-wide Academy of Art, with the laudable aim of improving artistic communications between the six states, although the Society of Artists, founded in 1895 in Sydney, had virtually fulfilled this purpose in the twenties and thirties. Under the guidance of the art patron and publisher, Sydney Ure Smith, the Society had set a good professional standard and had attracted work from the whole country. It was known that Mr. Menzies' taste was not for the avant-garde, but for the academic Australian impressionism of Streeton's late work and that of other similar artists. The apparently official support for the Academy seemed dangerous, and in reaction a Contemporary Art Society was formed in 1938, largely by George Bell. Its first exhibition was held the following year, and for this and other reasons 1939 can be regarded as the beginning of the modern period in Australian art.

A large exhibition of French and British modern art was shown in Melbourne and Sydney in 1939, giving Australians their first extensive sight of Cézanne, Gauguin, Van Gogh, Matisse, Picasso, and Dali. During the war the paintings remained in Australia and were shown in the larger cities on a number of occasions. Although the exhibition was influential on artists and had a great effect on public taste, it cannot really be regarded as a belated Armory Show.

In Sydney in that same year Frank Hinder and some colleagues held a group manifestation called "Exhibition I," where cubism was on the brink of geometric abstraction. This persisted as a thin stream until painterly abstraction swept Sydney in the fifties.

The year 1939 also saw the return of a number of painters from abroad. One was Eric Wilson, with further widely noticed cubist pictures. Another was his friend William Dobell (b. 1899).

Dobell today is the most famous painter within Australia, and his work commands the highest prices. This is partly a matter of notoriety. He won the 1943 Archibald Prize, a large annual prize for portraiture awarded by the trustees of the Art Gallery of New South Wales. The award was contested in the courts by two artists who claimed the painting was ineligible for the prize, being a caricature, not a portrait. The action, which was lost, attracted immense publicity. This was due to the large amount of money involved and to the fact that modern art had been "news" in Sydney for the past few years since the first Contemporary Art Society exhibition. Most newsworthy of all were the vicious attacks on the picture by some of the older members of the art establishment, including a former director of the Melbourne and Sydney state art galleries.

The portrait, which was lost in a fire in 1958, was of Dobell's fellow artist, Joshua Smith. Nobody denied that it was a brilliant painting; but it did show a certain amount of distortion. The neck was elongated, thin arms and tight suit were exaggerated, sensitive hands were enlarged, red ears stuck out, baggy eyes sagged, the seated pose placed the subject awkwardly in a corner of his chair. The painting was extraordinarily like the sitter in both character and appearance.

Its distortion may owe something to the example of Soutine's expressionist portraiture, in which Dobell's interest is recorded. Perhaps, also, one can find a faint trace of Lambert, the idol of Dobell's student days in Sydney before his departure in 1929 for ten years in Europe. Dobell's earliest work is very close to Lambert's. In Lambert's fashionable portraiture there were exaggerated poses, which appear more as affectation than characterization. Dobell has used similar devices, but for a deeper purpose and with an effect that does not irritate or pall.

Dobell spent some time in the Netherlands studying Rembrandt. He has also professed an interest in Daumier. There is no doubt that the portrayal of character and individuality is his chief aim, but he is also exceedingly interested in technique. This is finished, elaborate, and old-masterly and occasionally brings to his portraits a tension not unlike that of sixteenth-century mannerism.

Indeed, he is far from being a modern artist. The 1944 lawsuit was nevertheless seen as a victory for modern art, and no doubt it was to some extent. But it was more of a turning point for Australian art in general. Public apathy was replaced by interest, favorable or otherwise, and the case for art as discovery and expression, as opposed to innocuous decoration, was reestablished.

Stylistically, however, Dobell's influence has not been great. He is now somewhat aloof from current developments and is ungrudgingly given a place of eminence as well for the distress caused him by the lawsuit as for his splendid gallery of portraits. In these portraits he shows himself happier with men than with women and sometimes (unlike Lambert) more comfortable in vulgar society than polite. This reinforces the old image of Australia as a man's country, although with Dobell it is not golddiggers and stockmen, but the urban proletariat—tough journalists and piratical businessmen. His portrait of Mr. Menzies appeared on a *Time* magazine cover in 1960; another, of General Motors Chairman Donner, appeared in 1962.

Around 1950 Dobell paid a few visits to the Australian territories in New Guinea. The resulting paintings showed an occasionally obvious South Sea romanticism. There are also some landscapes of the delicate lakeside scenery at his home north of Sydney, but these are seldom more than relaxation pieces. His portraits remain his great contribution.

In the 1940's Sydney seemed to be the center of activity. The art books of the time deal almost entirely with Sydney painters, and in 1945 the newspaperman, Sir Keith Murdoch, who had brought out the 1939 French and British exhibition, organized a large showing of Sydney art for Melbourne. The Melbourne critics bowed to the Sydney school. Dobell, Drysdale, and Donald Friend were for a while almost a holy trinity, supported by a number of other painters who are now rudely christened the "Charm school" by a newer generation.

Donald Friend (b. 1915) had studied at the Westminster School in London. His work is charming, witty, and romantic, even lyrical; and marvelously proficient. He has lived in Nigeria, the tropical north of Australia, Florence, Ischia, and lately in Ceylon. He helped turn Hill End, a former gold-mining town 150 miles inland from Sydney, derelict but pretty, into something of an artist's colony. He was part of the Merioola Group of painters, acters, and writers which inhabited a down-at-heel Sydney mansion of that name around 1947. (Loudon Sainthill, now a brilliant theatre designer in London, was another of this group.)

More serious matters were stirring in Melbourne during the 1940's, but for a while Sydney romanticism was in the foreground. David Strachan's poetic still lifes and landscapes, Jean Bellette's figure compositions from classical mythology, Francis Lymburner's boys and girls, Elaine Haxton's happy Mediterranean art all contributed to this cheerful phase. An older man, Lloyd Rees (b. 1895) was not really part of the group, but his sometimes moody landscapes share the romanticism of the time and perhaps go rather deeper. He is even more painterly than the others and retains the respect of some of the new generation.

The style of these Sydney painters was in part a reaction to the more draftsmanlike or formalist style of the prewar avant-garde. It may also have been directly influenced by English wartime romanticism, for there are many apparent echoes of John Piper and Graham

361

Sutherland. They were interested in broken color and texture, not in the smooth simplifications of the thirties. They were perhaps deliberately cosmopolitan in subject matter in reaction against the persistent nationalism of earlier criticism and taste. In this, Paul Haefliger, the influential and informed art critic of the *Sydney Morning Herald*—the leading newspaper—would have helped considerably, since for over fifteen years he maintained a firm stand against parochial values.

Russell Drysdale (b. 1912), although always on close terms with Donald Friend and the rest of the group and sometimes showing affinities with their painting, concentrated on purely Australian subject matter. He was brought up in the country, studied under George Bell in Melbourne, visited Paris and London in 1938–1939, and settled in Sydney in 1940. His first Sydney exhibition in 1942 immediately established his reputation as the leading exponent of a new kind of national painting. Instead of an Australia Felix of rich grasslands and a forward-looking people, he showed a country which has often defeated man. He gives us careworn farmers and their families, pubkeepers in the silent country towns, Hill End with its deserted gold diggings, ambitious nineteenth-century streets and buildings standing forgotten, conquered houses decaying and returning to the soil, men working and children playing in the still emptiness, dead trees in man-made deserts. But his art is by no means morbid; he loves the ancient and powerful land, and he loves the people who have come to terms with it, their heroism and their dignity. His attitude is affectionate, admiring, and breaks easily into geniality.

Drysdale has been popularly regarded as the promoter of a harsh image of Australia. This is only a superficial view, but is understandable in terms of his first two important exhibitions of 1942 and 1945. In the first his landscapes contained excessively lean figures—but not starving ones, as his audience half-consciously assumed. The typical outback man is supposedly tall and lean, and this characteristic was only being emphasized. There was also a formal necessity for lean figures among veranda posts, thin trees, and wiry dogs. The 1945 exhibition was painted after he had been commissioned by the *Sydney Morning Herald* to illustrate the effects of an exceptionally severe drought in the far west of New South Wales. Dead trees became clawed monsters marching across an eroded desert or else took

on the form of bones. In these paintings there is an element of surrealist terror, but it must be remembered that the reality (attested to
by photographs) was scarcely different, and it should also be remembered that these paintings resulted from a commission. At no other
time has he been so savage.

Traces of surrealism occur elsewhere in his work. His student
friend Peter Purves Smith had used it in the thirties. Paul Nash and
Graham Sutherland have used it in a similar way for the English
landscape; certainly it has great usefulness for communicating the
strangeness and wonder of some aspects of the Australian landscape,
but it by no means serves to characterize Drysdale's art. His style is
grounded on the respect for rigorous formal organization taught in
George Bell's school and on his own special gift for drawing. He
works in the studio, slowly. His composition is always strong and
orderly. His color is symbolic rather than illusionist; although close
inspection reveals a variety of unusual purples, pinks, and soft blues,
the general impression of a room full of Drysdales is that they are all
red-gold—the color of hot earth and rock, even of the sky during
dust storms, in the endless plains of Australia.

His subject matter in the past ten years has no longer been taken
from the New South Wales in which he grew up, the areas of some
European settlement. He now devotes himself to the aboriginal north,
to half-castes, to native stockmen, and to the primitive life and ceremonial of the full blood. For these people he has an even deeper compassion than for the European settlers in the earlier paintings (it is a
question whether it sometimes becomes sentimental); for the landscape of the North and of the Center he shows an even greater awe
than for the more settled landscape.

Drysdale must be classed as a romantic painter of a profound kind.
This relates him to the lighter romanticism of his contemporaries in
Sydney, but he is best thought of in relation to Tom Roberts. These
two artists, one in the 1880's, the other in the 1940's, have made the
most important discoveries about Australian landscape and have expressed their love for it and its life most deeply. Both contain their
romanticism within a disciplined, orderly style, solid, methodical, and
sober. They represent the high points of a national Australian art.

While Drysdale was teaching Australians to see the beauty and
poetry of the outback, Sali Herman (b. 1898) was doing the same

for the congested innermost suburbs of Sydney. Swiss-born, Herman abandoned painting when young and took it up again when he came to Australia at forty. After some months at George Bell's school in Melbourne, he settled in Sydney in 1938. By the end of the war he was well known for his paintings of these crowded, exuberant nineteenth-century houses and streets. The popular response was angry at first—why paint slums when we have garden suburbs? This resembled the first response to Drysdale's outback paintings from people who were used to lush pastures and contented sheep. Within five years the message was through, and today it is becoming smart to live in Sali Herman's Sydney. He is a natural painter with an instinctive control of cheerful color, which he manages better than most of his contemporaries, and with a feeling for the solidity and volume of objects.

Another observer of cosmopolitan Sydney was Charles Doutney (1908–1957). The night clubs and shops were his preserve: a Toulouse-Lautrec subject matter and a Vuillard style.

With Doutney we have reached a painter who emerged in the fifties. By then Sidney Nolan was an established artist who had moved easily in the Sydney art world since his arrival from Melbourne in 1948. Nolan makes no appearance in the art books of the forties, most of which were published by Ure Smith in Sydney. His first important exhibition, of the Ned Kelly paintings, was in Melbourne in 1948. His first one-man show in Sydney was held a year later. Previously his earlier work was seen in various group shows, and in retrospect it has become important. If it is fair to consider that it was neglected, this perhaps signifies something of the difference between painting in Melbourne and Sydney over the past twenty years. Nolan, before his 1949 exhibition, would have seemed primitive and crude. In Sydney this would not have been excused on the grounds of the importance of his content; in Melbourne it might have been. In a general way, Sydney's art has been accused by its detractors of being well-painted triviality, Melbourne's of being badly painted literature.

The Melbourne avant-garde in the early forties was concerned with social realism and expressionism quite unlike Sydney's romanticism. The art-school postimpressionism of George Bell was rapidly

364

superseded, and those who favored the new forms of expression had captured the Contemporary Art Society from Bell by 1940. Albert Tucker (b. 1914) illustrates the change from Bell's postimpressionism. Perhaps influenced by the 1939 French and British Exhibition, his "The Futile City" (1940) is surrealist. At the same time James Gleeson, a consistently surrealist Sydney artist, was at his most Dalilike stage. But Tucker rapidly moved into a figurative German expressionism. Its appearance in Tucker's and Nolan's early work may owe something to the presence in Melbourne since 1937 of Danila Vassilieff (1898–1958), a Russian rolling stone who frequently exhibited childlike expressionist paintings. Many of Vassilieff's pictures were of Melbourne slums. Josl Bergner, an Austrian who now works in Israel, was in Melbourne during the early forties. He also was concerned, but in a more realist style, with the slums, with poverty, and with the refugees from Europe. So were some Australians, the most important being Noel Counihan, who began painting in 1941. The social realism of Counihan and his circle has been well received in Moscow and Leningrad recently, but it has lost the impact it had in the early forties.

Tucker's expressionism was a social expressionism concerned, however, with more lurid matters than those preferred by the social realists. In 1943 he began a series, "Night Images," or "Images of Modern Evil," inspired by the sudden flood of foreign troops into Australia and the consequent creation of an active night life, increasing prostitution and crime. Four years later, in 1947, Tucker left Australia for France, Germany, Italy, England, and America, where the Guggenheim Museum bought two paintings. He returned in 1960. He still works in long series of images of which the "Antipodean Heads" are the most successful. They stand for Australian explorers, bushrangers, or other heroic figures. Their surfaces take on the character of desert landscapes, scarred and cratered (the craters may also be boils), and in such a context the harsh ugliness of the actual paint work becomes meaningful.

These paintings belong to the new mythology of Australianism which is more generally associated with Nolan. Tucker, however, may have much to do with it. In 1943, as well as beginning his series of images, Tucker published an article, "Art, Myth and Society," in

365

which he wrote of the social usefulness of the myth and of the artist's ability to create it. Sidney Nolan shortly became the most imaginative Australian mythmaker.

Born in Melbourne in 1917 of Irish parentage, Nolan had worked as a commercial artist in the mid-thirties and first exhibited in 1939 with the Contemporary Art Society. His earliest paintings were abstract. In 1941 he changed to a primitive figuration, to gay childlike landscapes, none of which were serious enough for the social realists. They lasted until 1946. In that year the Ned Kelly series begins, and in it he sets about creating an Australian myth. The best myths require a narrative; the Ned Kelly story was both compact and eminently dramatic. Ned Kelly, an Irish-Australian bushranger, courteous to his family and neighbors and gallant to women, was driven to outlawry by police injustice. Finally, after an exciting chase, he was captured in 1878, wearing a suit of homemade armor. Nolan has stated that the ingredients for his series of paintings were "Kelly's own words, Henri Rousseau and sunlight." When first exhibited, they were received only moderately well; the primitivism was still perhaps an obstacle. Today they are often regarded as his best work.

The story of social injustice may not have been an important part of the success; the fact that the story is universally known in Australia and easily followed by all is perhaps more important. Nor is the artist committed to the story and the issues it raises. There is no greater demand on the spectator than that he enjoy it as a story. The rather absurd image of Ned Kelly helmeted becomes as lovable and as often demanded as a favorite doll. Also to be enjoyed is the apparent ease of painting and the fresh vision of sunny bush landscape as lyrical as the first landscapes of Streeton. These last two points are important in his success; perhaps more so is the setting in time. A nineteenth-century story, when well illustrated, apparently will suddenly make an Australian aware that he has a history. For a long time there was an attitude that Australia was too young a country to have such a thing; there was no interest in the country's past. In the last fifteen years or so this has changed, and there is now a flood of historiography. Paintings can, for some people, feed this new appetite even more effectively than books.

Nearly all of Australia's past lies within the Victorian period; Victorian architectural concepts, even Victorian morals, are still more pervasive in Australia than anywhere else in the world. Nolan's Australia is almost entirely a Victorian Australia. He unashamedly paints from Victorian photographs in the public archives. His two principal narrative series, the Ned Kelly and the Mrs. Fraser–Convict Bracefell series, are both based on events from the Victorian period. So are the Explorers and the Eureka Stockade series. The Queensland Outback series of 1947–1948, perhaps his finest, was painted after a deliberate search for the most old-fashioned parts of Australia. If figures appear in these pictures of old hotels or deserted mines, they are put into Victorian costume.

Drysdale's paintings also show a feeling for the Victorian past, but it is less frequent and less explicit. Nolan's 1947 trip to Queensland was the first time he had been able to visit the outback in the way Drysdale had been doing for some while—although he did hitchhike one hundred miles to the Ned Kelly country in 1946 for his material. He traveled to Central Australia in 1948 and two years later exhibited a great number of aerial views of the mountain ranges and deserts. He was commissioned by a Brisbane newspaper to make drawings of the 1952 drought in North Queensland, and this produced a series of soft-toned animal carcasses.

A year later Nolan left Australia permanently. He has since worked in Italy, Greece, and London. From 1958 to 1960 he was in America, a good deal of the time in Arizona. His subjects have included Greek and Italian landscapes, a series on the Greek myth of Leda and the Swan, and another series (synthesizing Greek landscape and Australian myth in the Gallipoli campaign) is in progress. The Fraser-Bracefell and the Ned Kelly series were repeated. Some of the post-Australian work appears glossy and repetitious in comparison with, say, the first Kelly series, and often less well painted.

Here one should mention the important part played in Melbourne by John Reed and his wife. Reed's active patronage and encouragement of Melbourne's avant-garde in the forties were of the greatest value. He bought many of Nolan's early paintings, and all the original Ned Kelly series was his until 1958, when he donated it as part of the nucleus of a Museum of Modern Art of Australia. Reed's sister, Cynthia, married Nolan in 1948. The Reeds clearly have a taste for figurative painting of a certain poetic kind. This must have something to do with the slow development of abstract art in Melbourne, but only in one instance does it seem to have provoked an art deliberately manufactured for their taste.

Abstraction has by now completely taken over in the Sydney avant-garde. A large official exhibition of French painting in 1953 helped prepare the way. It contained works by artists such as Soulages, Hartung, Manessier, and Vieira de Silva as well as the older men. Since then overseas exhibitions of contemporary art have become more frequent: Italian in 1956, Canadian and Northwest Coast American (with Tobey and Graves) in 1957, Japanese in 1958, and British in 1959 (with Alan Davie, Hilton, Frost, Gear, and others). The turning point came in 1956, when a large Australian exhibition containing a good deal of abstraction was sent aboard the S.S. *Orcades* to Honolulu, San Francisco, and Vancouver, and when, later, a small exhibition called "Direction I" was held in Sydney.

Before this, in the early fifties the Sydney "Charm school" entered an even more coloristic phase, almost neo-Byzantine. Justin O'Brien's religious subjects showed it before he won the first annual Blake Prize competition for religious art in 1950. Michael Kmit, a Polish artist who was in Sydney for eight years, was part of this movement and he also, in 1953, won the Blake Prize. Eric Smith, a third important colorist, has won the same prize four times.

At the same time the quiet work of two older painters, Ralph Balson and Grace Crowley, began to receive more attention. They had shared a geometric abstraction since about 1940. Balson, omitted from a major exhibition of Australian art in 1951, was included in the Arts Council of Great Britain's 1953 tour and has been represented in most significant exhibitions since then.

There were three other older men in the fifties whose formal excellence inspired the greatest respect and whose influence must have helped the tendency toward expression through form rather than content. They are Ian Fairweather, Godfrey Miller, and John Passmore.

Ian Fairweather (b. 1890) may be the best of them—perhaps even the best of all Australian artists—and his influence is now spreading. Scottish-born, he studied at the Slade School, and has spent much of his life wandering in China, the Philippines, and the East Indies, with periods in Australia since the thirties. For the past ten years he has sent an annual exhibition to Sydney from the island off the Queensland coast where he now lives and works. His paintings are seldom completely nonfigurative. There are references to the primitive art of Oceania. There are abstracted figure compositions. One also assumes an interest in Oriental philosophy, for besides his monogram, Chinese characters are sometimes inscribed on the paintings. But for sheer beauty of form and color, of linear and spatial rhythm, his basically cubist art, warmed by compassion and human understanding, is best compared to the serenities of Braque.

Godfrey Miller, who also traveled in the East, was born in 1893 in New Zealand, and in the thirties was at the Slade School. By 1948 he was in Sydney, where for some time now he has taught drawing at the principal art school. The example of his total dedication, his near-mysticism, is as important as his formal instruction. His lovely contemplative paintings—still lifes, landscapes, and nudes—have a particular spatial quality: air, trees, bodies, all are part of the same continuum, differing in density, color, and position, but ultimately unified into a universal whole.

John Passmore, the third and the youngest of these three elder painters, was born in Sydney in 1904. From 1933 to 1950 he was in Europe, mostly in England, where he did a good deal of commercial art. He brought back a style based on Cézanne, though with slightly more winning color. It has become, it almost seems, the property of every art student in Sydney. His subjects include landscapes, still lifes, and figure compositions. The last are often concerned with the beaches and water fronts, with the arguments and activities of fishermen. Passmore has a special facility for drawing and sometimes the more draftsmanlike paintings seem fresher than the systematic compositions. Sometimes one senses the artist's impatience with his own fine academicism; in some beautiful near-abstracts of 1959 the figurative image has been almost destroyed. His monumental figure compositions remain his best work.

Passmore's influence has been considerable—not only his style, but also his questing discontent. The most significant painter of the new generation, John Olsen (b. 1928), was his pupil. Master and pupil, their positions almost reversed, together with William Rose, Eric Smith, and the sculptor, Robert Klippel, formed the group "Direction I" whose exhibition in December, 1956, has already been mentioned as marking the turning point into abstraction, even though Passmore and Smith were still figurative.

The change was fairly sudden. Paul Haefliger, the art critic, early in 1955 thought that abstraction was an exhausted mode of expression. Perhaps he meant cubism or geometric abstraction, for later that year he had changed his mind about its possibilities in terms of abstract expressionism. In 1956 he highly approved of the abstract paintings in the S.S. *Orcades'* floating exhibition and of "Direction I." By February, 1957, he could write a long article announcing the arrival of the new art movement.

Some possible reasons for the change now emerge. The anti-parochial critical values of Haefliger, the formal strength of certain painters of the early fifties, and the influence of the 1953 French exhibition have been mentioned. The Contemporary Art Society's *Broadsheet* and its lectures consistently publicized new developments. There may have been no more than a healthy awareness that the newer forms of expression were the most likely to suit a new generation. It is not necessary at this stage to find further reasons, but besides their investigation of spatial form, there are hints of a philosophical attitude in the titles of some "Direction I" and *Orcades* exhibition paintings: "The Atman" and "View of the Western World."

Olsen has expressed himself clearly in these words: "I always endeavour to express an animistic quality—a certain mystical throbbing throughout nature." After "Direction I," he went abroad, with private backing, for three full years, which he spent in England, in Paris (at S. W. Hayter's atelier), and in Spain. He returned to Australia early in 1960.

In the meantime, abstraction had been consolidated in Sydney. When Haefliger confirmed its arrival in February, 1957, he called it abstract expressionism. This was not entirely accurate, but it is true that a painterly rather than a geometric abstraction was the rule. Ralph Balson had changed to it from his former geometric style. Many other established artists changed to abstraction: Douglas Watson (b. 1920) for instance, and Frank Hodgkinson (b. 1919). The latter, in 1958, won the first £1,000 Helena Rubinstein traveling scholarship. (Madame Rubinstein's career began in Australia, and she retains an interest in the country.) He returned in 1961 with

370

Tom Roberts. *Coogee Bay* (1888). Owner, National Art Gallery of New South Wales, Sydney.

William Dobell. *The Cypriot* (1940). Owner, Queensland Art Gallery, Brisbane.

Russell Drysdale. *Man Feeding His Dogs* (1941). Owner, Queensland Art Gallery, Brisbane.

Sidney Nolan. *Pretty Polly Mine* (1948). Owner, National Art Gallery of New South Wales, Sydney.

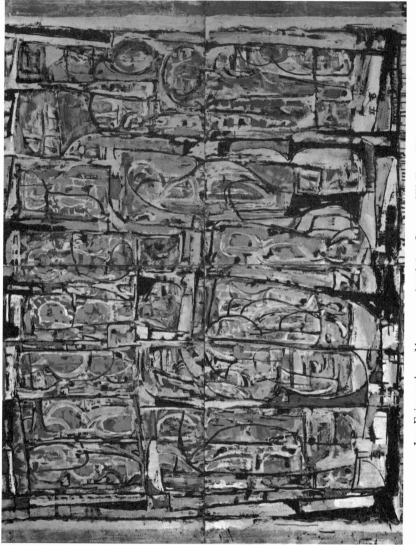

Ian Fairweather. *Monastery* (1961). Owner, Wallace Thornton.

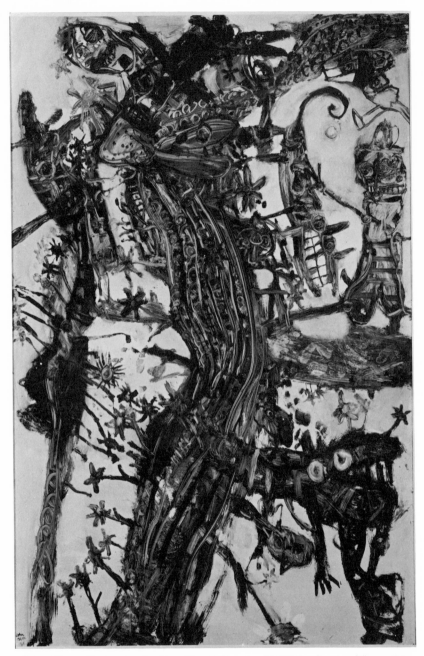

John Olsen. *Spring in the You Beaut Country* (1961). Owner, The artist.

Clement Meadmore. *More So* (1961). Steel. Owner, The sculptor.

Lenton Parr. *Orion* (1959). Steel. Owner, The sculptor.

House in Millswyn Street, South Yarra, Melbourne (c. 1880).

Walter Burley Griffin. Refectory, Newman College, University of Melbourne (1916).

The Australian Courtyard

Roy Grounds. Australian Courtyard, Cultural Center, Melbourne (1962).

ART

a fully assimilated New Spanish style. A number of young artists who emerged in 1957 were abstract from the beginning. They include Tom Gleghorn, John Coburn, and Leonard Hessing. Of these, the first two and many others practice an abstraction with definite landscape references, often with red images of heat and of deserts. Such pictures have a reasonable claim to be part of the Roberts-Streeton-Drysdale-Nolan tradition of Australian landscape.

Another young Sydney painter to emerge in the earlier fifties is totally different. Bob Dickerson, brought up in the industrial slums and once a professional boxer, is a self-taught painter who comments on urban society and its loneliness. He is not polemical like the Melbourne social realists, but compassionate like Drysdale; he is in some way an urban counterpart of Drysdale. All his pictures are of large-scaled figures, awkward, direct, and touching. It is not surprising that Melbourne appreciated him first; and he was the only Sydney member of the Antipodean Group which exhibited in Melbourne in August, 1959.

The Antipodeans consisted of seven painters and the art historian, Dr. Bernard Smith, who, from the artists' separate statements, compiled a manifesto in defense of "The Image." The appeal was for figurative art and Australian subject matter, on the grounds that nonfigurative art was incapable of communicating; in particular, that it could not communicate the Australian artist's experience of his time or his place.

In Sydney, there is, on a lower level, a connection between the figurative decorative romanticism of the 1940's "Charm school" and the romantic, decorative nonfiguration of some recent painting. But the claim of the best abstraction to express its own time or place as effectively as any figurative art would scarcely be denied anywhere in the world today, in Sydney, New York, or Barcelona. Nor should figuration be considered incompatible with decoration; some followers of the Antipodeans have already fallen into a decorative emptiness.

The seven Antipodeans, all born in the twenties, were Arthur Boyd, his brother David, and his brother-in-law John Perceval, with John Brack, Clifton Pugh, Charles Blackman, and the only Sydney member, Bob Dickerson. Dickerson has been discussed. John Brack is another social commentator, but intellectual, dry, and satirical;

371

his aim is directed on the conformism and drabness of middle-class suburbia. Blackman mostly paints large-scaled poetic figures. There have been series on Alice in Wonderland, on schoolgirls, and on his wife's blindness. He won the 1960 Helena Rubinstein traveling scholarship and is beginning to be fashionable in London. Clifton Pugh was perhaps the most admired of all in the 1961 exhibition of Australian painting at Whitechapel. His pictures are usually black and red studies of animal corpses, crows, and wild beasts, organized (with some spatial confusion) into striking decorative patterns and set among delicately painted naturalistic flowers and grasses. These landscape backgrounds insistently remind one of the lyrical farm-yard and bush scenes painted by Conder and McCubbin in the 1880's. The air of Victorianism is reinforced by Pugh's less frequent but excellent portraits, whose faces are obsessively photographic.

Nolan's Victorianism has been mentioned as part of his contribution to the Australian search for identity. The Antipodeans are, of course, his direct heirs. Most of them emerged in the fifties, but two —Arthur Boyd and John Perceval—were his close colleagues in the early forties. At that time Perceval was painting expressionist subjects from urban life. After the war he abandoned painting for pottery until 1956 when he became a plein-air expressionist. There can be no other avant-garde painter who still works on the motif. He completes his jovial and turbulent landscapes on the spot, in one sitting. Their quality is, in consequence, uneven. Sometimes they are of small boats or city water fronts; mostly they are tangled bush scenes, filled with wild flowers and butterflies.

Arthur Boyd is by far the best of the Antipodeans. He is the most painterly; he has real formal strength. Born into a family of land-scape painters, potters, and writers, he is otherwise self-taught. In the early forties he touched on surrealism and at the same time began his antiimpressionist Australian landscapes. Instead of being opti-mistic and pastoral, they are concerned with ragged bushland and lonely gulleys inhabited by horrid beasts and nasty humans. For a while Boyd submitted himself to the influences of Brueghel and Rembrandt, and at the same time he made a conscious effort to per-fect his technique. By the late forties he was in full command of his art.

Boyd's contribution to Australian landscape is original and of the

ART

greatest importance. He was a sound choice for representing Australia at the 1958 Venice Biennale. The crowded Brueghelian compositions, often religious, were set in scrubby Australian landscapes. Since then the landscape itself has predominated. The menacing grey bushland, typical of the mountains near Melbourne, has found an imaginative interpreter. Around 1950 he was also painting the bright wheatlands of the Wimmera. In both there appear the horrid animals and evil birds—black, blue, or red—which are no doubt a source for Pugh's art. In both there are clutching trees. Like Nolan, he has made the landscape old, even primeval; he is adding a little more to Australia's sense of the past.

Boyd has also painted on pottery plaques and has executed some excellent ceramic sculptures. In 1958, the same year that his landscapes were sent to Venice, he exhibited a series of figure compositions on the theme "Love, Marriage and Death of a Half-caste." In some, the large, simple figures, reminiscent of Chagall, appear against a landscape background; in most the landscape has been eliminated. The vivid, symbolic colors do not always seem well controlled, and one regrets the disappearance of the landscape. This half-caste series has been continued with considerable acclaim in London, where Boyd has lived since early 1960.

Antipodeanism provoked a further response in Sydney. When John Olsen returned from abroad shortly after the Antipodean exhibition he felt that Sydney abstraction should be provided with a focus of attention. Those whom he considered the best exhibited as a group in July, 1961. The group of eight painters and one sculptor styled themselves merely the "Sydney 9"; they cautiously avoided any form of manifesto. It was apparent that spontaneity and total seriousness about art were greatly prized. Besides Olsen there were two other veterans of "Direction I": Eric Smith, whose paintings had religious titles and nonfigurative imagery, and William Rose, whose beautiful, completely abstract constructions in space had scarcely changed in five years. Three older painters were Stanislaus Rapotec (b. 1912), Carl Plate (b. 1909), and Hector Gilliland (b. 1911). The first had been abstract for some time; Plate and Gilliland —the last in a more cubist manner—only since about 1958. Rapotec and two other exhibiters, Hessing and Upward, can be considered completely abstract, the two latter being perhaps the most elegantly cosmopolitan of all Australian painters. Hessing has a rococo zip in his line and uses fascinating offbeat color. Peter Upward (b. 1932) is a pure abstract expressionist, the nearest to New York of any, with his large, dark calligraphic gestures in polyvinyl acetate.

Olsen's "Direction I" paintings were probably based on industrial water fronts. Now, however, he seems to be placing himself more firmly within the Australian landscape tradition. His titles indicate as much: "Scrubby Country," "Yellow Country," "Journey into the You Beaut Country," or—from an earlier exhibition—"Australian Flux." The imagery is not always explicit, but the experience of landscape, as opposed to its appearance, is undoubtedly communicated by the brown-black colors and the line which marks a wayward track through various private signs and symbols. Klee and the Cobra group are influences. The probing, tentative lines and the exuberant, spontaneous ones are enough in themselves to communicate a full, physical humanity. The shapes and spaces created by the lines are equally active pictorially; the masterly color is always highly functional, neither decorative nor discordant. The joyful emblems of breast and buttock, wheels and ladders, bird and animal heads, or flowers only add to the general sense of euphoria. Few Australian paintings are so alive, so full of physical well-being. If they seem a very flattering expression of Olsen's time and place, they are still undeniably an expression of Olsen's particular personality.

Abstract landscape appears to be a dominant trend at present. Fred Williams, an excellent Melbourne painter, now practices it, as do Judy Cassab and Robert Hughes. One of the youngest artists, Ross Morrow, uses the techniques of abstract expression to build up a figurative landscape.

The principal exception is the powerful geometric abstractions of religious subjects by the Melbourne painter Leonard French (b. 1928). They are like murals or tapestries, and perhaps owe some debt to Leger; their fine craftsmanship transcends, but does not deny, French's beginnings as a sign painter.

There is, today, a good deal of pure abstraction in Melbourne, and its contribution may become as important as that of the now-scattered Antipodeans. Janet Dawson, young and Paris-trained, and Roger Kemp, an older man whose search has been long and sincere, could be the most interesting.

Henry Salkauskas is another Sydney artist who cannot be included in the abstract Australian landscape trend. His merit is certainly as great as most of the "Sydney 9" group, and his exclusion from it can only be a matter of his devotion to the more modest linocut and ink-drawing media. Within these media he achieves an assured largeness in his abstracts of snowy whites and velvety blacks. There are references to a universal nature, rather than to a particular Australian landscape.

It is worth pointing out that each capital city has some worth-while activity and that all art is not to be found in only Melbourne and Sydney. In Hobart, there is Carington Smith. In Perth, there is Guy Grey-Smith, whose landscapes have changed from Fauvism to abstraction. Adelaide has the close-up views of dead twigs and leaves of James Cant. In Brisbane, Jon Molvig practices a more European expressionism than any of the Melbourne school, and a much more painterly one than theirs. His portraits are the best since Dobell; and his outback subjects, resulting from the almost obligatory journey to the interior, carry on freely from Drysdale. Molvig, with French and Olsen, would generally be regarded as the best of the new generation.

Most abstraction has by now rejected the luscious, romantic color of its first years. It is possible that the New Spanish school, the product of a country whose landscape often resembles Australia's, will exert some influence in the near future. There are several texture painters at work, Elwyn Lynn in 1959 being the first to turn to this form of expression. Lynn also in the same year organized a neo-Dada manifestation, "Muffled Drums," and in 1962 three young men styling themselves the "Imitation Realists" introduced pop art assemblages of raw material from the gaudy vital world of the chain stores and mass advertising. Olsen too has begun to incorporate into his paintings figurative elements from the world of urban experience. This is one fruitful trend for the sixties which makes nonsense of the division between figurative and nonfigurative, as is also the use of abstract expressionist techniques by Morrow, Rapotec, and Daws to solve the perennial problems of interpreting the uniquely Australian outback landscapes.

To define, to dramatize, or to express this landscape has been a constant preoccupation for Australian art. To populate it with myths

375

and legends is a further task, best solved by figurative styles, in which there have been great successes as well as occasional absurdities. Against these purposes enough voices have been raised to avoid the dangers of provincialism or backwardness and to press the claims of painting in its purest forms. The groupings and their tensions seem ideally balanced. They have helped Australia become, in the art of painting, a genuine cultural contributor.

There was virtually no sculpture in Australia until two Englishmen came out to the gold fields in the 1850's. The first was Thomas Woolner, a member of the Pre-Raphaelite Brotherhood who spent the years 1852 to 1854 in Australia, during which he produced a number of sensitive portrait medallions. The other, Charles Summers, stayed longer (1853–1866) and executed a good deal of pleasant Italian Renaissance-style work. His most notable work is the large public statue in bronze that was erected in Melbourne in 1865 as a memorial to the explorers Burke and Wills. The poses of its two figures derive directly from Michelangelo.

The first Australian-born sculptor of note was Sir Bertram Mackennal (1863–1931). He was a successful expatriate, like the painters Bunny and Fox, though—unlike them—he worked in England rather than in France. He was the first Australian artist to become an associate and a member of the Royal Academy. After studying in London in the early eighties, he returned to Australia in 1887 to carve the reliefs on the Houses of Parliament in Melbourne, and he made other visits to Australia in 1901 and 1926. He did public statues, exhibition pieces for the salons, innumerable portrait busts, and statuettes. In his best bronzes there is a full-blown Edwardian charm: the portraits of Sarah Bernhardt and Lady Diana Cooper, for instance. Some of the later statuettes have a mild *art nouveau* flavor.

Web Gilbert (1866–1925) was another competent Melbourne sculptor who worked in a similar vein, but he spent little time abroad.

Between the wars, Daphne Mayo produced sound academic sculpture in Brisbane. Another woman, Ola Cohn, who had studied with the young Henry Moore at the Royal College of Art in London, changed the emphasis of Melbourne sculptors from modeling to carving in stone and wood.

376

Rayner Hoff (1894–1937), an Englishman who in 1923 became the first head of the Sculpture Department at East Sydney Technical College, was also a product of the Royal College of Art. He is certainly the most important Australian sculptor of the period. His carvings and bronzes are often excellent examples of the formal puritanism of the twenties. Besides portraits, he executed a number of public commissions and cinema decorations, many with the then-popular subject matter of fauns and satyrs. Rayner Hoff's position at the East Sydney Technical College is now filled by his pupil, Lyndon Dadswell, whose influence was important in the revival of sculpture after the Second World War, and whose winning design of a monolith to commemorate the late King George VI was the subject of considerable controversy because of its bold departure from the norm of commemorative sculpture in Sydney. Unfortunately, the monolith was never erected.

From about 1928 until 1948 little sculpture was produced in Australia. The carvings and bronzes of animals by Gerald Lewers in Sydney and Leonard Shillam in Brisbane attracted attention. Clive Stephen, a Melbourne surgeon who achieved real excellence as an amateur sculptor, also made small stone-carvings of animals. Various Melbourne expressionist painters produced sculptures. Danila Vassilieff's stone carvings of expressionist figures and abstract carvings have the same qualities as his paintings.

The Boyd circle of painters produces a great deal of ceramic sculpture. Arthur's have been of religious subjects; David builds personages out of wheel-thrown forms; and John Perceval is best known for his red-glazed figures of children, or "Angels."

Perhaps as a result of a British Council exhibition of Henry Moore in 1947–1948, interest in sculpture began to revive about 1950. Sculptors' societies were formed in Melbourne and in Sydney, the latter holding its first exhibition in November, 1951, in the open air of the Botanic Gardens.

There has never been a great demand for domestic sculpture in Australia, but commissions for modern architectural and outdoor pieces have increased enormously in recent years. Many sculptors are inevitably forced by their clients into figurative allegory, but in spite of such pressures, some of the new public sculpture is good.

Margel Hinder, the American wife of the constructivist painter

Frank Hinder, has done perhaps the best work in Sydney. She won a third prize in the 1953 international sculpture competition for the Unknown Political Prisoner. Her work is entirely nonfigurative and had been so even in the forties. Indeed, sculpture has in some ways been more advanced than painting, for the work of Robert Klippel, the sculptor member of "Direction I," had been abstract in 1950. He and Margel Hinder both make metal constructions in space. Klippel now works in the United States.

Clement Meadmore continues this kind of pure sculpture in Sydney. His constructions of welded steel planes with a rough but subtle finish achieve a fine masculine elegance. He was the one sculptor to be included in the 1961 "Sydney 9" group and is one of the best now working.

A more organic form of abstraction is found in Melbourne. Here is Lenton Parr, who has worked with Henry Moore. He is one of the best sculptors in Australia at present. His large steel constellations are spiky and sudden in their changes of scale and direction. Sometimes they are derived from insects; sometimes they create a new kind of abstract organism. Julius Kane and Norma Redpath also produce organic bonelike or human forms of some merit, while Vincas Jomantas does more strictly abstract carvings, of which the best are chunky monolithic forms in wood. The fundamental sculptural motif of the column is competently treated by Stephen Walker (b. 1927) who works in Hobart.

There are many other sculptors at work, but the general level is not high.

As in the case of sculpture, the first interesting Australian design was produced by a member of the English Pre-Raphaelite circle. Edward La Trobe Bateman (1816–1897) came out to the gold fields in 1852 with Thomas Woolner and remained in Melbourne for about fifteen years. He had worked with Owen Jones on the decoration of the Crystal Palace in London, and in Australia he designed domestic interiors and gardens and was perhaps the first person to employ native flora for decorative purposes—mainly in bookbinding and in tailpieces. Since Bateman, no one in Australia has established a reputation for bibliographic art; the few large collectors chose to augment their libraries rather than to have them bound artistically. Likewise, there has been no Australian typographer of note, although the books produced by the Sydney publishers Edwards and Shaw are most aesthetic. Adrian Feint has designed a great number of pleasing book-plates; and Norman Lindsay's book illustrations of the 1920's are brilliant. They are the happiest productions of a many-sided artist.

By the beginning of the twentieth century there were arts and crafts societies, whose members were nearly all women. Most of their work was *art nouveau* in style and used ornament based on native flora. The waratah was put forward in *The Australian Flora in Applied Art* (1915), a book addressed to students of technical colleges, as suitable for architectural capitals, glass bottles, electroliers, jewelry, chair backs and needlework, as well as for wallpaper, tiles, and painted pottery. Of Australian flora the gum leaf (eucalyptus) seems to have gained the greatest popularity, for it is still visible in the architectural enrichment of many early twentieth-century buildings and on municipal iron lampposts. The gum leaf also appeared in much of the ceramic decoration usually painted by the arts and crafts ladies on imported white porcelain vases.

Ceramics now are especially notable. The first Australian artist-potter was Merric Boyd (1889–1959), father of the painters Arthur and David. From 1920 he was producing earthenware with much fluid, naturalistic Australian plant and animal decoration, not only painted, but modeled. Today the work of David Boyd and John Perceval continues his exuberant style in Melbourne, where H. R. Hughan also produces excellent stoneware. Although he has been chiefly inspired by the Chinese celadons of the Sung period, Hughan's pots reflect something of the English work of Bernard Leach and Michael Cardew. He is perhaps the leading stoneware potter in Australia at present, but he is closely followed by a number of Sydney men. Ivan McMeekin and Peter Rushforth, both close to the contemporary English tradition, are the best, but good work is being done by Les Blakebrough, Ivan and Patricia Englund, Mollie Douglas, and Wanda Garnsey.

Australian design for industry has never been strong. Until recently most manufactures were imported, and now (when local manufacture of consumer goods is the rule) foreign designs are copied freely in preference to spending money to create local designs. Consequently, it is in the handcrafts that the most interest is found.

379

In some of the younger countries there has been considerable and praiseworthy work in wrought iron, stained glass, crystal—such as Steuben glass in the United States—silver (chalices and monstrances as well as domestic wares), tapestry, embroidery, and jewelry. In all of these arts or crafts there has been no notable achievement in Australia. An explanation may be found in the necessarily utilitarian nature of Australian society in the past or in the role of religion in that society—since most of these crafts are usually associated with religious institutions or are produced for a wealthy, leisured elite.

Work with textiles received some stimulus from Michael O'Connell, now well known in England. He arrived in Melbourne in 1920, and through the next two decades his modern hand block-printed curtains and fabrics became well known and were often included in exhibitions of avant-garde painting. During the Second World War, with imports cut off, Frances Burke specialized in textile design. Since then there has been little of note, though large manufacturers have occasionally commissioned prestige designs from famous artists, as Silk and Textiles Ltd. did in 1947 from Dobell, Drysdale, Margaret Preston, Douglas Annand, Alistair Morrison, and others.

Furniture is rather more interesting. In 1929, in Sydney, an exhibition of interior design included a few modern rooms, in which the style of the 1925 Paris Exhibition was clearly evident. Most of the furniture was designed by the painters Roy de Maistre and Adrian Feint. There were desks derived from the modern aeroplane hangar, chairs conforming to the curve of the human spine, tables based on the simplest primary forms—cylinders, cubes, prisms, and pyramids—and cabinets following in form the "set-back" architecture of the modern American skyscraper. Less fashion-conscious furniture was being made in Melbourne from 1927 by Frederick Ward in his own small factory. He preferred natural wood surfaces, not brightly lacquered ones, and a reticent style closer to the English arts and crafts tradition than to French jazz-modern. For a while, with Cynthia Reed and Michael O'Connell, he operated an influential shop. A few years later he was given a position with a large department store, the Myer Emporium, where he designed not only furniture and other products, but also packaging and interiors.

Fine cabinetmaking has been done in Melbourne since the 1940's by S. Krimper, and in the past ten years good furniture with Scandinavian or American influence has been designed by Grant Featherston, one of whose upholstered chairs has become something of a classic, and by Max Hutchinson and Clement Meadmore, who use metal and other modern materials with distinction. In Perth, an excellent version of a safari chair has been designed in Australian jarrah wood and kangaroo hide by David Foulkes Taylor. Unfortunately, the public art galleries have not yet fully recognized furniture design as overseas museums have done, except in Melbourne.

Immediately after the Second World War, the position of design appeared to improve. Courses in industrial design were introduced in the technical colleges, and in 1947 a Society of Designers for Industry was formed in Melbourne. An associated body was later formed in Sydney. At this period David Jones, a large Sydney department store, gave work to a number of designers, and for a while its packaging, advertising, window displays, and interiors presented a consistently high standard in the same way that the Myer Emporium had done under Frederick Ward in the thirties.

Gordon Andrews was the designer in charge at David Jones. He, Alistair Morrison, and Douglas Annand are probably the best designers working at present. The department store patronage indicates that successful work in Australia does not lie in the field of product design, where pirating from overseas magazines is normal, but in the fields of typography and interior design. Indeed, these designers—who are kept busy with exhibition stands and office interiors—tend to become at times interior decorators, even sculptors and painters, at the expense of industrial design.

In Australia, as in most countries, there are several large public art museums which, by displaying the best paintings, sculpture, and crafts available, endeavor to influence public taste and acknowledge contemporary changes in artistic idioms. The best public art collection in Australia is that of the National Gallery of Victoria, in Melbourne (founded in 1861). Largely as a result of a munificent benefaction from the estate of Alfred Felton (1831–1904), the Melbourne Gallery has been able to acquire numerous works by the great European masters: it has a fine Rembrandt collection and the only Cézanne in Australia.

Unfortunately, the Art Gallery of New South Wales, in Sydney (founded 1875), has no endowment comparable to the Felton bequest and traditionally has been severely limited in its acquisitions by a midget budget. It is unable to buy competitively overseas and accordingly exhibits principally Australian and British paintings and aboriginal art.

The art galleries in Adelaide (1880), Brisbane (1894), and Perth (1895) are smaller than those in Sydney and Melbourne. Adelaide has a well-balanced collection, and Brisbane's one-room museum has the only Picasso paintings in a public collection.

The most celebrated art prize offered in Australia is the Archibald Prize for portraiture; the Wynne Prize is offered annually for landscape painting. There are now about sixty annual art competitions in Australia.

Art education in the public schools was, until recently, regarded as a "frill." Elementary-school teachers are given some instruction in art and crafts during their teachers' college course of training, and they instruct their own classes in art; secondary-school art classes —in the past offered mainly to girls—are elective after the first year and are taught by specialist art teachers trained in the technical colleges. The University of Melbourne is the only Australian university that has a department of fine arts, although the University of Sydney has recently received a generous bequest to increase appreciation of advanced forms of the plastic arts. At present the art schools of the East Sydney and Melbourne technical colleges are the principal centers of training in painting, sculpture, arts, and crafts.

The architecture of the colonial period is now greatly loved in Australia. It is, of course, the tropical Indian variant of English Georgian with the veranda as perhaps the most significant feature— for the English regarded Australia as a tropical colony whose buildings needed protection from the sun. Thus the oldest surviving major building, the "Rum Hospital" in Sydney (built in 1811 during Governor Macquarie's administration in return for a rum monopoly), has a two-storied colonnaded veranda beneath a hipped roof and would be perfectly at home in Mauritius or the West Indies. It is now used as a government office building.

The second decade of the nineteenth century is associated, above

ART

all, with the architect Francis Greenway, already mentioned, whose buildings are still perhaps the most beautiful in the country. Greenway had been a pupil of John Nash. The challenge of providing a new country with its first public buildings caused a great improvement over his English work and sent him for his precedents to the English baroque architects—Hawksmoor, for instance, and perhaps Soane—rather than to Nash. These buildings are wide-eaved with gable ends treated as temple pediments similar to the west front of Inigo Jones's St. Paul's, Covent Garden. A barracks and two churches (St. Matthew's, Windsor—the more beautiful—and St. James's, Sydney) show a superb use of brick (almost primitivist in its directness), a subtle and precise articulation and, despite their small size, a monumental scale.

Exposed brick was not much used. Its low quality usually required stucco, which was after all the normal Regency material, and the country houses which resulted from the prosperity of the 1830's are either stucco or stone. The best architect of the thirties was John Verge, of whose typically Regency houses Camden Park and Elizabeth Bay House are sophisticated examples, making some play with oval spaces and semicircular bays. They are also very scenic and are beautifully related to their landscape settings. They have large French windows opening onto long verandas, a common enough Regency feature. With their outdoor living space in the form of verandas, such long, low white buildings as Camden Park, and more particularly its less consciously architectural contemporaries, have become exemplars for an occasional attempt at an Australian tradition of domestic architecture.

Tasmania also has, in Panshanger, a sophisticated long, low country villa of the 1830's; but on the whole its early architecture seems more English. Two-story houses were more common, and verandas were less used in this colder southern colony. Tasmania's churches and public buildings, built under the colonial architect John Lee Archer, are as interesting as New South Wales's in the thirties. Archer was happiest in the classical modes, but used Gothic and Tudor on occasion. Greenway indeed had built castellated stables for Government House, Sydney, but picturesque early Victorian eclecticism reached its peak around the year 1840 in the Tasmanian work of another convict-architect, James Blackburn (1803–1854).

383

His churches were neo-Norman, Italian Romanesque, Gothic, or Regency; some had Anglo-Saxon or Scottish features; a museum was pure Greek, and from his circle came a synagogue in the Egyptian style. All these charming buildings were small, and a golden freestone was the usual material. Tasmania's brief period of interest was almost over when Blackburn left for the new colony at Port Phillip in the forties and settled in Melbourne.

By the mid-fifties Melbourne had become the largest city and was to dominate Australian architecture. Before this, Edmund Blacket (1817–1883) emerged as Sydney's leading exponent of the Gothic Revival, though once or twice he used Norman. Blacket was self-taught; he arrived in 1842, three years later began to practice as an architect, and by 1849 was appointed colonial architect. Although it is in some ways imperfect, his work achieves a genuinely lyrical quality and shows a happy control of informal massing, one of the chief preoccupations of Victorian architecture. His churches, nearly all in the thirteenth- or fourteenth-century English Gothic, are his loveliest buildings, and of these St. Mark's, Darling Point, Sydney (begun in 1848) is the best known. The Great Hall of the University of Sydney (erected in 1852) is his most important work.

William Wardell (1824–1899) was another important Australian Gothic Revival architect. He arrived in Melbourne in 1858 with some memorable buildings already to his credit in England. Nickolaus Pevsner, the historian of European architecture, has pointed out that Wardell, in a young and wealthy nation, was able to build great cathedrals and to demonstrate the full possibilities of revived fourteenth-century English Gothic, while in England his friend Pugin, creator of the Gothic Revival, had to be content with parish churches only. The Roman Catholic cathedrals in Melbourne (designed 1859) and Sydney (designed 1865) are Wardell's. One in hard basaltic bluestone (a material which gives a distinct character to Melbourne's early warehouses and other buildings), the other in red-gold sandstone, they are perhaps a little archeological and cold in comparison with Blacket's churches. They are much bigger, however, than anything by Blacket, and they are unquestionably successes in the grandest manner.

The major Anglican cathedrals were usually built to designs sent out from England. St. Paul's in Melbourne (designed in 1877–1880 by William Butterfield) could have been as exciting as Keble College Chapel if the architect's designs had been followed. St. John's in Brisbane (designed in 1897), still incomplete, is a very suave Early English Gothic by J. L. Pearson and is the only cathedral to be vaulted in stone throughout. Another important English design carried out in Australia is Edward Blore's romantic Gothic Government House in Sydney (begun in 1837, completed in 1845).

Gothic was invariably used by Wardell for ecclesiastical work, but for other buildings it was a consciously artistic choice of style. By anonymous designers of the 1840's to the 1860's there are a few pretty white houses in Sydney with steep gables and ornamental bargeboards, and in Melbourne one or two in a more medieval Victorian Gothic. Perth developed a characteristic Tudor from its local red brick. Wardell himself supervised a number of Gothic branches of the English, Scottish, and Australian Bank, and in its head office in Melbourne (1885) he produced something of a masterpiece. It has a restrained exterior in which he again used the English decorated style of the fourteenth century for his window tracery. All the materials are luxurious, and the craftsmanship of iron doors and carved wood and stone is superb. The banking chamber is the most interesting of all, for in it the frankly expressed iron columns and joists are richly painted and given wrought copper capitals of naturalistic wheat and other Australian produce.

Renaissance Revival is far commoner than Gothic throughout the High Victorian period in Australia. In its various manifestations it still sets the character of most Australian cities, whose major buildings belong largely to the boom of the 1870's and 1880's. Wardell designed two fine Barryesque clubhouses in 1884 in Sydney, some banks, and, most conspicuously, Government House, Melbourne (1872–1876), a huge stuccoed Italianate mansion based on Queen Victoria's Osborne House. Nearly all the mansions in Melbourne of this period are similar. For extra richness and elaboration many banks favored Venetian Renaissance, and for town halls local governments often prescribed French Renaissance. Melbourne's Law Courts (completed 1884) are a handsome variant of the Four Courts in Dublin, but possibly the grandest of all these monuments is one of the earliest, Parliament House in Melbourne. Begun in 1856 to designs by two local architects, it closely follows Leeds Town Hall, and if its projected tall dome were ever built it would be almost a twin. Its palatial façade majestically terminates one of the principal streets, and its interiors, the reception hall, the two legislative chambers, and the library have a baroque profusion of gilt plaster allegorical decoration.

On a lower architectural level, and even more important to the predominantly Victorian character of Australia's cities, is the cast-iron ornament which adorns and indeed transforms miles of speculative housing and many hotels. The verandas of two-storied terraces or houses, or even single-storied ones, are the usual place for the openwork balustrades, spandrels, and friezes of cast iron which lighten the often clumsy houses with a lacy screen. Usually on symmetrical buildings, vaguely Georgian or Italianate, this ironwork was at first imported from England in the fifties during the labor shortages of the gold-rush years. (Some completely prefabricated iron houses, churches, and theatres were also imported.) Later it was manufactured in Australia, where native kookaburras and cockatoos were occasionally incorporated in the designs, though a naturalistic fern pattern was a more common local design. These verandaed houses have also been used as a basis by some present-day architects in search of an essentially Australian style.

Before the boom broke in the early nineties, Melbourne had built offices of twelve or more stories, with load-bearing walls, and serviced by hydraulic lifts (elevators). Such heights were not surpassed in Australia until the 1950's.

After the boom the most striking change was in housing. Scarcely any more terraces were built, and throughout the twentieth century single-story, single-family suburban houses have proliferated to give Australian cities perhaps the world's worst low-density sprawl. Stuccoed bastard Italianate styles gave way to "Queen Anne," which had nothing to do with Christopher Wren's formality. It was an informal picturesque style, in red brick, with white- or green-painted veranda woodwork. Red was also the color for the roof; the clumsy Marseilles tile has become since then a universal roofing material in Australian cities.

At its best, in some commercial and public buildings, this "Queen Anne" style of the nineties and the Edwardian years was the best of any urban Australian architecture. Roofs and skylines, street corners, and the relationship between building and pavement (sidewalk) appear to have been a serious consideration with their architects.

In Melbourne "Queen Anne" had a tendency toward *art nouveau* details. In Sydney, some schools have large round-arched windows and much terra-cotta ornament, and indeed a Richardsonian Romanesque in stone often became an alternative to red brick for offices and banks. The largest surviving Romanesque monument is the Queen Victoria Market building (1893), whose style was chosen because it was "now so largely employed by American architects." Here perhaps is the beginning of a steady American influence in commercial building and speculative housing.

Some large, expensive houses built in Sydney around 1900 are very like Richardson's domestic architecture. (Horbury Hunt, a romantic Sydney architect, had already used a less American Tudor-without-timbering.) Immediately before the First World War "Queen Anne" was superseded for smaller houses by the "California Bungalow." The exposed rafters sometimes took on an extra Japanese air. They have worn rather well, which is more than can be said for the "Spanish Mission" houses which arrived in the 1920's. Office buildings also went into American fancy dress between the wars; sometimes it was Hollywood Moorish, sometimes streamlined "Modern Gothic." The most conspicuous building in Melbourne until recently was the Manchester Unity Building (1935), a copy of the Chicago Herald-Tribune tower. English fancy dress was no less persistent. Timbered Tudor was popular for expensive houses for many years until the early thirties and was followed by a kind of Georgian, still favored today by some of the very wealthy.

In the early years of the century there were three or four architects of real interest. Robert Haddon (1866–1929), an Englishman who arrived in Melbourne in 1900, was responsible for many of the excellent *art nouveau* façades in that city. Desbrowe Annear (1866–1933) was one of the first significant Australian-born architects. In 1918 and 1919 he built Broceliande and Inglesby, the first of a number of elegant houses that look modern even today. They are white, unornamented, horizontal, almost flat roofed; the planning is open. In spite of an apparent debt to Voysey in certain details, there is an authentic Australian feeling.

387

PATTERN OF AUSTRALIAN CULTURE

An American, Walter Burley Griffin (1876–1937) is, with Green-way, perhaps the most important architect to have worked in Australia. An assistant of Frank Lloyd Wright from 1904 to 1908, he won the international competition for a plan for the new capital city of Canberra, and arrived in 1913. Canberra bears little trace of his hand in its actual buildings; it was in Melbourne that he practiced from 1915 until he moved to Sydney in 1929. Like Wright, he was a romantic exponent of an organic architecture. Castlecrag, his attempt at a unified suburb on the cliffs overlooking an arm of Sydney Harbor, still has some superb, small rough stone or concrete-block houses growing almost indistinguishably among the rocks and trees. Most are low, flat roofed, of rectangular or star-shaped blocks, thick walled but generously windowed; but some have tiny, circular, battlemented keeps attached. One of his earliest and best Australian designs, Newman College (1916) at the University of Melbourne, also allows itself a degree of medieval Gothic ornament, but on the whole the ornament of which he was so fond seems to derive from cubist painting. The outward-tilted gable ends and giant keystones that he often used show a tendency toward cubism, and in the interior of the Capitol Theatre, Melbourne (1924), he achieved a masterpiece. Not only are the walls and ceilings an acoustic labyrinth of prismatic forms in plaster, but the interpenetrating multilevel foyers and lounges have that spatial excitement which is the essence of architecture.

An Australian, Hardy Wilson (1881–1955), also had great significance at this time. After studying in America, as did many Australians of this period, he returned to discover the beauty of Sydney's colonial Georgian and to become its most ardent champion. By 1919 he had built the most exquisite of his Colonial Revival houses, for E. G. Waterhouse. He fancied that Australia was an Oriental country and that its architecture should show some affinity with that of China. This at least reinforced, for him, the emphasis on low horizontality; he also insisted on symmetry and proportion, on unornamented white walls shaded by native trees, on wide eaves for further shade, on verandas, and on Australian colonial details. His work is equal to the best of the contemporary Georgian Revival in England and far more constructive.

In the period from 1920 to 1940 Leslie Wilkinson (b. 1882), pro-

388

fessor of architecture at the University of Sydney, put forward a Spanish style as being the most suitable for Australia's Mediterranean-type climate. His houses, with their courtyards and loggias, are a thoughtful application of the theory and are a welcome relief from the Spanish Mission style of the speculative builders; but by 1940 it was becoming too late for any revivalism, except Australian, to be acceptable.

The modern movement—that is, the International Style—can be said to have arrived in Melbourne in the mid-thirties. The first to misapply the ideals of the Bauhaus was a dilettante architect, Sam Atyeo, in a conversion of 1935. Flat roofs, white concrete, and long sweeps of cantilevered balconies appeared in the hospitals designed by the Stephenson and Turner office. There were occasional factories and showrooms with glass curtain walls.

Roy Grounds (b. 1905) visited America and Europe in the thirties, but by 1940 he had built some modest flats (apartments) of the simplest form in which, instead of strict International Style, there was a trace of verandaed Australianism. At present he is perhaps Melbourne's leading architect, and rigid formalism and a degree of Australianism are still characteristic of his work. He likes perfect cubes or cylinders for his buildings and sometimes adds pyramidal or conical roofs. His best-known formalist building is the Academy of Science at Canberra (1959), a low, circular building under a dome that rises apparently from the ground, with no vertical walls to interrupt the spherical form. His National Gallery and Cultural Center designed for Melbourne in 1961 will be a blank-walled rectangle in the same bluestone as some of Melbourne's early warehouses, and an internal courtyard will be surrounded by "Australian" balcony verandas.

The other interesting trend in Melbourne is toward an antiartistic and unhistorical architecture based on new technology. It has already produced a most advanced tension structure: the Myer Music Bowl (1959) by Yuncken, Freeman Brothers, Griffiths, and Simpson, a gigantic open marquee of plywood and aluminum supported by steel cables, and the Olympic Pool (1959) by Peter McIntyre, a building requiring the maximum uninterrupted view, and which in a sense has no walls—the roof stretches across the pool and ties the two sloping banks of seats together.

Routine architecture—of office buildings, for instance—quite suddenly became a matter of general curtain walling about 1955. A transformation of the cities commenced. The work of very large offices, like Bates, Smart, and McCutcheon, or Stephenson and Turner, has maintained a good standard, and the building completed in 1961 for the Shell Oil Company in Melbourne by Skidmore, Owings, and Merrill suddenly made the majority of postwar office buildings look provincial. By 1961 it was realized that the glass box is an unsuitable fashion for so sunny a climate as Australia's, and solid cladding—or sun screening—is beginning to appear.

Smaller buildings have become so fancy—banks indistinguishable from motels—that Robin Boyd, sometime partner of Roy Grounds and now an architectural pundit, felt compelled to publish *The Australian Ugliness* (1960), a discussion of the consequences of recent prosperity, of "featurism," and "Austerica." Featurism is "the subordination of the essential whole, and the accentuation of selected separate features" always done in the name of beautification. Austerica is "a way of life where an austerity version of the American dream overtakes the indigenous Australian culture. It is also slightly hysterical . . . it lives by copying the American magazine, but not necessarily the best magazine, and never the latest copy."

Austerica is found mostly in Sydney and in the resorts. The choice by Saarinen of Jorn Utzon's romantic, exciting, avant-garde design (1956) for the Sydney Opera House now building is not Austerican, however. It was an original conception of world-wide significance.

There has been some good domestic architecture in Sydney in the past twenty years. From Sydney Ancher and his firm there is a low-slung Australianism with verandas. From Harry Seidler, who arrived in Australia in 1948 and studied with Gropius and Marcel Breuer, there is an architecture which makes fewer compromises with its landscape setting. Seidler has recently carried out some apartments and office blocks, which are perhaps the best large buildings in Sydney—clean, tidy, reticent, and well proportioned. A wave of younger men is, rather unfortunately, discovering Frank Lloyd Wright all over again.

In the 1960's Australians share the aesthetic discontent of most architects with an international architecture consequent on rapid communications. The curtain wall has failed in a hot climate; the relevance of the colonial heritage is doubtful. Because, like the southern areas of the United States, Australia is neither tropical nor frigid, its architects are largely eclectic; there are followers of Frank Lloyd Wright, Niemeyer, and Aalto. Only in Queensland, constantly humid as well as hot, is there a vernacular of light timber construction, always raised one floor above ground to catch every beneficial breeze. This was raised to full aesthetic quality in the work of R. S. Dods around 1910. This adaptability to climatic conditions may, one hopes, extend to the more temperate regions of Australia.

BIBLIOGRAPHY

Books

Badham, H. *A Study of Australian Art.* 1949.
Barrett, C. and Croll, R. H. *The Art of the Australian Aboriginal.* 1943.
Battarbee, Rex E. *Australian Aboriginal Art.* 1958.
Bonython, Kym, ed. *Modern Australian Painting and Sculpture, 1950–1960.* 1960.
Boyd, Robin. *Australia's Home: Its Origins, Builders and Occupiers.* 1952.
——. *The Australian Ugliness.* 1960.
Casey, Maie. *Early Melbourne Architecture: 1840–1888.* 1955.
Croll, R. H. *Tom Roberts.* 1935.
Ellis, M. H. *Francis Greenway.* 1949.
Herman, M. E. *The Early Australian Architects and Their Work.* 1954.
——. *The Architecture of Victorian Sydney.* 1956.
Heysen, Hans. *Water Colours and Drawings.* 1952.
Hoff, Ursula. *Masterpieces of the National Gallery of Victoria.* 1949.
MacDonald, J. S. *Australian Painting Desiderata.* 1958.
Moore, W. *The Story of Australian Art* (2 vols.). 1934.
Preston, Margaret. *Margaret Preston's Monotypes.* 1948.
Seidler, Harry. *Houses, Interiors and Projects.* 1949.
Smith, Bernard W. *Place, Taste and Tradition: A Study of Australian Art since 1788.* 1945.
——. *European Vision and the South Pacific.* 1960.
——. *Australian Painting, 1788–1960.* 1962.
Wilson, Hardy. *Old Colonial Architecture.* 1923.

Periodicals

Art in Australia. Monthly. 1916–1942.

MUSIC

A. L. MCLEOD

THE author of a recent *Current Affairs Bulletin* issued by the University of Sydney wrote that "music in Australia is a social experience. . . . We are audiences, not creators." Thus, succinctly, he epitomized the place of music in Australian life.

Australians are, indubitably, fond of music; they attend orchestral concerts in large numbers (but chamber music concerts and vocal or instrumental recitals hardly at all) and show genuine pride in those of their countrymen who succeed in musical careers overseas; Joan Sutherland is the most celebrated of a large contemporary group. It sometimes seems odd to observers that Australians are more eager to provide funds for their musically talented young people to study abroad than they are to provide suitable conditions for them to perform and teach in their homeland after they have gained experience and fame. Yet, collectively, Australians are among the least accomplished people in the world so far as ability to participate in music is concerned; they are, in short, audiences for rather than creators of music.

392

MUSIC

Almost all countries have a large body of folk songs that are sung by those unable to play some musical instrument; but this is not the case in Australia. Australians overseas invariably disappoint their hosts when they are invited to sing some Australian songs; the only ballad that most can sing is "Waltzing Matilda," which is as well known throughout the world as in Australia. Yet there is a considerable number of Australian ballads, as Dr. Russel Ward, Douglas Stewart, Dr. Percy Jones, and Nancy Keesing have recently shown by their researches. Some of the songs of the 1880's are particularly melodious and are eminently humorous in a dry, sardonic fashion; the American folk balladist, Burl Ives, was so impressed by them, in fact, that he has included some in his recitals and made a record of them. The art of folk singing, recently revived in both Britain and the United States, may yet popularize the great bulk of Australian ballads of the nineteenth century. Meanwhile, such American folk songs as "Yankee Doodle," "Shenandoah," and "Old Black Joe" are more familiar to Australians than their own "Click Go the Shears, Boys" and "Botany Bay," in spite of the national awareness of the outback.

Even more surprising, perhaps, is the general inability of Australians to play musical instruments, for orchestral concerts are vastly popular. There are great numbers of individuals who are able to carry on an informed, even quite knowledgeable, conversation about music history and literature, but there are few among the attentive, appreciative audiences at concerts who have any ability to play an instrument other than the piano.

The reasons for the dearth of instrumentalists in Australia are clear. First, there is a sociological disposition against music as a vocation. The feeling of the lower classes seems to be that an interest in music is a sign of effeminacy, the attitude among the middle classes is that music provides neither a secure career with reasonable remuneration nor the opportunity to achieve professional status, and the common belief among the upper section of society is that real achievement in music makes departure from the country imperative both for training and career purposes. Thus a vocation that is widely regarded as neither manly nor remunerative is unlikely to be particularly popular.

The second reason for the general inability of Australians to play musical instruments is the status of music education in the country. Instruction in instrumental music is not provided as a part of the normal school curriculum; schools have neither instruments to lend or rent to students nor teachers to give instruction. There are, accordingly, no school bands and orchestras. When musical comedies are presented by schools as part of their drama program, the accompaniment is usually provided by two pianos, and these are as often as not played by adults unconnected with the schools. Music programs, which are provided in almost all schools as an integral part of the curriculum, are usually concerned only with teaching part songs and the rudiments of music appreciation. In New South Wales, for example, the state Education Department mandates music instruction, but provides neither piano nor phonograph and record library for its implementation. The schools must, by devious means, raise the money necessary to purchase even the most essential instructional material.

Music can be taken as a high-school subject, but it has not until recently been accepted for purposes of university entrance. In a system in which high-school education has been regarded primarily as preparatory to university entrance, the failure to accept music as a matriculation subject has naturally militated against its wider election. Only in recent years have universities other than those in Melbourne, Perth, and Adelaide offered instruction in music, and it is not offered as a general education course, but only to those specializing in the subject. Few Australian public-school music teachers have enjoyed the rigorous and comprehensive training that is required of their counterparts in the United States, and rare indeed are those who can demonstrate proficiency on more than one instrument.

The unfortunate consequences of the national attitude to music as a career and of the parlous state of music education are readily to be observed. They intrude on the entire way of life. It is not uncommon to find, at public gatherings in Australia, that no one is able to play "God Save the Queen" on the piano. Festive occasions with public marches are often dull, unemotional rituals because of the absence of numerous, skillful, large bands. Dances are often held to the music of a trio composed of piano, saxophone, and drums. Dinner music provided by a string quartet is almost unknown. In Europe almost every town has its band and every city its opera house; in

394

Australia bands other than the few maintained by police, military, and Salvation Army units are almost nonexistent. In North America every high school, college, and university has its marching band of from 60 to 120 players; no educational institution in Australia has one. There are, however, a number of small highland pipe bands.

In the United States there are almost twelve hundred symphony orchestras, either professional or amateur. On a population basis, Australia could be expected to support about sixty, but it finds the utmost difficulty in maintaining six or seven at adequate strength. West Germany has, since the Second World War, built fifty-nine new opera houses; Australia (with a quarter of the population) is still building its first. There are no permanent opera companies or chamber orchestras in Australia; although there are universities that can rank with all but the very best elsewhere in the world, there is no college of music that could, in fairness, be compared to the Curtis Institute, the Royal Conservatory in Toronto, the Juillard School, or Oberlin Conservatory.

Notwithstanding the slight role that music plays in the cultural life of Australia, many Australians—most of whom have been singers —have achieved international fame in the world of music. A history of music in Australia becomes, essentially, an account of visiting artists, of the exodus of local artists, and of the commendable but sometimes shamefully unappreciated efforts of a few devoted souls to make music as essential an ingredient of the culture of their country as it is in other lands.

When one considers the rigors of travel from England to New South Wales and the premium on cargo space aboard the few ships that provided the veritable life line to the barely viable settlement at Sydney in its early years, it is noteworthy that, in 1790, H.M.S. *Sirius* landed a piano, the property of its surgeon, Mr. Worgan.

Within the year the instrument had been transported some forty miles away, to the home of Captain John Macarthur in the Cowpastures (now Camden). Writing to a friend in London, Mrs. Macarthur provided the first reference to music in Australia:

Our new house is ornamented with a new pianoforte of Mr. Worgan's, and he kindly means to leave it with me and now, under his direction, I have begun a new study. I am told, however, that I have done wonders in being able to play off "God Save the King" and Foot's "Minuet," besides that of reading the notes with great facility.[1]

For the next forty years there are very few references to music in the country's annals. Such items as are to be found indicate the slow growth of an activity too long and too frequently regarded as of peripheral concern in infant settlements in distant climes. In 1818 Robert McIntosh (perhaps a former regimental bandsman) advertised his availability for music lessons; in 1821 the *Hobart Courier* recorded the appointment of Mr. J. Livingstone as choirmaster of St. David's Church (where he soon organized a small wind ensemble, augmented by a cello and a viola), and in 1824 Robert Campbell opened, in Sydney, Australia's first music store.

During 1826 John Philip Deane arrived in Hobart from London to assume the duties of organist at St. David's Church, and he directed a public concert at which was performed "a new and beautiful Australian air in honour of Our Sister Colony of New South Wales" (presumably composed by either Livingstone or Deane). Deane quickly achieved distinction in Hobart and, after a decade, moved to Sydney where for almost fifty years he became one of the principal musicians and arbiters of musical taste.

Barnett Levey, the intrepid entrepreneur of theatre in colonial Sydney, was also a patron of musical entertainments. In July, 1829, he placed the following advertisement in the columns of the *Australian:*

A license having been granted to the proprietor of the Royal Hotel to hold and have concerts, etc., at his house, to be considered an Assembly Room, he therefore solicits such vocal talent, either with or without pay, to those who may please to step forward and lend their aid to this harmless amusement. . . . The public may rest assured that the strictest attention will be paid to preserve good order, and that such entertainment will only be presented as will amuse and instruct.

Decorum being assured, a polite audience attended the first concert on August 20, 1829, which included the overture to Cherubini's *Lodoiska* (probably played by the band of the Fifty-seventh Regiment), an anonymous quartet for flute and horns ("spoilt by the clinking of glasses," reported the *Australian* in its account of the

[1] From a letter in the Mitchell Library, Sydney, quoted in W. A. Orchard, *Music in Australia* (Melbourne: Georgian House, 1952), pp. 1–2.

evening), and several vocal numbers, including "Oh Lady Fair" and "Ye Banks and Braes." Subsequent concerts in September and October included overtures by Mozart and Weber, a duet for violins, and several part songs.

Apparently, interest in music developed apace, for in May, 1830, Mr. Bodenham, a Sydney auctioneer, advertised receipt of a shipment of Broadwood pianos, and six years later an importer announced the arrival of eight pianos, two violas, and two violins—one of which was a Stradivarius.

Sir Richard Bourke, eighth governor of Australia and an important and discerning patron of the arts, arrived in Sydney in December, 1831. With his general support, or under his specific patronage, concerts and musical organizations were soon promoted, among them the Philharmonic Society (1833).

Encouraged, no doubt, by the propitious atmosphere, in 1834 Levey promoted *Giovanni in London*, which he described in characteristic bombast as "an operatic extravaganza." The production was an unprecedented success, and Levey followed it with a concert version of Sir Henry Bishop's opera *Clari; or, The Maid of Milan*, which had had its premiere at Covent Garden in 1823. Levey engaged as his principal vocalist Australian-born singer-actress Elizabeth Winstanley, whose singing of the aria "Home, Sweet Home" assured the outcome of the venture. In the same year, Dr. John Lhotsky, a physician and botanist who spent five years in Australia, published what he described as "the first specimen of Australian music," a song of the women of the Monaro tribe of aborigines, arranged for piano and voice, which he inscribed to Queen Adelaide. This, like most other transcriptions of aboriginal songs, indicated that the native inhabitants used the pentatonic scale and that their melodies had a downward movement (usually beginning on the highest note) and a limited decorative tendency at the beginning. It is understandable that the transcription was neither popular nor influential, yet it remains an interesting curiosity of Australian music literature.

Throughout the thirties music developed rapidly in several ways. In January, 1836, Vincent Wallace, formerly an organist and violinist in Dublin, arrived in Sydney after a year's residence in Hobart, where he had given a series of concerts. He announced plans for

397

concerts to be held "in the saloon of the Royal Hotel, under the patronage and in the presence of His Excellency the Governor." The *Sydney Herald* described Wallace as "Professor of Composition at the Royal Academy of Music, London" and as a gentleman who "has ranked high among the musical society of Europe." But Wallace was then just twenty, and his name has never been located in any records of the London colleges of music.

Wallace was a versatile musician. At his opening concert he played a violin concerto by Mayseder, his own "Fantasia di bravura" dedicated to Paganini (news of whose death had recently been received in Sydney), performed in a piano duet, and played the piano accompaniment for several songs. The concert was, from all indications, a remarkable success. Within weeks Wallace opened, under viceregal patronage, an "academy for the instruction of young ladies in voice and instrumental music according to the system of Logier and Hertz." Assisted by his wife, sister, and brother, he undertook to instruct in flute, violin, guitar, piano, and voice as well as principles of music. But no sooner had Wallace's academy opened than J. P. Deane, also recently arrived from Hobart, announced in the press that he too was prepared to provide instruction—in piano, violin, violoncello, flute, voice, theory, and practice of music—and at about half the fees charged by Wallace. In addition, he was prepared to tune pianos "carefully and correctly at the shortest notice." Henceforth, both the Deane and Wallace families vied for public favor, offering several concerts and recitals both as commercial enterprises and as benefits for charitable and religious causes. They jointly sponsored a concert presentation of *The Messiah* and *The Creation* for the organ fund of St. Mary's Church.

For unknown reasons, Wallace soon left Australia for America and England. The *Sydney Gazette* of February 17, 1838, reported the musician's departure in unflattering terms: "Mr. Wallace, the Australian Paganini, left the Colony in a clandestine manner on Wednesday last, the 14th, and has sailed for Valparaiso, having contracted debts in Sydney amounting to nearly £2,000." After a peripatetic sojourn in South America, Wallace arrived in New York and, in 1842, was one of the principals in the founding of the New York Philharmonic Society. He later earned general acclaim for his opera *Maritana*. Although his stay in Australia was brief, his role in the development of public interest in music was noteworthy.

During the 1840's Isaac Nathan, a composer of several light operas who also set some of Byron's poems to music—to the poet's delight —was an influential member of Sydney's musical society. He organized several concerts of "grand oratorio," which included the work of Handel, Mozart, and Haydn, and composed an opera, *Don John of Austria* (1848), which was the first opera to be written, composed, and performed in Australia. Earlier in the decade Nathan and other impresarios produced concert and simplified theatre versions of several operas, including *The Barber of Seville* (1841), *La Sonnambula* (1843), *Der Freischütz* (1846), *The Bohemian Girl* (1847), and *Otello* (1848). By 1850, then, Sydney had become established as the center of music in Australia, largely as a result of the enterprise of Levey, Wallace, Deane, and Nathan.

The period from 1850 to 1914 might be called the choral and operatic period of Australian music, for during these years numerous large choirs—some apparently of consummate skill—were founded. And with an ample supply of voices trained in choral music, it was possible to produce opera on the grand scale.

The choral societies established after 1850 were legion, but mention should perhaps be made of some of the principal ones: the Adelaide Liedertafel (1858), the Melbourne Philharmonic Society (1853), the Royal Victorian Liedertafel (1868), and the Hobart Orpheus Choir (1859).

For the opening of the Great Hall of the University of Sydney in 1859 a grand concert was held which brought together the best musical talent of the nation, and the program (which included both *The Messiah* and *The Creation*) was performed by a chorus of 250 voices and an orchestra of 50—groups of impressive size for the time.

In 1861, W. Saurin Lyster, an Irish impresario who had formed an opera company in America, brought Henry Squires and Lucy Escott to Melbourne to sing the principal roles in *Don Giovanni, Maritana,* and *Lurline*. The season was a spectacular success, and Lyster took his company on tour of Adelaide, Sydney, Brisbane, and Hobart during the following year. In these cities they were applauded with equal enthusiasm. Encouraged by his initial success, Lyster under-

399

took to present additional operas in the following years: *Les Hugue-nots* and *The Beggar's Opera* in 1863, *Faust* and *Le Prophète* in 1864. For several years Lyster dominated the operatic theatre in Australia, maintaining high standards of production and an uncommonly catholic repertoire. He used increasingly elaborate scenery and costumes and featured such prominent European singers as Antoinette Link, who sang in *Lohengrin* (1877) and *Tannhauser* (1878), but he soon discovered that, satisfying as such operas were when produced on the grand scale, they were not financially feasible. To reduce his losses, he alternated grand with light operas and so made a businesslike accommodation between artistic enthusiasm and the economics of the theatre.

By engaging John Hill, a King's scholar of the Royal Academy, as conductor for his operas, Lyster ensured a high standard of musical achievement. His company's repertoire was speedily enlarged to include twenty operas. Among the singers whom Lyster brought to Australia were Lucy Chambers, Signora Coy, Signor Cecchi, Martin and Fanny Simonsen, and the brilliant Austrian soprano, Ilma de Murska.

Lyster went overseas in 1871, but returned to launch a new company with Alberto Zelman and G. B. Allen as its conductors.[2] New works offered included *Macbeth* and *La Fille de Madame Angot*, in which Edward Farley (a popular English baritone) and Armes Beaumont sang. Perhaps Lyster's greatest success was with *Carmen*, in the 1879 season, in which Madame Hersee sang the leading role. In 1880 Lyster engaged Camillo Urso and Carlotta Patti (the sister of Adelina), but his death in Melbourne brought that season to an early close.

Lyster's death caused a brief hiatus in opera in Australia until his nephew, George Musgrove, reorganized resources and staged *La Fille du tambour major*, an operatic extravaganza which ran for a season of 101 nights in Melbourne. Its star singer was Nellie Stewart, an Australian, for many years a favorite of local audiences.

J. C. Williamson, who had arrived in Sydney in 1874, was especially interested in legitimate theatre, but also sponsored Gilbert and Sullivan operettas. In 1885 he extended his interests to include

[2] Zelman settled in Melbourne, founded the Melbourne Symphony Orchestra in 1906, and conducted it with success for over twenty years.

opera proper, entered a partnership with Musgrove (which lasted until 1892), and imported the first of a series of Italian opera companies. As a result of the Musgrove-Williamson enterprise Australian audiences first heard *Cavalleria rusticana*, *I Pagliacci*, and *L'Amico Fritz*.

Two events of local significance were marked by concerts on a scale not hitherto attempted; the first was the Melbourne Exhibition in 1888, the other was the opening of the Sydney Town Hall in 1890. In Melbourne a music festival was planned as part of the Exhibition, and for it Frederick H. Cowen was brought from England as organizer. With his own ensemble as a nucleus he assembled an orchestra of over seventy players and presented a series of orchestral and choral concerts that were regarded as the most polished in Australian musical history up to that time. Perhaps the most celebrated event was the Australian premiere performance of Beethoven's Ninth Symphony. For the opening of the Sydney Town Hall and the dedication of its pipe organ (still the largest in the Southern Hemisphere) T. H. Best, the noted English organist, gave a series of recitals that were much praised.

Coinciding with the Federation festivities in 1900–1901, J. C. Williamson promoted another season of opera, his first for several years. The repertoire was more extensive and more sophisticated than that of the 1893 season, for it included *Aïda*, *La Bohème*, *Otello*, *Fedora*, and *La Giaconda*. Not to be outdone, Musgrove responded in 1901 with his own opera season, presenting *The Flying Dutchman*, *Lohengrin*, *Tannhauser*, *Carmen*, and rival productions of *La Bohème* and *Fedora*. The plethora of 1901 apparently satiated the public's appetite for opera for some years, for only an occasional opera was produced between that year and 1907 when the irrepressible Musgrove imported a German opera company to present *The Valkyrie*, *The Flying Dutchman*, and Engelbert Humperdinck's delightful *Hansel and Gretel*.

In 1911 Madame Melba, by then well established overseas as a singer, returned to tour Australia with John McCormack in a company under the direction of J. C. Williamson. Melba was, without doubt, the star of the season, and her performances in *Lohengrin*, *Otello*, *Samson and Delilah*, *La Bohème*, and *La Tosca* were memorable. The season was an unparalleled success, and Williamson was so encouraged that he engaged Thomas Quinlan to bring with him from Europe three companies of singers for the 1912–1913 seasons. Under his direction Williamson presented the complete Ring cycle and almost all the other Wagnerian operas, Debussy's *The Prodigal Son*, Puccini's *The Girl of the Golden West*, and Charpentier's *Louise*.

Opera had, by 1913, achieved its greatest success in Australia, and it almost immediately went into decline.

Late in 1913 J. C. Williamson died, and although his business successors were competent men, they were apparently unable to sustain the public interest in opera during the days of war and depression that lay ahead. Opera was produced occasionally, of course, as in 1924 when Melba's company presented sixteen works and in 1928 when both the Melba and Ganzales companies toured Australia. But it was not until 1948 that opera could be said to have returned to general favor.

For almost a decade after the beginning of the First World War there was a considerable truncation of musical, as of other cultural, activities. Opera languished, choral societies declined, overseas artists were infrequent visitors. Chamber music had never become popular in Australia, and so the slender musical fare was provided principally by military bands and local piano, violin, and vocal soloists. Gradually Australian musicians achieved recognition overseas—a few by virtue of their compositions, but most as singers—orchestral groups were established, and music eventually became part of the cultural pattern of the nation. It was not until the 1930's that Australia could claim to have adequate provision for the formal training of musicians, orchestras of some competence, composers who were known outside the country, and some individual artists of international caliber.

Before the turn of the century few Australian musicians had been acclaimed overseas; the most notable was perhaps Elizabeth Winstanley, the singer who subsequently turned to the theatre and to literature. But soon others were well known: Johann Kruse, violinist; Ernest Hutcheson, pianist, who later became dean of the Juillard School of Music; Frances Alda, who became a leading soprano at the Metropolitan Opera House for almost twenty years; Lempriere Pringle, bass, who sang with the Carl Rosa and Covent Garden opera companies; Percy Grainger and Arthur Benjamin, composers;

MUSIC

Peter Dawson, baritone; Gertrude Johnson, soprano; William McKie, organist of Westminster Abbey and master of the Queen's music; and Eileen Joyce, pianist.

As the nation began to take greater interest in music generally, it was natural that it should give some attention to the training of musicians. Although the universities in Sydney and Melbourne were opened in the early 1850's, they made no provision for instruction in music, and the public schools' only forray into music education was instruction (by classroom teachers virtually untrained in music) in vocal and choral music. It was not until 1887 that formal provision was made for higher education in music by the endowment of a chair of music at the University of Melbourne by Francis Ormond. To this professorship was appointed, in 1891, G. W. L. Marshall Hall, on the recommendation of Sir Charles Halle, who had visited Melbourne in 1890. Marshall Hall proved to be a most energetic person, and he soon organized a symphony orchestra which, after a series of fine concerts, helped establish the popularity of orchestral music in Victoria. Hall also established a music school (under university supervision, but privately financed) for training younger students. However, after some of his views were publicly criticized, Hall was denied a continuing appointment and was succeeded by Franklin Peterson. Most of Hall's faculty resigned in sympathy with him and joined the staff of his private music school. On Peterson's death in 1914, Hall was reappointed and continued as professor of music in the University of Melbourne until 1926. In 1890 the University of Adelaide appointed a lecturer in music and in 1897, its first professor of music, following a bequest by Sir Thomas Elder. But in Sydney and elsewhere, attempts to establish colleges of music were less successful. In 1902 a bequest was left to the University of Sydney for the promotion of music education, but it was not until 1948 that Donald Peart was appointed as first professor of music.

In 1914, however, the government of New South Wales, acting on the recommendation of the minister for education, Campbell Carmichael, decided to establish a state conservatorium of music. It invited applications for the position of director and, rejecting the application of Engelbert Humperdinck, whose *Hansel and Gretel* had long been a favorite of operagoers, appointed Henri Verbrugghen, a Belgian, whose string quartet had achieved some prestige in

Europe. The premises for the new conservatorium were not impressive: the former stables of Government House, slightly modified (still in use). Verbrugghen brought the other members of his quartet to Sydney, made several appointments to his staff (including Roland Foster and Godfrey Smith, until the last few years among the most active of Sydney voice teachers), and announced a series of twelve orchestral and twenty-four chamber music concerts for the 1916 season. In addition, he formed a select choir of seventy-five voices that gave a series of concerts, which included Beethoven's Great Mass. The Mass was so well received that it was taken on tour to Melbourne, Ballarat, Adelaide, Bendigo, and New Zealand. In 1922 Verbrugghen left Sydney to take an appointment as conductor of the Minneapolis Symphony Orchestra. He was succeeded in Sydney by Dr. Arundel Orchard, he by Dr. Edgar Bainton, and he, in turn, by Dr. Eugene Goossens.

Under the directorship of Dr. Orchard the Conservatorium Opera School was established and the Conservatorium Symphony Orchestra was expanded and put on a semiprofessional basis.

In 1934, Sir Hamilton Harty visited Sydney and conducted the Sydney Symphony Orchestra (which had been established in 1908, but had led a somewhat checkered career) for two seasons. He recommended the permanent establishment of the orchestra, and in 1936 the Australian Broadcasting Commission acted upon his recommendation. It went further and employed, in each state, a number of key musicians on an annual basis as the nucleuses of orchestras that could be used to provide both radio programs and public concerts. At first the music provided by these orchestras was light and popular, but it soon became more sophisticated. The Broadcasting Commission also decided to engage guest conductors each year. As a result, the infant orchestras had the advantage of being conducted by such persons as Sir Malcolm Sargent (1936, 1938–1939, 1945), George Schneevoight, Sir Thomas Beecham, Eugene Ormandy, and Sir Ernest MacMillan.

Between the wars numerous famous artists toured Australia: Moiseiwitsch, Heifetz, Spivakovsky, Galli-Curci, Kreisler, Toti dal Monte, Backhaus, Chaliapin, and Paderewski; but from 1940 until 1946 the pressing demands of national defense brought visits by

404

overseas musicians almost to a halt as concerts and recitals became infrequent and often unimaginative.

Even before the end of the Second World War the allied nations were planning for the postwar years. In Australia, as elsewhere, plans for educational and general cultural changes were being made. In 1944, Eugene Ormandy was invited by the Commonwealth government to report on the state of music in Australia and to make recommendations for future policy in respect to orchestral music. Ormandy reported:

My experience in Australia has shown . . . that the existing talent pool here is not large enough to supply all capital cities with symphony orchestras, but the general artistic level is high and some individual Australian artists are comparable with artists anywhere in the world. I think that first-class musicians, capable of taking key positions in orchestras and teaching younger players should be encouraged to come to Australia. These artists should not hold leading positions in orchestras, but should teach at conservatoria. This would inspire a new cultural drive as well as teach the next generation of native-born Australian artists.[3]

Ormandy's recommendations were not acted upon. Certain individuals objected that he had overlooked the fact that many Australian musicians were in the armed forces at the time; but Ormandy was well aware of this. That these musicians had not been playing for up to five years was perhaps an additional reason why his recommendations should have been accepted. But subsequent experience has inclined many persons to agree, albeit belatedly, with Ormandy's observations. The symphony orchestras in Tasmania, Western Australia, and Queensland, especially, have had the greatest difficulty in maintaining tolerable standards of performance and have no pool of trained musicians from which to draw replacements or additional members, so that their repertoires are severely restricted. Sydney and Melbourne, on the other hand, have been able to provide an adequate number of musicians for their orchestras, which now number eighty players each.

Apropos the staffing of the Australian conservatoria, Ormandy's comments had merit. Frankly, there are no outstanding teachers of music in Australia. There is not one teacher of vocal or instrumental

[3] Commonwealth Archives Office, Ormandy to Forde, July 11, 1944, p. 3.

music, of theory, or composition whom a student from overseas would make any effort to study under. The conservatoria in Adelaide, Melbourne, and Sydney have never gained the reputation enjoyed by so many colleges of music in North America, Britain, and Europe. Had Ormandy's recommendations been implemented, conditions for music education in Australia may well have been different—provided that eminent teachers could have been induced to take up even temporary residence there. As it is, any Australian of better than average ability must plan to leave Australia to further his training overseas. In Sydney, especially, the role of the state conservatorium is far from clear. Its teachers, though officially designated as professors, enjoy neither the salary nor the public status of university professors. They are partly public servants, partly private teachers. Their students range from precocious, talented children to mature though not promising adults. Occasionally they are able to devote time to advanced work with students who have been given adequate preliminary training elsewhere.

Early in 1946 the Commonwealth government (through the Australian Broadcasting Commission), the state governments, and the councils of the capital cities agreed to subsidize one permanent symphony orchestra in each state. These orchestras would be expected to give radio broadcasts, free public concerts, a regular subscription series, and free concerts for school children. The feature of this subsidy arrangement that has appealed to overseas observers is the total absence of any government interference in programming of concerts and music: it is a unique example of subsidy without interference in artistic matters and has proved to be eminently satisfactory.

In 1948, Eugene Goossens, formerly conductor of the Rochester and Cincinnati symphony orchestras, became the first permanent conductor of the Sydney Symphony Orchestra and during the eight years of his incumbency raised it at least to the level of the second-best American and European orchestras. Guest conductors were invited each season, and such celebrated musicians as Otto Klemperer, Rafael Kubelik, John Barbirolli, and Alceo Galliera praised the orchestra's versatility and achievement. Goossens' personal enthusiasm for his task and the vast popular support he received caused a veritable awakening of interest in orchestral music in Australia. Whereas in 1936 there were fewer than 800 subscribers to the Sydney orchestral concert season, in 1954 there were 12,000. Goossens was knighted in 1955 for his services to music in Australia; his departure for Europe in 1956 was a serious loss to music, both in Sydney and in Australia. But before he left he had managed to convince both the public and the government that his orchestra needed a permanent concert hall. With startling enthusiasm, the people endorsed a plan to build a combined opera house and symphony hall.

Dr. Nicolai Malko succeeded Goossens as conductor of the Sydney Symphony Orchestra and maintained the orchestra at near its earlier competence, though without the same public support.

The orchestras established in the cities other than Sydney have fared less spectacularly, principally because of their small size and, especially in Melbourne, because of their inability to hold any conductor for more than a year or two. The Melbourne orchestra lost, in rapid succession, Rafael Kubelik, Walter Susskind, and Kurt Woess. As a result of this rapid migration of its musical directors, the orchestra has lost much of its polish and its public following.

Since the war most of the great artists of Europe and the Americas have toured Australia under the direction of either the Australian Broadcasting Commission or of commercial managements. Even a selective list could become inordinately long, but the visits of Erna Berger, Isaac Stern, Walter Gieseking, Claudio Arrau, David Oistrakh, Hans Hotter, and Paul Badura-Skoda were immensely successful. From its inception the Australian Broadcasting Commission followed a policy of providing free concerts for school children, a practice begun in Melbourne by Bernard Heinze when he was professor of music in the university there. Today almost 200,000 school children attend free concerts during the year. In 1947 the Commission extended this policy and inaugurated a series of late-afternoon concerts for young adults from sixteen to twenty-five years of age at a nominal cost—about twenty-five cents a concert. Within seven years there were over 13,000 subscribers to the youth concerts. As a result of these youth and school children's concerts, in addition to the regular schedule of subscription concerts and tours of country districts, the demands on the six symphony orchestras are extremely

407

heavy, and it has been suggested on several occasions that the remedy lies in the creation of additional orchestras—perhaps in Newcastle and Canberra or in Sydney and Melbourne.

Examinations in music were formerly conducted by the Royal Schools of Music, by the Australian Music Examinations Board (from 1918), and by Trinity College, London, but in 1952 the Board replaced the British examining bodies entirely. Over 70 per cent of the candidates at these examinations are piano students—a figure which indicates the relative rarity of competent instrumentalists in Australia. Even the highest certificates of the Board are not recognized in either Australian or overseas universities for academic purposes. Adelaide and Melbourne universities award the B.Mus. degree in applied music, music theory, and music education.

In the postwar years opera has regained some of its earlier popularity. In 1948, J. C. Williamson Ltd. imported an Italian opera company which enjoyed considerable success and played for a season of unexpected length. Subsequently the New South Wales National Opera Company (a privately sponsored enterprise) and the National Theatre Movement in Melbourne promoted seasons of opera in 1951–1953, which introduced two works by Australian composers, *Endymion* by John Antill and *The Devil Take Her* by the expatriate Arthur Benjamin.

In more recent years there has been little opera worthy of mention. The Elizabethan Theatre Trust Opera Company played in four capital cities in 1958, its efforts, in the words of one local critic, ranging "from an attempt to produce *Carmen* to a splendidly simple production of *Fidelio*." Since then opera has retained its deficit-causing *ad hoc* status.

From 1954 the public demand for the building of a center for musical performances in Sydney grew, and it was given the unofficial name Sydney Opera House. The state government duly announced an international competition for a design for the building, and it is at present under construction, financed through state lotteries.

Designed by the Danish architect Joern Utzon, the building has aroused considerable controversy on account of its unconventional design, which has been described as resembling either the billowing sails of a ship or a collapsing circus tent. The roof line, of curved concrete shells, rather closely resembles the new Trans-World Airlines terminal at New York's Idlewild Airport. During 1962 Martin Carr, stage director of London's Royal Ballet Theatre, criticized the plans for the Opera House on the grounds that stage facilities would be inadequate for the presentation of spectacular ballet or opera. He said that at $27,000,000 it would be one of the most costly opera houses in the entire world, but that its main hall would be suitable only for concerts and small stage productions and that there was insufficient space for ancillary services. Because this is to be the first integrated music center in Australia, it will be of interest to describe its facilities. The Opera House will be a complex of four halls—a large auditorium with 2,800 seats, a second hall with 1,700 seats, an experimental theatre with 500 seats, and a 400-seat hall for chamber music recitals. The main hall will be the permanent home of the Sydney Symphony Orchestra, which until now has played in the cavernous Town Hall. There will be nine stage lifts, or podiums. It had been hoped that the Opera House would be completed in 1963, but recent estimates suggest 1965. As yet no director has been selected.

Some Australian composers have already been mentioned. To their number should be added the names of Alfred Hill, now an octogenarian, but regarded by many as the dean of Australian composers; John Antill, whose *Corroboree* ballet suite, based on aboriginal legends and melodies, has been recorded and performed overseas; Charles Mackerras, whose *Pineapple Poll*, based on Gilbert and Sullivan melodies, has gained some popularity; George Clutsam, composer of the operetta *Lilac Time* (renamed *Blossom Time*), based on the music of Schubert; and Dr. Edgar Bainton, whose opera *The Pearl Tree* has been performed in Sydney. Of these composers only Hill, Antill, and Bainton could be said to have displayed any originality in composition.

Chamber music has had little success in Australia. This can be accounted for, perhaps, by the generally low level of music appreciation in the community. The Musica Viva Society was formed in Sydney in 1946 to sponsor chamber music recitals, but it was forced to disband in 1952 through lack of support. Its quartet, which displayed commendable musicianship and interpretative acumen, disbanded, the cellist accepting the first chair in the Pittsburgh Symphony Orchestra. In 1955 the Musica Viva was revived as a management organization and has sponsored the Pascal, Hungarian, and Koeckert Quartets. In the last year or two it has found warm support from recent immigrants.

Visits by the Boyd Neel String Orchestra (1947–1948) and the Griller Quartet (1950) were well received, but these groups failed to produce any greater appreciation for chamber music among the great numbers of people who attended orchestral concerts than such local groups as the Phyllis MacDonald Players and the Queensland State String Quartet had produced. The University of Tasmania has recently announced its intention to support a string quartet.

Music criticism in Australia has not achieved any stature. The daily and weekly newspapers publish brief reviews of recitals, concerts, and operatic performances, but these are usually limited to two or three hundred words. Occasionally these reviews are ascerbic or astringent in character, and they could seldom be said to be either helpful to the musicians concerned or useful to the public. Only Lindsey Browne, music critic for the *Sydney Morning Herald*, could be said to have any regular following; yet he is often quite platitudinous in his comments or else acidulous while in error. His comments on the playing of William Kapell, in 1953, caused that eminent pianist to declare that he would never play in Australia again. It was on his return to the United States that he was killed in a plane crash.

On the other hand, Dr. A. E. Floyd, who for many years presented a Sunday evening radio program of music appreciation for the Australian Broadcasting Commission, has established himself as the paragon of music commentators in Australia.

Popular music, as broadcast on commercial radio stations, as played by bands, and as purchased on sheet music or records, is almost wholly American in origin, and American musicians have, in recent years, made highly remunerative tours of Australia, playing in Sydney and Melbourne for up to ten days at a time and before single audiences of almost 15,000. Among these musicians who have recently visited Australia have been Artie Shaw, Johnny Ray, Ella FitzGerald, Frank Sinatra, Elvis Presley, Burl Ives, and Gene Krupa.

Australian versions of American hillbilly music are especially popular in rural districts. Explanations of this popularity of an essen-

410

MUSIC

tially American music form are numerous. One recent writer has put it this way:

The lyrics romanticise the cowboy, the cattleman; his isolation and his confusion in cities; his triumph over city-slickers and the sorrow of his one true love; his good friend the horse, and his faithful dog. . . . At the very least, they are socially acceptable symbolic expressions of the sorrow that's too deep for tears and too self-consciously Australian to cause actual weeping.[4]

Recordings of this type of song by local performers, who often adapt the lyrics for Australian audiences, are in constant demand. A recent hit in Australia, "The Pub with No Beer," doubtless achieved its great popularity by virtue of its clear statement of Australian attitudes. But, in general, Australian popular music is slavishly imitative of United States models; it follows jazz, swing, rock and roll, calypso, or whatever is the current fashion in New York or San Francisco at a few months' distance.

In Australia, however, jazz (which has had a strong and constant following for many years) has produced some musicians of originality and uncommon versatility. The Australian Jazz Quartet spent almost five years on tour in both Europe and North America and was generously praised. In commenting on the jazz convention held in Adelaide in 1962, Edgar Poole has provided an informed account of the status of this musical form in Australia today:

The Australian jazzman does not have the same emotional make-up as Negro originators and it is not surprising that our jazz should have its own flavor. This is a solid earthiness of sound and a more consistent rhythmic base, with none of the subtle manipulations of beat or the delicate sprung rhythm of the Creole bands. However, modern recording processes have enabled us to hear much more easily the work of a much wider range of bands than was available in the late 'forties when Australian jazz really boomed and the earthiness, often heaviness, of much of our playing could be due to laziness or indifference as much as to more stolid emotions. And there is an unhealthily cultish feeling against any playing that strays too far away from the accepted norm. In fact, it was this lack of musicality and distrust of originality that deterred American cornet player King Fisher, undisputed star of last year's convention who was, unfortunately, unable to attend this convention, from remaining in Melbourne (which would have been lucrative) and led him to seek musical satisfaction (and find near-penury) in Perth.

[4] University of Sydney, *Current Affairs Bulletin*, Dec. 15, 1958, p. 56.

411

Good jazz singers are rare here and the defection to England of Paul Marks and Elvie Simmons has left us much the poorer, except for a promising young blues singer, Judy Jaques, in Melbourne. But the singing that made Ron Williams possibly the most popular individual performer at this convention was of a different order to the folk and classic blues of the others; it was not a singer's singing but a vocalisation of his bass playing, his phrasing chordal rather than overridingly melodic. This is jazz singing in the truest sense, a sense rarely experienced here, and then usually in the heat of very impromptu jazz making.[5]

Although great numbers of subscribers attend orchestral concerts in Australia, and although the country has produced a number of highly talented musicians, there is not the same vitality in music as in many of the other arts. There are no great musical artists who are also teachers; the really competent must leave for advanced instruction overseas, and when there they find that they must stay in order to exercise their talents. There have been periods in which large choral groups have excelled, periods in which opera was popular. At the moment orchestral music has taken the public's fancy. But it remains to be seen whether it, too, will be superseded in due course.

The weakest link in music as a cultural force in Australia remains the absence of adequate instrumental instruction as a part of public-school music education and the equivocal position of the conservatoria of music. Not until instrumental music instruction is provided as a part of the regular school program will schools be able to form orchestras and bands, will towns and cities be able to speak of their philharmonic orchestras, and will music be regarded as a worthy profession. Not until then will music be a force in Australian culture instead of the ornament that it now is.

BIBLIOGRAPHY

Brewer, Frank. *Drama and Music in New South Wales.* 1892.
Moresby, Isabelle. *Australia Makes Music.* 1948.
Orchard, W. Arundel. *Music in Australia.* 1952.

[5] *Bulletin*, Feb. 24, 1962, p. 28.

412

RECREATION

EDGAR WATERS

SCHOLARS, especially social scientists, are becoming increasingly more interested in what people do with their leisure, why they choose to do one thing rather than another, and what effect their leisure has upon them. There has been little scholarly investigation of leisure in Australia, so the following conclusions are impressionistic and tentative. However, on one fundamental point there seems to be general agreement, which apparently is justified: Australians place an unusually high value upon leisure. They take their right to leisure seriously.

It might reasonably be argued that it is not unusual for people to place a high value upon leisure, particularly people in relatively rich, highly industrialized countries like Australia. Do Australians, then, take their right to leisure more seriously than, say, Americans, Englishmen, Germans, Swedes? Since we cannot rely upon much more than impressions, those of outsiders may be worth more than those of Australians, and samples of comment which seem to be unanimous will be quoted.

413

PATTERN OF AUSTRALIAN CULTURE

John Douglas Pringle's *Australian Accent* is one of the more interesting of recent books about Australia written by an outsider. Pringle is a Scot and for five years was editor of the *Sydney Morning Herald*, the most august of Australian newspapers. He thinks that the great expansion of wealth over the last thirty years has corrupted a great many Australians, but not all. "The majority of the working class, for instance, remain amazingly contemptuous of material possessions which are well within their reach and continue to prefer their leisure to the chance of earning still more money." Pringle approves: "This refusal to be rushed into an endless competition for more and bigger cars, washing machines, radio sets, etc., has undoubtedly saved Australia so far from the worst excesses of American capitalism." [1]

A correspondent of the *Sydney Morning Herald*, apparently an American, writing on February 6, 1962 after a year's residence in Australia, sees the same tendencies and deplores them. He says, "The most striking difference between the American labour unions' demands and the Australians' is that the Americans demand more pay, more material fringe benefits, and more opportunity to earn overtime, while the Australian unions seem to concentrate on doing less and less work." The context makes it clear that he means working fewer and fewer hours.

If Australians do indeed place a rather remarkable emphasis upon abundant leisure as an element of a high standard of living or as a desired way of life, the reasons can probably be found in Australian history as much as in the present social and cultural pattern of Australian life. Half a century after the first settlement at Sydney, some observers already had the impression that Australians took their right to leisure seriously, and the impression has been received by outside observers at all times since.

Lieutenant Colonel Godfrey Charles Mundy, for example, was an English official serving in the colonial administration of New South Wales in the 1840's. Of this period, he wrote that it is strange, but

the well brought up and pretty maidens of the middle and servant classes of Sydney do not appear to be much sought in marriage. Yet it is undoubtedly in these classes that the well-known preponderance of males

[1] J. D. Pringle, *Australian Accent* (London: Chatto and Windus, 1958), pp. 101–102.

exists. The single men do not want wives, and the responsibilities and encumbrances of family life. They prefer working hard—working like slaves—four or five days, and "larking" the rest of the week.[2]

Of course, in Sydney in the 1840's some of the single young men were transported convicts; and it may be questioned whether very many even of the free men could afford two or three clear days of leisure in each week, no matter how hard they worked on the other four or five. Even so, Mundy's comment is striking as evidence of an early and now characteristic tendency to place a high value upon leisure.

It might be remarked, incidentally, that in Sydney at this time a rather high number of children were born out of wedlock. Perhaps this is partly to be explained by the fact that the young men, though not inclined to marriage, were fully inclined to "larking." However, if we can only guess that the young men devoted an important part of their free time to the pursuit of the pretty maidens of Sydney, we can be reasonably sure that they devoted a good deal of their leisure to the pursuit of outdoor games. A witness for this is John Dunmore Lang, a Scottish-born Presbyterian divine who became an important man of public affairs in Australia:

Let the reader turn over a file of the colonial newspapers for 1833 and he will find them stuffed almost to nausea with advertisements and accounts of races, cricket matches, boxing matches and regattas, with challenges to fight or to run or to row. The energy of the native mind seems of late to have been diverted almost exclusively into this frivolous channel.[3]

Let the reader turn over a file of the Australian newspapers for 1962—preferably looking at the issues of Monday mornings, with their reports of the sermons preached on Sunday mornings—and he will find clergymen still protesting vehemently that Australians devote a great deal too much of their energy to sport. But more than a century of exhortation from the godly has not caused Australians to abate their strong liking for this frivolous pursuit.

In fairness, it should perhaps be added that attacks on sport are made by a very small minority of clergymen and that they are not

[2] Godfrey Charles Mundy, *Our Antipodes* (London: Bentley, 1855), p. 189.
[3] Quoted in A. G. L. Shaw, *The Story of Australia* (London: Faber, 1955), p. 101.

generally aimed at sport per se. They may be attacks on playing games on the Sabbath, on the association of some sports with gambling, or part of a general charge that Australians are far too given to the pursuit of pleasure and—as part of this pleasure seeking—are excessively devoted to sport.

Lang may have exaggerated the colonists' devotion to sport. But there is plenty of other historical evidence to suggest that Australians have been markedly fond of outdoor sports all through their short history. A survey made in 1948 gives us some basis—not altogether reliable—for making numerical statements about participation in sport in Australia today. It would appear that in 1948 three Australians in every four watched outdoor games, at least occasionally, and that four Australians in every ten regarded watching games as an important leisure activity. About four Australians in every ten actually played one sport or another. Playing sports, it seemed, was the most favored way of using leisure for two Australians in every ten, while watching sport was the most favored way for one in every ten.

The figures for those who play sports and for those who regard sports as their favorite way of using leisure should probably be higher, for in the survey which produced these figures only adults were interviewed, and, of course, adolescents engage in more organized physical activities than their elders. Also, in the years since this survey was made, there seems to have been some decline in "spectator" sports, but probably a significant increase in "participation" sports.

A great many writers, not all of them Australian, have remarked on the "phenomenal" record of Australians in international sporting competitions. No doubt there are many factors involved in this record of success disproportionate to the size of the country's population. Superior methods of training, for example, are said to have something to do with the current eminence of Australians in swimming and tennis. No doubt the "star-making" system of certain Australian sports is a contributory factor, but this system is something that Australia shares with a good many other countries. No doubt the fact that so many Australians watch sport encourages the players. And, of course, in Australia as in other countries, the leading sportsmen and sportswomen win great fame and prestige, even knighthoods and regal honors. In the rather gloomy palace of culture in Melbourne which houses the State Library of Victoria and the best art gallery in Australia, there is also prominently displayed the stuffed hide of the race horse Phar Lap, regarded as among the greatest of winners of the Melbourne Cup. (Phar Lap was bred in New Zealand, but Australians have been happy to regard him—like a good many other New Zealanders—as Australian by adoption.) Australians may be rather remarkable in their attitude to race horses. But there is no reason for thinking that they are more inclined to idolize great sportsmen than are Americans, for example, or Frenchmen.

We should probably, then, look for additional factors to explain Australian success in international sporting competitions. It seems probable that the level of active participation in sport is higher in Australia than in most countries. It is difficult to find figures which allow firm comparisons, but there does seem to be some justification for the general Australian belief that in Australia more people play outdoor games than in any other country (relative to population, of course). Probably even more important than this is the fact that so many Australians play sport seriously, if not professionally.

A survey of leisure was made in Canada in 1946, of much the same kind as the survey made in Australia in 1948. Canada is a country which might reasonably be compared with Australia, though climatic differences might influence the level of participation in outdoor sports. Watching sports appeared to be the favorite use of leisure for 6 per cent of Canadians, as against 10 per cent of Australians. Playing outdoor games appeared to be the favorite use of leisure for 7 per cent of Canadians, but for 19 per cent of Australians. (The Canadian total may be increased if we add 4 per cent who regarded hunting or fishing as a sport. Even so, we would have a Canadian total of 11 per cent, against an Australian total of 19 per cent.)

We can assume that for most of the Australians interviewed sport and outdoor games were synonymous. Because of the scarcity of edible game, hunting as a sport is not of much importance in Australia. Certainly it is not nearly so popular as it is in Canada and the United States. Kangaroos are found only in the country districts —and they are not good eating. Fishing, also, is not so important

417

in Australia. It is true that here, as in a number of other countries, there appears to have been an increase in the number of people actively participating in sport and that an important part of the increase has been in sports which are not—or not primarily—competitive games: boating, skin diving, skiing. But there has also been an increase in the numbers of people playing competitive games. There has been a decline, probably a very considerable decline, in the numbers playing tennis, which in 1948 was by far the most often played of all outdoor games; but this has been offset in large degree by a remarkable increase in the numbers playing squash. And though tennis was much the most popular game in 1948, large numbers of Australians played other games; out of every hundred Australians, it appeared that three played bowls; three, football; four, cricket; and five, golf. It is unlikely that the numbers playing cricket have fallen; it is probable that the numbers playing football have risen; and it is certain that the numbers playing golf and bowls have risen. (By bowls here is meant the outdoor game that Drake is reputed to have played before sailing out to give battle to the Spanish Armada; American-style indoor bowling has been introduced into Australia only very recently; it gives indications of becoming popular.)

The evidence of these surveys is not to be relied upon too heavily, and the comparisons which can be made between Australia and countries other than Canada can be relied upon even less. But so far as the evidence goes, it does suggest that, in comparison with other countries, very high numbers of Australians take an active part in outdoor sports, and more especially in competitive games.

These things probably go a long way toward explaining Australian success in international sporting competitions. How, though, are we to explain this level of interest in playing sport and this emphasis upon competitive games?

No doubt these things are in part a cultural heritage from the British Isles, where so many sports were invented or developed. No doubt they are also to be explained partly in terms of the climate, which favors outdoor activities the year round in most places, especially in the coastal fringes where the greater part of the population lives. The Tasmanian winters are cold, but not cold enough to discourage football; the Queensland summers are hot, but not hot enough to discourage cricket.

Probably one should also look for explanations in terms of personality traits. It has been suggested there may be a connection, in the case of some men, between participation in outdoor games and fear of being thought, or of thinking oneself, to be homosexual or overfeminine (with the assumption that there is frequently a close relationship between feminine personality traits in men and homosexuality). The history of Australian attitudes to homosexuality has not been explored, but it is one which would probably pay exploration. At an early period, conditions of life caused homosexuality to be both widespread and tolerated in sections of the working class. Today, Australian attitudes toward homosexuality appear to be more repressive than English or American attitudes. It seems quite possible that a study of homosexuality in Australia and of attitudes to it could throw interesting light on Australian attitudes to certain games.

Some observers consider Australians to be markedly aggressive; this might help to explain the emphasis on competitive games. On the other hand, competitive games—especially ones like golf and tennis, but also some team games such as cricket—are often played in an atmosphere of pleasant sociability rather than of fierce competitiveness.

Possibly the aggressive egalitarianism which many Australians believe to be a distinctive feature of the national character may help to explain the origins of the emphasis on competitive games. At the beginning of the nineteenth century the playing of organized sport was a pastime of "gentlemen" more often than of workers. The native-born Australian worker of the time does seem to have been very much inclined to assert that he was as good as any English officer and gentleman, if not better. Sport was one of the forms of upper-class culture which lower-class Australians could readily adopt and in which they could hope to prove themselves as good as or better than men of superior social standing.

It has become common for people in many countries to feel that success of their country's sportsmen in international competitions is a great cause for national pride. It may be that feelings of this kind have been especially powerful in Australia (which is said to

419

possess an overgrown national inferiority complex) and particularly in relation to sporting matches between Australia and England. Many Australians still believe that Englishmen are prone to patronize them, to treat them as colonials; and this assumed attitude is, of course, resented. At times, remarkably intense national feelings have been aroused by the cricket matches between Australia and England. For quite a long time Australian delight at outshining the English in cricket may very well have been a stimulus to making that game popular; the same kind of stimulus may have been at work helping to make other games popular at various times.

Cricket seems to have the longest recorded history of any team game in Australia. A match was played in Sydney in 1826. Cricket is played throughout the country, and it is played by men of all social classes. A cricket team in a country town is likely to be a very mixed bunch in terms of social grouping, status, and income. Most Australian men have at least some idea of how to bowl or handle a bat, and even if they play virtually no sport at all, they may still take part in at least one annual "social" cricket match. Matches of this kind may be arranged between two institutions or between different parts of one institution (two departments of a university, for example) or between different groups of workers in an institution— professional staff against clerical staff, teachers against students, and so on. A social match of this kind is much more likely to be cricket than any other form of sport.

Cricket is one of the more important spectator sports, but it has nothing like the popularity of football. Even enthusiastic cricketers can sometimes be induced to admit that the game is, if not actually boring, at any rate "a bit slow to watch." Nevertheless, attendances at important matches are quite large, and the Australian Broadcasting Commission finds it worth-while to televise interstate and international games, or parts of them; cricket is a leisurely game, and a Test Match (or international contest) may last three or four days. At times, international matches have drawn enormous crowds of spectators, and they always arouse considerable general interest even though the numbers who actually go to watch the games may be rather small. Queries about the progress of the Tests and comments on performances challenge comment on the weather as the chief item of small talk; newspaper offices erect boards outside their buildings and show the changing scores in all the detail that cricket requires; radio stations announce the latest scores in the intervals between programs. It is hard to say just how many people pay more than casual attention to this constant stream of information, but it is clear that most men and a good many women do give it at least casual attention.

Cricket matches between Australia and England have been going on for a long time. An English team toured Australia in 1861–1862, and an Australian team first toured England in 1878. In 1882 an Australian victory occasioned the remark that English cricket was dead, and its ashes could now be carried to Australia. The ashes—a figure of speech only—remain the symbol of victory in the Tests between Australia and England.

It has already been suggested that Australian feelings about cricket matches against England probably reflected tensions in Anglo-Australian relations. Feelings about the Tests and attendance at them were never so high as in the early 1930's. This was, of course, a time of acute social tension and frustration within Australia; these feelings seem to have caused a flare-up of the old feeling that Australian troubles were due to English machinations. And if the intense Australian desire to win the Tests probably reflected suspicion and resentment of England, the matches themselves helped to generate further ill-feeling toward the English; Australians claimed that the English body-line bowlers were deliberately trying to cause physical damage to the Australian batsmen. It is unlikely that Test cricket will ever again arouse such intensity of interest, unless some new and unexpected cause for tension in Anglo-Australian relations should emerge.

Tests against other cricket-playing countries are also arranged from time to time. The desire that Australia should win, which still shows itself fairly strongly when Tests are being played against England, is not so evident when Australia is playing India or the West Indies or New Zealand. A West Indian team which toured Australia in the summer of 1960–1961 played dashing and light-hearted cricket and attracted unusually large numbers of spectators. There seemed to be a quite general feeling that it was a pity that

421

they lost the Test series; even the Australian captain, in a television interview, seemed slightly apologetic about having led the winning team.

Football is by far the most important spectator sport in Australia. In 1948, two men in every five and one woman in every five said that they sometimes watched a football match, and about six men in every hundred actually played the sport.

Australians play three forms of football. Soccer, the most popular form of football throughout most of the world, has been the least important in Australia. Australians have evolved one form of football which is played nowhere else in the world, as Americans have also done; it is called Australian rules, or simply rules, and is by far the most popular form of football in some of the larger centers of population.[4] Consequently, such international success as Australia has had in football competitions has been in Rugby, which is played with enthusiasm in only a few countries. In Australia, Rugby is played chiefly in New South Wales and Queensland, Australian rules football in Victoria.

Soccer in the past has been the least important form of football in Australia. It has been widely played in only a few areas—mostly coal fields and steel towns—where working-class migrants from Great Britain settled in solid groups. Its chief centers have been in New South Wales. But soccer is the favorite spectator sport of many of the postwar migrants from Europe, and this has led to a great increase in its popularity. Soccer also seems to be growing in popularity among young native-born Australians in some places, probably at the expense of Rugby. This may be related to the fact that soccer is a less violent form of football.

Because it is the chief spectator sport, football has suffered from the recent general decline in spectator attendance at sports matches.

The 1948 survey showed that many more people played tennis than any other outdoor game. It was the one game played by women more than men; it was also predominantly a middle-class game. Since 1948, tennis has declined somewhat in importance, and there has been a considerable decline in the numbers watching competition

---

[4] It has been claimed that Australian rules is derived from Rugby; another suggestion is that, like American football, it is a descendant of a form of the game common in Ireland.

tennis; today, in Sydney at least, the numbers who watch tennis are not much higher than the numbers who watch soccer. But there has also been a decline in the numbers playing tennis. This has been explained in a number of ways; for instance, it is said that the boom in urban land values has resulted in a great decrease in the number of privately owned tennis courts. This is no doubt true, but tennis courts overgrown with weeds are no uncommon sight on the suburban periphery and in the country areas. At the same time there has been a remarkable increase in the number of people playing squash, which is the nearest rival to tennis. In 1955 there was one public squash court in Sydney; by 1961 there were more than ninety. The shift from tennis to squash is perhaps not much more than a change in fashion, a shift from one game to another closely related game. However, squash does seem to have attracted more men than women away from tennis. Many players, and probably more men than women, think of playing sport largely as a way of keeping fit. One brief game of squash, especially to a busy person, may appear more desirable than a leisurely game of tennis because it more rapidly uses up the same amount of energy and presumably prevents the formation of the same amount of superfluous and socially undesirable fat.

In any case, despite the inroads of squash, tennis remains the most played of all athletic games in Australia. But, in addition to squash, golf, bowls, and various water sports are becoming increasingly popular, and they are all probably affecting the popularity of tennis in some degree.

Fifteen years ago, golf was apparently played by one Australian in twenty; a few years later, one writer remarked of Australia that "the prevalence of public golf courses is exceeded only in Scotland." Golf is undoubtedly growing in popularity in Australia. A general increase of wealth in the community is making the game available to more groups, and golf is losing the association it once had with high-income or socially exclusive groups. Nevertheless, some Australian golf clubs maintain their social exclusiveness; a few golf clubs, for example, exclude Jews, though such overt anti-Jewish discrimination is very rare in Australia.

Outdoor bowls is a middle-class game which is most often taken up in middle age, perhaps in late middle age, and continued into old age. Bowls is a competitive team game, but a rather gentle one, and

423

its purely social aspects seem to be fairly important. There has been a remarkable increase in the number of women playing the game: in New South Wales the number of women belonging to bowling clubs increased from fewer than 4,000 in 1952 to more than 24,000 in 1961.

The increasing popularity of bowls is no doubt one element in a significant shift in habits among Australians in late middle age and old age. This shift is associated with a complex of factors, including changes in family relationships and income distribution, which it is hardly possible to consider here. But, in general, it may be said that it is part of a developing pattern of life in which older adults lead a much more active social life outside the family circle than they once did.

A few other team games—hockey, baseball, polo, basketball—attract relatively small numbers of players. In one or two cities, night baseball has achieved some popularity as a spectator sport during the winter. The players are sometimes cricketers who are "keeping their eye in" during the off season. Softball, basketball, and one or two other games are played to a limited extent in schools and to an even more limited extent by adults. Field athletics flourish in the schools and, to a lesser extent, in the universities; outside these institutions, they are encouraged only by a small number of adult clubs. Australian success in track athletics is due primarily to a small number of gifted young men and women, stimulated by the glamour of big international competitions and the associated star-making.

Competitive swimming is mainly an activity of school children and adolescents. The success of Australians in international swimming competitions—as in field athletics and tennis—is due to the selection and intensive training of a small number of highly gifted performers. But swimming, like tennis and unlike field athletics, is a highly popular participator sport with adults as well as with children. All the largest Australian cities are on the coast, with easy access to beaches, and enjoy climates that make swimming an enjoyable activity for several months of the year. Away from the sea, most towns of any size have public swimming pools. In the public schools of many states it is obligatory for children to learn to swim, and there are few Australians who cannot swim.

Beaches are patrolled by young men organized into surf lifesaving

424

clubs. Surf carnivals—with competitions between clubs in such things as the technique of rescuing swimmers, swimming, and surf-boat racing—attract numbers of spectators, but perhaps largely because a ready-made audience is often assembled on the beach.

Recreational swimming appears to have been popular in Australia, at least among men, almost from the beginning of settlement. In Sydney in 1849, one writer noted that there was "a bathing cottage at Government House, a large hulk moored and fitted as a public bathing-house in Wooloomooloo Bay, and every villa near the harbour possesses a like convenience." [5] In that year, apparently for the first time on record, a swimmer was attacked by a shark in the harbor. "Not many days later I saw a foolhardy fellow swimming about in the very same place with a straw hat on his head and a cigar in his mouth!" [6] Today only the very foolhardy (or the ignorant new arrival from Europe) would swim in Sydney's harbor, except in areas that are enclosed with sharkproof netting.

Although swimming seems to have been popular so early, surfing from the ocean beaches established its great popularity only in the present century. Prudish laws about bathing in public places helped to cause this delay, and brief bathing costumes on the beaches still cause an annual agitation. The arts of surfing, shooting the breakers, and riding surfboards seem to have been learned only gradually and from Pacific Islanders. The first Australian to learn to shoot the breakers is said to have been taught by an Islander named Tommy Tanna, who worked as a gardener in the Sydney suburb of Manly. Tommy Tanna was used as a generic name in Queensland for Melanesian indentured laborers, but the distinction between Melanesians and Polynesians was probably not widely drawn by Australians, and this Tommy Tanna may have been Polynesian. The art of surfboard riding was certainly learned from Hawaiians.

Another water sport, skin diving, has established its popularity only since the end of the Second World War. The numbers of skin divers and spear fishermen have increased remarkably over the last few years—naturally, not so much in the colder waters of the southern states as in New South Wales and Queensland—and it looks as though their numbers will continue to increase at a rapid rate. Fatal encounters with sharks have been very rare, and the occasional kill-

[5] Mundy, *op. cit.*, p. 195.   [6] *Ibid.*, p. 196.

ings do not seem to deter skin divers any more than they do surfers.

Sailing has long been a popular Australian sport, and Sydney has developed its own special class of small sailing craft. Ocean yacht racing on any considerable scale is a more recent development, reflecting postwar affluence. The course of the more important races is now followed with much general interest, especially the annual Sydney to Hobart race. Large crowds gather to watch the yachts leaving Sydney, sailing down the harbor, and out through the Heads. Aerial cinematography keeps television viewers aware of the progress of the race.

Postwar affluence has also caused a great increase in the popularity of power boating and, along with it, water-skiing. Australia is not well endowed with rivers and inland lakes suitable for these sports, but man-made dams help, and along the coasts there are many lagoons and sheltered inlets and estuaries. Over the past few years, cars with boat trailers attached have become a common sight, and the boom in this sport gives every sign of continuing to grow.

Where so much of the population lives along the coast, sea and estuary fishing has naturally always been a popular form of sport. In many Australian families the breadwinner takes his annual holidays during the summer school vacation, and the whole family spends a week or two at the seaside. For adult males, fishing is perhaps the most important aspect of such a holiday. Native Australian freshwater fish are not of the kind that greatly excite the fisherman-sportsman. Fishing in streams has always been an important form of relaxation for many men, especially for men in lower income groups, and it has the added motive of providing cheap food or a welcome change of diet. Mountain streams in Tasmania and the southeastern mainland have been planted with trout for a long time now, and trout fishing is growing in popularity, especially among men in higher income groups.

Hunting is much less important than fishing as a sport for a number of reasons: the relative lack of interesting game, the lack of hunting grounds near the main centers of population, and the stringent laws governing licenses for the possession of firearms. There is a good deal of rather casual shooting of small game by country dwellers; duck shooting is undertaken in a more planned and definitely organized fashion. A few, sufficiently wealthy and sufficiently adventurous in temperament, shoot buffalo or crocodiles in the Northern Territory. In many pastoral districts big kangaroo shoots are sometimes organized, as much for utilitarian reasons—keeping down the numbers of animals which compete with sheep and cattle for grass—as for sport.

Bushwalking has attractions for some city dwellers. This may mean a fairly gentle day's ramble along well-worn tracks, carrying nothing more than food for one or two meals. Or it may mean a week in rough mountainous country, finding one's way along little-used tracks, perhaps needing to do fairly expert map reading, and carrying on one's back large quantities of food, a sleeping bag, and a tent. There are no professional guides, but bushwalking clubs do their best to dissuade beginners from venturing into difficult country except in the company of veterans. Bushwalking is chiefly carried out in the hills and sometimes in fairly heavily wooded country. There is no lack of suitable country close to the major cities. In the next few years it is possible that there will be a development of guided horseback tours through some of the areas that are already popular with bushwalkers (for example, the Snowy Mountains and the Victorian high plains), but so far there is very little of this.

There are a few spectator sports which we have not yet mentioned. Boxing and wrestling attract relatively small and decreasing audiences. Bicycle racing was once an important spectator sport, but with growing affluence it has largely disappeared, though its place is partly taken by motorcycle racing. Motorcar racing has not been of any great importance until very recently, but is now growing in popularity. The enthusiasts are proud of the fact that, though the sport is so little developed in Australia, the country has already produced one world champion driver, Jack Brabham. Since about 1960 Australian competitions have attracted a few leading drivers from overseas.

In the 1860's there was a gold rush to Kiandra in the Snowy Mountains. Skis had already been introduced into this country for utilitarian purposes; the miners took up skiing for sport during the winter months when digging was difficult. They formed what is reputedly the oldest ski club in the world. Despite this early start, and despite the fact that the Australian snow fields exceed those of Switzerland in area (though the snow lies on them for a relatively short period of months), skiing did not develop much until after the First World War. The reason was partly that the snow fields, though they lie in the southeast, the most heavily populated region of Australia, are considerable distances from the major cities. (It is about three hundred miles from Sydney to the snow fields of the Snowy Mountains, though Melbourne is closer to the Victorian fields.) Since the Second World War, better communications with these isolated mountain areas and greater wealth in the community have brought about a remarkable increase in the popularity of snow sports among people living in the southeast. The influence of European migrants has also helped to bring about this popularity, and large-scale hydroelectric engineering projects in the snow country have helped to improve communications. But snow sports remain expensive and out of the reach of most Australians.

Horse racing occupies a position all its own. It is an important spectator sport, but not nearly so important as a number of others. Yet it is a common charge of Australian moralists that their fellow countrymen display an interest in horse racing that amounts almost to a mania and certainly to a great national vice. Press and radio would give the impression that there is a good deal of truth in the charge. The newspapers devote a major part of their sporting pages to news about horse racing; the majority of radio stations devote most of each Saturday afternoon to broadcasting descriptions of the races.

One race, the Melbourne Cup, is greeted every November with a tremendous display of interest throughout the country. The race was first run in 1861; by 1865 some public servants and bank officers were given a half-day holiday on the day of the Cup; today it is a public holiday throughout Victoria. And throughout the whole country, the pace of work slackens for a few minutes and busy city streets momentarily appear almost deserted, as everyone who can crowd near a radio does so to hear a description of the race. Even in schoolrooms, transistor radios whisper under desks; and pupils as well as teachers have organized a sweepstake on the Cup. The Sydney headmaster who gave his pupils a half-day holiday for the Cup of 1960 was thought to have gone a little too far, however, and was reprimanded for it.

An observer in the 1880's argued:

428

The popularity of the Melbourne Cup is largely due to its being the great gambling event of the year. Every township in the remote bush has its guinea sweepstake over the Cup, every town hovel its half-crown one. . . . Everybody backs his fancy, if only because, unless he is a strict Methodist, it would be peculiar not to do so.[7]

Just so, today, almost everyone gambles a small amount on the Cup, if only because it would be peculiar not to do so. But gambling will not pass as the explanation of the popularity of this race above all others; that remains a mystery. A very high proportion of the people who bet on the Cup do not bet on anything else during the whole year.

Gambling explains the peculiar importance of horse racing in Australia. Australians gamble on the results of horse racing as the English gamble on the results of football games. Off-the-course betting flourishes, though it is illegal in some states and was in others until recently. An "S. P. bookie" (starting price bookmaker) may be found operating in the bar of a great many Australian pubs on Saturday afternoons. Housewives can sit at home and do their betting by telephone. And the spectators at horse races are often more interested in gambling than in horses. A good many of them attend night greyhound races with the same enthusiasm as they attend daytime horse races, and again because their chief interest is gambling.

It has been estimated from a public opinion poll that rather more than half the Australian population gambles on horse racing. Close to 90 per cent of the population buy tickets in lotteries, most of which are state-run. But many of the people who regularly invest small sums in buying lottery tickets hardly regard this as a form of gambling and perhaps do not indulge in other forms. Some of them would indignantly condemn other forms of gambling, or gambling in the abstract. And, though the figure for betting on horse racing is high, it must be remembered that this is much the most important form of gambling in Australia. Card playing does not seem to be as important a form of leisure activity in Australia as in some other countries, though it is certainly not unimportant; however, it seems likely that it is seldom accompanied by gambling involving significant amounts of money. Other gambling games that seem to

[7] R. E. N. Towpeny, *Town Life in Australia* (London: Eliot Stock, 1883), p. 213.

be of some importance in other comparable countries—dice and bingo, for example—are either virtually unknown or else unimportant in Australia. Two-up, a gambling game using coins which is of English origin, has had a long history in Australia and figures largely in the country's folklore. But it is illegal, and although some large "schools" (regular games) exist in most cities and it is sometimes very important in such places as construction camps or army camps during wartime, it seems in fact to be an important form of gambling for very small numbers of people.

It is difficult to obtain reliable information about the real extent of gambling in Australia, or in most other countries, partly because important forms of gambling are often illegal. It is clear enough that gambling is an important leisure activity of Australians, but there does not seem at present—despite the claims of the moralists—to be clear evidence that Australians are significantly more addicted to it than are people in other comparable societies. There is even less evidence that Australians are more likely than Englishmen or Americans to gamble on a scale which has important consequences for their economic situation.

Night sport is not greatly developed in Australia. Trotting, dog racing, boxing, and wrestling are the chief night spectator sports, and these are not the most important of spectator sports. Night baseball is important in one or two places, chiefly, perhaps, in Adelaide; the reason for this is rather obscure, since Adelaide shows, in general, much less sign of American cultural influence than many other cities in Australia. In some places, a trial is being made of night football, but it can hardly be said to have firmly established itself as yet. Tennis and squash are the participator games most widely played at night, though American-style tenpin bowling is becoming popular very rapidly.

Visiting friends in their homes—perhaps just to sit and talk, perhaps to play cards, sometimes to look at the slides of someone's holiday trip—is an important leisure activity for many, especially for older adults. Parties in private homes are also important, and they are probably becoming considerably more important for younger adults and adolescents, especially in middle-class groups. At such parties, there is often dancing to music provided by a phonograph. Formal balls, in public rooms of one kind or another, are important social occasions for some people. The dance "palais," where public dances were held on two or three nights of each week, was once important in the lives of many Australians, especially of the working class and lower middle class. It has undoubtedly lost a great deal of its importance over the last twenty years or so. Nineteenth-century observers noted that Australians seldom took much trouble to acquire skill in dancing; and that, at least, has not changed. Probably most Australians can get through a waltz or a fox trot, but relatively few of them can perform such simple and well-established dances at all well. Even fewer would essay the more recently introduced and more intricate Latin-American ballroom dances. An attempt was made a few years ago to popularize American square dancing; its popularity was brief. It is probable that more recent innovations—rock and roll and the twist—also will not survive relatively brief spells of popularity, chiefly among adolescents.

A decade or so ago listening to the radio was the most favored way of spending the evening. Since then, television has become available in the chief cities, and thus to a majority of the people of Australia. Although radio is now relatively much less important than television, it is still an important medium of both information and entertainment. There have been changes in the kinds of programs broadcast, as a result of the competition from television. Above all, and especially in the cities, there is an increasing emphasis upon the broadcasting of popular music. In some cities, programs of popular music take up almost half of all broadcasting time and more than half in the case of some stations. Most of this music is provided by recordings of American performers. Many of the "soap operas" broadcast in the morning programs intended for housewives are also of American origin. American radio comedy, in contrast, never seemed to have much appeal for Australian audiences, though some English radio comedy seems to have great appeal for the minority audience which listens to the stations controlled by the Australian Broadcasting Commission.

Television stations began operating in Sydney and Melbourne in 1956 and 1957 and were established in the capital cities of all the states by 1960. Television very rapidly established itself as a most important source of entertainment for a great mass of Australians. Sydney, for example, is a city of a little more than two million

431

people. Its first television station began broadcasting at the end of 1956; since 1957 there have been three stations in operation. By the end of 1960, it was estimated that the television audience at peak viewing hours was approaching one million—almost half the people in the city. Because of the concentration of Australia's population into a few urban centers, the introduction of television into six cities meant that broadcasts could be received by a majority of homes. During 1962 and 1963, television stations will begin broadcasting in a number of provincial cities and country towns.

During the lengthy public discussions which preceded the introduction of television into Australia, many pious statements were made—by spokesmen for government and the television industry, among others—about the need to broadcast as many Australian-made programs as possible. In practice, the financial interests of the commercially owned stations led them to use an increasing number of filmed programs, purchased from overseas. According to a report of the Australian Broadcasting Control Board, "by December 1959, the majority of commercial stations televised practically nothing but imported films between 7:30 P.M. and 9:30 P.M. on any evening, and only one station presented a regular weekly local programme (of 30 minutes duration) between those hours." According to the same report, "approximately 88 per cent. of the films were imported from the United States of America, and 10 per cent. from the United Kingdom."

During 1960 the Commonwealth government offered some advice and gave some instructions to the television stations, both intended to bring about an increase in the amount of Australian material broadcast, but the position has not greatly altered. The greater part of the Australian material broadcast by the commercial stations consists of news or of programs like quiz shows. At the peak viewing hours in the evenings, the greater part of the material broadcast is still American. The commercial stations have been under constant attack for this policy, notably from the Labor party and from those who might hope to gain employment if there were more Australian television production. They have also been under attack because most of the metropolitan stations are under the control of metropolitan daily newspaper companies and because of further links with radio broadcasting networks. It is argued that this concentration of

432

control of the chief media of public information is dangerous. None of these attacks has had much effect, either on the stations or on the conservative Commonwealth government; but it is conceivable that there may be many changes in Australian television if a Labor government comes to power in Canberra.

In addition to the commercial stations there are radio and television stations, controlled by the Australian Broadcasting Commission, that cater to a minority audience, for example, the audience for "serious" music, which is almost entirely ignored by the commercial stations. The Commission provides educational programs for schools and many service programs for rural listeners. It broadcasts the debates in the Commonwealth parliament and operates a short-wave station, aimed chiefly at listeners in Asia. It broadcasts more Australian material than do the commercial television and radio stations, and its overseas material is more often English than American.

In Australia, as elsewhere, the growth of television has led to a considerable decline in movie-going. In 1950, Australia had more cinema seats, in proportion to population, than any other country in the world except the principality of Monaco. Some figures from Victoria will illustrate the effect of television upon movie-going. This state has a population of less than three million. In 1956–1957 —when television was beginning in Victoria—cinema attendances were thirty-four million. In 1960–1961, the figure had dropped to sixteen million. In the last few years, a large number of cinemas have been closed, some of them to be converted into bowling alleys. (The economy involved here, in the taking over of existing buildings, may have played some small part in the rapid development of this sport in Australia.)

Before the coming of television, the films shown in Australian cinemas were overwhelmingly of American production, with a few coming from England and fewer still from European countries. Today, the great majority of films shown are still American, but an increasing number of smaller cinemas specialize in the showing of European films. This may partly be explained by the rapid postwar growth in the European-born part of the population, but it is also partly a response to the competition of television. With much of their mass audience drawn away, the cinemas now depend more on a minority audience of sophisticated film lovers. This audience ex-

433

isted before the days of television, but its demands were not met because it was much more profitable to please the mass audience.

There are night clubs, of course, most of them in Sydney and Melbourne, and in the past year or two there have also been burlesque shows—though these have met with considerable discouragement from the police and the courts. Neither of these forms of entertainment seems to attract large numbers of Australians. It is possible, however, that night clubs will soon become more popular in Australia, as recordings of some American night club comedians are proving popular. But the reluctance of governments to grant liquor licenses to night clubs hampers their development.

From a survey made in 1947, it appeared that reading books or magazines was the preferred evening leisure activity of twenty-seven Australians in every hundred. This figure is probably lower now that television is available to most of the population. In any case, very little is known about the reading habits of Australians. Sociologists have begun to study this question, but it is only very recently that one or two universities have set up departments of sociology.

The Australian book trade is chiefly in books printed in England. The relatively small numbers of books published in Australia are almost entirely about Australia; and many novelists prefer to seek English publishers because of the small size of the local market. Most books are still sold in specialist bookshops, but the "paperback revolution" has come to Australia, and paperback books are sold by some general retail stores and by the small stalls that deal primarily in newspapers and magazines. Most American books still circulate in English editions, but in recent years many American paperbacks have been imported. Australians buy more books than do people in most countries, but this may be partly due to the poor development of public lending libraries. A public opinion poll in 1953 suggested that two-thirds of Australian adults read an average of twenty-eight books each year. Mostly they read popular novels. Such figures are very unreliable, but at least it is certain that a very high proportion of the books read by Australians are popular novels by English and American authors.

Comic books are widely read by Australian children and adoles-

434

cents. Most of these are American, some of them directly imported from the United States, others reprinted in Australia. This represents a significant change in reading habits over the last twenty or thirty years. Before this change, most children's reading matter of a popular kind was imported from England; although it included comic strips of pictures, it also included a high proportion of periodicals which printed chiefly straightforward narrative stories, with pictures merely as incidental illustrations. The influence of comic books has received little objective study in Australia, but they have nevertheless been the subject of a great deal of heated and hostile comment. Some states have introduced laws ostensibly aimed at the censorship of such forms of literature, but it is not evident that these laws have been very effective. No doubt comic books are read to some extent by Australian adults, but there does not seem to be any evidence of the extent of this habit.

A large number of popular magazines are imported into Australia from England and the United States. Two or three American journals, such as *Time* and *Reader's Digest*, print local editions, with slight modification of their contents. But Australian popular magazines also flourish. They are of kinds familiar in other similar countries, as a few titles chosen at random will perhaps sufficiently indicate: *Pix, People, Man, Wheels, Nation, Australian Home Beautiful, Australian Women's Weekly*.

Australians seem to be fairly avid readers of daily newspapers. In proportion to population, there are more issues of daily newspapers printed in Australia than in most countries, including the United States (though not so many as in England and one or two of the smaller European countries). Within each state of the Commonwealth the daily newspapers produced in the capital city have a dominating influence. The metropolitan dailies—and especially the morning papers—circulate throughout the state. Because of this, there has been a tendency for the provincial newspapers to disappear and for the survivors to concentrate on local news; the smaller ones serve to some extent as supplements, rather than alternatives, to the metropolitan papers. There has also been a tendency toward concentration in each metropolis. Sydney, for example, with more than two million people, has four daily newspapers controlled by three organizations. (A few years ago they were controlled by four organizations.) There is also a growing tendency toward overlapping in newspaper control and ownership from state to state.

The quality of Australian newspapers is often commented upon adversely by visitors from other countries. Most such comments seem to mean that there are no Australian newspapers which give such ample coverage of international news as do the more serious American and European newspapers. This is widely admitted, but the counterargument is sometimes given that there is also no mass "yellow" press in Australia and that none of the Australian newspapers reaches the level of triviality of, for example, the London afternoon papers. Recently, however, some of the Australian newspapers have clearly been trying to imitate the London popular press.

Sunday newspapers are long established in some states, but in others Sabbatarian influence still prevents their publication. Most Sunday newspapers are versions of daily papers, modified by a relative lack of topical news and addition of numerous features like reviews of records and films, stories about television, film, and sporting stars, and gardening notes. In some cases, the lack of topical news is a matter of necessity, since the "Sunday" newspaper is on sale early Saturday evening.

Detailed and comprehensive analyses of newspaper reading habits in Australia are not yet available. It seems fairly certain, however, that the sections of newspapers most widely read are the main news stories, the sporting pages, and the comic strips. In the more "popular" newspapers the main news stories, whether local or international, are likely to be treated in a rather sensational and sometimes misleading manner. Information about horse racing is prominent in the sporting pages, and on race days many papers print a "form guide," chiefly for the benefit of gamblers. The comic strips are largely of American origin, though a few are from England. A number of Australian strips—most of which attempt to be *comic*—have maintained their popularity over the years, but it can hardly be said that Australians have been very successful in this form of popular art. Indeed, the only Australian who has been notably successful in this line now works for a London newspaper and draws upon the English background (though his strip is published in one or two Australian newspapers). On the other hand, the brilliant tradition

436

of black-and-white art which was established in the 1890's is by no
means dead. The standard of the topical cartoons in the daily newspapers is generally fairly high, and at least two of the Australian
practitioners of this art are very good.

In the eyes of most Australian moralists, drink and gambling
would appear to be the two great national vices. In practice, figures
for alcoholism and the number of traffic accidents caused by drunken
driving are unreliable, and only an antiliquor crusader would make
confident statements about the amount of damage caused in Australia by alcohol. However, Australians certainly consume a good
deal of alcohol. As a national average, they drink small quantities
of wine (little more than a gallon each year), and even smaller
quantities of spirits (less than a third of a gallon each year), but
they drink about twenty-two gallons of beer a year. This figure
(and the figure for wine consumption) is about twice what it was
immediately before the Second World War; it is estimated by
treating the whole population as drinkers. Thus a good many Australian men must consume thirty, forty, or fifty gallons of beer each
year. Australian beer is high in alcohol—two to three times that
of most English or American beers.

A certain amount of wine and beer is drunk with meals, a certain
amount in homes during visits between friends, and a good deal at
parties. But traditionally, beer has been drunk mostly in pubs. Although the Australian pub is an offshoot of the English institution,
it is very different in character. Most Australian pubs are large,
and the drinking is done standing at bars in large barrooms which
are often very crowded. It is still a very common habit with many
men to drop into a pub to drink one, or two, or several social beers
with friends after work or on Saturdays. In the past, in many states
the law required pubs to close at 6:00 P.M., and this led to a rush
for drinks as that hour approached which many observers thought
squalid. Today in most states the pubs are open until 8:00 or 10:00
P.M.

Changes in social-drinking habits, especially perhaps the increase
in public drinking by women, has led to changes in the pubs. There
are now more lounges and beer gardens where beer is drunk sitting
at tables. In states where pubs are open until 10:00 P.M., there may
be entertainment offered in the lounges by singers and musicians

437

(who are often rather amateurish performers); there may also be dancing. Such entertainments are likely to be offered only on Friday and Saturday evenings.

In recent years some states have made liquor licenses fairly readily available to clubs (which are generally required to serve liquor only within the same hours as pubs). This has resulted in a spectacular increase in the membership of such licensed clubs. Often these are associated with sporting bodies or with ex-servicemen's organizations, but membership in the club is often widely available to people who have no special interest in its formal objectives. Membership in the club is sought because of its social amenities and for drinking, dancing, and playing slot machines. The development of clubs has drawn considerable numbers of patrons away from the pubs. It seems probable that these clubs will develop into very important centers for the use of evening leisure time.

Activities of a more or less markedly sexual kind are presumably important in the leisure of any community. In Australia parties, dances, visits to beaches, and occasions of mixed social drinking in clubs or beer gardens are undoubtedly valued partly for the opportunities for sexual encounter and flirtation. But it is difficult to decide just how far they are valued for these rather than other reasons. Some recent observers from Britain have commented upon the lack of erotic display by Australians in public. Certainly, some European male migrants seem to amaze and amuse Australians by their frank public display of erotic interest (of course, the overt amusement might conceal envy, disapproval, or any number of unadmitted reactions). The native observer may feel that he sees signs of erotic interest and attraction and of sexual tension between men and women, which the outside observer misses because he is looking for other and more obvious signs. At any rate, it would be dangerous to take relative lack of public erotic display as an indication of lack of erotic drive or of the repression of sexual activities.

These visitors might also have commented upon the relative lack of public signs of prostitution.

However, there has been virtually no sociological investigation of Australian sexual behavior. An Australian-born medical man, Dr. Norman Haire, who was prominent in movements for sexual reform in Britain some years ago, endowed fellowships for sexual research in the University of Sydney. Only one seems ever to have been taken up, then only for a short time and for psychiatric research. This is a rather remarkable demonstration of lack of interest in a subject which engages a good deal of scholarly attention in other countries. It is of a piece with the severe censorship of books and films which are considered to be obscene. Obviously, there are powerful influences in Australian society and culture which inhibit the investigation and discussion of sexual activities. Whether they also inhibit sexual activities themselves in the same degree is another matter. In the absence of careful investigation, the observer can only record impressions. For what it is worth, this observer—deeply involved in his own society, but with some experience of others—records his impression that sexually motivated activities occupy a good deal of the leisure time of Australians and not notably less than in some other similar societies.

It will be clear from what has been said that a great deal of Australian entertainment is imported directly from the United States, in the form of printed matter, films, and sound recordings. In addition, many local entertainers copy American styles, sing songs or play music written in America, and so on. This state of affairs is a matter of considerable concern to some Australians. There are many reasons for resentment of American influence in popular culture: a dislike of the American popular arts, for moral or aesthetic reasons; a nationalist desire to see a distinctively Australian popular culture; a fear that the influence of American culture will lead Australians to adopt American values and an Americanized style of life which is disliked, misunderstood, or distrusted.

It is clear enough that in many obvious respects the pattern of Australian society and culture is coming to resemble that of the United States more closely than it did in the past. It is natural to assume that this is largely due to the influence of American popular culture. On the other hand, one could produce an argument which would go something like this: American and Australian society are proceeding along roughly parallel lines of development in economic and social organization; this is primarily due to the existence of similar forces inside each society; Australian society would proceed in this direction even if there were no direct American influence upon Australia. Americans are producing forms of cultural

439

expression which reflect the kind of social and economic organization they have achieved. These forms of cultural expression are readily accepted by Australians because they reflect the kind of social and economic organization which Australians will themselves achieve, just a little later than Americans. On this kind of argument, Australia could be seen as partly overcoming its own cultural lag—the lag of cultural development behind economic and social development—by taking over cultural forms from a society which is proceeding in the same direction, but keeping a little bit ahead.

One can without doubt say that Australian society and culture today are more like American society and culture than they were fifty years ago. But one can also say that Australians are still very different from Americans, just as they are very different from Englishmen. Thirty or forty years of intensive exposure to American cultural influence has not destroyed the distinctive Australian ethos or the distinctive Australian style of life.

BIBLIOGRAPHY

Clark, J. F., and Olley, A. *Pre-television Social Survey: The Interests and Activities of Families in Sydney.* 1958.

Elkin, A. P. *Marriage and the Family in Australia.* 1957.

Mackay, I. K. *Broadcasting in Australia.* 1957.

Mackenzie, Jeanne. *Australian Paradox.* 1961.

Oeser, O. A., and Emergy, F. E., eds. *Social Structure and Personality in a Rural Community.* 1954.

——., and Hammond, S. B., eds. *Social Structure and Personaltiy in a City.* 1954.

Pringle, J. D. *Australian Accent.* 1958.

Taft, R., and Walker, K. F. "Australia," in *The Institutions of Advanced Societies,* ed. by Arnold M. Rose. 1958.

Towpeny, R. E. N. *Town Life in Australia.* 1883.

THE CULTURE OF

THE ABORIGINES

J. H. BELL

THE aborigines occupied Australia for thousands of years before the first European settlement came in 1788. It is now accepted that the aborigines did not originate in Australia, but migrated from across the sea to the island continent. Exactly when they entered Australia is not known, but it seems to have been between 10,000 and 20,000 years ago. This places their arrival during the late Pleistocene period. Prehistory in Australia has been neglected until recently. Its development will undoubtedly throw light on the important question of man's arrival in Australia.

Where the ancestors of the aborigines came from is still debated. The theory that they originated in Europe is now rejected, and increasing evidence seems to point to Asia. Just *where* in Asia is not known, but places as far apart as the Mediterranean seaboard and southern India have been suggested. Another opinion favors southeast Asia, which is geographically closer to Australia. The ancestors of the aborigines not only spread to Australia, but throughout Asia

441

and Melanesia as well. Small pockets of people sharing ancestors with the aborigines are found in these regions today.

At what points the aborigines first entered Australia is not known, but it is more than likely that there were several sites because there must have been a series of migrations covering centuries. It seems certain that the aborigines entered Australia along the northern coast—the Cape York Peninsula, the Kimberley region, and the Arnhem Land coast being particularly favored. From New Guinea it would have been an easy matter to cross the narrow island-dotted Torres Strait to Cape York. Further, from Asia the aborigines could sail to Arnhem Land and the Kimberley coast in canoes and on rafts because the sea was shallower than it is today and more islands existed.

A series of migrations to Australia and a resulting population pressure forced those aborigines who had arrived earlier to move away from the northern coast and down the eastern and western coasts. In time, others were forced into the interior. Just how long it took the aborigines to spread across the face of Australia is unknown, but it would have been a slow movement even though they made use of the inland river system to facilitate their journey.

The Australian aborigines have sufficient physical features peculiar to them to constitute a racial category, which is called Australoid. The Australoid is now accepted as one of the four main races of mankind, the others being the Caucasoid, the Negroid, and the Mongoloid. Originating somewhere in Asia, the Australoids—according to a theory which is gaining support—can number among their ancestors the famous *Sinanthropus pekinensis* of China and the equally famous *Pithecanthropus erectus, Homo soloensis,* and *Homo wadjakensis* of Indonesia.

The aborigines are not the only Australoids in the world today. Other groups of people in Asia and Melanesia are classified with them. These include the Ainu of northern Japan, the pre-Dravidian hill tribes of southern India, the Veddas of Ceylon, the Sakai of Malaya, and other small remnants in Indonesia and in New Guinea.

The physical characteristics of the aborigines are distinctive. Skin color varies, but most are chocolate brown. The aborigines are never as dark as Negroes. In form their hair is wavy and curly, never woolly or frizzy as in the Negro; in color it ranges from brown to black. In inland Australia aboriginal children often have blond hair which changes color when adulthood is reached. Adult males have an abundance of body hair. The aborigines have a retreating forehead and a narrow head. Their eyes, dark brown in color, are deepset, and the eyebrow ridge is very heavy. They have a wide nose— some, indeed, are almost flat—and in profile the nose has a Semitic appearance. They have projecting jaws, a wide mouth, and full lips, but their lips are not everted as found in the Negro. The aborigines are a slender and muscular people, the average height of males being five feet six inches and of females five feet one inch.

One of the great mysteries of Australia is the extinct Tasmanian aborigines, who had died out by 1876. They are important because they were probably the first people to enter Australia. Racially, the Tasmanian aborigines were not Australoids as are those of the mainland. One theory is that they constituted a distinct racial category called Tasmanoid, but the consensus now favors their classification as Negroid. In physical appearance the Tasmanian aborigines shared characteristics with the Melanesians and the Papuans, both of whom are classified racially as Negroid. It is likely that they originated in New Caledonia.

One suggestion is that the Tasmanian aborigines preceded the Australoids into Australia, and that with the coming of the latter they were pushed southward and finally forced out of the mainland across Bass Strait onto the island of Tasmania. It seems more likely, however, that they occupied both Australia and Tasmania before the arrival of the Australoids, and that later those on the mainland were either absorbed or annihilated by the invaders while those on the island remained untouched (being protected from contact by Bass Strait). The cultures of the Australoids and the Tasmanian aborigines had very little in common, which suggests a lack of contact between them.

When the Europeans came to Australia in 1788, it is estimated that the aboriginal population numbered about 300,000.[1] This figure

[1] A. R. Radcliffe-Brown, "Former Numbers and Distribution of the Australian Aborigines," *Official Year Book of the Commonwealth of Australia*, No. 23, 1930 (Melbourne: Government Printer, 1931), pp. 687–696.

is small in comparison with the size of the continent, which is about three million square miles in area—about the same size as the United States of America. On the basis of these figures, the density of the aboriginal population of the whole of Australia in 1788 would have been about one person to every ten square miles. But there was considerable variation in the density of the aboriginal population in different parts of the continent because of varying geographical and climatic conditions. The Great Australian Desert in the interior of the continent had a density ranging from one person to every fifteen square miles in Northern Territory to one person to every thirty-eight square miles in South Australia. Half of this desert region receives less than ten inches of rain a year and the rest from ten to twenty inches, and it is everywhere subject to severe droughts. On the other hand, the well-watered coastal fringe of the continent and the great river systems could support a larger population. In these regions the density was as high as one person to every 6½ to 7½ square miles.

The small total of 300,000 aborigines was determined by the available food supply because these people are food gatherers and hunters, not agriculturalists or pastoralists. They are parasites on nature, being solely dependent on what it produces unaided. For this reason the aborigines kept their population in check by practicing infanticide and abortion.

Thus the climatic and general geographical conditions of the Australian continent controlled the size of the aboriginal population and its distribution. These factors affected not only their economic life, but were formative in their social and religious life.

One of the two most important effects that contact with European settlers has had on the aborigines has been the great decrease in their numbers. It has been estimated that between 1788 and 1880 the aborigines had decreased by almost three-quarters.[2] By this time many whole tribes in southeast Australia had completely disappeared. This depopulation came about partly by the indiscriminate destruction of many aborigines by European settlers. Guns, poison, and punitive expeditions were used against them, but many more fell victim to diseases (such as smallpox, influenza, measles, and tubercu-

[2] E. J. Foxcroft, *Australian Native Policy* (Melbourne: Melbourne University Press, 1941), p. 109.

444

losis) introduced by Europeans. Unbalanced diet, high infant mortality, liquor, and psychological malaise have also been suggested as additional causes of their depopulation.

The second important effect of European contact was the appearance of the mixed-blood aborigines or, as they are popularly though erroneously called, half-castes. These are aborigines with varying admixtures of European blood. From the first days of settlement until well into the nineteenth century there was a great disproportion in the sexes of the settlers, a fact very noticeable on the frontiers. The shortage of European women led to sexual relations between European men and aboriginal women, the result of which were the mixed-blood aborigines.

The appearance of mixed-blood aborigines is another factor explaining the decrease in full-blood numbers in that some full bloods mated with mixed bloods, and, instead of reproducing themselves, they produced more mixed bloods.

Today the aboriginal population includes both full-blood and mixed-blood aborigines and totals approximately 78,000. There are approximately 46,000 full bloods and approximately 32,000 mixed bloods distributed throughout Australia, as Table 2 indicates. From this table it will be seen that the aborigines are scattered over the whole of the continent, but that the majority are concentrated in Western Australian, Queensland, and Northern Territory. It will also be seen that in the states of New South Wales and Victoria the aboriginal population is essentially a mixed-blood one. The figures

Table 2. Aboriginal Population and Distribution in Australia, 1961

State or territory	Full-blood aborigines	Mixed-blood aborigines	Total
New South Wales	250	13,000	13,250
Victoria	208	1,069	1,277
Queensland	9,100	7,211	16,311
South Australia	2,139	2,983	5,122
Western Australia	20,338	5,896	26,234
Tasmania	—	214	214
Northern Territory	13,900	1,247	15,147
Australian Capital Territory	—	100	100
Total	45,935	31,720	77,655

in the table refer only to aborigines known to the authorities. There are other mixed-blood aborigines of very light castes, such as octoroons and lesser castes, who are lost in the general population and numbered with it. No official attempt has been made to trace these people.

All told, the aboriginal population constitutes only about 0.8 per cent of the total population of Australia, which is now over 10,000,000. But aboriginal numbers, both full-blood and mixed-blood, are increasing. Evidence from mission stations in northern Australia indicates that full-blood numbers are definitely increasing. For example, on Bathurst Island (off the Arnhem Land coast) the population is now about 800 and is increasing. However, the largest increase is found among mixed-blood aborigines. For example, in one study carried out in New South Wales it was estimated that the average number of live births per mixed-blood aboriginal woman was 5.2.[3] On the other hand, in New South Wales as a whole the average number of children per existing union is about 2.9. Although this increase in aboriginal numbers is partly explained by improved medical care and welfare activities generally, it also reflects that the aborigines are at last making an adjustment to the presence of Europeans in their country.

Among the aborigines different patterns of social structure have been found, but comparison shows that they are only variations of a general type, the main features of which are described hereunder.

The largest unit in the social structure is the tribe. Before the coming of the Europeans, it is estimated that there were about 500 aboriginal tribes, the membership of each ranging between 100 and 1,500 and averaging about 500 to 600. An aboriginal tribe is a group of people who speak the same language or dialects of that language, who have a unity of social customs, and who inhabit and own a definite area of territory. But it is sometimes impossible to tell whether a particular group is a tribe, a subtribe, a local group, or a combination of tribes. This is because of real differences of dialect within the group or because contiguous tribes sometimes have marked similarities in language and customs.

The tribal territory varies in size depending upon the nature of

[3] A. P. Elkin, "Position and Problems of the Aboriginal Mixed-Bloods in Australia," *Proceedings of Seventh Pacific Science Congress*, VII (1953), 629.

the region in which the tribe lives. On the fertile coastal fringe of the continent where food is relatively plentiful, the tribal territories are small, some being no more than 1,700 square miles. On the other hand, in the desert region a tribal territory might be as large as 40,000 square miles. Tribes are usually separated from each other by natural boundaries such as rivers, creeks, gullies, and mountains; but where none exists, they are separated by a no man's land.

A tribe may or may not have a name. Some tribes have the same names as their languages; others take as a tribal name the word for "no" in their languages. Still other tribes originally had no names for themselves, but were named by their neighbors on the basis of the points of the compass, and these names eventually came to be accepted by the tribes so named. Other tribes have been named by anthropologists who have worked with them. In the late 1920's the noted American anthropologist, William Lloyd Warner, worked with an unnamed tribe in northeastern Arnhem Land and, needing some name by which to refer to them, extended the name of a local group within the tribe to the whole tribe. In this way the Murngin tribe got its name.

The aboriginal tribe is not a political unit. It has no central authority or warmaking function. Despite the popular fallacy, the aborigines do not have tribal chiefs. The members of a tribe never assemble together at any one time for political, economic, or other purposes. In short, no more can be said than that a tribe in aboriginal Australia is a territorial and linguistic group with its own peculiar customs.

Each tribe is divided into a number of local groups, sometimes spoken of as hordes. It is the local group which is the important social, economic, political, and religious unit for the aborigines. The statement made above that the tribe owns a definite territory has now to be qualified, because it owns this territory only inasmuch as it is composed of a number of local groups, each of which has its own territory. In other words, the tribal territory is the sum total of all the territories of its constituent local groups. This is one of the keys to an understanding of tribal unity, the tribe not being politically organized.

The local group is small in number, fifteen or so members, and inhabits a definite territory with well-known boundaries. The members of the local group are kinsmen related through the male line. Thus children belong to the local group of their father and paternal grandfather. Not only is descent patrilineal, but residence is patrilocal. This means that males remain members of their natal local groups all their lives, whereas females leave their natal local groups at marriage and take up residence in the local groups of their husbands. The local group tends to be exogamous in that members have to take their spouses from outside the group. This "law" of exogamy produces important social and economic ties among local groups which are illustrative of the reciprocity that characterizes aboriginal life in all its spheres.

The local group is politically autonomous. Political control or authority lies in the hands of the elders, the old men, who are full of experience and have a detailed knowledge of sacred mythology and ritual. A council of the adult males decides community problems on the basis of precedent, the part played by each member depending upon his age and degree of initiation. The summing up or the consensus of the council is expressed by a headman. Each local group has a headman who is usually the oldest man in the group, providing he still retains all his faculties. Additionally, the headman's position depends upon support from the other old men, his wisdom, his intimate knowledge of different aspects of the life of the group, and his place in the sacred life. More often than not the headman is also the medicine man in the group. The headman has no special rights or privileges and does not live any differently than other members of the group. The headmen of contiguous local groups confer together with the old men of the several groups on matters of common interest, and on such occasions they are aided by the initiated men. Political life is no more complex than this. As already mentioned, the aborigines do not have chiefs or kings as is sometimes popularly supposed. Further, there is no institution of rank.

The local group is composed of two, three, or more closely related families—depending on the fertility of the country. A family consists of a man, his wife or wives (the aborigines are polygynous, being allowed more than one wife), and their children—own or adopted. As with most peoples, the family is the important socializing agency. It teaches the child his roles in the social and economic scheme of things. The family is the basic social and economic

448

unit. For most of the time it is economically self-contained, husband and wives cooperating in the food quest. On other occasions, both for social and economic reasons, several families within the local group live together and seek food together.

The aboriginal family is the basis of an elaborate kinship system which spreads not only to the boundaries of the tribe, but far beyond. Indeed, every aboriginal with whom another comes into contact, whether a member of the tribe or not, is regarded firstly as a relative and secondly as a particular kind of relative and is treated accordingly even though the relationship is more often than not fictitious. It follows that it is impossible for an aboriginal to have anything to do with another aboriginal who is not related to him either factually or fictitiously.

The aborigines provide an illustration of a people among whom the very widest possible recognition is given to genealogical relationships. They are able to do this because each tribe has a classificatory system of kinship terminology. This means that relatives are divided into a number of different classes and that one kinship term is applied to all relatives found in each class. For example, one's father and all his brothers (that is, one's paternal uncles) are all called "father" by the aborigines, and one's mother and all her sisters (that is, one's maternal aunts) are all called "mother." From this beginning the consequential relationships are traced out.

From this follows the principle that there is a certain pattern of social behavior for each class of relative which is strictly observed and in this way the kinship system regulates every aspect of aboriginal life.

Although it is possible to speak of a basic aboriginal kinship system, some important variations in kinship structure are found among the aborigines. Indeed, it is now agreed that there are five main variations of the basic aboriginal kinship system in Australia. These variations are referred to as kinship types, and each is named after one of the tribes which exhibits it. They are the Kariera, Karadjeri, Aranda, Aluridja, and Ungarinyin. Each type is characterized by variations in marriage rules and in social behavior.

The kinship system regulates the whole social life of the aborigines, including marriage. As an aboriginal is "related" to every other aboriginal with whom he comes into contact, it follows that no matter whom he marries he will marry a relative. But, according to the "laws" of his tribe, he can marry only persons who stand to him in a specified relationship. For example, in one tribe he is required to marry *any* cross-cousin, in another a *particular* cross-cousin, in another a *second* cousin, and so on.

The remaining important social groupings are age grades, sex groups, clans, moieties, sections, and subsections.

Males pass through five age grades during their lives. These are childhood; adolescence, which is characterized by the first of a series of initiation rites; early manhood and married life; eldership, during which they take an active part in controlling life within their group; and finally, old age. Females pass through four stages: childhood; early married life; later married life; and old age. Aboriginal women are not the chattels or slaves that early anthropologists thought them to be. True, the society is male-dominated, but women are not without status. Women live in their husbands' local groups and improve their status in these groups by their food-gathering and childbearing roles. The successful food gatherer and mother of several children enjoys a high status. Old age greatly improves a woman's status because the aborigines respect age irrespective of sex.

The aborigines are divided into two groupings on the basis of sex. In some parts of Australia this division is acknowledged in that each sex has a totem peculiar to it. For example, the males of a tribe might be symbolized by one type of animal or plant and the females of the same tribe by another. These sex groupings are dependent upon each other for economic and biological purposes, but they are mutually exclusive in other spheres of activity—especially the political and the religious. The religious life is secret and for the men alone. The men travel great distances from the camp when secret rituals are to be performed, and the women are warned against following them under pain of death. The rituals, however, are performed by the men for the whole group (including the women) and not for themselves alone. In other words, the men assume responsibility for the group's religious life.

The composition of the clan has already been noted. It consists of people related in one line only, either the male or the female, but not both. If descent in the tribe is patrilineal, a person of either sex belongs to the clan of his father and paternal grandfather; but if descent is matrilineal, a person belongs to the clan of his mother and maternal grandmother. All members of a clan are related in that they claim descent from a common founding ancestor. Such a claim may be fictitious or real.

Many aboriginal tribes are divided into two moieties, an important division for social and ceremonial purposes. The moiety, like the clan, is a totemic grouping and takes its name from its totem. It is also similar to the clan in that all its members are related either patrilineally or matrilineally. In some tribes the moieties are exogamous, but in others they are not. Where marriage is permitted within the moiety the partners, however, must come from different clans and different local groups within the moiety. Thus it is not possible to say that the function of the moiety division within a tribe is to control marriage. Rather, the local group, the system of kinship, and the clan are the primary mechanisms controlling the establishment of the marital union. The chief function of the moiety system is ceremonial. When large numbers gather to perform ceremonies, the moiety division is seen in camping arrangements and in the actual performances. The members of one moiety will camp together, spatially removed from the camp of another. Further, each moiety has its part to play in the ceremonies associated with initiation, the increase of native fauna and flora, and funerals. Moieties can be seen as opposing social groups, but the parts they play in ceremonies are to be seen as complementary.

Some tribes are further divided into four sections and others even further into eight subsections. Sections and subsections are one and the same thing and may be discussed together. A man, his wife, and their child are each in different sections or subsections, but all the children of a woman are in the one section. The section or subsection into which a person automatically falls, while different from his mother's, depends on it. Because of this, sections and subsections may be loosely spoken of as being matrilineal. In the Nyul-Nyul tribe of northwestern Australia, for example, the four sections are named Panaka, Burong, Karimba, and Paldjeri. The children of a woman of the Panaka section are always in the Karimba section, and vice versa; similarly with the Burong and the Paldjeri sections. Diagrammatically, this may be represented as follows:

$$\overset{\curvearrowright}{\underset{\curvearrowright}{\begin{array}{c} \text{Panaka} \times \text{Burong} \\ \text{Karimba} \times \text{Paldjeri} \end{array}}}$$

On the basis of this, sections and subsections may appear to regulate marriage and descent, but this is only superficially so. There are many tribes, for example, without these divisions in which marriage and descent are controlled quite simply in other ways, some of which have been noted. Actually, the primary purpose of sections and subsections is to divide relatives into different groups for various social purposes and to separate certain types of relatives, such as cross-cousins and parents and children.

Generally speaking, then, the aborigines have developed a complex social structure in contrast to other aspects of their life which are poorly developed, such as material culture. But not all tribes have the complete set of social divisions described above. The coastal tribes of southeastern Australia, for example, have no moieties, sections, or subsections, and other tribes with sections and subsections do not have totemic clans.

The aborigines are hunters and food gatherers; in coastal regions and along rivers they are also fishermen. They do not practice agriculture, pastoralism, or any food production whatever. Before the coming of the European settlers, the aborigines had no knowledge of how plants grew. They never realized that the seeds they collected from plants to eat, and from which they made a kind of rough flour, were the origin of the plants themselves. Further, Australia had no indigenous cereals suitable for cultivation. With regard to pastoralism, the aborigines had no domesticated animals, apart from the dingo or wild dog which they trained to hunt. The dingo is not indigenous to Australia, but was brought to the continent by the ancestors of the present-day aborigines. The dingo rapidly increased and spread quickly throughout the country far in advance of the aborigines themselves. Australia had no indigenous animals capable of being domesticated for pastoral purposes.

Living on an island continent and cut off from the rest of the world, the aborigines had no contact with the agricultural and pastoral peoples of southeast Asia and Melanesia. Hence they did not have the opportunity to learn about such economic pursuits or to import cereals or animals for domestication.

452

THE CULTURE OF THE ABORIGINES

Because of their hunting and food-gathering activities, the aborigines are nomadic. But they are not true nomads because their wanderings in search of food are confined within their tribal territories—more particularly within their local group territories. It is, therefore, better to describe them as being seminomadic.

The local group and the family are the important economic units. The size of the local group's territory varies with the fertility of the country and ranges between fifty and several hundred square miles. Not only food gathering, hunting, and (where applicable) fishing rights, but all raw materials (timber, mineral deposits) in the territory are owned by the members of the group. The members of neighboring local groups, even though closely related, cannot hunt over the territory without permission. Whether permission is granted depends on the prevailing season. Trespassers are severely dealt with.

The economic importance of the family has been referred to. It is within the family that the simple economic division of labor on a sexual basis, which is fundamental in the aboriginal economic pattern, is seen most clearly. The man is the hunter and fisherman, and his wife (or wives) the food gatherer. This division is strictly adhered to. Small boys accompany their mothers on the food quest, but when they become older they accompany their fathers, who teach them the necessary hunting and fishing skills. The economic roles of the sexes are to be seen as complementary.

No matter how large the residential group becomes, for example, when the season is good and several families live together, this sexual division of labor prevails. On such occasions the men who are physically able go hunting together or in small groups under the direction of the headman. They may stay away for a day or more, depending upon how successful they are or how far they have wandered away from the camp. They hunt kangaroos, wallabies, opossums, wombats, and birds. The women also wander about together, seeking edible vegetable foods such as yams, small game, witchetty grubs, ants, caterpillars, and so on, but they always remain relatively close to the camp and always return to it at the end of a day's food gathering. Sometimes the men return empty-handed, and the camp is then solely dependent on what the women have collected. When the men are successful, their game is divided up according to the strict

453

rules of kinship for the distribution of food, and a hunter and his family rarely get anything that he has killed. But the aborigines' existence depends on reciprocity, and the hunter and his family will share in the distributions made by other hunters.

Depending on nature, the aborigines are close to it and have an expert knowledge of their physical environment. This has enabled them to live for centuries in harsh desert regions where lost Europeans lacking such knowledge perish within a few days. Season by season, the aborigines know exactly where within their local group territory food is to be obtained, and they make for such locations at the appropriate times of the year.

The aborigines have a paucity of material possessions because of their nomadism. As they are moving most of the time, they have no need for permanent shelters and cannot cope with many possessions. They possess only things that are essential and can be carried. Their material possessions are confined to those things which are important in the economic and religious life. Types of possessions vary from region to region, but any list would include wooden spears, spear throwers, stone axes, shields, wooden bowls, bark bags and baskets, grinding stones, digging ticks, throwing sticks, fire sticks, and sacred objects of wood, stone, and quartz. Where appropriate, the aborigines have fishing gear—bone hooks and lines and nets of vegetable fiber. Some tribes, but not all, have boomerangs. Many people may be surprised to learn that the boomerang is unknown to the aborigines in parts of Western Australia, South Australia, and Arnhem Land. Those having boomerangs put them to different uses. The famous "returning" boomerang is occasionally used for hunting, but its chief use is as a toy or plaything. There are special hunting boomerangs and fighting boomerangs, and in some tribes they are used only as musical instruments for tapping out rhythms.

Housing is not found among the aborigines. Since they are almost continuously on the move, it would be a waste of time to construct permanent shelters to be abandoned after a few months when the season changes. The aborigines make do with a crude shelter of branches called a wurley or mia-mia or with a lean-to of bark. Sleeping in the open is preferred, even in cold weather, when they keep warm by building fires throughout the camp. Along the northern Queensland coast, as a precaution against mosquitoes, the aborigines sleep on platforms over smoke fires.

The aborigines are a naked people. Clothing is unknown, but in regions where the winter and the nights are exceptionally cold, use is made of the skins of animals such as the kangaroo and opossum. These skins are not fashioned into garments, but are simply thrown over the shoulders or wrapped around the body. The aborigines migrate from regions where the winter is severe. Tiny pubic tassels of fur, pearl-shell pendants, or waist belts of humain hair are worn by males—not as coverings, but as signs that they have been initiated. If of marriageable age, females wear fringes or belts of bark. On ceremonial occasions the aborigines paint their bodies with various colored raw ochres, and in sacred rituals the performers decorate themselves with human blood, animal fur, and bird down.

The adaptation that the aborigines have made to nature is not only economic and social, but religious as well. They are spiritually tied to their tribal land, which is the home of their preexistent spirits. Their religious life is keyed to nature and clearly shows their dependence on it as food gatherers and hunters. They perform rituals for rain and for the increase of the native flora and fauna. They are not only concerned with the present and the future, but also with the past, because it is the culture heroes, the mythical ancestors of the "dreamtime" of long ago, for whom the rituals are performed and who alone can make rain and animals and plants appear. This religious adaptation to nature is called totemism.

Totemism, in general terms, is a system of relationships between the individuals or groups within a society on the one hand, and the animals and plants that are socially important on the other. The relationships are demonstrated by the term for the totem being applied to the individual or group. Thus one group is linked to a particular species, say, the kangaroo, another group to the emu, and so on. In this way, society and nature are looked upon by the aborigines as sharing a common life and belonging to the one moral order.

The aborigines are famous in the general study of totemism because it is found everywhere among them and in all its possible forms, both with regard to distribution and function.

Distribution and function are the two ways in which totemic phenomena among the aborigines are classified. Distribution is the types of totemism found. These types are associated with particular social groups, each linked with some natural species limited to it. They may be local groups (the membership of each being determined by being born at a particular place associated with some particular natural species which becomes the totem of the local group), clans, or other social and ceremonial divisions of the tribe, such as moieties, sections, sex groupings, and cults, each of which will have its own totem.

Function is the part played by totemism in the life of the tribe. Totemism has two important functions among the aborigines. The first is to link together certain persons who are closely related in the female line but who do not live together. These people claim that a certain natural species, their totem, is their "flesh." That is, it is one of themselves. They therefore respect their totem as if it were their own mother or some other close female relative. They will not injure it. On the other hand, the totem acts as their guardian, warning them of approaching dangers by appearing in their dreams or even materializing before them. Further, social totemism (as this is called) helps to regulate marriage in that persons of one "flesh" (that is, possessing the same totem) cannot marry. The second important function of totemism is to group males of the same locality who share the same conception totem into religious cults. Each cult has a totem which is regarded by the members, not as their "flesh," but rather as their "dreaming." In other words, this particular totem is not believed to be one of themselves as in social totemism, but as representative of a culture hero of the "dreamtime."

The "dreamtime" was a period long ago at the beginning of the world when the culture heroes roamed the countryside making natural phenomena, such as mountains and rivers, and creating the natural species. The aborigines recreate the "dreamtime" by recounting myths about the period which tell how things became what they are, and they act out these myths in the form of rituals. These performances bring the cult members into close contact with the culture heroes and provide for continuity with the socially important past. The "dreamtime" is socially important because the aborigines believe that it was also in this time that the rules for present-day social behavior were introduced by the culture heroes. A breach of such rules is an offense against the heroes, and here lies the sanction.

Associated with these cults are two very important ceremonies. They are increase ceremonies and initiation ceremonies.

In the myths of the "dreamtime," the heroes tend to be associated with animals and plants—some of which become the totems for the different cults. In each local group territory there are certain sites, believed to have been associated with the culture heroes, at which ceremonies for the increase of the native fauna and flora have to be performed. The aborigines, knowing nothing of the general biological process of reproduction, believe that such ceremonies replenish the supply of animals and plants. They believe that the spirits or souls of such animals and plants—and, for that matter, of man himself—preexist in the spirit centers in the present dimension of the "dreamtime" and are incarnated or reincarnated by such ceremonies.

Initiation ceremonies are performed to initiate males into the heroic cults. It is during such ceremonies that the secrets or mysteries associated with the cults are made known to the neophytes by the old men, who are the custodians of the religious and magical secrets. Initiation, which takes the form of some physical operation, such as tooth evulsion, cicatrization, or circumcision, takes place for all males, usually at the onset of puberty. It is regarded as a ritual death and rebirth. The neophyte is taken by force from the women, with whom up till this time he has always been associated, and is taken to the ceremonial ground, initiated, and told some of the secrets of the cult. He is also shown sacred stone symbols believed to have belonged to the culture heroes. To give his wounds time to heal, and in order to impart more secrets to him, he goes into seclusion for some weeks. He is then regarded as "dead." Emerging from seclusion signifies his rebirth—not as a child, but as a man ready to take his place in adult life. From now on he must associate with the men because he is one of them and must only have contact with women as is allowed by "law."

Funeral rites vary in different parts of Australia. The principal method of disposing of the dead is burial, but the bodies of important old men are either exposed to the elements or mummified. In mummification the corpse is dried in the sun or over fires and then

457

carried about for many months by the mourners. Finally, it is exposed or, to a far lesser extent, cremated. In exposure, the body is placed in a tree and left until only the bones remain. These are then painted and buried in totemic ground. Rituals accompany all forms of disposition.

The aborigines believe that the chief cause of death is sorcery, which includes pointing the bone.[4] They also believe that before a burial can take place the deceased must be avenged. The sorcerer is usually determined by the medicine man, who holds an inquest after which either a revenge expedition to kill the sorcerer is organized or compensation is demanded from the sorcerer's group. In aboriginal Australia the sorcerer is always believed to be outside the deceased person's local group. Fear of sorcery is so strong among the aborigines that the belief that it could be performed within the local group against a fellow member would have a disintegrative effect on the group. Further, only when the dead person is avenged is his soul believed to depart and leave his kinsmen in peace. When he has been avenged and the funeral rites have been performed, the soul returns to the "dreamtime" where it awaits reincarnation. The belief regarding the souls of both sexes is the same.

The aborigines are a preliterate people. They have no literature, but like primitive people the world over, record their past in myths and legends and express themselves through dancing, music, singing, and art—all of which have both sacred and secular forms.

Each tribe has many myths and legends which are told around the

[4] Pointing the bone is widespread in aboriginal Australia and, requiring no special skill, can be practiced by anybody. It is, however, a risky business and is performed in great secrecy because, should a person catch another pointing a bone at him, he is justified in killing him on sight. This is a form of self-defense upheld by aboriginal "law." The pointing bone ranges in length from three to twelve inches, is pointed at one end, and at the other has a knob of resin to which human bait is attached. To be effective, the bone has to be "sung"; that is, endowed with evil magic. This is done secretly in the bush. A curse, such as "may your head split open," is whispered over the bone, and it is then buried for several days. The actual pointing may be performed well away from the intended victim or in close proximity to him. The performer squats, clutches the bone in both hands, jerks it in the direction of the victim, and whispers a spell so that the evil magic will leave the bone and enter his victim's body. Very soon afterward the victim suffers great pain and eventually dies, unless saved by a medicine man who is able to diagnose his trouble and suck the evil magic out of the patient.

campfires in the evening or are confined to the religious activities of the men. The myths and stories are usually very long and full of the most minute details. Their telling is an art which takes many years of practice and becomes the specialization of certain old men. The aborigines love nothing better than a good story well told.

Dancing is also either sacred or secular. Sacred dancing is restricted to the secret religious ceremonies of the men, but both men and women participate in the secular, or ordinary, dancing corroborees. These are staged on well-worn dance grounds, and once going they continue night after night for about two weeks. The dancing is repetitive, but to the aborigines never monotonous. Corroborees are much enjoyed and are the most important social form of entertainment. They give the young people a chance to show off before the opposite sex.

Dancing of both types is always accompanied by music and singing. The aborigines have a limited number of musical instruments; the most elaborate is the didjeridoo, which is made from the slender branch or trunk of a tree, the center of which has been eaten out by white ants. The player blows into the instrument and produces a throbbing, rhythmical, one-note sound. The longer the didjeridoo, the deeper the tone. The only other musical instrument is tapping sticks, pieces of wood about a foot in length made from hard wood, which are simply tapped together in time with the singing and the drone of the didjeridoo. Sometimes boomerangs are used in place of sticks.

Aboriginal songs are really myths which are sung by songmen only. These are old men who specialize in songs in the same way that other old men specialize in the telling of myths and legends. The songman's principal role is to direct the sacred ceremonies and to sing the appropriate myth in order to explain to the audience the actions of the performers. Each ceremony has its own songs, which are very simple and repetitive.

Ethnomusicology has made a late, but impressive, start in Australia, and an exhaustive study of the aboriginal music of Arnhem Land has been made by Professor A. P. Elkin and Trevor Jones.

Aboriginal art takes a variety of forms. There are outline rock engravings, paintings on the walls of caves and rock shelters where they are protected from exposure, bark paintings, incised engravings on wooden weapons and tools. Secular art can be seen by all, but sacred art by the men alone. Sacred art is found in secluded places known only to members of the cult.

In painting, the materials used are red and yellow ochre, charcoal, and gypsum. The material is crushed and mixed with grease or water and is painted onto the rock or bark using the finger or a stick which has been chewed at one end. In making rock engravings, crude stone chisels are used to make the outline.

The subject matter of aboriginal art is confined to hand stencils, animals, plants, human beings, and geometric designs; concentric circles are the most popular. Under the influence and training of European artists, a few aboriginal artists from Central Australia have found acceptance in world art circles. The late Albert Namatjira is an example. These artists have concentrated on landscape paintings, but lately some have commenced to include animals and human beings in their work—mainly under pressure from European buyers.

When the first Europeans arrived in eastern Australia to establish a settlement, the aborigines proved to be shy and harmless. They made no attempt to prevent the settlers from landing and erecting their tents on the shores of Sydney Harbor. Gradually, some of them were coaxed into the new settlement, and they willingly helped the settlers in small ways when asked. Their behavior toward the settlers was doubtless based on the fallacious assumption that they were temporary trespassers only. But as time passed and the settlers increased in number, the aborigines were to realize that the Europeans had come to stay, and so their behavior toward the newcomers changed.

Contact with European civilization has played havoc with aboriginal culture in many parts of Australia. The breakdown of the culture came about not so much by direct attacks on it, but indirectly as a consequence of the way of life that the Europeans were establishing. Aboriginal customs were directly interfered with only when they impeded white settlement. Nor did the aborigines want to discard their culture for that of the settlers.

The aborigines, completely satisfied by the operation of their own culture, were not an inquisitive or acquisitive people as far as European culture was concerned. They showed no curiosity about it and no inclination to discard their own way of life and to imitate that of the Europeans. Their lack of interest in what the Europeans regarded as a superior way of life was misinterpreted by the settlers and led to the formation of the general opinion that the aborigines were incapable of being civilized. The Europeans failed to realize that the attitude of any native people to an intruding culture is determined by their own cultural background and value system. The cultural backgrounds and value systems of the Europeans and aborigines were almost diametrically opposed. They had very different social, economic, religious, and political organizations. The Europeans lived a sedentary life, the aborigines a seminomadic one. The Europeans valued material possessions, the aborigines did not. The Europeans, wrongly believing that acquisitiveness was a universal human trait, criticized the aborigines because they seemed to lack it. The conviction of cultural and racial superiority characterized European relations with the natives. The Europeans believed that the aborigines were a worthless people with no culture. Further, the isolated retaliatory attacks by aborigines on settlers alienated sympathy for them. At a public meeting in Sydney in 1826, it was declared by men of position that the aboriginal was not a human being and that there was therefore no more guilt in shooting him than in shooting a dingo.

Basically, the two cultures were incompatible. Both could not exist in the same region, and one had to give way. The Europeans won the day. They had come to settle the country, and they forcibly alienated the land of the aborigines. In doing so they shattered the aboriginal culture, which was fundamentally based on tribal land. The livelihood of the settlers, who were farmers and graziers, depended on huge tracts of land, and there was no room for an aboriginal food-gathering economy in the midst of an agricultural and pastoral settlement. Large areas were put out of bounds for hunting and food-gathering activities. The aborigines were driven away or destroyed, and no consideration was given to any rights that they had in the land taken or to their interests generally. The development of even some of the resources of the country in the interests of the native people was never contemplated.

Further, being scattered and nomadic, with no centralized political organization or weapons to match those of the Europeans, and faced with a decreasing food supply as a result of the deliberate killing of native fauna and the clearing of land by Europeans, the aborigines were powerless to resist the intrusion. They had not experienced anything like the new situation before. They could attack the settler in his lonely hut, but they could not deal with an increasing number of settlers.

The density and rate of European settlement in the early years of contact are important factors in understanding the contact situation. At the several centers of settlement both the density and rate were high. In less than a generation the European population had far surpassed the total aboriginal population.

Aboriginal culture broke down not because the aborigines wanted European culture, but because European settlement, with its usurpation of hunting and food-gathering areas, undermined the aboriginal economic life which was the foundation upon which the social and religious life rested. When the food-gathering-and-hunting base was swept away, the social and religious life were without points of reference or meaning and they, too, collapsed. Thus the change wrought in the natural environment disorganized the aboriginal way of life. With the breakdown of the economic system, the validation for the social structure disappeared.

Another important factor leading to the breakdown of aboriginal culture was depopulation, the causes of which have already been noted. This demographic change had important effects on the social structure and distribution of the aborigines. Lacking the proper numbers of performers, the traditional patterns of social interaction broke down. Many of the groups formerly important in the social life were wiped out, and only the remnants of others remained. Very important, of course, was the destruction of the local organization which was the core of the aboriginal way of life.

Of the changes in social structure that took place, the most important was the emergence of the camp as the major unit in the social structure replacing the former local groups. These camps grew up near, but not as a part of, European settlements, on which at first they became partly economically dependent and later totally so. The camps were considerably larger than any former groups had been because the members were no longer dependent solely on what nature provided. Further, their locations were often permanent, a quality none of the former local groups possessed. These locations were determined by the permanent nature of European settlements and by the fact that the camps became the distribution centers for government rations. The camps were composed of heterogeneous local group and clan remnants, and membership was not governed by rigid rules as these latter groups had formerly been. Their composition was not stable. Membership not being automatic, members could change their camp affiliation, their choice being determined by personal preference. There was much movement between the camps. Although the camp sites became permanent, the aborigines did not become a sedentary people but were able to continue their "walkabout" activity in an attenuated form. Their mobility was reinforced by the new conditions which did not make for economic stability.

As the camps were composed of the remnants of different local groups and clans, the breakdown of such distinctions and sentiments is implied. This breakdown resulted not only from depopulation and economic changes, but also from the prohibition of warfare. This last point meant that aborigines could travel through and live in camps in former hostile territories. In time, the heterogeneous elements were welded together by intermarriage and resultant kinship ties.

Intimate social life changed also. Although subject to changes, the family, the most intimate unit of living, continued, fitting just as well into the camp as into the former local group. Descent was no longer strictly unilineal. This came about partly by the numbers of mixed-blood aborigines, the progeny of white men, who (lacking fathers) were absorbed into their mothers' groups and reckoned their descent accordingly. This had a very important effect on the formerly patrilineal groups. Further, because exogamy broke down, men now frequently married women from the same camp, with the result that both lines of descent became important. Kinship lost some of its functions. Its importance as a referent for marriage deteriorated, and nonkinship groups emerged. Even so, kinship retained much of its social and economic importance and facilitated wanderings between camps.

Changes in marriage took place. Polygyny gave way to monogamy. In the early years this was not because of missionary influence,

463

but because of the change in economic life which meant that a man could not support more than one wife. In the traditional tribal system, plural wives provided much of their own keep and contributed to that of their husband by their food-gathering activities. In short, they were economic assets. With the collapse of the traditional economic system, women played a decreasing role in economic life and became dependent upon their husbands and male relatives. Plural wives, then, became economic liabilities in the contact situation.

Prescribed marriage rules broke down. This came about through depopulation, the disappearance of the spatially separated local groups, the emergence of the large camp, and the outlawing of killing among the aborigines by European authorities which removed the most powerful sanction supporting the traditional marriage rules. The decline in the authority of the old men was another contributing factor. Accompanying this was the breakdown of the patrilocal nature of the groups in some regions. Females now remained with their parents and married men from the same camp or from other camps who came to live with them. This improved the status of women because, by remaining with their parents in their own camps, they were not the outsiders they had been in the traditional groups.

The authority of the old men was weakened by European contact. Young men who worked for the settlers were put in a strong position in that many people, including the old men, became partly dependent on the rations they received from their employers. The authority of the old men was also weakened by the decay of the religious life, particularly initiation, in which they had been able to impress their authority on the young men. Young men working for Europeans could successfully resist the painful initiation operations or could simply move to some other camp. This meant the disappearance of the distinction between the initiated and the uninitiated as well as the groups based on these statuses. But the attitude of these young men cost them their tribal birthright because the old men did not entrust them with the sacred knowledge of their people. They lost their spiritual retreat. They lost their "dreaming."

For a time, and with certain reservations, the aborigines were left in control of their own affairs. In New South Wales, the government's policy was to leave the aborigines in charge of their own affairs and to allow their "laws" to operate, except in matters of murder among themselves and in any matters involving Europeans. Such matters were to come before the local European magistrates. Further, the military was empowered to prevent the aborigines from warring among themselves and to keep law and order between them and the Europeans. The administrators at the time, like so many before them, wrongly believed that the aborigines had chiefs, and the military commanders were instructed to bring to the notice of these chiefs their responsibility for maintaining law and order in the camps. Some man in each camp was subsequently charged with these duties. The system failed, of course, because chieftainship was alien to the traditional tribal structure. The chiefs appointed by the European authorities were not recognized by the aborigines. Further, the mobility of many aborigines and the continuous movement to and from the camps weakened such a system of control. The system of chiefs was also weakened by European settlers who never recognized them, even if the authorities did, and dealt with the aborigines as individuals and not through the appointed chiefs.

With the establishment of official aboriginal reserves throughout the country, political control passed to government officers, missionaries, and the police. In some ways the reserves were similar to the camps. They had permanent locations and in some cases were composed of heterogeneous remnants. But they had amenities and permanent supervision by European officials, both of which the camps lacked. The reserves replaced some camps, but others persisted, and in most states in Australia today both reserves and camps are found.

With regard to changing the culture of a primitive people like the aborigines, three factors have been suggested as significant. One is the type of people having contact with the primitives. In Australia in the early years these included itinerant timber getters, gold diggers, farmers, graziers, soldiers, and convicts, none of whom was expressly interested in changing aboriginal culture. Three notable omissions among the Europeans in contact with the aborigines were missionaries, schoolteachers, and women.

At first missionary activity was not officially encouraged, and any which did take place failed miserably. Later missionaries were encouraged, and today they play an important part in the acculturation of the aborigines in every state and in the Northern Territory.

The early missionaries, in their zeal and ignorance, believed that the aborigines were without religion and morality and that clothing the natives was the first important step toward changing them from heathens into Christians. Today enlightened missionaries realize that it is better for the aborigines to go naked than to wear clothing which is never washed or changed. Further, they realize that Christianity will come slowly, but that they can be of immediate service in the fields of aboriginal health, welfare, and education. Aboriginal education was virtually neglected until the last few decades.[5] In some states education was left to the supervisors of reserves, who were frequently not academically equipped for the task. Further, their supervisory activities left them little time to devote to education. The small number of European women among the settlers in the early years of the colony and on the frontiers even today militated against aboriginal acculturation in that aborigines were never given the opportunity of learning about the customs and morality of European domestic life. Aboriginal women were, and are, rarely employed as domestic servants.

The second factor is that acculturation partly depends on what has been called the inherent communicability of alien cultural elements. The usefulness of some of the material goods (such as food, axes, knives, blankets, and tobacco) brought by the Europeans was clearly seen by the aborigines, and items better than the indigenous products were accepted in time. Hence metals and cloth replaced stone, wood, and bark, with the result that certain aboriginal stone and woodworking techniques disappeared. In the case of food, the aborigines were compelled by circumstances to accept the white man's food. Other material goods, however, did not appeal. The aborigines were very slow to take over European forms of shelter, and still today there are many regions where such housing is shunned. On the other hand, immaterial items of European culture such as religion, morality, and social customs, which require detailed teaching, are very slow to get across to primitives even with the help of teachers and missionaries.

The third factor is that the social distance and lack of contact between the peoples will impede cultural transmission. The social

[5] J. H. Bell, "Aboriginal Education in New South Wales," *Australian Quarterly*, XXXIII (June, 1961), 30-34.

distance between Europeans and aborigines was most marked. In the first place, the mutually incompatible economic systems led the Europeans to try to get rid of the aborigines by destroying them or driving them away. In some regions this was successful, but in others the administration intervened but made no efforts to save the aboriginal economic structure. Rather, the administration was only concerned with maintaining a system of regulated avoidance between the two peoples.

The collapse of the aboriginal economic system destroyed this relationship of regulated avoidance because aborigines became more and more dependent on Europeans. The men combined their rapidly diminishing food-gathering activities with working for the settlers who needed casual labor on their farms and sheep and cattle stations. Further, because of the great disproportion in the sexes of the Europeans, particularly in frontier settlements, aboriginal women were desired for sexual purposes. This meant that Europeans and aborigines had limited need for each other, and their relationship became one of mutual exploitation. Each took advantage of the other's weakness, but they remained foreigners to each other and shared little. The semi-independence of the aborigines passed in time, and they became wholly dependent on Europeans. This produced a new relationship of superordination-subordination. The Europeans now took full advantage of aboriginal weaknesses, and the aborigines were unable to retaliate.

For aborigines in many parts of Australia, such contact with Europeans reduced them to a state of pauperism. They moved from camp to camp and from reserve to reserve eking out an existence as best they could. Casual and intermittent work from Europeans coupled with government bounty was their fare. From parasites on nature, they became parasites on the settlers.

Although there was little direct action by Europeans to change aboriginal culture, extensive changes came about indirectly. The history of contact shows that European influences, for the most part casual and haphazard, penetrated diffusely. Cultural borrowing between Europeans and aborigines was one-sided. Europeans regard the aborigines as primitives and inferior and having nothing to offer them. One of the few things borrowed from aborigines was place names—and many of these have been spelled incorrectly!

467

Fewer and fewer aborigines are now living the traditional tribal life. Those who do are found in northern Australia and in the desert regions of Western Australia. It is estimated that there are today 6,500 aborigines in these two regions living in a tribal state beyond the confines of civilization. But even these have a limited contact with Europeans—government patrol officers, missionaries, scientific expeditions, and so on—and this contact has produced certain changes in their way of life. From the almost inaccessible desert regions, the aborigines periodically go to mission and government stations for medical aid or when food or water are in short supply. Sometimes they leave their children to attend settlement and mission schools. Gradually, these aborigines will settle around government and mission settlements as others have done, and within about another generation the traditional, seminomadic way of life will be no more. So it can be said that there are no aborigines in Australia today who have never seen a white man. All the aborigines have some contact with Europeans, and many live in close proximity to them.

The Second World War did more than anything else to reduce the number of "untouched" aborigines. The navy, air force, and particularly the army penetrated everywhere. Maps were drawn and photographs taken, and large army camps grew up almost overnight in formerly unexplored regions. Although the armed forces treated the aborigines well, their very presence had a shattering effect on aboriginal culture.

For most aborigines the traditional life has gone or is ebbing away. The most pressing aboriginal problem facing Australia today is not those still living the traditional tribal life, but those who, through contact with Europeans, are either losing contact with the ancestral way of life or have lost contact with it and can be spoken of as detribalized. There are approximately 70,000 such aborigines distributed throughout the continent. Of this number, some 32,000 are mixed-blood or part-aborigines. The problem is heightened because the mixed bloods are tending toward rapid natural increase.

These detribalized aborigines constitute a problem because they neither live the traditional aboriginal life nor the life of the European population, but something in between. Theirs is a hybrid culture, incorporating features of both aboriginal and European cultures in varying degrees depending upon the amount of contact that the aborigines of different regions have had. Roughly, these can be divided into two categories. The first contains tribal remnants who still speak their own languages and observe as far as possible their social rules, but who live permanently on government and mission settlements removed from large European centers. These people work on the settlements, or nearby cattle stations, and in mines owned by Europeans. On the settlements, they have permanent dwellings and their children attend the settlement schools. Most of them are found in Western Australia, Northern Territory, and Queensland. The second category contains mixed-blood aborigines who live in New South Wales and Victoria on government reserves or in conspicuous, unofficial, and substandard camps of shacks on the edges of country towns and in settlements in the slums of cities. In such camps the aborigines have no conveniences. They move around frequently, visit agricultural fairs, do a few odd jobs, spend lavishly what they earn on taxis, change *de facto* spouses quite often, and neglect their children's education. Those who live on government reserves have better conditions, houses and other amenities being provided. Economically and socially, however, their lot is little different from that of the camp dwellers. Residentially, culturally, and socially these aborigines are a marginal people. They live on the fringes of towns, participate to a very limited extent in the cultural and economic life of modern Australian society, and find little, if any, social acceptance by Europeans near whom they live.

Mention should be made of those mixed-blood aborigines in New South Wales and Victoria who have never personally experienced tribal life in any form and who speak no aboriginal language. Only skin color distinguishes them from the European population, but they are predominantly quadroons and lighter castes. These people are found in the suburbs of metropolitan areas living a life no different from Europeans'.

Responsibility for the aborigines is divided between the Commonwealth government, which is directly responsible only for those in the Northern Territory, and the several state governments, each of which is directly responsible for those within its own boundaries. The problem is further complicated by the differences in legislation in the various states and the Northern Territory and, within this legislation, differences on such matters as the definition of "aboriginal." However, the policy pursued toward the aborigines, both full blood and mixed blood, in all states and territories is one and the same, namely, that of assimilation. But this policy has a short history, beginning in the early 1940's. Before this time the policy was one of protection by segregation.

In 1788, the policy of the British government toward the aborigines was in keeping with its reason for founding the colony in Australia.[6] The aim was simply to establish a penal settlement to accommodate the overflow from English prisons. The government had no missionary or civilizing aims with regard to the aborigines. To prevent interference with the establishment of the colony, the aborigines were to be protected from the convicts and settlers. They were to be regarded as British subjects, but were to live apart from the Europeans. The policy was not to acculturate or assimilate them, but to protect them by isolation. In other words, the administration saw its role as being to maintain law and order between the aborigines and the settlers—and nothing more.

In 1825 the policy toward the aborigines changed. They were now to be civilized and converted to Christianity. The change in policy was a result of that facet of the humanitarian movement of the nineteenth century concerned with the effect colonization was having on the native peoples of the British Empire. The new policy was ignored in Australia. The administration had more pressing problems, and public opinion did not favor a change in policy. The lack of interest displayed by the aborigines in European culture, which has already been noted, confirmed the popular opinion that they were incapable of being civilized and that they were poorly endowed with intelligence.

From the middle of the nineteenth century the several states were granted responsible government, and with it came responsibility for the aborigines within their respective boundaries. The general policy adopted toward them was a continuation of protection by a system of isolated reserves. This policy was legally constituted in Victoria in 1860, in South Australia in 1880, in Western Australia in 1886, in Queensland in 1897, in New South Wales in 1909, and in North-

[6] J. H. Bell, "Official Policies toward the Aborigines of New South Wales," *Mankind*, V (1959), 345-356.

ern Territory in 1911. This policy remained unchanged until the 1940's.

The 1930's, however, saw much criticism of the protection policy. It was a negative policy because the aborigines apparently were dying out. The policy had been designed to protect the aborigines who remained from abuses by Europeans; actually, it failed. Atrocities and massacres continued in this period of "protection," particularly in Central and Northern Australia where the full-blood aborigines lived in larger numbers. Further, the attitude that the aborigines were an inferior people continued. By the late 1930's, it was realized that they were not doomed to extinction and that a positive policy designed to promote their progress was necessary.

The new policy came out of the Canberra conference of 1937, attended by all aboriginal authorities. The conference resolved that the destiny of the mixed-blood aborigines lay in their assimilation into modern Australian society. Not too much later, the same recommendation was made with regard to full bloods. By the early 1940's, every government concerned with aboriginal welfare had modified its policies and administration. The policy of assimilation is also supported by the various Christian missions.

The policy of assimilation means that all aborigines and part-aborigines are expected eventually to attain the same manner of living as other Australians and to live as members of a single Australian community enjoying the same rights and privileges, accepting the same responsibilities, observing the same customs, and influenced by the same beliefs, hopes, and loyalties as other Australians.

The policy of assimilation does not include intermarriage, but there are no legal restrictions against it. Some aboriginal-white unions have taken place, and others will doubtlessly take place in the future. Intermarriage is regarded as a purely personal matter and is neither officially encouraged nor discouraged. Nor does the policy mean that aborigines have to lose their identity as aborigines, or that there is no place for items of their culture (myths, legends, art forms) in the wider Australian culture. (In fact, in recent years aboriginal art motifs have been exploited commercially, and bark paintings and artifacts have been used for interior decoration.) What the policy aims at is simply to avoid having an isolated racial mi-

471

nority which finds no acceptance by the European majority and is consequently at a disadvantage.

Each state has a government agency to implement the official policy. In New South Wales this agency is the Aborigines' Welfare Board, a body of eleven members, constituted under the Aborigines' Protection Act. Among its members are experts in anthropology and agriculture and officers of the Departments of Public Health, Education, and Police. Two positions for aborigines, one for a full-blood aboriginal and the other for a mixed blood, are also provided. The Board has field officers headed by a superintendent of aboriginal welfare. Welfare officers are stationed in different parts of the state, and the Board controls twenty aboriginal stations and numerous reserves, most of which are supervised by a manager and a matron. About 5,000 of the state's 13,000 aborigines live on the stations and reserves.

Millions of pounds are being spent throughout Australia on aboriginal health, hygiene, housing, education, and training for employment. For every seventy aborigines there is one government officer or missionary working full time in the field. Notwithstanding, no aborigine has yet graduated from a university.

In addition to being British subjects, the aborigines are also Australian citizens by virtue of the Nationality and Citizenship Act of 1960. But in order to protect those not capable of fending for themselves, certain restrictions can be imposed on them. Like minors under the age of twenty-one years, some cannot exercise full citizenship rights. In most states and territories aborigines cannot buy liquor legally, and in some states they are denied full franchise rights. However, in some aboriginal acts provision is made to overcome restrictions on the exercise of citizenship rights. In New South Wales these restrictions are overcome by issuing suitable aborigines with certificates which exempt them from the provisions of the Aborigines Protection Act. These certificates were made legal under the provisions of the Aborigines Protection (Amendment) Act 1943; since then some 877 have been granted. Similarly, South Australia has exempted a large number of mixed-blood aborigines from the provisions of the Aborigines Act, 1934–1939, and some 1,900 aborigines have been freed from the provisions of the Welfare Ordinance in the Northern Territory.

472

THE CULTURE OF THE ABORIGINES

The implementation of the policy of assimilation has been hindered by a number of factors.[7] One is the relative youth of the policy compared with one hundred and fifty years of the diametrically opposed policy of protection by segregation which preceded it. This latter policy had a marked success, and it has been difficult to counteract its effects.

Another factor is race prejudice. Administrators and students of the aborigines recognize that assimilation is being hindered by prejudice toward aborigines. In some regions, the aborigines and Europeans share common living areas and use the same local utilities, but relationships between them, apart from stereotyped and limited ones such as service relationships, are nonexistent. They do not share a common life. Sometimes they have to work together, but they keep to themselves in their leisure hours. In some regions the aborigines are easily segregated socially because they are segregated spatially—living on reserves or in camps on the outskirts of towns. It is not unknown for attempts to be made to prevent aborigines from taking up residence in towns. Townspeople say that they do not want aborigines as neighbors because they have a depreciating effect on property values. The objection is that aborigines do not know how to live in houses properly and have low standards of hygiene.

Criticisms of the aborigines are numerous, but many of them are unproved stereotypes which are used by Europeans to rationalize the prevailing extensive social distance between themselves and the aborigines. Prejudice is noticeably more marked in regions where aboriginal numbers are larger.

This barrier to assimilation, however, is not an insuperable one. It is clear that assimilation will not be reached unless the Europeans want it and are willing to help the aborigines achieve it. This means that Europeans have to be willing to grant equal rights and responsibilities to the aborigines. Enlightenment has proceeded slowly since the 1930's, and anthropologists have contributed a great deal to shattering the myths and stereotypes held by Europeans about the aborigines. Further, the reports of the several aboriginal agencies indicate that progress is being made in overcoming prejudice.

A third barrier is the group life being built up by pockets of

[7] *Proceedings of the Conference on Welfare Policies for the Australian Aborigines* (Armidale, N.S.W.: University of New England, 1960), pp. 71–87.

detribalized aborigines all over Australia. These aborigines live together in a fairly compact, isolated fashion on reserves or in camps. Finding no acceptance by Europeans, these encampments have, over the years, been turned into highly integrated social groups. In these groups the aborigines live an intimate social life characterized by continuous face-to-face, personal, informal, and inclusive relationships of equality. Each group is characterized by a strong spirit of cooperation, mutual aid, generosity, and hospitality among its members, but these do not extend beyond the group. As indicated, in these groups the aborigines live a life that is neither truly aboriginal nor truly European in its characteristics, but is a combination of both. The attenuated features of the traditional life that persist, however, become barriers to the assimilation of the members because Europeans see them as alien to their own culture and give them a low social rating. Realizing that assimilation means the breakup of these groups, the aborigines resist the new policy despite the social and economic advantages that they would achieve from it.

These small groups of aborigines are localized and ethnocentric. They are social, not political, in significance. There is no over-all aboriginal solidarity, and so long as the marked ethnocentrism of local groups exists, no such solidarity will be achieved. The few unsuccessful associations formed by individual mixed-blood aborigines in the eastern states to champion the cause of aborigines generally on a state-wide or nation-wide basis is evidence for this. These associations have had very short lives because aborigines from one region refuse to cooperate with those from another. The reason for this is either that the ancestors of the two peoples were traditional enemies or that a fear of sorcery lingers on. The dislike of unknown aborigines is found to be common among mixed-blood groups. Even mixed-blood aborigines living in the Sydney metropolitan area claim to dislike the mixed-blood aborigines of the north coast of New South Wales and those from western New South Wales. They describe them as "bad mobs," as "full of fight," and as thieves. Aborigines refuse to vote for another from a different region who stands for election to one of the Aboriginal Welfare Boards, claiming that the candidate would do nothing for them. There seems little likelihood of aboriginal solidarity being extended to the national level as long as such local, insular feelings exist. If it

474

were achieved, another barrier to assimilation might be erected because such a movement would be bound to have political concomitants which might not be appreciated by the European population.

Finally, there are certain administrative difficulties which have hindered the implementing of the assimilation policy. The new policy was introduced at the beginning of the Second World War and had to contend with financial and personnel shortages. These shortages carried over into the postwar years and are still to be found in some states today. The greatest difficulties are financial, and these hinder welfare activities. These administrative difficulties are real ones, and their importance is not to be underestimated in the list of factors hindering assimilation.

The factors mentioned, however, are not eternal barriers to assimilation, nor should they be interpreted as demonstrating that assimilation is the wrong policy for the aborigines. There is proof in the achievements of individual aborigines that assimilation is possible. Present developments throughout Australia give hope for an increasing movement of aborigines into the main body of the Australian community. It should be clear that assimilation is the only feasible policy because the former traditional tribal life has either passed or is passing away. The rate of its passing varies according to the region and the types of aborigines. Lighter-caste aborigines, such as quadroons and octoroons, have a better chance of being assimilated than darker aborigines. The aboriginal uniform or badge of color is an important factor in hindering assimilation. Lighter-caste people who dissociate themselves from the aboriginal population find little difficulty in being assimilated as individuals. The number of light-caste aborigines who have been lost in the general community over the past fifty years must be considerable, but at any one time the number is not great. Metropolitan areas and large towns provide the best opportunity for assimilation and small country towns the least, especially if an aboriginal camp or reserve is in the vicinity.

It is clear that assimilation will be a slow process and that it will take a long time to achieve. Gradual assimilation is the keynote of the policy because great social dangers would arise if assimilation were forced and rapid. It is also clear that assimilation will be achieved in certain spheres of Australian life before others. Economic assimilation will come first. This phase has already begun, but it has a long way to go. Aborigines unable to lead their former economic life are offering their services to European employers and are being accepted in increasing numbers. At present they are low in the occupational status hierarchy, being employed as manual laborers and often only on a temporary or casual basis. But this is often their own fault because, although no longer required to be nomadic for economic reasons, they continue to be a very mobile people. Whenever they feel the urge to do so, they give up their jobs, spend their earnings in fares, and abandon many of their material possessions. Political assimilation will come next. Mixed-blood aborigines of half-caste and less have the federal franchise, and full bloods enjoy the right to vote in New South Wales, Victoria, and South Australia. In 1961, a Commonwealth parliamentary committee, set up to investigate the question of aboriginal voting, recommended that the federal franchise be granted to all full bloods without restriction. Recently, the aborigines became entitled to all social service benefits administered by the Commonwealth government. The aborigines pay taxes, must obey the law, and receive free and compulsory education. Compulsory education is a relatively new thing for the aborigines, and it is seen as one of the most important factors that will foster assimilation generally. It is through education that the aborigines will come to appreciate European culture. Social assimilation will come most slowly of all. It is hindered principally by three factors: cultural differences, prejudice on the part of Europeans, and the highly integrated group life of the detribalized aborigines.

BIBLIOGRAPHY

Books

Battarbee, Rex. *Modern Australian Aboriginal Art.* 1958.
Berndt, R. M., and Berndt, Catherine. *From Black to White in South Australia.* 1951.
Chaseling, W. S. *Yulengor: Nomads of Arnhem Land.* 1957.

Commonwealth of Australia, Department of Territories. *Our Aborigines.* 1957.

——. *Progress towards Assimilation: Aboriginal Welfare in the Northern Territory.* 1958.

Elkin, A. P. *Studies in Australian Totemism.* Oceania Monograph No. 2. 1933.

——. *The Australian Aborigines: How to Understand Them.* 1954.

——., and Jones, Trevor. *Arnhem Land Music.* Oceania Monograph No. 9. 1958.

Foxcroft, E. J. *Australian Native Policy.* 1941.

Harney, W. E. *Life among the Aborigines.* 1957.

McCarthy, F. D. *Australia's Aborigines: Their Life and Culture.* 1957.

——. *Australian Aboriginal Rock Art.* 1958.

Mountford, C. P. *Records of the American-Australian Scientific Expedition to Arnhem Land: Volume I, Art, Myth and Symbolism.* 1956.

Parker, K. L. *Myth and Symbolism.* 1957.

Radcliffe-Brown, A. R. *The Social Organization of Australian Tribes.* Oceania Monograph No. 1. 1931.

Robinson, Roland. *Australian Legendary Tales.* 1953.

——. *The Feathered Serpent: The Mythological Genesis and Recreative Ritual of the Aboriginal Tribes of the Northern Territory.* 1956.

University of New England. *Proceedings of the Conference on Welfare Policies for the Australian Aborigines.* 1960.

Warner, W. L. *A Black Civilization: A Social Study of an Australian Tribe.* 1958.

Wells, Annie E. *Tales from Arnhem Land.* 1959.

Periodicals

Oceania: A Journal Devoted to the Study of the Native Peoples of Australia, New Guinea and the Islands of the Pacific Ocean. Quarterly. 1930– .

Oceania Monographs. Occasional. 1931– .

BIOGRAPHICAL NOTES
ON THE CONTRIBUTORS

※

SIDNEY J. BAKER was born in Wellington, New Zealand, but has lived in Australia for many years. In addition to the books listed in the bibliography for the chapter on speech and language, he is author of *New Zealand Slang, The Gig* (a novel), *The Man Who Was Sung* (a play), a biography of the navigator and explorer Matthew Flinders, the sections on language in the *Australian Encyclopedia* and *Encyclopaedia Britannica,* and articles in the *Journal of General Psychology, Psychiatry, Psychiatric Quarterly.* He has been awarded research grants by the government of New Zealand, the Commonwealth of Australia, and the Australian Council for Educational Research to allow him to pursue studies in the psychological implications of language.

G. W. BASSETT, M.A., Dip.Ed., Ph.D., is Professor and Dean of the Faculty of Education in the University of Queensland. After teaching in the public schools of New South Wales, he became Lecturer in Education at Sydney Teachers College and later Principal of Armidale Teachers College. At Armidale, Professor Bassett was also Head of the Department of Education in the University of New England. Dr. Bassett studied under Professor Sir Fred Clarke at the University of London. He has contributed a number of articles on teacher education to professional

478

journals and was made a Fellow of the Australian College of Education in 1961 for his services to Australian education.

J. H. BELL, Associate Professor and Head of the Department of Sociology and Anthropology in the University of New England, was formerly Senior Tutor in Anthropology in the University of Sydney. He holds the M.A. degree of the University of Sydney and the Ph.D. degree of the University of London. His doctoral thesis was written on the subject of mixed-blood communities in New South Wales.

CECIL HADGRAFT, Reader in English in the University of Queensland, has been Commonwealth Literary Fund Lecturer in Australian literature in 1951, 1960, and 1961. During 1949 he was engaged in postgraduate studies at the University of Manchester, and in 1956 he was on the faculties of the University of Omaha and Louisiana State University as a John Hay Whitney Fellow. Mr. Hadgraft is the author of five school textbooks in English, of *Queensland and Its Writers* (1959), and of *Australian Literature* (1960). At present he is preparing a critical edition of Henry Savery's *Quintus Servinton* and a study of Wallace Stevens.

D. J. MacDOUGALL, LL.B., graduated with first-class honors in the University of Melbourne and entered legal practice in Melbourne, having been admitted as a barrister and solicitor of the Supreme Court of Victoria. He subsequently accepted a teaching appointment with the University of Melbourne Law School. In 1959 he was awarded the J.D. degree of the University of Chicago, where he had studied as a Fulbright Scholar and British Commonwealth Fellow. At present, Dr. MacDougall is Senior Lecturer in Law in the University of Sydney. He has contributed articles to legal and business journals in England and Australia and is joint editor of the *Sydney Law Review*.

A. L. McLEOD is a graduate of Sydney, Melbourne, and Pennsylvania State universities, and holds the B.A., M.A., Dip.Ed., B.Ed., and Ph.D. degrees. He has taught in teachers' colleges in Australia, was Associate Professor of English and Speech in the State University of New York at Fredonia, and is now Professor and Chairman of the Department of English and Speech at Lock Haven State College, Pennsylvania. Dr. McLeod is author of a book of verse, *Beyond the Cresting Surf* (1959), editor of *The Commonwealth Pen* (1961), and a contributor to *Collier's Encyclopedia*.

JOHN A. PASSMORE, Professor of Philosophy in the Institute of Advanced Studies, Australian National University, graduated B.A. from the University of Sydney with first-class honors in both philosophy and English literature. He was Lecturer in Philosophy in the University of Syd-

479

ney from 1935 until 1950. In 1940 he was awarded the M.A. degree (Sydney) for his thesis on Hume. During 1948 Professor Passmore worked with Karl Popper at the London School of Economics, and in 1955 he studied at Oxford as a Carnegie Fellow. In 1950 he was appointed to the Chair of Philosophy in the University of Otago, New Zealand; he accepted the Chair at the Australian National University in 1956. Professor Passmore is a member of the Institute Internationale de Philosophie, the Australian Humanities Research Council, and the Australian Social Science Research Council. He is, in addition, a consulting editor of the *International Encyclopedia of Philosophy*.

DANIEL THOMAS is Assistant Curator of the Art Gallery of New South Wales, and is especially interested in contemporary Australian painters. He is the author of *Sali Herman* (1962).

SIR SAMUEL MacMAHON WADHAM, Kt., holds the M.A. degree from the universities of Cambridge and Melbourne, the Diploma in Agriculture (Cantab.) and the LL.D. (Melbourne). A Scholar of Christ's College, he became Demonstrator in Botany at Cambridge after graduation and was appointed Professor of Agriculture in the University of Melbourne in 1926—a position he held with great distinction until his retirement in 1957. Sir Samuel has been a member of the Royal Commission into the Wheat Industry, the Commonwealth Rural Reconstruction Commission, the Australian Universities Commission, the Immigration Planning Council, and other government bodies. He is a Fellow of the Australian Institute of Agricultural Science, a Trustee of the Royal Society of Victoria, and President of the Australian and New Zealand Association for the Advancement of Science. In 1956 he was knighted for his services to science and education.

JOHN M. WARD, M.A., LL.B., Barrister-at-Law of the Supreme Court of New South Wales, has been Challis Professor of History in the University of Sydney since 1949. He is now Dean of the Faculty of Arts and Chairman of the Extension Board of the university, a member of the Social Science Research Council of Australia, and a member of the Australian Humanities Research Council. In 1951 Professor Ward was Dominion Fellow of St. John's College, Cambridge University; in 1957–1958 he visited Britain, Canada, and the United States on a Carnegie Corporation Traveling Fellowship; he has been appointed to a Visiting Professorship in History at Yale University for 1963. Professor Ward's publications include *British Policy in the South Pacific, 1786–1893* (1948), *Australia's First Governor-General: Sir Charles FitzRoy, 1851–1855* (1953), and *Earl Grey and the Australian Colonies, 1846–57* (1958).

RUSSEL WARD, Associate Professor of History in the University of New England at Armidale, N.S.W., was awarded the Clark Prize when he graduated B.A. in English at the University of Adelaide. He subsequently obtained the M.A. with double honors, in English and history, from Adelaide, the Dip.Ed. from the University of Melbourne, and the Ph.D. in history from the Australian National University. Dr. Ward is an associate editor of *Meanjin*, editor of *Poems Grave and Gay* (1953), and author of *Man Makes History* (1952), *Britons Make an Empire* (1953), and *The Australian Legend* (1958), which was awarded the Ernest Scott Prize of the University of Melbourne as "the most distinguished work in Australian and New Zealand or British colonial history in the Pacific" published in the biennium 1958–1959. In addition, Dr. Ward has written the Australian section of the UNESCO study, *History of the Scientific and Cultural Advancement of Mankind.*

EDGAR WATERS is a graduate in history and philosophy of the University of Sydney. He has taught in England and has lived in Europe. In recent years he has contributed to journals in Australia. At present he is lecturer in English literature in the School of General Studies of the Australian National University, completing work on the Ph.D. degree. His research has been undertaken in the area of the history of the popular arts in Australia.

INDEX

INDEX

484

INDEX

485